JOURNAL FOR THE STUDY OF THE OLD TESTAMENT
SUPPLEMENT SERIES
420

Encountering the Divine

Theophany in Biblical Narrative

George W. Savran

T&T CLARK INTERNATIONAL
A Continuum imprint
LONDON • NEW YORK

Published by T&T Clark International
The Tower Building,   15 East 26th Street,
11 York Road,   Suite 1703,
London SE1 7NX   New York, NY 10010

www.tandtclark.com

British Library Cataloguing-in-Publication Data
A catalogue record for this book is available from the British Library

ISBN 0 567 04391 6 (hardback)

Typeset by Tradespools, Frome, Somerset
Printed on acid-free paper in Great Britain by MPG Books Ltd, Bodmin, Cornwall

CONTENTS

FOR BELLA

ויהיו בעיניו כימים אחדים
(Gen. 29.20)

ABBREVIATIONS

AB	Anchor Bible
ABD	*Anchor Bible Dictionary*
AEM	*Archives épistolaires de Mari*
ANET	*Ancient Near Eastern Texts Related to the Old Testament*, ed. J.B. Pritchard, 3rd. ed. Princeton: Princeton University Press, 1969
ARN	*Avot deRabbi Natan*
AV	Authorized Version
BASOR	*Bulletin of the American Schools for Oriental Research*
BDB	*A Hebrew and English Lexicon of the Old Testament*, ed. Frances Brown, Samuel R. Driver, Charles A. Briggs.
BM	*Bet Miqra*
BT	*Babylonian Talmud*
BZ	*Biblische Zeitschrift*
BZAW	Beihefte zur Zeitschrift für die alttestamentliche Wissenschaft
CAD	*Chicago Assyrian Dictionary*
CBQ	*Catholic Biblical Quarterly*
CBQMS	Catholic Biblical Quarterly Monograph Series
Deut. Rab.	*Deuteronomy Rabbah*
EI	*Eretz Israel*
EJ	*Encyclopedia Judaica*
EM	*Encyclopedia Miqra'it*
Exod. Rab.	*Exodus Rabbah*
Gen. Rab.	*Genesis Rabbah*
FOTL	Forms of Old Testament Literature
GKC	*Gesenius' Hebrew Grammar*, ed. E. Kautsch, trans. A. E. Cowley
HAR	*Hebrew Annual Review*
HTR	*Harvard Theological Review*
HUCA	*Hebrew Union College Annual*
ICC	International Critical Commentaries
JAAR	*Journal of the American Academy of Religion*

JANES	*Journal of the Ancient Near Eastern Society of Columbia University*
JAOS	*Journal of the American Oriental Society*
JBL	*Journal of Biblical Literature*
JCS	*Journal of Cuneiform Studies*
JJS	*Journal of Jewish Studies*
JNSL	*Journal of the Northwest Semitic Languages*
JPS	The Holy Scriptures, Jewish Publication Society, 1917
JQR	*Jewish Quarterly Review*
JR	*Journal of Religion*
JSJ	*Journal for the Study of Judaism*
JSOT	*Journal for the Study of the Old Testament*
JSOTS	Journal for the Study of the Old Testament Supplement Series
JTS	*Journal of Theological Studies*
KJV	King James Version
LXX	Septuagint
LXX^L	The Lucianic recension of the Septuagint
Mish.	*Mishnah*
Mid. Teh.	*Midrash Tehillim*
MT	Masoretic Text
NJPS	*Jewish Publication Society Tanach*
OTL	Old Testament Library
OTS	*Oudtestamentische Studiën*
PR	*Pesikta Rabbati*
PRE	*Pirkei DeRabbi Eliezer*
RB	*Revue Biblique*
RSV	Revised Standard Version
Sam.	*Samaritan Pentateuch*
SBL	Society of Biblical Literature
SJOT	*Scandinavian Journal for the Old Testament*
Targ.	*Targum*
TDOT	*Theological Dictionary of the Old Testament* ed. G. J. Bottenweck and H. Ringgren
Tos.	*Tosephta*
VT	*Vetus Testamentum.*
VTS	Vetus Testamentum Supplements
WBC	Word Biblical Commentary
WCJS	World Congress of Jewish Studies
ZAW	*Zeitschrift für die alttestamentliche Wissenschaft*

INTRODUCTION

This study is a result of thinking about the unusual ways in which contact between the human and the divine is addressed in the Bible. More than ten years ago, in a course entitled 'Strange Encounters in the Bible', I began to examine some of the texts discussed here. What at first seemed to be simply a collection of odd stories gradually took shape in my mind as reflections of an overarching pattern of communication between God and man/woman in the Bible. I am not speaking of techniques of divination, nor am I referring to the notion of prophecy; itself a hugely complex and uncommon means of divine–human communication. Rather, I am alluding to texts which speak of visitation, of actual meeting between human and divine. While such matters are always of interest to students of religion, these particular narratives deserve special consideration insofar as they reveal something about both actors, about the possibility for interaction between the two spheres, and about the effects of the one upon the other.

Much of the study of theophany has concerned itself with the mythic origins of theophany motifs in biblical poetry, and their suggested origins in the language and imagery of the Divine Warrior in the Ancient Near East. While these traditions have clear reflexes in poetic texts such as Hab. 3, Ps. 18, and elsewhere, the attempt to connect all expressions of biblical theophany to this warrior model has led to some rather forced interpretation. Although some of the imagery of theophany in a text like Exod. 19 is similar to what is found in traditions related to the storm god, most of the Sinai traditions lack these images. Beyond the abbreviated narrative of Josh. 5.13–15 it is difficult to find traces of this militaristic theme in the theophany narratives themselves. Attempts have also been made to tie together theophany images under the rubric of the throne vision, with its description of judgment in the divine council. While this is suited to texts like Isa. 6 and Dan. 7, one is hard pressed to find this motif in most other theophany stories, which are about initiation, promise, intercession and annunciation. A third avenue of approach has been offered by the form-critical study of the prophetic call narratives, which sees the origin of these texts in the pattern of commissioning a messenger or in the election of a leader. While this model is appropriate to certain call narratives, it is not successful in explaining the differences between the wide variety of texts which fall under the rubric of theophany narratives.

Whatever their antecedents may have been, it seems that the biblical writers have created something quite new and different. Using dream reports, mythic depictions of theophany and the upheaval of nature, promises of divine guidance, and prophetic oracles, the literary genius of the biblical narrative developed a new way of discussing the interaction between the human and the divine, in a way which reflected the biblical concern with the special relationship between YHWH and Israel. In order to accomplish this, the writers had to negotiate the tension between divine transcendance and anthropomorphism. On the one hand, the Diety's autonomy was carefully guarded, by the suddenness and unpredictability of the Deity, and by the absolute nature of the Deity's decisions. The theophany was most often left to the discretion of the Deity regarding place, time, and the form of manifestation. There developed as well a number of unique strategies for the depiction of the visual presence of the Deity, reflecting a religious sensibility which abhorred graven images yet clung to the idea of divine immanence. At the same time the second part of the equation, YHWH's concern for the individual and for Israel was expressed in various ways. The approach to the individual was made in a graduated fashion which allowed for a process of recognition. The reactions of the individual to theophany were taken into account, and objections and responses of doubt and skepticism were treated carefully. In addition, the societal effects of the theophany were also given their due, as the connection between the theophanic encounter and larger societal concerns was developed. The divine–human encounter was not described simply to enhance a particular individual, but was always done with larger societal (and covenantal) concerns in mind. The results of these efforts and concerns was the development of a unique literary structure, the theophany narrative, which brought together these disparate elements in a way which expressed both the writer's respect for the autonomy and power of the Deity, and his perceptive depiction of the dynamics of interaction between the human and the divine.

The bulk of this study is given over to exploring these theophany narratives as a literary category in themselves. Chapter One lays out the literary model of the type-scene as the schema for the analysis of the theophany narratives. The next four chapters flesh out the implications of this analysis with a close reading of the texts under discussion, suggesting strategies which are employed by the narrator to address certain problems. Rather than read each text in its entirety, we have chosen to treat each type-scene element separately in order to gain a greater understanding of the dynamics of a given element, and not simply an understanding of a single text. Chapter Two will discuss the question of preparations for theophany, both the narrator's literary *mise en scène* as well as the question of human initiative. Chapter Three will deal with strategies for the visual depiction of YHWH in these texts. A central issue is the degree of flexibility regarding the delineation of the distance between YHWH and humans, and the bridging of that gap. We will explore the restrictions placed upon the visual representation of the numinous, and the diverse mechanisms for dealing with these limitations. We will restrict our discussion primarily to the visual aspect and pass over the verbal revelation, as this element has been the subject of the many studies which are concerned more with the content of the revelation than with the process described. Chapter Four will explore the range of human responses to the encounter with the divine, from positive acknowledgement of the power of the numinous to the various expressions of hesitation and anxiety. The emphasis here will be on the interactive elements of the theophany, and will include discussion of YHWH's 'response to the response'. Chapter Five will take up the question of how the protagonist is transformed by the experience. In some texts the protagonist makes a self-reflective statement about the experience, as does Ezekiel in Ezek. 3:15 or Daniel in Dan. 7. But in most cases we must resort to other means for evaluating what the implication of the theophany are for the protagonist. The most productive means will be the examination of the ways in which the protagonist rejoins the society he has left temporarily, and what his new role in that society will be. Included in this discussion are ritual reflections of the theophany, the emergence of the prophet, and the birth of the promised son. We wish to ask how these texts allow for 'continuity' of the experience, i.e., the transformation of the revelatory experience into communal structures for ongoing communication with the divine.

The final three chapters will take up a number of issues which emerge from the analysis of the motifs. Chapter Six will address the question of the potentially (and actually) lethal nature of encounters with YHWH. What is the connection between the threat of danger as a theme in other theophany narratives and its actualization in these texts? We will analyze the appearance of subjective factors in assessing the lethal quality of the encounter, and suggest explanations for the absence of this concern in other texts. Chapter Seven will explore the intertextual implications of our analysis, with particular attention to the use of allusion, as seen in the relationship between Elijah's theophany at Horeb in 1 Kgs. 19 and Moses' Sinai theophany in Exod. 33. The final chapter will discuss directions taken by the theophany narrative in late biblical and post-biblical literature, most noticeably in its transformation within apocalyptic literature (e.g. Daniel and *1 Enoch*), in the development of inspired interpretation, the apocalyptic theophany as seen in Daniel and *1 Enoch*, and the emergence of the tour of heaven as a new literary genre.

Many people have contributed to this project since its inception. First among equals are the long-time members of my weekly study group, Henry

Abramowitz, Shlomo Naeh, Jonathan Price and Eliezer Schwartz, who over the years have been a regular source of intellectual support, and have engaged in specific discussion of some of the texts analyzed in this book. The Schechter Institute has provided me with a comfortable base from which I was able to work productively, and gave me the opportunity to teach much of the material contained in this study over the past six years. I owe much to my colleagues and students for their assistance and their feedback. Sections of the book were read and helpful comments offered by Diane Sharon, Penina Galpaz Feller and David Frankel. I am also thankful for the assistance of a fellowship from the Kekst Foundation, which enabled me to devote more of my time to writing than would otherwise have been possible. A different version of the first chapter was presented at the World Congress for Jewish Studies in Jerusalem in August, 2001, and was published in *Prooftexts* in 2003. I thank the editors for permission to reproduce some of that material here. I would also like to thank the editors of the series for their willingness to publish this study, and Rebecca Vaughan-Williams and Slav Todorov of T & T Clark for their help and expertise in preparing the manuscript for publication. Conversations with a number of people contributed substantially to shaping this study, and to firming up my ideas about the texts and issues discussed here. My sincere thanks to Jack Feldman, Art Green, Ed Greenstein, Lori Lefkowitz, David Levine, Adi Savran, Yossi Turner, Eli Weisstub, and others who I may have forgotten to mention.

Most of all I owe an innumerable debt to my wife and partner in all things, Bella, who offered me constant support and feedback, both intellectual and emotional. Without her steady help the completion of this project would have been much more prolonged and difficult.

ערב ראש השנה, תשס"ה
Jerusalem
George Savran

Chapter 1

THEOPHANY AS TYPE-SCENE

The otherness of the God of Israel in relation to the human world is one of the most powerful defining characteristics of biblical thought. The prohibition against any physical representation of the Deity, the insistence on YHWH's essential difference from man/woman or from crafted representations, and the autonomy and independence of the Deity reinforce this basic idea. Yet, at the same time, this Deity remains in constant contact with the world. Indeed, one of the most common conventions of biblical narrative portrays the God of Israel speaking with human beings in normal human discourse, with no particular speech markers to indicate the exceptional nature of the dialogue.[1] The willingness of biblical narrative to portray YHWH as a God with human attributes – speech, thought, emotions, even representations of hand, arm, and mouth[2] – undercuts this otherness, and tends to place the Deity on the same narrative level as his human interlocutors. Precisely because certain conventions of biblical style minimize the difference between the human and the divine, those narratives which depict the revelation of the divine to a human audience are of particular importance in their ability to bring out certain aspects of the essential difference between the divine and the human.[3] And since they often recount first-time experiences, theophany narratives reveal to the reader something of the shock and surprise of the encounter with the divine. In these texts the individual is jolted sharply out of his or her normal existence in the face of something which he does not

---

1. This similarity is limited to the conventions of biblical speech, and does not pertain to the question of divine omniscience, which is one of the major points of difference in the portrayal of the human and the divine. Cf. M. Sternberg, *The Poetics of Biblical Narrative* (Bloomington: Indiana University Press, 1985), pp. 322–5; G. Savran, *Telling and Retelling* (Bloomington: Indiana University Press, 1988), pp. 88–94.

2. Cf. M.C.A. Korpel, *A Rift in the Clouds: Ugaritic and Hebrew Descriptions of the Divine* (Muenster: Ugarit-Verlag, 1990).

3. There is no shortage of biblical scenes in which YHWH is depicted in splendid isolation, as in certain narrative sections of Gen. 1–11. But among those texts where YHWH is shown in interaction with the human world, theophany narratives are exceptional in displaying the sharp difference between the human and the divine.

fully grasp at first, but which ultimately induces a sense of self-awareness (and awareness of the Other) which is nothing short of transformative.

1. *The Nature of the Texts to be Discussed*

Insofar as theophany refers to the appearance of the divine before a human audience, our discussion of the topic could include any of the many stories which involve an encounter between the two spheres. There are hundreds of such encounters in the Hebrew Bible, beginning with the primeval history and continuing in the patriarchal narratives in Genesis. Moses alone conducts numerous conversations with YHWH, not to mention the many subsequent leaders and prophets. However the term 'theophany' is used here not in its figurative sense of 'encounter with the divine', but, in keeping with the Greek φαινειν, 'to appear', it implies the presence of a visual component in addition to verbal interaction.[4] In all the texts we will consider the visual element is present in some form, though it is not necessarily the dominant manner of revelation.[5] Moreover, the term 'theophany narrative' applies only to those encounters in which the narrative framework is apparent. It is precisely such a framework that offers contrasting points of view, temporal progression, and the development of character, providing a portrait of how the Bible understood the peculiar dynamics of such an encounter. Conversely, although the rich tradition of poetic descriptions of theophany has much to contribute to the biblical understanding of such appearances of the divine, it will serve only as background for the major part of our discussion, since these texts lack the narrative framework which describes the reception of theophany.[6]

---

4.   F. Polak distinguishes between theophany as displaying an 'outside perception', while simple divine address (not a theophanic experience) involves what Polak calls an 'inner light'. See 'Theophany and Mediator', in M. Vervenne, *Studies in the Book of Exodus*, pp. 113–47 (113 n. 4). N.F. Schmidt and P.J. Nel ['Theophany as Type-Scene in the Hebrew Bible', *Journal for Semitics* 11 (2002), pp. 256–81], distinguish between theophany and epiphany as denoting respectively divine presence and divine power (260).

5.   Cf. J. Lindblom, 'Theophanies in Holy Places in Hebrew Religion', *HUCA* 32 (1961), pp. 91–106 (106).

6.   E.g. Judg. 5.4–5, Hab. 3.3–7, Pss 18.8–16, and 29.3–9. For discussion of various aspects of theophany not dealt with here see: J. Barr, 'Theophany and Anthropomorphism in the Old Testament', *VTS* 7 (1959), pp. 31–8; T. Hiebert, 'Theophany in the OT', *ABD* vol. VI, pp. 505–11; J. Jeremias, *Theophanie: Die Geschichte einer alttestamentlichen Gattung* (Neukirchen-Vluyn: Neukirchener Verlag, 1965); K. Kuntz, *The Self-Revelation of God*, (Philadelphia: Westminster, 1967); T.W. Mann, *Divine Presence and Divine Guidance in Israelite Traditions* (Baltimore: Johns Hopkins University Press, 1977); S. Talmon, 'The Concept of Revelation in Biblical Times', *Literary Studies in the Hebrew Bible* (Jerusalem: Magnes, 1993), pp. 192–215; F.M. Cross, *Canaanite Myth and Hebrew Epic* (Cambridge: Harvard University Press, 1973), pp. 147–94.

The unique character of each of these narrative encounters is brought out in a variety of ways. In many of the texts the theophany event presents a new development in the life of both parties, marking the beginning of a relationship.[7] Despite certain similarities between some of the texts, in no two is YHWH presented in the same fashion. Sometimes the human response is more standardized (e.g. הנני), but the individuality of the human characters is carefully drawn, as in much of biblical narrative.[8] In all cases the dramatic encounter between human and divine is prefatory to a major change in the life of the character. Texts of initial encounter we will consider which fall in this category include Jacob's dream (Gen. 28.10–22), the calls of Moses (Exod. 3–4), Samuel (1 Sam. 3), Isaiah (Is. 6), Jeremiah (Jer. 1), Ezekiel (Ezek. 1.1–3.14) and Gideon (Judg. 6.11–40.), annunciation texts (Judg. 13 and Gen. 18.1–15), and the double revelation to Hagar (Gen. 16.7–14; 21.17–19). Our discussion will also include a number of texts which describe theophanies that are not first time meetings. These include Jacob's struggle with the angel (Gen. 32.24–32), Moses' pleading with YHWH in the aftermath of the golden calf episode (Exod. 33.12–23), Joshua's encounter with the angel (Josh. 5.13–15), Elijah at Mt. Horeb (1 Kgs 19.1–18), and the account of Balaam and his ass (Num. 22.22–35).[9]

In all the texts to be discussed the theophany serves as the central focus of the text, and not as a secondary motif.[10] For this reason this discussion necessarily cuts across accepted categories of genre, for it is the theophanic encounter which defines and shapes the story. For example, a text like Gen. 28.10–22 has not been discussed in the same context as call narratives such as Exod. 3, since Jacob isn't 'called' as a prophet, nor does he receive a commission, only a general promise from YHWH concerning his future. Moreover, Gen. 28 has been classified as a dream-report, and has therefore been linked with other theophany dreams such as 1 Kgs 3.4–15

---

7. Adam in Gen. 2–3, Cain in Gen. 4, Noah in Gen. 6 all speak with YHWH, but these encounters lack the dramatic sense of visual encounter, and the reader has little sense of the stages of perception of the divine, or of the character's reaction to the encounter. A text like Gen. 12.1–8 shows us only YHWH's command to Abraham, and Abraham's external reaction. We know nothing of Abraham's astonishment at being addressed in this way, much as Abraham's immediate reaction to being commanded to sacrifice his son in Gen. 22.1 is withheld from the reader.

8. See R. Alter, *The Art of Biblical Narrative* (N.Y.: Basic Books, 1981), pp. 114–30; S. Bar-Efrat, *The Art of the Biblical Story* (Tel Aviv: Sifriat Poalim, 1979), pp. 73–111; A. Berlin, *Poetics and Interpretation of Biblical Narrative* (Sheffield: Almond Press, 1983), pp. 33–42; Sternberg, *Poetics*, pp. 342–64.

9. Other theophanies which have a minimal narrative context, such as those to Jacob in Gen. 32.1–3 and 46.1–4, will not be explored in detail.

10. As in Exod. 16 and Num. 11.4–35.

and Gen. 20.6–7.[11] As a result the relationship between Gen. 28.10–22 and a text like the story of Moses and the burning bush in Exod. 3.1–6 has not been given appropriate attention. In a similar fashion, the accounts of the promise of a child in Gen. 18.1–15 and Judg. 13.2–25 have been examined primarily in relation to other annunciation stories such as 2 Kgs 4.8–37.[12] While this has led to valuable insights about the annunciation stories, it should be recognized that the theophanic element in Judg. 13 and Gen. 18 brings these stories into the orbit of texts like the revelation to Hagar in Gen. 16.7–14, and sheds light on the notion of revelation to women in the narrative.

2. *The Type-Scene and Form Criticism*

In order to illustrate some of the limitations of prior discussions of the narratives under consideration, it will be useful to consider approaches to the group of theophany narratives known as prophetic call narratives. Form-critical discussions of the call narratives found in Exod. 3.1–4, Judg. 6, Jer. 1, Isa. 6, and Ezek. 1 have focussed on the basic structural similarity of these texts, and have arrived at a variety of conclusions about the nature and origin of these stories. While there is general agreement as to the commonality of a number of elements in most of the texts, the precise number and definition of these elements remains in dispute. Thus N. Habel proposed six such elements: divine confrontation, introductory word, commission, objection to the commission, reassurances and promise of assistance, and the sign. He reached the conclusion that the formal model of the charging of a messenger lies behind the prophetic narratives. In Habel's estimation this charge is best exhibited by Gen. 24 (despite the absence of theophanic elements in that text), and this 'secular' form was adapted to the prophetic call narrative. W. Richter defined a similar set of components, but saw the purpose of the form as establishing a model for the commissioning of a saviour for Israel, and includes the account of the choosing of Saul in 1 Sam. 9–10. W. Zimmerli, sensitive to variations in the narratives, developed a two-tiered model, the first reflected in the

---

11. R. Gnuse, *The Dream Theophany of Samuel*, (Lanham MD, University Press of America, 1984), p. 140; R. Fidler, 'The Dream Theophany in the Bible', (doctoral dissertation, Hebrew University, Jerusalem, 1996) (Hebrew) pp. 152–53; C. Westermann, *Genesis 1–11* (Minneapolis: Augsburg, 1984) pp. 452; J-M Husser, *Dreams and Dream Narratives in the Biblical World* (Sheffield: Sheffield Academic Press, 1999), pp. 123–38.

12. J. Cheryl Exum, 'Promise and Fulfillment: Narrative Art in Judges 13', *JBL* 99 (1980), pp. 43–59; Y. Zakovitch, *The Life of Samson* (Jerusalem: Magnes, 1982), pp. 74–84 (Hebrew); R. Alter, 'How Convention Helps us Read: The Case of the Bible's Annunciation Type-Scene', *Prooftexts* 3 (1983), pp. 115–30.

narratives of Moses, Gideon, Saul and Jeremiah, and the second revealed in the calls of Isaiah, and Micaiah ben Yimlah in 1 Kgs 22.[13]

The criticism of previous form-critical suggestions offered by Uriel Simon is coupled with his own suggested criteria for understanding the call narratives.[14] In his discussion of 1 Sam. 3 Simon objects to the omission of Samuel's encounter from the list of call narratives, and offers an alternative to the above mentioned schema. In contrast to Habel's six elements Simon proposes a five-part structure for understanding the call narratives:

1. The establishment of the initial fitness of the candidate, which may be inferred by miraculous birth (Samson), by a deed of heroism (Moses), or by divine service (Samuel).

2. An initially erroneous identification of the divine. This is illustrated by Moses' first observation of the bush (Exod. 3.3), by Samuel's failure to understand who is calling him, and by Saul's reluctance to inquire of the seer and his lack of recognition of Samuel in 1 Sam. 9.

3. The expression of apprehension and misgivings. This may include doubt or refusal, as in Moses' response in Exod. 3.11–4.17, but can also be implied from encouragement formulae which are apparently addressed to this doubt, as in Ezek. 2.6.

4. The imposition of the mission by YHWH despite the desire to avoid it. This is most explicit in YHWH's response to Moses' objections in Exod. 3.11–4.17, but Simon includes Eli's adjuration of Samuel (1 Sam. 3.18) as well as YHWH's command to Ezekiel to eat the scroll (Ezek. 2.8).[15]

5. The initial recognition of the appointed figure as divinely authorized. This is seen in the people's response to Joshua 'We will obey you' (Josh. 1.16–18), in the disciples' acceptance of Elisha in 2 Kgs 2.15, and in Samuel's recognition by Eli (1 Sam. 3.18) and by the people (3.20).[16]

While this schema provides some attractive refinements which, together with Simon's sensitive and nuanced reading of 1 Sam. 3, advance our understanding of the story considerably, these criteria are not as uniformly

---

13. N. Habel, 'The Form and Significance of the Call Narratives', *ZAW* 77 (1965), pp. 297–323; W. Richter, *Die sogennanten vorprophetischen Berufungsberichte* (Gottingen: Vanderhoek und Ruprecht, 1970); W. Zimmerli, *Ezekiel I* (Hermeneia; trans. R.E. Clements; Philadelphia: Fortress, 1979), pp. 97–100. Cf. also B.S. Childs, *The Book of Exodus* (Philadelphia: Westminster, 1974), pp. 53–6, R.K. Gnuse, *The Dream Theophany of Samuel*, pp. 133–42 and J. Van Seters, *Abraham in History and Tradition* (New Haven: Yale University Press, 1975), pp. 261–62.

14. U. Simon, *Reading Prophetic Narratives*, (Bloomington: Indiana University Press, 1997) pp. 51–8.

15. It seems that Simon would include Habel's fourth category, the commission, as implicit in the imposition of the mission, even though it is not explicit in 1 Sam. 3. Cf. *Prophetic Narratives*, p. 55.

16. Simon, *Prophetic Narratives*, pp. 54–5.

applicable to the call narratives as Simon argues. While the fitness of the character of Moses is clearly established by his actions in Exod. 2.11–22, in the case of prophets like Jeremiah, Isaiah and Ezekiel there is no (prior) indication as to why this particular individual is chosen.[17] Placing these texts in the larger framework of theophany narratives, however, would allow for the understanding of some of these phenomena in a more satisfying context. As will be discussed below, theophany scenes usually begin with a more prosaic *setting of the scene*, which has more to do with the circumstances surrounding the theophany and its purpose than with the fitness of the character. When judged against other theophany narratives, Simon's second element, the 'initial error', seems less a mistake than an incomplete perception. Moses at the bush does not err in his initial reaction to it so much as reveal his limited understanding of what he sees. Indeed, this limited perception is an essential element in the refocusing of the protagonist's understanding that is common to theophany narratives. It often reflects the essential shift in the individual's perception of reality when confronted with a manifestation of the divine. Not only is the protagonist's grasp of the situation partial, but the narrator's general reluctance to describe divine manifestations in anything but general terms adds to this sense of incompleteness, and points to its being a stage in the character's progression toward a new level of knowledge.

Simon's third category of apprehension and misgivings is indeed common to a number of the narratives we will discuss, but here it may be more helpful to distinguish between two distinct types of human reactions. The more widely discussed is the prophetic objection to accepting the task set before him. Yet in the framework of theophany stories more significant are the protagonist's reactions to the encounter with the divine (and not to the commission itself).[18] In many cases this will be reflected in the protagonist's bipolar response to the numinous as both attractive and frightening, at once drawing him closer, and yet provoking anxiety about the potentially lethal nature of encountering YHWH. The fourth category, the imposition of the mission despite the desire to avoid it, is appropriate to many (but not all) prophetic call narratives (e.g. Isa. 6), but, as we shall see, not to many other theophany stories.[19] Jacob's dream in Gen. 28.13–15, for example, is about divine promise and support at a time when Jacob is leaving his home.

17. It is also desirable to distinguish between the establishment of the protagonist's character in the larger narrative (e.g. Moses in Exod. 2.11–22, or Samuel in 1 Sam. 2) and the absence of such an indication within the theophany tale itself.

18. On this distinction see G.Y. Glazov, *The Bridling of the Tongue and the Opening of the Mouth in Biblical Prophecy* (JSOTS 311; Sheffield: Sheffield Academic Press, 2001), pp. 37–53.

19. As will be discussed below in chapter 4, Eli's adjuration of Samuel in 1 Sam. 3.18 can be seen as a pale reflection of this idea.

Simon's final category, the initial recognition of the divinely appointed figure, is indeed appropriate to Samuel in 1 Sam. 3.19–21, but it is not very common in other narratives. Here, too, defining the phenomenon more broadly will be helpful in understanding its function not simply as the final stage of the prophetic call, but as reflective of a larger dynamic in theophany narratives. In most cases the theophany moves from a private, intimate encounter to a more externalized perspective reflecting the potential public ramifications of the experience. In the case of prophetic call narratives this may include popular acceptance of the prophet's role, but in most cases the call narrative gives no indication of this. Rather, the opposite is emphasized: Jeremiah and Ezekiel are told to expect harsh opposition from the people, and Isaiah's commission to deceive the people in order to bring about their destruction (Isa. 6.9–13) is hardly the sort of behaviour calculated to lead to popular acclaim. That the prophets did eventually achieve such recognition may owe little to the call narratives themselves and more to their rhetorical abilities.[20] Rather, these narratives commonly display an externalized expression of what has been up to this point an internal process. The type of externalization we are speaking of may be reflected in the public recognition of Samuel, but it may be seen equally in Jacob's anointing the stone where he dreamed, and in his promise to build a temple at Bethel, to mark publicly what he had experienced on a private level (Gen. 28.18–22). The bringing of the people to Sinai by Moses and his central role in the revelation can be seen as a public restatement of Moses' private experience for the entire people.[21] This certainly fits Simon's category of public recognition, though it is not initial recognition. Thus the public/private dichotomy, or the inside/outside dialectic of the theophany, is often reflected in this element as well.[22]

While the form-critical approach has provided important insights about the structure of the call narrative and the possible origins of these texts, the limitations of this methodology have been rehearsed many times in recent

---

20. R. Carroll ([*Jeremiah* (OTL; Philadelphia: Westminster, 1986) p. 100]) understands Jeremiah's call narrative to be directed at a later audience than the one to whom the prophet may have actually spoken. Such an understanding of the function of the call narrative may well be appropriate for Isaiah and Ezekiel as well.

21. Following the interpretation of Exod. 3.12 as referring to the Sinai revelation; cf. M. Greenberg, *Understanding Exodus* (N.Y.: Behrman House, 1969), pp. 75–8.

22. Polak's idea of the 'relic' as a physical reminder of the theophanic experience also reflects this inside/outside dynamic. Cf. F. Polak, 'Theophany and Mediator', p. 116. Moses' staff is certainly a good example of this, but even in cases where no concrete relic exists there is still a movement from private experience to public expression. In addition to the example of Sinai mentioned above, this is also demonstrated in the externalization of Moses' private theophany in Exod. 33.12–23 in the episode of Moses' veil in Exod. 34.29–25.

studies.[23] Most relevant for our concerns is the observation that the uncovering of a hypothetical Ur-form of the story may be of only limited assistance in deciphering a given call narrative.[24] The interrelationship of the stories may owe as much to intertextual influence as to reliance on a basic formal model. The emergence of literary approaches has been instrumental in advancing a more nuanced understanding of these texts, as can be seen from Simon's treatment mentioned above. Frank Polak's analysis of the theme of theophany and mediator in the book of Exodus attempts to bring together a number of different types of theophany stories under the literary rubric of 'theme'.[25] Thematic analogy and variation in motif are a richer source of literary meaning than purely formal considerations, and open up the biblical text in important ways.

But it is the idea of the type-scene which will be most helpful to bridge the gap between formal structural connections between the narratives and the particular dynamics of each story. I will use the term to refer to a recurrent scene within a story whose repetitions reveal both identity and difference: identity in the basic plot sequence which is described, and difference in the deployment of certain motifs in varying fashion. Robert Alter's innovative use of the concept of the type-scene to illustrate the richness to be found in betrothal stories and annunciation stories represents an important advance beyond form-critical methodology.[26] S. Gelander considers the wilderness complaint stories in Exodus and Numbers to constitute yet another type,[27] and one might also point to the

23. See A. Berlin, *Poetics and Interpretation*, pp. 122–9; Alter, *Biblical Narrative*, pp. 47–50; Polak, *Biblical Narrative*, pp. 381–66.

24. Kuntz, *The Self Revelation of God*, pp. 58–71, suggests a form-critical schema for a theophany Gattung which is interesting for its originality, but suffers from the same limitations as other form critical constructions.

25. F. Polak, 'Theophany and Mediator', p. 116, outlines a series of 'determinant components' common to all theophany tales which combine to form a matrix of ideas. The elements which Polak identifies are:
a. The dimension of the theophany (location, addressee).
b. The question of direct contact with the Deity versus mediated contact.
c. The relationship of verbal and visual elements.
d. The relationship of the theophany to manifestations of nature (thunder, fire).
e. The purpose(s) of theophany (commissioning, revealing the essence of the Deity, transmitting a specific message).
f. The significance of physical remains (relics) after the theophany (e.g. Moses' staff).
All of these elements are indeed present in theophany narratives to one degree or another, but they more accurately describe dynamics within the narrative than actual building blocks for a narrative structure.

26. Alter, *Biblical Narrative*, pp. 50–62; idem, 'How Convention Helps us Read', pp. 115–30. See also the discussions in Polak, *Biblical Narrative*, pp. 381–86, and S. Gelander, *Art and Idea in Biblical Narrative* (Tel Aviv: Hakibbutz Hameuchad, 1997), pp. 136–42 (Hebrew).

27. Gelander, *Art and Idea*, pp. 138–141.

wife-sister stories in Genesis, or to the recurring account of the return of a messenger, particularly one bearing disastrous news.[28] One of the advantages of this tool over the form-critical method is in its eschewing a diachronic analysis which would establish a primary text which serves as a prototype for all the other appearances of the same scene. Since biblical research of the past few decades has not succeeded in providing greater consensus regarding the relative dating of narrative texts, there is great value in being relieved of the burden of a diachronic model of literary development.

Like the examples discussed by Alter, theophany narratives exhibit a set number of recurrent motifs around which the story is based: The setting of the scene, the appearance and speech of YHWH, human response to the presence of the divine, the expression of doubt or anxiety, and externalization of the experience. While most of the elements of the call narrative can be seen to fall within the theophany narrative, the theophany theme so transforms these texts that the term 'call narrative' is insufficient to describe them accurately. We would propose that the net must be cast wider, and that these call narratives be seen as a particular subset of initial theophany narratives. The form-critical definitions discussed above are accurate as far as they go, and history of traditions analysis may also reveal important trends in the development of the stories. But in the context of the literary study of the Bible the type-scene will be a more useful tool for demonstrating the interrelationship of these stories. Through such an approach we will demonstrate how biblical tradition has encoded variety within these texts in order to address a complex range of situations.[29]

28. Cf. D.M. Gunn, 'Narrative Patterns and Oral Traditions in Judges and Samuel', *VT* 24 (1974): 286–317.

29. Most recently, Schmidt and Nel ['Theophany as Type-Scene in the Hebrew Bible'] suggested an approach to the topic quite similar to that described here. They propose a five-part type-scene consisting of background, manifestation, dialogue, intrigue, and conclusion, and offer readings of Exod. 3–4; Exod. 19–34; Num. 22–24, and 1 Kgs 19. While some elements dovetail quite nicely with our analysis (e.g. 'manifestation', 'dialogue'), others are too broadly conceived (e.g. 'background', 'conclusion'), and the element of intrigue does not function consistently as a plot element in the scene, but serves different purposes depending upon the context. The approach taken here will be more rigorous in its definition of categories, broader in the range of theophany narratives to be considered, and more nuanced in our reading of those texts.

3. *The Essential Components of the Theophany Type-Scene*

a. *Preparation for Theophany: Setting the Scene*
While the exposition is a common element in many stories, its importance here is in establishing some basic parameters of the nature of the divine–human encounter. In theophany stories the primary function of such a *mise en scène* is to separate the protagonist from family or others in preparation for what in most cases is a solitary experience. Jacob's departure from his family (Gen. 28.10) forms the backdrop to his dream at Bethel, and his isolation is central to the message of the dream. Similarly Jacob's aloneness at the Jabbok is underscored in Gen. 32.24 in order to separate him from his family and to accentuate the heroic aspects of his struggle with the angel. Moses' separation from Jethro's family is emphasized by his pasturing the sheep אחר המדבר – in the far part of the desert (Exod. 3.1).[30] The call of Samuel (1 Sam. 3) plays off against this tendency in significant ways – Samuel is alone, yet close enough to Eli to hear his voice (or to imagine that he hears his voice). Yet despite his proximity it is clear that Eli hears neither the call nor YHWH's oracle. Hagar's first meeting with the angel of YHWH in Gen. 16.7–14. comes after she has fled the difficulties of life with Sarah and Abraham; the subsequent theophany in Gen. 21 takes place after she has been driven out of Beer-sheba.[31] Manoah's wife is alone on both occasions when the angel appears to her (Judg. 13.3,9), her husband's subsequent involvement being solely the result of his own insistence. The angel who appears to Elijah in 1 Kgs 19.5 arrives after he has dismissed his servant.[32] In the case of Balaam (Num. 22), the narrator uses this solitary aspect as a foil for mocking the prophet's inability to perceive what his ass sees.

This focus on the solitary aspect of theophany highlights the unusual nature of divine–human encounters, suggesting that there is something about the appearance of the divine that is antithetical to human company. This is a highly private experience, even though it always has public ramifications. This solitude also increases the sense of mystery and sanctity surrounding the encounter. Insofar as it is a highly uncommon occurrence, the recipient of the experience must separate himself from his everyday reality as a precondition for the encounter. This underscores the unusual

---

30. Cf. W.H.C. Propp, *Exodus 1–18* (AB; N.Y.: Doubleday, 1998), p. 197.
31. Even though Ishmael is with her, the revelation of the *malakh* comes only after she has distanced herself from her son as well (Gen. 21.16).
32. The solitude of the prophets Isaiah, Jeremiah and Ezekiel is not specified, but the terms of the call indicate a private experience in all cases.

nature of group revelation in the Bible, and points toward one of the exceptional aspects of the revelation at Mt. Sinai.[33]

A second significant function of the setting of the scene is the determining of location. Frequently this is connected to an aetiological element later in the story in relation to a specific sanctuary (Bethel, Gibeon, Shiloh,) and the subsequent importance of the holy place.[34] This in turn is often tied to what we will describe as the final aspect of the type-scene, the creation of structures for the continuation or extension of the experience. In the case of both Moses (Exod. 3) and Jacob (Gen. 28) the revelation takes place at a holy site, though the protagonists themselves apparently have no knowledge of this, a fact which subsequently becomes important in judging their reactions to their experiences. In the case of the two theophanies involving Hagar, the location of a well serves as an important landmark, especially in Gen. 21.19, where her perception of the well marks a life-saving event and has an aetiological function.[35] An additional aspect of spatial signification is found in stories in which the location has internal relevance to the story. The location of Gideon's theophany under a tree (Judg. 6.11) is an everyday, almost ordinary scene, but at the same time the action of concealing produce from the Midianites is indicative of the problem of oppression; Y. Amit goes so far as to suggest that Gideon himself is hiding from the Midianites.[36] In the case of Isaiah 6, the prophet's vision isn't located spatially, but a sharp contrast between divine and human leadership is drawn by the notation 'In the year of the death of King Uzziah' in Isa. 6.1; the imagery of the vision, however, suggests some connection to the Temple in Jerusalem.[37] A third type of significance can be seen in Ezekiel's call narrative, where the prophet's situation in exile is clearly related to the nature of the chariot vision and to the message he is told to transmit. Thus we see how the setting of the scene is not simply a formal requirement of the narrative structure, but is essential to the purpose and experience of the theophany which follows.

---

33.   Here, too, however, there are aspects of separation – the physical distance from Egypt, the refraining from sexual activity, and the theological aim of Israel becoming 'a kingdom and priests and a holy nation'.

34.   Cf. Lindblom, 'Theophanies in Holy Places', pp. 91–106.

35.   Despite the significance of mountains as a locus of revelation in the Bible, only those theophany narratives associated with Sinai (Exod. 3, 19, 33, I Kgs 19) have a mountain setting. Cf. Hiebert, 'Theophany', pp. 505–9.

36.   Y. Amit, *The Book of Judges: The Art of Editing* (Jerusalem: Mossad Bialik, 1992), p. 235 (Hebrew).

37.   On the connection between the vision and the Jerusalem temple cf. B. Uffenheimer, 'Isaiah 6 and its Rabbinic Exegesis', in Uffenheimer, *The Bible and Jewish History*, pp. 18–50 (34) (Hebrew). One might also point to the outside/inside dichotomy set up by Abraham's receiving his guests (and the attendant annunciation) outside his tent.

b. *The Appearance and Speech of YHWH.*

The emergence of the Deity in theophany narratives may be marked by a vision or a dream, or by the appearance of a divine emissary. The *malakh* is depicted as a visual manifestation in the cases of Abraham (Gen. 18), Jacob (Gen. 32.2–3,24), Balaam (Num. 22), Joshua (Josh. 5.13), Gideon (Jud. 6.12), and Manoah's wife (Jud. 13). In initial theophanies this visual element always occurs first, even though the subsequent verbal revelation proves to be the primary means of conveying the message.[38] In his dream (Gen. 28.11–12) Jacob sees a *sullam* with angels ascending and descending, prior to hearing a voice which delivers a message of protection and accompaniment. Moses' revelation (Exod. 3.1–6) begins with the visual awareness of the bush (or a *malakh*), and is only then followed by YHWH's verbal address.[39] Isaiah sees YHWH enthroned, encircled by angels singing praises, prior to YHWH's question 'Who will go for us?' (Isa. 6.8). And Ezekiel's highly complex vision of chariot and Deity is but a prelude to the commissioning speech in Ezek. 2.1. The group revelation at Mt. Sinai in Exod. 19 begins with visual and sensual elements of smoke, fire and cloud prior to the speech of the Deity.

In theophanies such as Exod. 33 and 1 Kgs 19, which are not initial encounters, the visual aspect does not introduce the divine, but is preceded by verbal interaction. This seems to emphasize the priority of visual revelation for attracting the attention of the protagonist, but once communication has been established the visual element is of lesser import.[40] In all of these texts the message of the divine is delivered in words, whether this be a commission in the call narratives, the promise of the birth of a child in annunciation stories (Gen. 16.10–12; 18.10; Judg. 13.3–5), or the affirmation of blessing to Jacob (Gen. 28.13–15; 32.28; 46.2–4) and to Hagar (Gen. 21.17–18). The relationship between the visual and audial elements is an important part of the theophany, and the two should not be seen as entirely separate elements. This is illustrated well by the relationship between Moses' vision of the burning bush and his subsequent commission. The bush ablaze reflects both Moses' role as prophet (enlivened by fiery inspiration) as well as his task as national

---

38. In 1 Sam. 3 the visual element is diminished and its mention in 1 Sam. 3.15 may coincide with the verbal message. Solomon's dream at Gibeon relates verbal interaction, but uses the verb נראה to describe the revelation (1 Kgs 3.5). Jer. 1.4–19 has no reported visual component, and the revelation begins verbally. On the question of the visual element in Jeremiah's call see below pp. 81–4.

39. On the relation between the bush and the *malakh* see Propp, *Exodus 1–18*, p. 198; Greenberg, *Understanding Exodus*, p. 70.

40. In the case of Hagar the revelation of the angel is described verbally in both Gen. 16 and 21, but in the first occurrence the visual element becomes apparent only in the aetiology of the well in Gen. 16.13.

liberator (Israel caught within Egypt).[41] Likewise, Isaiah's perception of the transcendence of the divine in Isa. 6.1–4 foreshadows the subsequent divine speech which seeks to separate Isaiah from human society and join forces with the heavenly pantheon.[42]

This visual representation of the Deity is subject to limitations which are reflected in the narrator's depiction of the numinous as well as in the character's perception of the divine. As a rule, the visual depiction of the divine begins with some marker of the sense of distance between the Deity and the protagonist. This may be reflected by the appearance of a *malakh* as an intermediary or as a precursor of YHWH, as in the encounters of Abraham (Gen. 18), Jacob (Gen. 32.2–3,24), Balaam (Num. 22), Joshua (Josh. 5.13), Gideon (Judg. 6) and Manoah's wife (Judg. 13). Conversely, there may be a graduated process of depiction, as demonstrated by the series of three הנה clauses in Gen. 28.12–13, delineating what Jacob saw in his dream. The focus moves from an image which indicates the possibility of connection between heaven and earth, to angels which represent the very process of communication, and culminates in the appearance of YHWH. The tripartite focus is meant to indicate both the reality of communication between the divine and human spheres, as well as the transcendence of the Deity, whose otherness is temporarily overcome in the theophanic moment. Similarly, in his call narrative Ezekiel first describes the chariot in 1.4–24, and only in 1.25–27 does he delineate the figure enthroned thereon, giving the impression of gradual approach, revealing more and more detail as it draws near to the prophet.[43]

Not only is the speech of the Deity generally heard after the visual component of the revelation is complete, but once the discourse begins there is no further reference to the visual. After YHWH speaks to Jacob the *sullam* ceases to be an object of reference, as does the burning bush after YHWH's call to Moses.[44] The physical departure of YHWH's chariot after the commission of Ezekiel is presented in audial terms (Ezek. 3.12–13), despite the extensive physical description in the first part of the narrative. In this sense the verbal has taken precedence over the visual, for in the biblical world it represents truer communication with the divine.[45] At the same time, the close relationship between the two modes of

---

41. Cf. Greenberg, *Understanding Exodus*, pp. 70–1; Propp, *Exodus 1–18*, p. 222.

42. M. Weiss, 'Image and Voice in Prophetic Vision', *WCJS* 6 (1973), pp. 91–9 (Hebrew).

43. M. Greenberg, *Ezekiel 1–20* (AB; N.Y.: Doubleday, 1983), p. 52. The audial element is mentioned in 1.24, but there are no spoken words until 2.1.

44. J.P. Fokkelmann, *Narrative Art in Genesis* (Amsterdam: van Gorcum, 1975), p. 54.

45. While Deut. 4.33 and 5.23–27 do speak of hearing the Deity as an exceptional and potentially lethal experience, exposure to the voice of YHWH is generally not subject to the same types of representational limitations as in the visual dimension. Cf. L. Kochan, *Beyond the Graven Image* (London: Macmillan, 1997), pp. 7–10, 159–70.

communication creates a unified message, and represents a higher level of revelation than the symbolic dream (e.g. Gen. 37.6–7,9), in which the object is beheld but not explained. In Gen. 28.13–15 YHWH does not explicitly spell out the meaning of the vision of the *sullam*, but its significance becomes evident as a result of YHWH's speech.[46] Likewise, in the call narrative of Ezekiel, the intricate description of the divine chariot in 1.4–28 is not deciphered by YHWH's speech to the prophet, but its import is clear enough.[47]

Thus, for all the Bible's reticence about describing YHWH in visual terms, and despite the obvious preference for spoken revelation over visual disclosure, the theophany narratives reveal something of the significance of visual representation of the Deity. The fact that many of these spectacles are first time theophanies may reflect the sense that the visual is important for initial experience, but that deeper communication is primarily verbal. Yet, at the same time, Moses' most daring request of YHWH in 33.18 is הראני נא את כבדך – '*Show* me your glory' – a visual revelation to which YHWH is unwilling to agree.[48]

c. *Human Response to the Presence of the Divine.*
i. *Fear and Fascination.* One of the chief distinguishing characteristics of theophany stories is the reaction of the protagonist to the appearance of the divine. Though they may differ in the form of expression, these responses are characterized by an unusual display of humility or fear, an awareness of 'creature consciousness'. The external contours of these reactions include bowing (Exod. 24.1, 34.8; Num. 22.31; Josh. 5.14; Jud. 13.20), hiding the face (Exod. 3.6), exclamation (Gen. 28.16), or even the simple הנני, 'ready', as a statement of willingness to respond to the divine (Gen. 46.2; Exod. 3.4, 1 Sam. 3). In certain cases these expressions are accompanied by a sense of thankfulness for not having perished as a result of the encounter with the divine, sometimes coupled with an explicit fear of death. In Gen. 32.30, after he realizes that he has been wrestling with an angel, Jacob declares 'My life was spared'; after being told in no uncertain terms that the angel was ready to kill him, Balaam responds in Num. 22.35 with an appropriate sense of fear and chastisement. Upon the departure of the angel who has been speaking with him Manoah declares 'We will surely die' (Judg. 13.22). Hagar's reaction to her encounter with the angel in Gen. 16.13, 'Have I gone on seeing after seeing him', expresses a similar anxiety at having come close to death. And Isaiah's comment in Isa. 6.5,

---

46. Fokkelmann, *Narrative Art in Genesis*, p. 54.
47. Greenberg, *Ezekiel 1–20*, pp. 58–9.
48. The theophany in 1 Kgs 19, culminating in a 'still small voice' and not in a visual representation, may well be a reaction against ocular description of YHWH, in the spirit of Deuteronomy 4–5.

אוי לי כי נדמיתי, describes not simply Isaiah's shocked silence after his vision of the heavenly throne, but his actual conviction that he is going to die as a result of this experience.[49] This conviction that visual contact with the divine is lethal is well grounded in the Bible, finding expression in the Sinai traditions[50] and in the untimely deaths of Nadav and Abihu (Lev. 10.1) and Uzzah (2 Sam. 6.7).[51]

At the same time, we can recognize in many of these texts a dual response which R. Otto has characterized as *fascinans et tremendum*, a simultaneous fascination with the divine balanced by mortal fear of the implications of such an encounter.[52] Following his initial awareness of the fiery bush in Exod. 3.3 Moses declares his intention to turn aside and draw closer to the numinous, even before he fully understands the nature of what is before him. In 3.4 YHWH instructs him to stop, to remain suspended in a liminal state, symbolized by the removal of his shoes. The apprehensive aspect of Moses' reaction is seen only in v. 6, where he hides his face out of fear of the divine. Similarly, Jacob's initial response upon waking from his dream in Gen. 28.16 is amazement, focusing on the presence of the numinous in the place where he has lain down. Only in v. 17 does he respond with fear – 'And Jacob was afraid and said, "How awesome is this place!"'. Isaiah is drawn to gaze at length at the spectacle of YHWH enthroned and the pantheon of seraphim who praise him (Isa. 6.1–4), and subsequently is shaken with the fear of death in 6.5. In the case of Ezekiel one sees the initiate's fascination in the elaborately detailed description of the chariot. Yet when he actually sees the figure on the heavenly chariot he faints, not out of rapture, but out of fright in the face of the numinous. This combination of reactions is unique to the encounter with the divine, and constitutes one of the clearest markers of the theophany tradition.[53]

---

49. Note also Exod. 33.20; Judg. 6.22–23, and the related mortal anxiety in Exod. 4.24.

50. Exod. 20.19; 24.11; Deut. 4.33; 5.23–26.

51. One can see this idea of the lethal nature of the encounter with the divine extended to appurtenances and precincts associated with divine worship in the Priestly code. Cf. M. Haran, *Temples and Temple Service in Ancient Israel*, (Oxford: Oxford University Press, 1978), pp. 175–88; I. Knohl, *The Sanctuary of Silence*, (Minneapolis: Fortress Press, 1995), p. 150. See the discussion of the awareness of the lethal character of the encounter in chapter 6.

52. R. Otto, *The Idea of the Holy*, (London: Oxford University Press, 1950), pp. 12–40. See also H. Pedaya, 'Seeing, Falling, Song: The Yearning to See God and the Element of the Spirit in Early Jewish Mysticism', *Asufot* vol. 9 (1985), pp. 242–4 (Hebrew).

53. As with other type scene motifs, the narrator may occasionally de-emphasize this theme, as in the case of Samuel in 1 Sam. 3. Instead, the element of fear is displaced onto Eli, reflecting both Samuel's youth and the complexity of his relationship with his mentor. Cf. Simon, *Prophetic Narratives*, p. 68.

ii. *The Expression of Doubt or Anxiety*. Another aspect of this response to the divine is reflected in the reluctance to accept the prophetic mission. This is considered to be an essential component of the prophetic call narratives (and the call of Gideon) by both Habel and Simon. It is certainly prominent in the calls of Moses, Gideon, and Jeremiah, but it is not as prevalent as their analysis might lead one to assume. Isaiah's statement 'How long' (Isa. 6.11) may indicate reluctance, but this is hardly in the same category as Moses' lengthy series of five objections in Exod. 3.11–4.17. Ezekiel is silent throughout his call narrative, and the ascription of such reluctance to him is imputed from the various statements of divine encouragement which are presumed to address such fears.[54] Simon is correct in pointing out that Samuel's reluctance to speak is related to his relationship to Eli, but this is not the same phenomenon as Moses' or Jeremiah's reservations.[55]

The type-scene framework can be helpful in understanding the apparent absence of this theme from certain texts by viewing it in a broader context. While in some commissioning narratives this reluctance may be a sign of modesty,[56] it may just as likely reflect a degree of psychological uncertainty about the nature of the experience undergone. Voicing doubt or uncertainty as a reflection of this incredulity is common to a spectrum of theophany narratives wider than the call narratives. In the annunciation stories, for example, Sarah's skeptical response to the promise of a son is clearly stated (Gen. 18.12), and the text employs the unusual technique of 'corrective quotation' to reflect a divine response to this.[57] In the story of Samson's birth, Manoah's wife does not display any overt indication of skepticism, but this role is taken over by Manoah himself, as he raises question after question about the angel's identity and the promise of a son.[58] A related type of skepticism may also be reflected in Jacob's vow in Gen. 28.20–22, if one follows the conditional reading of Jacob's promise,

---

54. Cf. Greenberg, *Ezekiel 1–20*, pp. 75–6. W. Zimmerli *Ezekiel I* (trans. R.E. Clements; Hermeneia; Philadelphia: Fortress Press, 1979), pp. 98–100 sees a closer connection with the call represented in Micaiah's vision (1 Kgs 22.19–21) than with those of Moses and Jeremiah.

55. Cf. n. 53 above.

56. E.g. Saul (1 Sam. 9.21); Moses (Exod. 3.11 following Rashi), and Gideon (Judg. 6.15).

57. Savran, *Telling and Retelling*, p. 73.

58. Cf. Y. Amit, ' "Manoah Promptly Followed his Wife" (Judges 13.11): On the Place of the Woman in the Birth Narratives', in Brenner (ed.), *A Feminist Companion to Judges*, pp. 146–56 (148–50). Zakovitch, following Josephus ties this to Manoah's anxiety about his wife's fidelity, but here too the skepticism voiced by the women themselves in other annunciation stories (Abraham in Gen. 17.17; the Shunammite in 2 Kgs 4.16) would indicate that a basic uncertainty about the promise may be an integral part of the story. See Zakovitch, *The Life of Samson*, p. 78.

namely that his acceptance of YHWH as his god is dependent upon fulfillment of his promise to Jacob.[59]

How can this skepticism go hand in hand with the reactions described in the previous section, which are characterized by a powerful sense of acceptance of the authority of the divine? We would hypothesize a model for the theophany in which the elements we have described are aligned as follows: After an initial separation from the human world (element a) in order to encounter the divine (elements b and ci), there is a graduated return to the human world, reflected in elements (cii) and (d). The shock of encountering the divine in elements (b) and (ci) completely overwhelms the human recipient of the theophany, temporarily obliterating the self, and silencing any sense of opposition. As the experience continues, however, the protagonist begins to return to him/herself, the ego reasserts itself, and critical sensibility may emerge in the form of the skepticism we have outlined above (cii). Whereas the human response to the divine discussed in (ci) reflects the protagonist's closeness to the numinous and the attendant reactions of encountering the divine presence, the sense of doubt or disbelief referred to in (cii) suggests a distancing from the initial experience. Seen in this light, the reluctance/skepticism motif may have different functions. It may serve to heighten the sense of the miraculous, as in Gen. 18 and Judg. 13. It may by used to provide a critical perspective on the protagonist, specifically on his lack of understanding or faith (Jacob, Balaam, Manoah). Or it may express genuine anxiety at the prospect of undertaking the given prophetic or military commission (Moses, Jeremiah, Gideon). In all these cases the reflection of skepticism is understood as a natural human response, which may have a positive or negative coloration.

There is an interesting counterpart to this human reluctance in a number of narratives in which YHWH refuses a request by the protagonist to act in a certain way. The most noticeable example is Moses' request in Exod. 33.18, 'Show me your glory', to which YHWH does not accede, for reasons related to the lethal nature of the divine presence: 'No man can look upon me and live' (33.20). In I Kgs 19 YHWH refuses Elijah's request to punish the people, and instead dismisses the prophet by commanding him to anoint Elisha as his successor. (1 Kgs 19.15–18).[60] In Gen. 32.29, the angel declines Jacob's request to reveal his name, as does the angelic messenger to Manoah and his wife in Judg. 13.[61] As the human reluctance to accept the divine commission or promise has been ascribed to human frailty or anxiety, an essential component of the human condition, so these divine

---

59. See the discussion of Gen. 28.20–22 in chapter 4.

60. Cf. Y. Zakovitch, '"A Still Small Voice": Form and Content in I Kings 19', *Tarbitz* 51 (1982), pp. 329–46 (342) (Hebrew).

61. On this refusal see A. Reinhartz, 'Samson's Mother: An Unnamed Protagonist', *JSOT* 55 (1992), pp. 25–37.

refusals can be seen as indicative of something in the makeup of the Deity which cannot sanction various human requests.[62] YHWH's nature does not allow him to be perceived beyond a limited sense, and the *malakh* seems to be possessed of a similar set of limitations regarding angelic identity. The rejection of the requests of Jonah and Elijah for divine punishment are likewise seen as contrary to the nature of the Deity. Thus the theme of human reluctance, when read in the framework of theophany narratives reveals a divine complement. In both situations something of the protagonists is revealed, be it an element of human nature or the limitations placed on human understanding of the divine.

d. *Externalization*

The theophany narrative describes a movement from the human world to the divine and back again, from public to private to public, reflecting the dynamic of a temporary meeting between the two separate spheres of existence.[63] As the narrative begins with the separation from the societal context of the protagonist, so it finds its conclusion in the return of that protagonist to the world, but in a transformed manner. As there was a temporary eclipse of human characteristics such as speech and will in the drawing near to the divine, the concluding stage of the theophany narrative is marked by an increased awareness of the public sphere, by the establishing of a social role or a ritual structure for translating the private experience into an ongoing collective framework. In the case of Jacob's dream, the final element of Jacob's vow in Gen. 28.22 is a promise to build a temple on that site. This is a continuation of the process of externalization which was begun by Jacob's pouring oil on the stone in 28.18. What he has erected as a stele is to be expanded further into a temple, and the promise to tithe his possessions in 28.22b reflects the

---

62. While not containing an actual theophany narrative, the book of Jonah contains both prophetic refusal to accept a commission (Jonah 1.3) and YHWH's refusal to accept Jonah's request to destroy the Ninevites (4.10–11).

63. It may be useful here to make reference to an anthropological model of ritual. The structuralist pattern of separation and aggregation is used by a number of writers to describe the function of ritual as a means of mediation between the human and the divine. Cf. E. Leach, 'The Logic of Sacrifice', in B. Lang (ed.), *Anthropological Approaches to the Old Testament*, pp. 136–48 (137–39); J.W. Flanagan, 'Social Transformation and Ritual in 2 Samuel 6', in Meyers and O'Connor (eds.), *The Word of the Lord Shall Go Forth: Essays in Honor of David Noel Freedman*, pp. 361–72 (367–68). In the theophany accounts themselves there are few ritual elements, but the process of departure from and return to a normative social framework is clearly analogous to such a model. In place of human ritual activity, it is the Deity whose appearance and words act upon the human subject. See also H. White, 'The Initiation Legend of Ishmael', *ZAW* 87 (1975), pp. 267–306, who posits an initiation legend at the core of Genesis 21.

continuation of his relationship to the Deity at that precise spot by means of a ritual framework – from stone to stele to temple.[64]

An analogous ritual framework can be seen in the tradition of Moses' shining face in Exod. 34.29–35, which concludes the theophany to Moses in Exod. 33–34.[65] Moving from a focus on YHWH's face, which Moses is not permitted to see, the text proceeds to describe the creation of a ritual structure whereby Moses' face also cannot be viewed directly by the people immediately following his contact with YHWH. Moreover, the tense of the verbs involved mark habitual behavior, making it clear that just as Moses continues to have contact with YHWH on an ongoing basis, so the ritual use of the veil is not simply a one time improvisation, but an established practice.[66] As with Jacob's dream of the *sullam*, a singular experience becomes the basis of a continuing relationship. In Gen. 32.32 the prohibition against eating the גיד הנשה is a result of Jacob's being wounded in his struggle with the angel; as he is limited in his mobility, so the Israelites are to be limited in their diet.[67] Gideon builds an altar to YHWH (Judg. 6.24) as a response to his experience in Judg. 6.11–23. Here too the text states expressly that the altar continued to serve the Israelites 'to this day', beyond the immediate confines of the theophany experience. Thus in each of these cases the type scene of the theophany does not end with the departure of YHWH, but includes a significant external reaction which indicates an ongoing ritual relationship which grows out of the theophany.[68]

Regarding prophetic figures, this externalization is reflected in the emergence of the protagonist in his role as prophet. In the case of Samuel

---

64. Cf. Fokkelmann, *Narrative Art in Genesis*, pp. 66–9, 79.

65. The connection between the theophany and this pericope is the result of editorial design. Cf. R.W.L. Moberly, *At The Mountain of God* (JSOTS, 22; Sheffield: Sheffield Academic Press, 1983), pp. 177–80.

66. Note the similar use of habitual verbs in the related ritual description of the tent of meeting which precedes the theophany in Exod. 33.7–11. On the significance of the mask as a mark of social authority see T.B. Dozeman, 'Masking Moses and Mosaic Authority in Torah', *JBL* 119 (2000), pp. 21–45.

67. Cf. C. Westermann, *Genesis 12–36* (trans. J.J. Scullion; Minneapolis: Augsburg, 1985), p. 520; S.A. Geller, 'The Struggle at the Jabbok', *JANES* 14 (1982), pp. 37–60 (56).

68. Other forms of externalization include the aetiology of the well באר לחי ראי by Hagar in Gen. 16.14, and the birth of the son as an external affirmation of the promises made in Judg. 13 and Gen. 18. At the same time we should notice an important difference between theophanies to men and those to women. For the men the theophany marks the beginning of an ongoing relationship with YHWH, but for women such an continuing relationship with YHWH is not described. No female prophet is given a call narrative, women do not serve as cultic functionaries, and the matriarchs remain, like Sarah, 'within the tent'. Cf. T. Frymer Kensky, *In The Wake of the Goddesses* (N.Y.: Free Press, 1992), pp. 118–43; P. Bird, 'The Place of Women in the Israelite Cultus', in Miller *et al* (eds.), *Ancient Israelite Religion: Essays in Honor of F.M. Cross*, pp. 397–419. (See also pp. 153–56 on annunciation stories).

the process of externalization is begun by his opening the doors of the sanctuary in 1 Sam. 3.15,[69] continues with his revealing the oracle to Eli in 3.18, and reaches its culmination by public recognition (and ongoing revelation) in 3.19–21. For Isaiah, Jeremiah and Ezekiel this emergence is implicit in the prophetic message which they are told to impart, and, for the latter two figures, in the anticipation of human resistance to their role. The most fully developed instance of this idea concerns the depiction of Moses as mediator of the covenant, as he is seen in both Exodus and Deuteronomy. Already in Exod. 3.11 the focus of the prophet changes dramatically from the divine to the human, as reflected in Moses' objection that the Israelites won't believe him.[70] The response he receives in 3.12 points to the Sinai theophany as the ultimate goal of this private experience, reflected in the understanding of the bush as a foreshadowing of Sinai.[71] YHWH's rejoinders to Moses' subsequent objections point to increasingly externalized responses: from the revealing of YHWH's name (3.14–15), to the transformation of the staff into a snake (4.1–4), to the appointment of Aaron as Moses' second (4.11–14). And at the culmination of the Sinai theophany, Moses is designated by the people to continue the dialogue with the Deity (Exod. 20.19). The Deuteronomic reworking of the Sinai traditions extends the experience beyond the immediate moment into the future, to become a model for the continuing process of revelation by YHWH to Israel by means of Moses ('Would that they always had a heart to fear me' – Deut. 5.29). If, in Exod. 20.20, the purpose of the theophany is to put the fear of YHWH into the hearts of the people then and there, in Deut. 5.28–29 it is to make the fear continue throughout Moses' career as lawgiver and mediator.[72]

While these four motifs are the building blocks of the theophany type-scene, it should be clear that not every narrative develops each of them in equal fashion. In some cases the initial vision is described at length (Ezekiel), while in others only briefly (Moses) or not at all (Jeremiah). As a rule, the human reaction to the appearance of the Deity is of central importance (Jacob in Gen. 28), but in the case of Samuel the reaction to the divine is unremarkable. Various writers will emphasize certain elements

---

69. J.G. Jantzen, '"Samuel Opened the Doors of the House of Yahweh" (1 Sam. 3.15)', *JSOT* 26 (1983), pp. 89–96.

70. Even in his request regarding the name of the Deity in 3.13, Moses asks the question with regard to an anticipated difficulty with his public role, and not out of a desire to draw closer to YHWH.

71. Cf. above, n. 21.

72. R. Polzin, *Moses and the Deuteronomist* (N.Y.: Seabury, 1980), p. 50; A. Toeg, *Lawgiving at Sinai* (Jerusalem: Magnes Press, 1977), pp. 48–51 (Hebrew). This future orientation is extended still further in Deut. 18 to include the institution of prophecy to be continued after Moses' death. Cf. Savran, *Telling and Retelling*, pp. 114–15.

in order to bring out unique aspects of the individual theophany. Thus the elaboration of Ezekiel's chariot vision brings out the message of divine mobility in an exceptional manner – theophany can take place outside the land of Israel. The absence of Samuel's reaction to the presence of YHWH comes to highlight how his concern with Eli's response to this message stands at the center of his consciousness. It is precisely because of the centrality of this reaction in other theophany narratives that we can understand the significance of the suppression of the motif in the story of Samuel. Equally revealing is the placement of the statement about the lethal nature of the divine presence in the mouth of YHWH in Exod. 33.20. In all other cases the statement reflects human anxiety about exposure to the face of the divine, but here Moses is unafraid, and it is YHWH who imposes the limitation on him. The contrast between this revelation to Moses and all other theophanies could not be clearer.

4. *Varieties of Theophany Scenes*

While the above schema applies generally to the theophany type scene, a limited classification of these texts will be useful for further discussion. The criteria considered here include the timing of the event in the life of the individual, the nature of the recipient of the theophany, and the place of the theophany in the structure of the narrative.

a. *Type A: Initiation and Identity.*
The most common theophany texts are those which involve an initial or initiatory encounter with YHWH which is central to the definition of the protagonist's role or identity. From among these we would single out Exod. 3.1–4.17, Gen. 28.10–22, 1 Sam. 3.1–21, and Judg. 6.11–24. All four of these texts establish a narrative context in which the protagonist is situated before and/or after the call, thereby bringing the theophany into sharper focus. This narrative framework is highly developed with a clear sense of before, during and after, both within the pericope and in the surrounding narrative as well. In contrast to these 'embedded' theophanies are the call narratives of Isaiah (Is. 6.1–13), Jeremiah (Jer. 1.1–21) and Ezekiel (Ezek. 1.1–3.15). These contain similar elements to the initial encounter type scene, but the absence of a precise narrative context raises questions about the place of the theophany in the life of the prophet and the way it impacts upon his person. While they form a backdrop for subsequent prophecies, these theophanies are not necessarily integrated into the larger framework of the prophet's life.[73]

---

73. At the same time they retain significant literary ties to other chapters throughout the book. On Isaiah cf. J.L. McLaughlin, 'Their Hearts Were Hardened: The Use of Isaiah 6.9–10 in the Book of Isaiah', *Biblica* 75 (1994), pp. 1–25; B.D. Sommer *A Prophet Reads Scripture*

The story of Balaam's ass in Num. 22 is similar to the initiatory theophany in certain ways: Balaam is placed in an isolated location, fails to recognize the initial signs that a divine emissary is present, but once he does see the *malakh* he is overcome with fear and self-abasement. However, since Balaam has already had a number of conversations with YHWH in 22.10,18, the episode of the ass also bears some resemblance to the subsequent category of midlife calls.[74]

The annunciation narratives can be seen as a variation of the initiatory narratives, but here the protagonist is the mother (and/or father) of the child. Within the patriarchal framework of the biblical narrative, a clear distinction is made between the call or promise to men regarding their public roles, and the revelation to women about their corresponding private role, namely the bearing of a child. Women are not 'called' by the Deity for any purpose other than the bearing of children. Moreover, there is little or no additional contact between YHWH and these women after the birth of the child.[75] Nonetheless, despite their secondary status, a number of women are the subject of individual theophanies, and these are among the few texts in the biblical narrative where women are singled out for contact initiated by YHWH. This is felt very clearly in both Judg. 13 and Gen. 18, though each text describes the theophanic experience in different ways. The narratives about Hagar in Gen. 16 and 21 resemble this type of narrative in that both center around her childbearing role and the fate of her son. Gen. 21 also has certain points of similarity to the type of theophany seen in the binding of Isaac in Gen. 22, in which the purpose of the theophany is the protection of the beloved son.[76]

(Stanford: Stanford University Press, 1998), pp. 93–6; 178. On Jeremiah cf. J.R. Lundbom, *Jeremiah 1–20* (AB; N.Y.: Doubleday, 1999), pp. 227–9; E. Davis Lewin, 'Arguing for Authority; A Rhetorical Study of Jeremiah 1.4–19 and 20.7–18', *JSOT* 32 (1985), pp. 105–19. On Ezekiel cf. D. Halperin, 'The Exegetical Character of Ezek. X.9–17', *VT* 26 (1976), pp. 129–41.

74. R. Fidler discusses the inferior quality of Balaam's revelation in its relationship to dream theophanies to non-Israelites. See 'The Dream Theophany in the Bible', pp. 98–105.

75. One need only compare the promise of a child to Abraham in Gen. 17.15–16 with the promise to Sarah in Gen. 18. Within Genesis 17 the division between the promise to Abraham (17.1–14) and to Sarah (17.15–16) contrasts the public role of Abraham in carrying on the covenant with the external sign of circumcision, with the role of Sarah, whose sole task is to bear Isaac. When the promise is made again to her in Gen. 18, there is no mention of any public or ceremonial aspect. See further E. Fuchs, *Sexual Politics in the Biblical Narrative* (JSOTS, 310; Sheffield: Sheffield Academic Press, 2000), pp. 49–65.

76. F. Landy ['Narrative Techniques and Symbolic Transactions in the Akedah', in Exum, *Signs and Wonders*, pp. 1–40 (29)], points out the striking parallel between Hagar's seeing of the well in Gen. 21.19 and Abraham's seeing the ram in 22.13. For more on the connection between Genesis 21 and 22 see J.D. Levenson, *The Death and Resurrection of the Beloved Son*, (New Haven: Yale University Press, 1993), pp. 82–110.

b. *Type B: Redefinition in Midlife*

In a second grouping of narratives the theophany takes place in the middle part of the character's life (or later), and serves a different function from the previous texts. These encounters do not constitute a call to action, or an initiation into a calling, but may reflect something of a crisis in the life of the individual (or the nation).[77] Jacob, returning from a twenty-year sojourn in Aram, has a physical confrontation with an angel in Gen. 32.24–32 (which prefigures his subsequent encounter with his brother Esau) and in which he is renamed as Israel. While this encounter resembles the previous category in that YHWH initiates the meeting, the other two instances reveal a new phenomenon, theophany as a result of human initiative. Elijah, after being threatened by Jezebel following his slaughter of the Baal prophets, flees to Mt. Horeb in 1 Kgs 19.1–21 for an encounter with YHWH. The result of this meeting is an unusual type of 'recommissioning', in which Elijah is essentially dismissed by being told to anoint his successor.[78] In marked contrast to this (and intertextually related to it) is the encounter between Moses and YHWH following the golden calf episode. In Exod. 33.12–17 Moses pleads for divine favor towards Israel in the face of a communal crisis. The subsequent personal request in 33.18–23, to behold the divine *kavod*, is in a class of its own among theophany narratives, as indicated above.[79] All three texts are marked by a striving for further contact with YHWH which is frustrated in some way by the Deity. Each of these stories offers a reflection upon the tension between human presumption and the accessibility of YHWH, indicating the limits of human perception of, or contact with, the divine.

c. *Type C: Group Theophany*

As noted above, the majority of biblical theophanies are individual occurrences, but the phenomenon of group theophany is present as well. The primary instance of this is the revelation at Mt. Sinai in Exod 19.1–20.18, 24.1–18 (cf. also Deut. 4.1–5.30), a highly composite set of traditions, which contains elements of both type A and type B.[80] While this theophany

---

77.   On the life of the nation read along the model of the life of the individual cf. I. Pardes, *The Biography of Ancient Israel* (Berkeley: University of California Press, 2000), esp. pp. 64–99.

78.   Cf. B.P. Robinson, 'Elijah at Horeb', *RB* 98 (1991), pp. 513–36. A more severe rebuke in the context of a theophany can be seen in YHWH's reaction to Aaron and Miriam's criticism of Moses in Num. 12.2, where Miriam is physically afflicted with leprosy.

79.   See the discussion of these texts in chapter 7.

80.   For discussion and bibliography on the Sinai theophany see Childs, *The Book of Exodus*, pp. 340–75, 497–509; Toeg, *Lawgiving at Sinai*, pp. 32–59; Dozeman, T.B., *God on the Mountain* (Atlanta: Scholars Press, 1989); J. Licht, 'The Revelation of God's Presence at Sinai', in Avishur and Blau (eds.), *Studies in the Bible and the Ancient Near East Presented to Samuel Loewenstamm*, vol. 1, pp. 251–67 (Hebrew).

is an initiatory event for the Israelites, Moses' role is more complex; at times he serves as a representative of YHWH, and at times he is identified more fully with the Israelites. Here too we find the setting of the scene with the arrival at Sinai,[81] a visual appearance by YHWH followed by a verbal message,[82] an anticipated reaction of fascination[83] and fear by the people,[84] followed by externalization in the appointment of Moses to act as the intermediary for all future revelation. The Sinai theophany has unique characteristics as well: a greater focus on the ritual and sacrificial elements, the role of the priests and the sanctuary, the appointment of Moses as mediator of the covenant, and a heightening of the lethal element. While this text represents the fullest development of the group theophany one should also note the priestly theophany in Lev. 9.1–10.7 (including the deaths of Nadav and Abihu),[85] as well as the appearance of the divine in Num. 14.10, 16.19, 1 Kgs 18.38, and 2 Chron. 7.3. In contrast to the Sinai theophany these narratives use conventional symbolic representation of the divine (fire, *kavod*), and contain no spoken element addressed directly to the people.[86]

There are a number of texts which include theophany as a limited motif in the larger narrative, without the detailed development of the appearance of the divine or the human reaction. In these cases the theophany does not occur at the beginning of the narrative, but is subordinated to other matters more central to the story. In Num. 11.4–35, for example, we find frequent interaction between YHWH and Moses, as well as the 'prophesying' of the seventy elders and of Eldad and Medad, which certainly reflects the human reception of the divine. But the story itself is concerned with issues of human leadership and the complaints of the

---

81.   This may include a variation on the notion of separation as well. The movement away from Egypt into the desert sets the Israelites off against their surroundings, and the theological ideal of 'a kingdom of priests and a holy nation' (Exod. 19.6) may indicate a sense of separation implied by chosenness. In addition, prior to the revelation itself, Moses enforces segregation between the men and the women (19.15), which can be seen as yet another permutation of the notion of separation.

82.   Deuteronomy presents a modification of the visual theophany, redefining it as a primarily verbal experience. Cf. M. Weinfeld, *Deuteronomy and the Deuteronomic School* (London: Oxford University Press, 1972), pp. 206–8; Toeg, *Lawgiving at Sinai*, pp. 117–44.

83.   As reflected in the instruction not to allow the people to ascend the mountain to see YHWH (Exod. 19.12–13,21).

84.   Cf. Exod. 20.15–16.

85.   See the discussion in J. Milgrom, *Leviticus 1–16* (AB; N.Y.: Doubleday, 1991), pp. 571–640.

86.   Cf. B. Schwartz, 'The Priestly Account of the Theophany and Lawgiving at Sinai', in Fox *et al* (eds.), *Texts, Temples, and Traditions: A Tribute to Menahem Haran*, pp. 103–34. I. Knohl notes the presence of *fascinans et tremendum* in the people's response in Lev. 9.24 – וירנו ויפלו על פניהם. Lecture, Schechter Institute, Nov. 1, 2001.

Israelites, and the theophanic elements are utilized in the service of these larger themes.[87] YHWH appears and speaks in many contexts, but the interaction between him and the one receiving the revelation is not as central. In some cases these might be considered truncated theophany stories, or narratives in which the intertextual element is pronounced, as in the relationship between Gen. 32.24–32 and Exod. 4.24–6.[88] And even though only one or two elements of the type-scene may be found in these texts, one can discern similar dynamics among those elements which do occur.[89]

87. Cf. B. Levine, *Numbers 1–20* (N.Y.: Doubleday, 1993), pp. 319–27, 337–8; J. Milgrom, *Numbers* (Philadelphia: Jewish Publication Society, 1990), pp. 376–86; D. Jobling, *The Sense of Biblical Narrative*, (Sheffield: Sheffield Academic Press, 1978), pp. 27–62.

88. Cf. Geller, 'The Struggle at the Jabbok', pp. 57–60.

89. E.g. the segregation of the 70 elders from the rest of the camp in Num. 11.24, or the separation of Aaron and Miriam from the camp in Num. 12.4.

Texts	Solitude	Location	Visual	Message	Response	Lethal	Skepticism	Externalization
Gen. 16:7-14	+	+	*malakh*	after	thanksgiving	+	?	aetiology, birth of son
Gen. 18:1-16	+	+	3 men	after	Abe –	–	–	birth of son
					Sarah – laughter		+	
Gen. 21:14-21	+	+	–	speech only	–	–		well, water, growth of son
Gen. 28:10-22	+	+	dream	after	fear, understanding	–	vow?	stele, temple
Gen. 32:24-33	+	+	man (darkness)	after	aetiology	+	–	aetiology, sciatic nerve
Exod. 3:1-6(+)	?	+	*malakh*, fire	after	hiding face/fear	?	–	signs/rod/prophet
Exod. 19-20, 24	+	+	fire, smoke	after	fear	+	+	appointment of Moses
Exod. 33:12-23	+	+	Deity	before	'Show me your glory'	+	–	tablets, mask
Lev. 9:23-10:4	–	+	fire	–	death	+	–	removal of bodies, restrictions
Num. 12:1-16	–	+	cloud	after	prayer for Miriam	–	–	leprosy, outside the camp
Num. 22:2-35	?	–	*malakh*	before and after	bowing/fear, understanding	+	+	prophet
Josh. 5:13-15	+	–	man	after	bowing	–	–	removing shoes?
Judg. 6:11-22	+	+	*malakh*, Deity	after	understanding, fear of death	+	reluctance	altar
Judg. 13:2-25	+	–	*malakh*	after	Manoah + bowing, understanding	+	Manoah	altar, birth of son
1 Sam. 3:1-21	+	+	vision	after?	–	–	telling Eli	opening gates, prophet
1 Kgs. 3:4-15	+	+	–	+	thanksgiving	–	–	sacrifice
1 Kgs. 19:1-18	+	?	*malakh*, fire	before and after	hiding face	–	–	anointing Elisha
Isa. 6:1-13	+	–	Deity	after	fear, volunteer	+	?	prophet
Jer. 1:4-19	+	–	?	before	'I can't speak'	?	+	prophet
Ezek. 1:3-3:15	+	+	chariot	after	falling on face	?	?	prophet

Chapter 2

PREPARING FOR THEOPHANY

How does one prepare for a theophanic encounter in the Bible? Are there set patterns of behaviour which precede the encounter with YHWH, a preference for certain locations, for a certain stage in the life of the protagonist? While the Bible provides precious little information, an examination of this first stage of the theophany narrative, the setting of the scene, can offer some insight into these questions. While the exposition can serve many different functions in biblical narrative,[1] its most significant purpose in the theophany narratives is the separation of the protagonist from other human company prior to the theophanic experience. Given the radical otherness of YHWH in the Bible we should not be surprised that there would be an antithetical relationship between the presence of human fraternity and the appearance of the divine. We might ask, however, to what extent does the recipient of the theophany wish to be distant from human company, and to what extent is he or she seeking to draw close to the divine?

As the encounter with the divine is most often a first-time experience, the protagonist is unaware that the encounter is about to take place, and the separation is usually the result of some earthly motivation. Certain texts speak of actual flight from human oppression, as with Hagar's running away from Abraham and Sarah in Gen. 16. There is no preparation for the theophany on the part of Hagar, and no indication that her flight will lead to a meeting with a *malakh*. Moreover, the theophany does not come to affirm her flight, but to argue for her return. Jacob's departure to Haran is motivated by Esau's threat prior to his encounter in Bethel in Gen. 28.10–22. In other cases the context supplies the notion of flight, as with the Midianite oppression described in Judg. 6.1–10 prior to Gideon's encounter in Judg. 6.11–24.[2] In those texts which do not describe an initial encounter one finds a more conscious movement towards the divine.

---

1. On the function of the exposition in biblical narrative cf. Amit, *The Book of Judges*, pp. 112–24; Sternberg, *Poetics*; Gelander, *Art and Idea*, pp. 37–44; Polak, *Biblical Narrative*, pp. 115–16.

2. Amit, *The Book of Judges*, p. 235, suggests that 6.11 should be understood as 'hiding wheat' from the Midianites, which may indicate that Gideon himself is in hiding.

In some cases the movement towards YHWH is combined with a sense of flight, as with Elijah in 1 Kgs 19, and Israel's departure from Egypt and movement towards Sinai in Exod. 19.[3] In other cases the individual explicitly seeks out contact with YHWH, not out of a desire for refuge, but in search of a specific divine response (Moses in Exod. 33; Solomon in 1 Kgs 3.1–15). Insofar as we are concerned with the transformation of the protagonist, it will be useful to distinguish between conscious and unconscious preparation in order to better judge the nature and extent of this transformation.

In many cases the text seeks to establish a liminal space in which a meeting of the divine and the human can take place. To this end, a related function of the exposition in certain narratives is the determination of the location as significant for subsequent divine-human contact. This can be seen in the emphasis on מקום in Gen. 28.11–12 in relation to the establishment of a sanctuary in Bethel, in the mention of הר האלהים as a reference to Sinai in Exod. 3.1, and the naming of the well at באר לחי ראי in Gen. 16.13–14. The sense of a sacred space is developed within the story, though the site itself may be named for aetiological reasons or because of its association with the establishment of a cultic center at that place (e.g. Bethel).[4] On certain occasions the location is centered around a natural phenomenon such as water (Hagar, Jacob at the Jabbok, Ezekiel) or a tree (Abraham, Gideon), with no cultic site attached.[5] The existence of multiple revelations at a variety of unexceptional sites underscores a central point: sacred space owes its sanctity exclusively to the Deity, and his appearance at a given site reflects the autonomy of the Deity, not the inherent sanctity of the place.[6]

There are, additionally, a few cases in which there is no indication of any preparation, conscious or unconscious for the theophanic experience (e.g. Isa. 6, Jer. 1). In these cases while there is no contextual setting for the theophany, biblical criticism has supplied one in the form of a call narrative.[7]

---

3. The connection between Exodus and Sinai is reiterated throughout the Exodus story. Cf. Exod. 3.18; 5.1,3; 9.13, etc.

4. Despite the prominence of the mountain as a site for theophany outside the narrative tradition (Deut. 33.2–5; Judg. 5.4–5; Hab. 3.3), its presence in the texts to be dealt with here is limited to the Sinai traditions. See the literature referred to by Hiebert, 'Theophany', pp. 505–8.

5. Hiebert, 'Theophany', p. 508.

6. See S. Japhet, 'Some Biblical Concepts of Sacred Space', in B.Z. Kedar and R.J.Z. Werblowsky (eds.), *Sacred Space: Shrine, City, Land*, pp. 55–72.

7. In Ezek. 1 it is clear that the prophet's situation in exile in Babylon is directly connected to the chariot vision, and to the message he is to deliver. Though the text makes no explicit

1. *Flight*

1. *Genesis 28*. When he appears in Gen. 28.10, Jacob is in flight from his brother Esau on the way to Haran. Other than the reference to Jacob's seed in 28.14 and Jacob's mention of his father's house in 28.21, everything in the text focuses exclusively on Jacob and YHWH, emphasizing instead Jacob's complete separation from his familial context. Verse 10 itself gives no indication that this pause in his journey is related to anything other than nightfall and the need for a place to rest. Gen. 28.11, however, introduces greater complexity. On the one hand, it would seem that the beginning of the verse, 'He arrived at the place', emphasizes the ordinary, indefinite quality of the location, calling it simply המקום. While the term can refer to a specific place of sacrifice or worship, as in Gen. 22.3–4, here it seems to mean nothing more than 'he came to the place (where he would spend the night)'.[8] But this apparent anonymity is undercut by the repetition of מקום three times with the definite article in a single verse.[9] Since Gen. 28.19 informs us that this 'place' does in fact have a name, the persistent use of this definite/indefinite term draws attention to itself. On one level, this tension between the ordinary and the extraordinary simply foreshadows the future naming of the site in v. 19.[10] However, beyond the aetiological aspect of the story, the repetition of מקום highlights the significant connection between it and the stone Jacob chooses.

---

mention of physical separation from those around him, the end of the vision in 3.14–15 is marked by Ezekiel's rejoining the exilic community, indicating that the vision occurred as a solitary experience.

8.   Only in the Rabbinic understanding is מקום a name for the divine; cf. *Gen. Rab.* 68.9. Regarding its use as a term for the divine in the Bible (notably in Esther 4.14) see M. Fox, *Character and Ideology in the Book of Esther*, (Columbia, SC: University of South Carolina Press, 1991), p. 63. At the same time the term is pregnant with sacral possibilities, as will become apparent in the continuation this narrative. See also *TDOT*, vol. 8, pp. 537–9; Vanderhooft, 'Dwelling Beneath the Sacred Place', pp. 625–33). The verb פגע reflects a similar ambivalence. While it means simply 'to arrive at' in Exod. 23.4; Josh. 16.7; 17.10; 19.11,22,26, it may also refer to an encounter of particular moment, as with Saul's meeting with the band of prophets in 1 Sam. 10.5, or Moses' and Aaron's hostile encounter with the Hebrew overseers in Exod. 5.20. Most striking is its occurrence in Gen. 32.2 regarding Jacob's meeting with angels in Mahanaim.

9.   The use of the definite article in the first occurrence is particularly surprising, for how can a place be 'the place' with no prior indication? One might have expected something like מקום אחד (Gen. 1.9). Cf. the suggestions by Fidler, 'Dream Theophany', p. 165; Fokkelmann, *Narrative Art in Genesis*, p. 63 n. 38.

10.   On the aetiological significance of the story cf. C. Westermann, *Genesis 12–36*, pp. 452–3; N.M. Sarna, *Understanding Genesis* (New York: Schocken, 1965), pp. 192–4. On the polemical avoidance of the name of the place here see Y. Amit, 'Bochim, Bethel, and the Hidden Polemic (Judg 2,1–5)', in G. Galil and M. Weinfeld (eds.), *Studies in Historical Geography and Biblical Historiography*, pp. 121–31 (126).

He came to a certain place.	(A)	ויפגע במקום
He took one of the stones of the place.	(B)	ויקח מאבני המקום
He lay down in that place.	(C)	וישכב במקום ההוא

In its first occurrence (A) the 'place' stands by itself, with no identifying characteristics other than the direct article. In (B) it appears as part of the phrase מאבני המקום which gives the equally indefinite stone[11] an identity, combining the vagueness of מקום with the specificity of the אבן and anticipating the interrelationship of 'stone' and 'place' which will be developed in vv. 18–19. The unusual detail of the choosing and placement of the stone is exploited in vv. 17–18, but its function in 28.11 is not at all clear. On the one hand we find utilitarian readings: the stone offered protection for Jacob's head,[12] served as a pillow,[13] or as a place for sitting or eating.[14] In contrast to these practical explanations, which indicate Jacob's lack of awareness of the sanctity of the place, R. Kutscher sees it as a stone chosen for the express purpose of incubation.[15] This interpretation attributes to Jacob greater awareness of the nature of the place, where he actively seeks out an oracle of protection or guidance with regard to his journey to Haran. However, the setting of the scene in other initial theophanies is often marked by habitual behavior, usually related to one's occupation – Moses tending his flock, Gideon beating out wheat, Samuel tending the lamp in the temple at Shiloh. In each case a connection can be drawn between the activity and the message of the theophany, but none of these indicate prior awareness of the significance of the location. It is true that in Gen. 28.18 a subsequent connection is made between Jacob's actions before and after the theophany. But Jacob's reactions in vv. 16–17 clearly indicate his surprise at the theophany, making it very unlikely that his choosing the stone was directed towards a theophanic experience.[16] The deliberateness of the act in 28.11 is highlighted in the text, but its purpose

---

11. Or stones – the Hebrew lends itself to the plural, but v. 17 refers to a single stone. Cf. *Gen. Rab.* 68.11.

12. Rashi *ad loc.*

13. S.D. Luzzato, *Commentary to the Pentateuch* (Tel Aviv: Dvir, 1965), p. 117 (Hebrew).

14. Sforno *ad loc.*

15. Cf. R. Kutscher, 'The Mesopotamian God Zaqar and the Pillar in Jacob's Dream', *Beer Sheva* 3 (1988):125–30 (Hebrew); R. Gnuse, *Dream Theophany*, pp. 35, 67–8; R. Fidler, 'Dream Theophany'; Y. Peleg, 'Going up and Going Down: A Key to Interpreting Jacob's Dream' (Hebrew), unpublished doctoral dissertation, Schechter Institute of Jewish Studies, Jerusalem, 2000, pp. 143–52 (Hebrew).

16. Fidler ('Dream Theophany', pp. 181–8) argues that while such an awareness on Jacob's part may have been present at an earlier stage of the story, in the present redaction the idea of incubation has been suppressed.

is to set the stage for subsequent transformation as marked by Jacob's new awareness in vv. 16–17 and by the anointing of the stone in v. 18.

In (C) the place is more specifically identified as במקום ההוא, *that* place, its greater definition the result of Jacob's actions and the stone itself. Thus the place where Jacob sleeps (C) is the meeting point of the stone and Jacob's head, a joining together of the 'place' which he has come upon by chance (A) and the specific site of the stone and of Jacob's preparations in (B). The effect of this is to create a sense of the liminal quality of the place, between the sacred and the mundane, between the human and the divine, between the old (Luz) and the new (Bethel). This combination of general and specific meanings of 'place', of chance encounter and directed action, will find its counterpart in the continuation of the narrative, specifically in YHWH's words to Jacob in v. 13. But despite this intimation of future importance, at this point Jacob remains unaware of this significance, setting the stage for the great recognition of transformation indicated by his reactions in 28.16–17.

ii. *Exodus 3.1*

And Moses tended the flock of his father-in-law Jethro, the priest of Midian.	(A)	ומשה היה רעה את צאן יתרו חתנו כהן מדין
He drove the flock into the wilderness,	(B)	וינהג את הצאן אחר המדבר
And he came to Horeb, the mountain of God.	(C)	ויבא אל הר האלהים חרבה

While the description of Moses as shepherd anticipates his subsequent role as leader of the people,[17] its proximate function in this narrative has more to do with Moses distancing himself from his immediate surroundings. Whereas Exod. 2.11–22 focused on Moses' escape from Egypt, Exod. 3.1 translates this flight into movement towards the divine. On the one hand, the text emphasizes Moses' connection with his new family by mentioning Jethro's name and familial connection at the very beginning of the verse. But though he is tied to Midian by his wife and son, he is, like Jacob, estranged from his original home. If Jacob's theophany in Gen. 28.10–22. was intended to guarantee his return to his land, the focus of this theophany will be the return of Moses to his people. In both cases the departure is a necessary interlude to preserve the life of the hero, and to enable the encounter with the divine.

17. On the role of the shepherd in the Bible and the ancient Near East see Propp, *Exodus 1–18*, pp. 221–2.

The structure of Exod. 3.1 highlights the distance between Moses and
Horeb – they form the first and last words of the verse which bridges the
gap between them. The separation from his family is accomplished by the
use of two consecutive verbs ('he drove', 'he came') to indicate both time
and space and by the unusual phrase אחר המדבר to mark the distance from
his familial framework. The phrase indicates the far part of the desert,[18]
and serves as the mark of separation between the family (A) and the
mountain of God (C). While it may also call to mind Moses' encounter
with God's אחור in Exod. 33,[19] by itself it indicates nothing about Moses'
own perceptions. In spite of the fact that the location he arrives at is
termed הר האלהים, there is no indication that Moses is aware of the sanctity
of the place, or that he has come in search of contact with the divine. In
contrast to Gen. 28, the place is named before the theophany takes place.
Nonetheless, in the ensuing account Moses does not at first grasp what he
sees, nor is he aware that he has been designated by the narrator for a
unique role. To be sure this designation is implicit in the birth narrative
and miraculous salvation of Exod. 2.1–10. But Moses' lack of awareness at
this point serves to highlight the transformative aspect of the theophany by
making a clear distinction between 'before' and 'after'. Thus, while the
sanctity of the site is unknown to Moses there is nonetheless a sense of
Moses distancing himself from the ordinary.[20] Moses begins this story as a
shepherd, with no clear agenda beyond his relation to his father-in-law and
his flock; the story concludes with a focused return to Egypt, a reunion
with his brother Aaron, and a designated role as prophet and leader of the
people.

iii. *Genesis 32.24–32*

In Gen. 32.24 Jacob's aloneness is highlighted by the explicit expression
ויותר יעקב לבדו, which also indicates the suddenness of this solitude.
Attempts to explain this suddenness have contextualized the setting of the
scene within the narrative framework of Jacob's return to Canaan and his
encounter with Esau. Here Jacob is not actually in flight, though he does
see himself in mortal danger. Our narrative is placed at a central point
between the preparations for his meeting with Esau in Gen. 32 and the
actual reunion in Gen. 33.[21] Not a few commentators have suggested that
this theophany comes to foreshadow Jacob's meeting with his brother,

---

18.   Propp, *Exodus 1–18*, p. 197; Greenberg, *Understanding Exodus*, p. 68.

19.   Carroll, 'Strange Fire', p. 41. On the phrase itself see Propp, *Exodus 1–18*, pp. 197–8.

20.   The midrash explained this in terms of Moses' desire to provide better care for his
sheep (*Tanhuma* Shemot, 7; *Exod. Rab.* 2:2). Here too Moses is unaware of the location he
arrives at.

21.   The brief encounter in 32.2–3 with the group of angels further contextualizes the story,
giving the impression that this meeting too will be fortuitous. Moreover, the chiastic structure

highlighting his anticipation of a hostile and life-threatening encounter.[22] Jacob's response to the struggle with the angel in 32.30, 'I have seen God face to face and my life was spared', is closely connected to his use of פנים in 32.20–21 and 32.31.[23] The use of אבק/חבק in 32.24–25 and 33.4 draws the connection still tighter,[24] as does the physical request for a blessing in 32.26 (ברכתני) and the giving of a 'blessing' in 33.10–11.[25] Indeed, Jacob's response in v. 30 – ותנצל נפשי – makes the theophany seem like the answer to the prayer he voiced in 32.11– הצילני נא. Yet it is never clear why Jacob separates himself from the company of his family. In 32.22–23 he transports all of his family members across the river, while he himself remains alone on the other side.[26] The suddenness of the attack by the 'man' in v. 23 indicates that Jacob has no expectation of such an encounter.[27] While in Gen. 28 and Exod. 3 there is some discrepancy between the reader's expectations of an encounter and the protagonist's lack of awareness, in Gen. 32 the reader is taken by surprise no less than Jacob.

Despite these attempts at contextualization, the story is set adrift by unanswered questions. Why is Jacob attacked here by a divine emissary, where the context would lead us to expect protection? If it is a response to the return from a foreign land, like Exod. 4.24–26,[28] then this has very little to do with the meeting with Esau. In demanding a blessing in Gen. 32.26, we might expect Jacob to ask for protection from Esau as he does in 32.11, but there is no indication of this. Moreover, if the wound to his thigh

---

of the larger Jacob narrative hints at the complementary nature of these two meetings. See M. Fishbane, 'Composition and Structure in the Jacob Cycle', *JJS* 26 (1975), pp. 15–38; Fokkelmann, *Narrative Art in Genesis*, pp. 208–23.

22. N.M. Sarna, *Genesis* (JPS; Philadephia: Jewish Publication Society, 1989), p. 404; Fishbane, 'Composition and Structure', p. 28; Fokkelmann, *Narrative Art in Genesis*, p. 220.

23. In 32.20 Jacob hopes 'that I will his (Esau's) face and he will forgive me', and in 33.10 he declares that seeing Esau's face 'is like seeing the face of God'.

24. Note also the sound play on יבק as well; cf. Y. Zakovitch, 'Yabok, Penuel, Mahanaim, Bet El', *Ariel* 100–101 (1994), pp. 191–204 (192); Fokkelmann, *Narrative Art in Genesis*, p. 210.

25. Jacob uses the term ברכה to refer to his gift to Esau, but the irony is unmistakable. Cf. Fishbane, 'Composition and Structure', p. 28.

26. The reasons for Jacob's aloneness here are far from clear. Rashbam offers a psychological explanation based on Jacob's anxiety about meeting Esau: Jacob was looking to run away from the encounter, and the angel came to strengthen his resolve.

27. Westermann [*Genesis 12–36*, p. 516] maintains that this is not about an encounter between Jacob and God, but between Jacob and some hostile demon. While this may have been the case for an earlier stage of the story, in its present form the blessing indicates that this is a divine emissary who comes to Jacob. This is brought out most clearly by Jacob's recognition statement in v. 31. The phrase פנים אל פנים is used exclusively for contact between the human and the divine (Exod. 33.11; Deut. 5.4; 34.10; Judg. 6.22; Ezek. 20.35).

28. Cf. Geller, 'Struggle at the Jabbok', p. 57; Westermann, *Genesis 12–36*, p. 517.

suggests a threat to Jacob's fertility,[29] why is Jacob injured *after* he has sired all his children, and the question of fertility is no longer pressing? The limping and the aetiological notice about the sciatic nerve also have no direct connection to this context, both in their concern with dietary matters, and in their mention of 'the children of Israel' for the first time in Genesis.[30] All these points make it clear that the meaning of the narrative cannot be sought only in a contextual reading, but the story must also be seen as an independent theophany narrative with themes which are independent of the encounter with Esau.[31] The tension between these two positions would indicate that Jacob's preparation in 32.22 should be read both as an escape from his apprehension about his upcoming meeting with his brother, as well as an anticipation (if not an actual prefiguration) of that meeting. According to the former, Jacob's separation from human company results in assurance from a divine emissary that his blessing is intact, while according to the latter his struggle with an איש indicates his ultimate success over his brother.[32]

2. *Approach*

Less frequently the protagonist is fully aware of the theophany which will follow, and in fact seeks out contact with the divine by physical or ritual means. In certain cases the separation is straightforward, and the intention of the protagonist to initiate contact with YHWH is clear from the text. For instance, the theophany which Moses experiences in Exod. 33–34 is the result of his own perseverance in the aftermath of the golden calf episode. Here the separation from the human community is not described explicitly by physical movement towards YHWH, as, for example, in 32.31. However the terms of the theophany described in 33–34, and the description of Moses' return to the Israelites in 34.29 make this separation apparent. Likewise, Solomon's dream theophany at Gibeon in 1 Kgs 3 follows upon a deliberate visit to the shrine at that site and offering a large number of sacrifices, whether for propitiation or for purposes of incubation.[33] Other texts, however present a more complex picture of this dynamic.

---

29. Geller, 'Struggle at the Jabbok', p. 50 n. 37.
30. Westermann, *Genesis 12–36*, p. 514.
31. The story might also be seen as a contextual response to Jacob's leaving Laban. Is Jacob's promise not to oppress Laban's daughters (Gen. 31.50) not violated by the division of his camp into two halves? The possibility of multiple contextualizations emphasizes the independence of the pericope from its immediate setting.
32. Cf. Geller 'Struggle at the Jabbok' p. 54 and the discussion below, chapter 4.
33. 1 Kgs 3:4–15 is considered to be the prime (if not the only) example of incubation in the Bible. Cf. A.L. Oppenheim, *The Interpretation of Dreams in the Ancient Near East*

i. *1 Kings 19.* Understanding the preparations for Elijah's theophany at Horeb is fraught with problems, not the least of which is approach (twice) by an angel *prior* to the theophany at Sinai. On the one hand, these preparations recall the model of flight from oppression discussed above. Elijah's hasty escape to the desert distances him from Jezebel and the danger she poses, but his dismissal of his servant in 1 Kgs 19.3 leads to an equally dangerous situation, as the establishment of his solitude directly precedes his request to die in 19.4. While the appearance of an angel in the desert as a divine response to the threat of death recalls the situation of Hagar in Gen. 21, here Elijah quite deliberately heads toward his own death. In contrast to all other theophany narratives, Elijah's desire to die signals a most extreme form of separation from the people.

But in the continuation of the narrative in 19.8 it is clear that Elijah is equally deliberate about moving towards a meeting with YHWH, though it is not clear at whose initiative this is to take place. If we understand the angel's statement in v. 7, כי רב ממך הדרך, as referring to the way to Horeb, then the process of theophany is initiated by YHWH sending his *malakh* as a response to Elijah's flight. But if the angel's statement is a call to Elijah to return to his people in the North, then it is Elijah himself who decides to defy this and seek out YHWH at Horeb.[34] YHWH's question to Elijah in 19.9 – 'What are you doing here Elijah' – would seem to favor this reading.[35] If the latter is the case, then Elijah separates himself from human society in order to actively seek out an encounter with the divine. In this way Elijah's situation is located somewhere between flight and approach.[36]

ii. *Exodus 19–20.* In addition to the fact that the Sinai pericope in Exod. 19–20 is the most complex theophany narrative in the Bible,[37] it also raises problems regarding the idea of preparation. While group responses to divine manifestation are found also in Lev. 9.24 and 1 Kgs 18.39, these are limited to a worshipful reaction to the appearance of heavenly fire on the

(Transactions of the American Philosophical Society, n.s. 46; Philadelphia: American Philosophical Society. 1956), pp. 188–90; E.L. Ehrlich, *Der Traum im Alten testament* (*BZAW*, 73; Berlin: Topelmann, 1953), pp. 13–57; S. Bar, *A Letter That Has Not Been Read: Dreams in the Hebrew Bible* (Cincinnati: HUC Press, 2001), pp. 223–32.

34. See Robinson, 'Elijah at Horeb', p. 519

35. The phrase מה לך is frequently used in contexts where a person appears (often before YHWH or before the king) without having been summoned, and is asked to explain his (unexpected) presence. Cf. Gen. 21.17; 2 Sam. 14.5; 1 Kgs 1.16; 2 Kgs 6.28; Est. 5.3.

36. An unusual aspect of preparation here is Elijah's not eating for 40 days, a practice which at once emulates Moses in Exod. 34 and Deut. 9, and looks forward to the later practice of fasting as a preparation for a divine oracle (Dan. 9). There may be an echo of this practice in Exod. 24:11, which mentions eating and drinking following theophany.

37. See the discussion in chapters 3 and 4.

altar.[38] In other texts such as Exod. 16.7,10, Num. 14.10; 16.19; and 20.6 the *kevod YHWH* also appears, but there is no popular reaction recorded, and God addresses himself only to Moses on these occasions. Only in Exod. 19–20 is there verbal contact between God and the Israelites, as well as a clear reaction to the numinous other than bowing down.[39]

Moreover, much of this theophany is mediated through Moses, which creates an even odder situation: while this is an initial theophany for the Israelites, Moses has experienced an initial theophany in Exod. 3, and has conducted numerous subsequent conversations with YHWH. For this reason this theophany has an unusual dual purpose. Like other initial theophanies we have studied, its primary function is to transform the Israelites and initiate them into a new sort of relationship with YHWH. But at the same time, it will also serve as verification of Moses' role before the people, a process of official recognition which is spelled out in 19.9: 'I will come to you in a thick cloud, in order that the people may hear when I speak with you and so trust you ever after'.

The tension between these two functions is reflected already in the preparation stage of the theophany. Unlike other initial theophanies, the site of the theophany, as well as the timing of YHWH's appearance, is made known to all. The notion of preparation here is clearly very different from the previous texts, which suggest an opposition between the presence of the divine and human company. Instead the Sinai narrative translates this into symbolic and ritual terms. The introductory speech in 19.4–6 declares the purpose of the theophany with language which reflects both the intimacy of a direct encounter as well as the larger goals of this new covenant relationship. The journey to Sinai is seen as a continuation of the separation from Egypt. The phrase אלי אתכם ואבא – 'I brought you to me' – in particular indicates a drawing near to the divine which has been initiated by YHWH. This symbolic sense is further emphasized by the demand for the Israelites to be a 'kingdom of priests and a holy nation' in contradistinction to all other nations, a further symbolic representation of the process of separation.[40] On a ritual level this is manifest in the various proscriptions delivered by Moses to the people: not to ascend the mountain or to touch it (19.12,21); the separation between the priests and the rest of the people (19.22); the laundering of clothes (19.10) and sexual

---

38.   In both texts one finds ritual preparation for the theophany: In Lev. 9 the offering of numerous sacrifices related to the dedication of the tabernacle, and in 1 Kgs 18 the repair of the altar and the preparation of a sacrifice.

39.   For a discussion as to whether or not the Israelites actually heard YHWH speak at Sinai cf. B.D. Sommer, 'Revelation at Sinai in the Hebrew Bible and in Jewish Theology', *JR* 79 (1999), pp. 422–51.

40.   Cf. Childs, *Exodus*, pp. 366–7 and the literature cited there.

abstinence (19.15). The idea of separation here is coupled with the priestly notion of separation – washing clothes imitates ritual immersion; sexual abstinence recalls the priests during their service of the divine. All of this is meant to enact the idea of a kingdom of priests on a symbolic level.[41]

Yet none of this is accomplished without the guiding hand of Moses. We hear of no independent acts of preparation by the people; in fact they are warned explicitly not to attempt contact with the mountain except by means of Moses (19.12,13). The fact that Moses is constantly ascending and descending the mountain, that each communication with YHWH is both forecast and reported without any of the usual ellipsis in repetition[42], comes to illustrate just how essential Moses is to this entire process. The conclusion to this process is found in 20.18–19, where Moses is empowered by the people to return to YHWH and to act as spokesperson. Thus in both Exod. 19–20 and 1 Kgs 19 there is a curious admixture of flight and approach, of distancing oneself from danger and being summoned to encounter the divine. In both cases the fact of prior knowledge about the encounter makes it more difficult to asses the extent of the character's transformation.

3. *Hybrid Forms*

While the above texts define the basic parameters of flight/approach, other theophany narratives display an unusual combination of the above dynamics. These texts exhibit a more developed narrative exposition which precedes the actual theophany. The process of moving toward an encounter with the divine is lengthened, while the protagonist remains largely unaware of the significance of the encounter. In each of these cases this admixture takes a different form, but in all three cases the notion of solitude is compromised by the presence of another sentient being who is also a potential or actual recipient of the theophany.

iii. *1 Samuel 3*. Insofar as this is an initial theophanic experience, we expect no awareness of the approach of the divine on Samuel's part. Indeed, Samuel is clearly ignorant of YHWH's call when it comes, and he needs explicit instruction by Eli before he can receive the revelation. Precisely at this point lies the rub: though Samuel is physically isolated in preparation for the theophany, he will seek Eli's company a number of times before he responds to the call. Only here of all the individual theophanies does the protagonist have a human helper, without whom he cannot achieve

---

41. Dozeman, *God on the Mountain*, pp. 98–101; Nachmanides on Exod. 19.10.
42. See Sternberg, *Poetics*, pp. 376–8, on the structure of repetition.

contact with YHWH. In a physical and symbolic sense Samuel can be seen to be 'approaching' the divine, by his location in the throne room of the temple.[43] This is intensified by Samuel's attention to the light in the temple, which is contrasted with Eli's blindness and distance from the divine.

The unusually long exposition in preparation for the theophany plays an important role in establishing this complexity by contrasting Samuel and Eli on a number of levels.[44] 1 Sam. 3.1 provides general background to the story while vv. 2–3 describe the situation on the night of Samuel's call.

Young Samuel served YHWH under Eli.	(A)	והנער שמואל משרת את ה' לפני עלי
In those days the word of YHWH was rare;	(B)	ודבר ה' היה יקר בימים ההם
Prophecy was not widespread.	(C)	אין חזון נפרץ

Two issues are taken up in 1 Sam. 3.1: the relationship between Eli, Samuel and YHWH, and the dearth of prophecy at this time. The independence of the three clauses allows for a variety of interpretations of the relationship between these two ideas. On the one hand, the relationship of clauses (A) and (B) could be taken as causative. Samuel serves God as an apprentice to Eli, and *therefore* prophecy is rare – the true spiritual light is subject to an inferior teacher.[45] Eli is the cause of the scarcity of prophecy, and Samuel's challenge in the story will be to liberate himself from Eli's noxious influence. According to this reading Eli is not much better than his

43. In addition a number of readers have seen indications of incubation in Samuel's sleeping in the temple. See the discussion in R. Fidler, 'The Shiloh Theophany – A Case Study of a Liminal Report', *WCJS* 12 (1999), pp. 99–107 (101) (Hebrew); Gnuse, *Dream Theophany*, pp. 139–42.

44. The context of 1 Sam. 1–2 also plays an important role in setting up this tension. Eli's blindness, both moral and spiritual is developed in the previous two chapters, though he is also seen as a somewhat positive figure. The negative portrait of Eli in 1 Sam. 1 consists primarily of his inability to perceive what is going on within Hannah and his sharp rebuke to her in 1.14. While he responds more positively in 1.17 after Hannah's explanation of her plight, he nonetheless remains somewhat tainted by this first response. In 1 Sam 2.22–25 Eli is revealed to have appropriate moral sensibilities, but his rebuke is insufficient to discipline his sons and change their behavior. In both cases, the narrator portrays him more as ineffective than as truly negative. This characterization is present in our text as well, but there is a much more positive presentation of him, particularly in his words to Samuel in vv. 17–18. On the dimming of Eli's eyes compare Isaac in Gen. 27, and the use of the phrase כהה רוח in Isa. 61.3 and Ezek. 21.12 to denote spiritual deadness.

45. On the language of (A) as descriptive of levitical work cf. Exod. 28.35, 43; 29.30; 30.20; Num. 1.50; 3.6, 31; 4.9, etc. See Y. Amit, Y., 'The Story of Samuel's Commission to Prophecy in Light of Prophetic Thought', in B.Z. Luria (ed.), *Sepher Moshe Goldstein*, pp. 29–39 (30) (Hebrew).

sons in chapter 2, casting a negative pall over the temple at Shiloh.[46] As the chief priest of the sanctuary he bears responsibility for the actions performed by all other priests including his sons. This interpretation would be in keeping with the negative oracle he receives in 2.27–36, and is further supported by the depiction of his blindness in 1 Sam. 3.2.

There is, however, contextual evidence to the contrary: In 1 Sam. 1–2 Eli may be inept at diagnosing Hannah's distress and ineffective in disciplining his sons, but there is no indication that he himself is a pernicious influence. Nor does the continuation of the narrative in 1 Sam. 3 support this, for it is Eli who is responsible for Samuel's ultimate reception of the revelation, and who then compels Samuel to reveal the prophecy he has received.[47] But neither is Eli wholly benign. The question of his influence is developed further by the description of the hierarchy of service in (A). Samuel is termed an inexperienced נער who is unable to serve as a source for prophecy.[48] Moreover, Samuel serves God לפני עלי. The phrase implies that it is only through Eli's instruction that Samuel serves God, so that the absence of widespread prophecy relates directly to Eli's questionable leadership.[49] Moreover, clause (C) is not simply repetitive of (B)[50] but amplifies it: prophecy was not only rare in frequency,[51] but it was also not widespread. The few oracles that occurred didn't circulate beyond the immediate recipient of the oracle, with the result that people remained untouched by the prophecy.[52] Prophecy, though rare, is not unknown, as we see in 1 Sam. 2.26–

---

46. L. Eslinger [*Kingship of God in Crisis* (Decatur, GA: JSOT Press, 1985), pp. 145–6] notes that in contrast to 2.11, Eli is no longer given the title priest in 1 Sam. 3. The description of Samuel as a נער serves to set him off further from Eli's sons, with whom he has been contrasted so clearly in chapter 2.

47. Alternately, the clauses could be read cumulatively, (B) adding to (A) by suggesting that, although Samuel served God, prophecy was scarce. Despite the fact that Samuel's service of God was correct, no oracles were forthcoming, and Samuel was thus unaware of the proper responses, and had yet to be taught by Eli. (Samuel's status as נער would be further support for this reading). The blame for the scarcity of prophecy reflects a general sense of divine disfavor.

48. On the meaning of נער see M. Elat, *Samuel and the Foundation of Kingship in Israel* (Jerusalem: Magnes Press, 1998), p. 25 (Hebrew); *TDOT* vol 9, p. 480.

49. See Amit, 'Samuel's Commission', p. 30.

50. If the word of the Lord is rare, clearly there isn't widespread vision. Amit, 'Samuel's Commission', p. 31, sees the repetition as referring to first audial, then visual revelation.

51. This meaning for יקר is otherwise unattested in the Bible, though Is. 13.12 – אוקיר אנוש מפז may suggest this. *TDOT* vol 6. p. 281, suggests this meaning for Job 28.16: a single precious stone might therefore be considered rare.

52. Since the verb פרץ has the sense of 'multiply' (Gen. 30.30; Exod. 1.12; 1 Chron. 4.38; Job 1.19; Prov. 3.10), it is often taken here to indicate frequent vision. But since the niphal usage of this root is unique, one might equally point to 2 Chron. 31.5, where the verb means 'to become public knowledge'.

36. However, given the negative sentiment of the oracle it is hardly surprising that Eli would have preferred that its substance would not be made public outside of a limited circle of people. This reading attributes to Eli some of the blame for the scarcity of prophecy, but at the same time implies his importance. Any change in this situation will not be only Samuel's doing, but will have to involve Eli in some crucial way. The tension within this reading highlights the centrality of Eli and the difficulty Samuel must overcome to emerge as a prophet in his own right.

On that day Eli lay down in his place.	(A)	ויהי ביום ההוא ועלי שכב במקומו
His eyes had begun to fail;	(B)	ועינו החלו כהות
He could barely see.	(C)	לא יוכל לראות

Verse 2 brings us closer to the immediate situation of the story, moving from 'those days' to 'that day', and presenting three clauses which focus exclusively on Eli. Eli lies in his place, though unlike Jacob's מקום it is not the site of revelation. If (B) is primarily a statement about ageing, as in Gen. 27.1 and Deut. 34.7, Eli lies in his place because he can't see,[53] and is therefore physically unable to attend to the lamp in verse 3.[54] However, if the double emphasis on not seeing in (B) and (C) develops the criticism of Eli implicit in v. 1, Eli's inability to see reflects his passivity (שכב) and his benightedness. Eli cannot see well enough to function in the Temple, nor is there widespread vision in the sense of prophecy.[55] Whereas in (B) Eli's eyes have only begun to darken, in (C) his functional blindness is established. The sense of a worsening situation raises the specter that prophetic vision will also decline further. What emerges from these verses is a degree of ambivalence as to Eli's role and character. It is unclear if he is to be understood as a negative force against which Samuel must struggle, or if he will simply be a foil against which Samuel's transformation will be measured.

The lamp of God had not yet gone out.	(A)	ונר אלהים טרם יכבה
Samuel was sleeping in the temple of YHWH,	(B)	ושמואל שכב בהיכל ה'
Where the ark of God was located.	(C)	אשר שם ארון אלהים

---

53. Cf. R. Yosef Kara *ad loc.*

54. Simon [*Prophetic Narratives*, p. 62], noting that blindness can be coupled with prophetic vision (Gen. 48.10–19; 1 Kgs 14.4–6) suggests that Eli is only physically disabled. But despite Eli's 'moral courage' in the continuation of the story, he is not gifted with prophetic vision. Perceiving someone else's call is hardly identical with the gift of prophecy.

55. Eslinger, *Kingship of God*, p. 147.

Over against this uncertainty verse 3 offers some hope, as a counterpoint to the negative appraisal offered so far. As opposed to the darkness of v. 2 and the lack of vision of v. 1, a light still burns, reflecting Samuel's daily task in the sanctuary.[56] If there isn't widespread vision, there is at least some degree of contact with the divine. Samuel's reclining posture (שכב) is no different than Eli's, but his location is crucial – he is within the sanctuary rather than 'in his place'.[57] Here, too, the syntax of the concluding relative clause also offers some relief from the previous darkness. The lamp may simply indicate the night-time hours, a sense of quiet, a time of receptivity to revelation.[58] Samuel is positioned in the Temple to attend to the flame; it remains lit because of Samuel's devotion and presence. In either case the symbolic association of Samuel with light is the antithesis of Eli's association with darkness in the previous verse, and develops the contrast between the two characters. Symbolically opposed to one another as light and darkness, they are bound together by their mutual presence in the sanctuary, and by their interdependence upon one another – Eli as Samuel's essential mentor, and Samuel as Eli's surrogate son and successor. Fokkelmann develops the connection between the progressive nature of Eli's blindness and the lamp of the temple which is close to being extinguished.[59] As all of v. 2 and its attendant focus on darkness is associated with Eli, so all of v. 3 – the lamp, the ark, the sanctum – is tied to Samuel.[60] Thus vv. 1–3 have clearly established the contrast between Samuel and Eli, and have accomplished the requisite separation for the

---

56. Cf. Exod 27.21; Lev. 24.3; Fidler, 'Theophany at Shiloh', p. 101.

57. Traditional Jewish commentary had difficulty with Samuel, a non-priest, being in the central section of the sanctuary. The Targum, for example, places him nearby; cf. *BT* Qiddushin 78b. But the sense of the text is that he was near the ark, 'like a servant before his master'. See the discussion in Simon, *Prophetic Narratives*, pp. 63–4, on literal and metaphorical understanding of the verse. Simon himself prefers to read היכל as indicating not the Holy of Holies, but as referring to the entire temple area.

58. Fidler, 'Shiloh Theophany', p. 100, n. 5. K.P. McCarter, *I Samuel* (AB; Garden City, N.Y.: Doubleday, 1980), p. 98, says this refers to a time before dawn. Simon, *Prophetic Narratives*, p. 63, notes the congruence with the menorah of Exod. 27.21. V.A. Horowitz ['Eli's Adjuration of Samuel's Initiation Oath (I Sam. 3.17–18) in Light of a "Diviner's Protocol" from Mari (AEM I/1,1)', *VT* 44 (1994), pp. 483–97 (497) discusses the hour in light of the significance of early morning dreams in Mesopotamia.

59. J.P. Fokkelmann, *Narrative Art and Poetry in the Books of Samuel* vol. 4, *Vow and Desire* (Assen: Van Gorcum, 1993), pp. 160–1.

60. Thus, while we accept Simon's criticism of the metaphoric understanding of the verse, one should not ignore the implicit symbolism of light and darkness as positive and negative indicators in these verses. Amit's point about the essential quality of both characters is well taken: 'Eli the blind priest, who will understand but not see, and Samuel, who doesn't understand, but will see and hear.' 'Samuel's Commission', p. 31. Samuel's transformation will therefore focus upon the point at which he understands as well as hears, for this will mark the completion of the process.

approach of the divine. But they have also made it clear that Samuel's proximity to the divine is to be enabled by Eli, as seen in the continuation of the narrative. Samuel approaches the divine and distances himself from Eli, but not in a black and white fashion.

iv. *Numbers 22*. A somewhat different situation obtains in the case of Balaam's ass in Num. 22. While the episode of the ass in 22.21–35 may have originated as an independent narrative,[61] the story is best understood in the context of the surrounding story. Prior to his encounter with the *malakh* in 22:21–35, Balaam converses with YHWH a number of times in 22.9–12. in night-time visitations, with no visual element reported.[62] Moreover, the tone and language of the conversation leads one to believe that this is not the first time they have conversed.[63] By contrast, the theophany in 22:21–35 takes place during the day, after Balaam has concluded his night-time conversation with YHWH, and after he has joined the company of Balak's ministers. The context emphasizes that Balaam is not alone, though the presence of these ministers plays no part in the subsequent theophany in vv. 21–35. Rather than fleeing human companionship, he seems to have joined it in the context of the messengers. Moreover, although 22.21–35 is not an initial revelation to Balaam, the story itself has the usual indications of an initial theophany – lack of expectations about encountering the divine; incomplete awareness of the revelation; surprise and *tremendum* in the presence of the divine. In this sense the story presents revelation as perceptible on different levels. At the highest level in the story is Balaam, who is capable of perceiving the divine in both visual and verbal terms. Second is the ass, who is temporarily elevated over Balaam,[64] but ultimately is not the recipient of verbal revelation. At the lowest level are the ministers of Balak; they have no contact with YHWH, and are not even mentioned in the actual theophany in 22.21–35. They have no possibility of communication with YHWH without the help of a human intermediary, and thereby represent *in nuce* the role that will be assumed by Balak in the continuation of the story.[65] The narrator's decision to represent theophany as being perceived

61. Cf. A. Rofe, *The Book of Balaam* (Jerusalem: Simor, 1980) (Hebrew), pp. 10–26.

62. See the discussion in Fidler as to the nature of these visitations: 'Dream Theophany', pp. 123–1.

63. R.W.L. Moberly, 'On Learning to Be a True Prophet: The Story of Balaam and his Ass', in P.J. Harland, and C.T.R. Hayward, (eds.), *New Heaven and New Earth: Prophecy and the Millenium*, pp. 1–17 (2).

64. The vision of the she-ass is privileged in that she is allowed to see the angel before Balaam.

65. See G. Savran, 'Beastly Speech: Intertextuality, Balaam's Ass and the Garden of Eden', *JSOT* 64 (1994), pp. 33–55 (35).

simultaneously (or not perceived) in a number of different ways conforms to the theme of the wider Balaam narrative.

v. *Genesis 18*. In Gen. 18.1–2a, as Abraham is approached by the divine visitors, v. 1a, 'YHWH appeared to him', gives the impression that Abraham will recognize them. The use of the term נצבים to describe their presence is a further clue to the reader of the presence of the numinous.[66] When Abraham runs toward them in 18.2b we have the momentary impression that he understands the nature of his visitors, and that we have entered a preparation scene of the 'approach' type described above. But Abraham remains unaware of the nature of his guests, certainly during the initial stages of their dialogue as well as through the entire scene of preparing food and feeding them.[67] The beginnings of such an awareness are found in the question of 18:9, 'Where is Sarah your wife?'; it becomes more pronounced with the annunciation in v. 10, and is unequivocal with the narrator's use of YHWH in v. 13.[68] Moreover, the figure of Sarah, present but hidden within the tent, compromises the solitary nature of the revelation, especially when compared with the previous revelation about the birth of Isaac in Gen. 17, which is entirely solitary. It would seem that the demands of the annunciation narrative condition these changes: in all cases the message is to be delivered to the women, but there is a complex hierarchy between YHWH, husband and wife which demands the husband's presence in the scene, even if his role is ultimately peripheral to the action. Thus while Abraham certainly stands at the center of the action in this story, there is a deliberate reduction in his role once the annunciation comes in v. 10.[69] Here there is no flight, only approach, but it is the divine who approaches the human protagonist.

In each of these hybrid cases the notion of solitude is compromised in that each recipient of the theophany is given a helper, without whom the theophany would not take place. In each case the helper is granted a special level of awareness which falls somewhere between knowledge and ignorance. If the helper is initially more aware than the recipient of the

66. Cf. *TDOT* vol. 9, p. 528.

67. Cf. T. Rudin-O'Brasky, *The Patriarchs in Hebron and Sodom (Genesis 18–19)* (Jerusalem: Simor, 1982), pp. 48–61 (Hebrew), esp. the discussion of the pointing of אדני on p. 52.

68. Rudin-O'Brasky, *The Patriarchs*, p. 57.

69. Rudin-O'Brasky, *The Patriarchs*, pp. 63–6 follows Gunkel in claiming that an earlier version of the story made a direct connection between Abraham's hospitality and the promise of a son. She develops this further (pp. 66–74) in comparing the two motifs in the story of the Shunammite in 2 Kgs 4.8–37 and Ovid's account of the annunciation of Orion. But the present form of the story greatly weakens this equation of gift for gift, and in doing so minimizes Abraham's significance in the story.

theophany, he is ultimately left behind when the theophany occurs: Samuel surpasses Eli, Balaam surpasses the she-ass, and in Gen. 18 Sarah ultimately supersedes Abraham as the object of YHWH's attention.

Chapter 3

THE VISUAL REPRESENTATION OF THE DIVINE

The Israelites said to Moses:
'It is our desire to see our king,
For the one who hears cannot be
compared to the one who sees'.
(*Mekhilta de-Rabbi Ishmael*, Bahodesh 2)

Theophany narratives are not exceptional in stressing the visual appearance of YHWH in the Bible. Despite the strong aniconic tendencies in biblical religion, and despite the clear preference in the Bible for spoken over visual revelation, there is no shortage of texts describing visual apprehension of the Deity. Throughout the biblical narrative YHWH is frequently described as having appeared to various personages (נראה אל).[1] Although the fear of seeing YHWH is a powerful taboo, a number of these texts describe encountering YHWH 'face to face' (Gen. 32.30; Exod. 33.11; Deut. 5.4; 34.10; Judg. 6.22).[2] While Deut. 4.12 protests that the Israelites 'saw nothing but a voice', the anxiety about seeing and being seen is an essential part of the Sinaitic experience in Exod. 19–20.[3] Job is convinced that he will behold YHWH (19.26–27), and after YHWH's speech out of the whirlwind he exclaims 'Now I see you with my eyes' (Job. 42.5).[4] The *k'vod YHWH* is described consistently as a visible and palpable manifestation of the divine, which appears (נראה) in plain sight of all Israel.[5] The *malakh YHWH*, another representation of numinous presence, is most often described as visibly apparent to those

---

1. Gen. 12.7; 17.1; 18.1; 26.2,24; 35.1,9; 46.29; 48.3; Exod. 3.2; 6.3; 16.10; Lev. 9.23; Num. 14.10; 16.19; 17.7; 20.6; Judg. 6.12; 13.3; 1 Sam. 1.22; 3.21; 1 Kgs 9.2; 2 Chron. 1.7; 3.1; 7.12.

2. The phrase is also used in contexts such as Exod. 33.11 and Deut. 5.4 (speaking to YHWH face to face), which attempt to undercut the visual origins of the phrase.

3. Cf. especially 19.21, 20.18–20.

4. See the discussion of seeing in Job in E.M. Good, *In Turns of Tempest* (Stanford: Stanford University Press, 1990), pp. 373–5.

5. Cf. Exod. 16.7, 10; Lev. 9.6, 23; Num. 14.10, 22; 16.19; 17.7; 20.6; Deut. 5.24; 2 Chron. 7.3.

who are addressed by him.[6] In both prophetic literature and in the psalms YHWH's appearing is frequently described in terms of visual apprehension.[7] Poetic expressions of theophany often describe visual apprehension as part of the experience.[8] Passages in the psalms such as Pss. 11.7; 17.15, 27.4,13, 42.3, 63.3 speak of 'seeing God', an expression which has been subject to varying interpretations, from the judicial to the cultic to the visionary.[9] While the term *panim* as a manifestation of divine presence has a number of different meanings, it can also indicate visible presence. If YHWH could 'cause his face to shine upon you' (Num. 6.25), then under exceptional circumstances that face might be visible to human sight as well.[10] As with the Pentateuchal injunction 'to see the face of YHWH' three times a year, the phrase may well indicate something between the experiential and the cultic.[11] While some of the above instances may refer to metaphorical 'seeing', the wide range of texts which make use of visual expressions is striking, and indicate the centrality of the visual in the encounter with the divine.[12]

The most common terms used to represent the divine presence are the *malakh*, the *kavod*, and the *panim* of YHWH.[13] None can be reduced to a

---

6. Note the exceptional case of Hagar in Gen. 21.17, where the phrase 'from heaven' is added to indicate that this is purely an audial revelation; cf. Westermann, *Genesis 12–36*, p. 342; G. von Rad, *Genesis* (OTL; Philadelphia: Westminster, 1972), p. 243.

7. Ps. 77.17; 84.8; 97.4,6; 102.17; Isa. 6.1–8; 40.5; 60.2; 66.18; Jer. 31.3; Ezek. 1, 10, Zech. 9.14. Note also Isa. 38.9.

8. Deut. 33.2, Judg. 5.4–5., 2 Sam. 22.8–51 (=Ps. 18–50); Hab. 3.3–6, Mic. 1.3–4, Isa. 19.1, Ps. 68.8–9. Cf. Hiebert 'Theophany', pp. 505–11; J. Jeremias, *Theophanie*, pp. 3–15; Kuntz, *The Self-Revelation of God*, pp. 28–40.

9. Cf. Smith, 'Seeing God', pp. 173–6; idem, *Pilgrimage Pattern*, pp. 100–9.

10. M.S. Smith, ' "Seeing God" in the Psalms: The Background to the Beatific Vision in the Bible', *CBQ* 50 (1988), pp. 171–83 (176); idem, *The Pilgrimage Pattern in Exodus* (Sheffield. Sheffield Academic Press, 1997), p. 101; A.R. Johnson, 'Aspects of the Word Panim in the OT', in Fück (ed.), *Festschrift Otto Eissfeldt*, pp. 155–60; *TDOT*, vol. 11, pp. 595–608.

11. MT 'be seen', but a majority of scholarly opinion supports reading the verb in the *qal* conjugation. The phrase is often compared to the similar Akkadian phrase *amaru pan ili* which refers to visiting a sanctuary. Cf. Childs, *Exodus* p. 451; J.H. Tigay, *Deuteronomy* (*JPS*; Philadelphia: Jewish Publication Society, 1996), p. 159; Smith, *Pilgrimage Pattern*, pp. 101–2; cf. Exod. 23.17; 34.23; Deut. 16.16; 31.15; Isa. 1.12.

12. See further the discussions of the visual in the Bible in E. Wolfson, *Through a Speculum That Shines* (Princeton: Princeton University Press, 1994), pp. 16–28; W.W.G. Baudissin, ' "Gott schauen" in der attestamentliche Religion', *Archiv für Religionswissenschaft* 18 (1915), pp. 173–239; S. Terrien, *The Elusive Presence* (San Francisco: Harper Collins, 1983); J.D. Levenson, 'The Jerusalem Temple in Devotional and Visionary Experience', in Green (ed.), *Jewish Spirituality*, vol. 1, pp. 32–61.

13. Eichrodt, *Theology*, vol. 2, p. 23, refers to these as forms of the 'spiritualization of the theophany', in the sense that they indicate an 'indirect, weakened appearance' of the divine presence. Eichrodt adds the revelation of the name of YHWH as the highest form of this

single phenomenon; each has its own complex history and semantic range and serves to represent some aspect of the divine. The *malakh YHWH* can be messenger, representative, advance party, or in one case, a term for a fiery manifestation of the divine (Exod. 3.2).[14] *Panim* implies something like 'presence', but this can vary from a metonymic term for the 'entire' deity, a description of divine attentiveness, a source of blessing, or a cultic meaning, perhaps connected with pilgrimage.[15] While the *k'vod YHWH* is the term used for the figure on the chariot which Ezekiel sees in Ezek. 1.28, it is also that which YHWH will not reveal to Moses in Exod. 33.18–23. Moreover, the *kavod* can refer to a publicly discernible presence which is visible to all Israel at certain moments.[16] The fact that we cannot define these terms precisely reflects something of the general biblical strategy for representing the divine. These phrases are primarily reserved for indicating the divine presence, but nowhere are they defined in unambiguous ways. All three expressions play a role in averting the attention of the reader from the precise depiction of the divine, and in exchanging a more precise description for a conventional one.[17]

Despite this plenitude of visual experience of the divine, very few texts go into much detail about what was observed. None of the passages in the Psalms about seeing YHWH describes what aspect of the numinous the worshipper hopes to see. Depictions of theophany in biblical poetry are equally reticent, preferring to describe the approach of YHWH, or manifestations of his presence in nature, rather than a description of the divine persona *per se*.[18] For the most part, while YHWH may be beheld, he is not to be described except by a number of conventional expressions, or by the attendant quaking of the natural world. Visual experience may be the primary stuff of religious experience, but verbal revelation is usually the predominant medium for explaining the meaning of the encounter. Seeing YHWH is the ultimate experience in biblical theophany, but

spiritualization, in part because it has no anthropomorphic element within it. But see the observations of M.S. Smith, *The Origins of Biblical Monotheism*, (N.Y.: Oxford University Press, 2000), pp. 74–5, concerning the idea of name as a form of manifest presence of the deity.

14. Eichrodt, *Theology*, vol 1, pp. 23–9; *TDOT* vol. 8, pp. 315–24.

15. W. Eichrodt, *Theology* vol. 1, pp. 35–9. S. Ahituv argues for the meaning 'angel' in Exod. 33:14; see 'The Countenance of God' in Cogan *et al.* (eds.), *Tehillah LeMoshe: Biblical and Judaic Studies in Honor of Moshe Greenberg*, pp. 3*-13* (Hebrew).

16. E.g. Exod. 16.7,10; Lev. 9.23; Num. 14.22; 16.19. Cf. the discussion in Milgrom, *Leviticus 1–16* pp. 58–9; 574–7; 588–90; *TDOT* vol. 7, pp. 29–34; Eichrodt, *Theology*, vol 1, pp. 29–35.

17. Cf. Korpel, *A Rift in the Clouds*, pp. 91–6.

18. The larger question of anthropomorphism as such is of secondary interest here. For discussion of the topic see R.J. Zwi Werblowsky, 'Anthropomorphism', *Encyclopedia of Religion* (N.Y., 1987), vol. 1, pp. 316–20; Eichrodt, *Theology*, vol. 1, pp. 16–22; Barr, 'Theophany and Anthropomorphism', pp. 31–8; Wolfson, *Through a Speculum*, pp. 16–24.

hearing YHWH will decode that experience and give it a transmittable form. As opposed to poetic texts like Ps. 29 which present the visible side of theophany, the theophany narratives offer the reader both the visual and the audial experience, usually in an interdependent manner.[19]

Theophany narratives allow us to explore the visual representation of the divine from a unique perspective. Since the eye observing the theophany is situated in a narrative context which describes the experience in a temporal framework, the reader is better placed to examine the stages of this revelation, and to evaluate the experience from the clearly identifiable point of view of the protagonist. Within these texts visual contact with the divine is not simply important, but represents a fundamental form of validation of the theophanic experience.[20] In many theophany narratives an initial visual encounter is essential to the experience of the divine, and seems to be an integral part of the process of initiation into further (usually verbal) contact with the divine. Moreover, the language used to describe the divine in theophany narratives differs from the conventional representations mentioned above. While the *malakh YHWH* appears in six of nineteen theophany narratives, *kavod* appears but twice, and *panim* only once, offering a different perspective on the visual representation of the divine.[21] Rather, we find unusual scenes like Isaiah's throne vision, and Ezekiel's chariot vision. Sometimes the visual component may be a description of a mediating element, such as Jacob's ladder, or Moses' thornbush.[22] And although some of the texts reveal very little of what was actually glimpsed, careful

19. For discussion of relationship between apprehending the Deity and its relationship to the aniconic tradition in the Bible, see Wolfson, *Through a Speculum that Shines*, pp. 16–28; J.L. Kugel, *The God of Old* (N.Y.: Free Press, 2003), pp. 71–107. H. Pedaya has discussed the dynamics of seeing and hearing God in Jewish mystical texts, with attention to the biblical background of these dynamics. See *Vision and Speech: Models of Revelatory Experience in Jewish Mysticism* (Los Angeles: Cherub Press, 2002) (Hebrew). For discussion of the visual mode in apocalyptic and Rabbinic sources see Wolfson, *Through a Speculum*, pp. 28–51; I. Chernus, 'Visions of God in Merkabah Mysticism', *JSJ* 13 (1982), pp. 123–46; D. Boyarin, 'The Eye in the Torah: Ocular Desire in the Midrashic Hermeneutic', *Critical Inquiry* 16 (1990), pp. 532–50,

20. Cf. Pedaya, 'Seeing, Falling', pp. 237–9; idem *Vision and Speech*, pp. 5–15. This contrasts with (and probably predates) the Deuteronomic focus upon hearing as a superior sense of experience of the divine. Cf. S. Geller, *Sacred Enigmas*, pp. 38–51; Wolfson, *Through a Speculum That Shines*, pp. 24–28.

21. *Kavod* appears in Exod. 33.18 and Ezek. 1.28. *Panim* also appears in Exod. 33.18–23, (though the phrase 'face to face' occurs in Gen. 32.30 and Judg. 6.22). *Malakh* appears in Gen. 16, 21; Num. 22; Judg. 6, 13, 1 Kgs 19. The usage of *malakh* in Gen. 28.12 and Exod. 3.2 is of a different nature, as will be discussed below.

22. Isaiah's throne vision alludes to elements which have a basis in the cultic life of ancient Israel – the throne, the cherubim, etc. Cf. Haran, *Temples and Temple Service*, pp. 247–59; Uffenheimer, 'Isaiah 6', pp. 34–41; Smith, *Origins of Biblical Monotheism*, p. 77.

study will reveal some basic dynamics of the Bible's understanding of the visual encounter with the numinous.

Characteristic of all the examples we will discuss below is the quality of limitation of vision. The divine is never the subject of unqualified vision, but the perception of the numinous is always marked by a holding back, whether of the description provided by the narrator or the observing character, by limitation of the perception of the divine by an external source (Isaiah), or by focusing upon some aspect of divine manifestation prefatory to the actual appearance of YHWH (Gen. 28, Exod. 3, Ezek. 1). Whether this is a reflection of the inability of finite human language to describe the infinite, or of the limited ability of humans to perceive the numinous, or of theological reservations regarding the narrator's authoritative privilege, the result is an awareness of limitation. We will explore a number of different literary strategies for presenting this sense of limited vision.

We are not interested in attempting to assess the various theophanies according to the quality of the revelation, or to offer judgment as to whether a given theophany describes a lesser or a fuller experience of the divine.[23] While certain general tendencies are recognizable throughout the Bible, such as the superiority of direct revelation to dreams,[24] the appearance of the *malakh YHWH* in place of the deity as in Judg. 13, or the superiority of Mosaic revelation to all others, we cannot state that Isaiah saw 'more' or 'less' of the Deity than did Jeremiah or Ezekiel.[25] While it is likely that individual background and subsequent editing have influenced the details of their descriptions, these questions are beyond the purview of this study. Rather, we are concerned with how these differences reflect a variety of literary strategies for dealing with the dilemma of representing the presence of the divine in visual form.

Our treatment of the revelatory aspect of the theophany will contain relatively little discussion of the verbal element, as that material has been discussed in great detail in the commentaries and the critical literature. The visual aspects, on the other hand, have not been examined along the lines developed here. The discussion will proceed in accordance with the way the visual presentation is organized, and how it is perceived by the character. The appearance may be sudden or gradual, and the perception of the protagonist may also be immediate or delayed. We have not grouped

23. So Eichrodt, *Theology*, vol. I, pp. 16–39.

24. Cf. Num. 12.6–8, and the discussion in R. Fidler, 'Dream Theophany', pp. 48–55.

25. The rabbinic comment in *BT* Hagiga 13b which explains the differences between Isaiah's and Ezekiel's descriptions of theophany as a reflection of each prophet's background may be equally satisfactory as a response to the question of difference. Apart from the commonly accepted observation that Ezekiel's vision is influenced by his priestly background, we will not attempt this type of analysis here.

these visual characteristics according to what aspect of the Deity is seen, but rather according to strategies of perception. The reasons for this are twofold. First, as mentioned above, the lack of clarity and precision in the language of theophany often makes it nearly impossible to determine what was actually seen. For example, in Exod. 33.18–23, one is hard pressed to understand the precise difference between *kavod* and *panim*, which are forbidden to Moses, and YHWH's 'goodness' (33.19) and his 'back' (33.23), which are revealed to him. Secondly, what is disclosed of what was actually observed is very limited. Ezekiel's vision in Ezek. 1 is exceptional in presenting the various facets of the divine chariot in great detail, but in other cases we have only a hint of what the visual experience may have consisted, as with Samuel in 1 Sam. 3.15. In a text like Exod. 24.9–11 the seeing is explicit, but the corresponding description of what is seen in 24.10 describes only the bottom half of the picture: 'under his feet was the likeness of sapphire stone'. The characters saw something more, but the reader is not privy to their view.[26]

1. *Gradual Revelation and Gradual Recognition*

The first strategy we will discuss is that of gradual revelation of the divine by means of a series of visual depictions which increase in intensity in anticipation of the ultimate stage of visual revelation. The goal of the description is to convey a full sense of the viewer's visual perception without, at the same time, revealing 'too much' of the essence of the divine. On the one hand, the premium which is placed on conveying the visual perception of the viewer reflects the intention of the narrative to validate his experience in the most reliable sense (the visual). Yet how, in the face of such direct visual perception, is the mystery of the numinous to be preserved?

i. *Ezekiel 1.4–28*. In the case of Ezekiel chapter 1, the visual aspect of the prophet's call far exceeds what can be found in any other theophany narrative, both in length and in specificity. While elsewhere the visual element is usually limited to a few verses at most, here the divine chariot is disclosed in stages, and in great detail, in no less than 25 verses. Ezekiel's narration describes an increasingly intense connection to the divine. The visual elements begin at a distance in v. 4, with a minimum of specificity. The storm imagery which usually suffices as a depiction of the approach of the divine in other texts here marks only the beginning of the vision; it also reappears at the end, serving as a frame for the entire vision. This

---

26. Job 4.12–16 presents the reader with a stunning example of the emotions and sensations surrounding a moment of revelation, but the reader is left in the dark as to what was seen. See D.J. Clines, *Job 1–19* (WBC; Waco, Texas: Word, 1989), pp. 128–31.

reappearance is marked by reference to thunder in v. 25, to the fiery aura (ונגה לו סביב) in v. 27, and to the final simile of the rainbow in v. 28.[27] Within the framework of the storm theophany the object appears distinctly, gradually drawing closer to Ezekiel, who is able to discern more and more as it approaches.[28]

Throughout this first person account we are constantly reminded of the prophet's focalization of the experience: אראה in vv. 4, 15, 27, and 28, אשמע in vv. 24 and 28.[29] From a general apprehension of a cloudlike entity in v. 4, the vision proceeds to the shape of the creatures in vv. 5–8,[30] to a description of their interactive movement in vv. 9–14 and the curious wheel structures in vv. 15–21. The verbs of motion through v. 12a all refer to internal movement of the elements on the throne, but 12b–14 emphasizes the movement of the entire object through the sky. That the object is moving closer to Ezekiel becomes clearer as the vision progresses. While the verbs הלך and נשא indicate horizontal and vertical movement respectively throughout the vision, vv. 22–23 represent a closer focal point, depicting a 'firmament', or a platform, as well as the first mention of the creatures covering themselves. This may serve as an indication of proximity to the Deity. The double use of עמד in vv. 24–25 indicates that the approach has ceased and the chariot is stationed close by to Ezekiel, enabling him to hear the thunderous sound in v. 25 and to observe the shape on the chariot more closely.

The intensity of this approach is also heightened by the presence of an auditory effect from v. 24 onwards, first the sound of the wings of the creatures, then the sound of something else above the firmament, associated with the Deity itself in v. 25.[31] These audial elements are not

27.   It is most likely that Ezekiel partakes of the storm theophany traditions mentioned above – Exod. 19, Ps. 29, Ps. 18, Hab. 3, etc. Cf. B. Uffenheimer, 'Ma'aseh Merkavah', *EM* vol. 5, pp. 199–203 (200) (Hebrew); L.C. Allen, 'The Structure and Intention of Ezekiel 1', *VT* 43 (1993), pp. 145–61 (147–49); H. Van Dyke Parunak, 'The Literary Architecture of Ezekiel's *Mar'ot 'Elohim*', *JBL* 99 (1980), pp. 61–74 (63).

28.   For discussion of aspects of the vision not addressed here the reader is referred to the commentaries by Zimmerli, *Ezekiel 1*; Greenberg, *Ezekiel 1–20*; L.C. Allen, *Ezekiel 1–19* (WBC; Waco, Texas: Word, 1994); D.I. Block, *The Book of Ezekiel: Chapters 1–24* (Grand Rapids, MI: Eerdmans, 1997), and the bibliographies therein.

29.   The term הנה strengthens the focalization in vv. 4 and 15; cf. S. Kogut, 'On the Meaning and Syntactical Status of הנה in Biblical Hebrew', in Japhet, *Studies in Bible*, pp. 133–54.

30.   In Ezekiel 10 the creatures are referred to as כרובים, but this may well reflect a later interpretation of the vision. See Halperin, 'Ezekiel X:9–17', pp. 129–41.

31.   This is often identified with thunder; Block, *Ezekiel 1–24*, p. 104, sees this as an allusion other storm theophanies, such as the sevenfold קול of YHWH in Ps. 29. This distinction between the sounds of an approaching theophany followed by a distinct but non-verbal divine קול recalls the description of the Sinai theophany in Exod. 19–20.

verbal, but, like the sounds in Exod. 19, indicate the growing proximity of the Deity.[32] The use of three similes to express the intensity of the sound reflects the prophet's attempts to interpret what he hears. The first of these, 'many waters', often has cosmic overtones, though here it may simply indicate the amplitude of the sound.[33] The second, 'like the sound of Shaddai', may reflect Ezekiel's understanding of the chariot as a divine vehicle, or may simply utilize the divine name as a superlative, as in Ps. 36.6.[34] These images effectively capture the power inherent in the vision, but with no requisite sense of premonition. Rather, it is the third epithet, 'the sound of an army', which conveys something of the terrifying aspect of what he sees, and hints at the negative aspect of YHWH's appearance. Not only does the chariot vision indicate the absolute freedom of the divine presence to move in whatever direction it will, but the imagery of the chariot is as warlike as it is majestic, presaging destruction, as will be made explicit in the second appearance of the vehicle in the vision in Ezek. 8–11.[35] In all three cases the similes can be read as references to human or natural phenomena, but they also hint at a divine or cosmic interpretation of the chariot. This double-edged quality[36] allows for a delay in Ezekiel's identification of the chariot with the Deity until v. 28.[37]

The high point of the vision comes in vv. 26–28, as Ezekiel describes what he sees above the chariot. The refocusing of the prophet's gaze is made clearer by the fact that once he concentrates on this figure, he makes

32. Note the increase in volume and intensity from Exod. 19.16 to 19.19.

33. Cf. H. Mays, 'Some Connotations of *Mayim Rabbim*', *JBL* 74 (1955), pp. 9–21, but note Greenberg's qualification about Ezekiel's use of the term (*Ezekiel 1–20*, p. 48).

34. Though other divine epithets are used in this way, It is questionable whether שׁדי is employed in this fashion. Radak points to Isa. 13.6 and Job. 22.25 for a similar usage, but the context in Isaiah favors a pun on Shaddai as 'destroyer', and in Job the term clearly refers to God. Zimmerli, *Ezekiel I*, p. 130, notes that the simile is lacking in the LXX, and sees this as a late addition influenced by Ezek. 10.5.

35. Cf. Allen, 'Ezekiel 1', pp. 152–5. See the imagery in Joel 2.11 as an intertext for our phrase here. המלה has destructive connotations also in Jer. 11.16. Zimmerli (*Ezekiel I*, p. 131) sees a connection with Isa. 17.12–14, but the sense here is contrastive with that text. If, in Isaiah, the roaring of the sea and the din of the people represent a foreign force which YHWH will silence, in Ezekiel the din is that of YHWH's own assembly.

36. Simile, in describing what something is like, also describes what the object is *not*.

37. Ezekiel markedly refrains from any explicit mention of the Deity before v. 28. The reference to מראות אלהים in 1.1 may be taken as either a general overview of the entire experience, part of the introduction in vv. 1–3, or else as 'mighty visions', where the term אלהים is to be read as a superlative. Greenberg notes that for Ezekiel אלהים is 'usually an appelative "divinity", not the proper noun "God"' (*Ezekiel 1–20*, p. 41). Cf. also Block, 'Text and Emotion: A Study in the "Corruptions" in Ezekiel's Inaugural Vision (Ezekiel 1.4–28)', *CBQ* 50 (1988), pp. 418–42 (28).

no further mention of the vehicle.[38] From v. 22 on the 'firmament' has become the constant reference point for the prophet's focus, mentioned repeatedly in vv. 22, 23, 25, and 26. The relationship to this term illustrates well the change in perspective of the prophet. Most commentators take the term רקיע as a platform or a plane, based on the occurrence of the verb רקע with the sense of 'flattened out' or 'stretched out'.[39] Since all other occurrences of רקיע refer to the heavenly firmament, it is reasonable that this meaning might resonate here as well.[40] It seems that both meanings are applicable here, and are used to mark Ezekiel's change in perception as the vision reachers its climax. As long as Ezekiel focuses on the lower part of the chariot, in vv. 22–23, the רקיע marks the upward limit of the prophet's vision, as do the heavens.[41] But once his attention is drawn *above* the firmament – first by sound in v. 25, then by sight in v. 26 – the same רקיע seen from *above* now becomes a platform on which the throne is resting. This gives a near-literal interpretation to the expression 'the heaven opened and I saw מראות אלהים' in v. 1. In this sense the term has a dual function, representing both the heavens themselves and the more specific platform on which the throne rests. The chariot now dominates his attention so completely that it virtually replaces the actual sky in his vision. The focus on the term indicates Ezekiel's exceptional position vis-a-vis the vision that he perceives. The spatial coordinates of the prophet's position are altered in order to allow him a glimpse of the divine.

The description of the enthroned figure in vv. 26–27 describes both the upper and lower halves of this divine body in parallel fashion, but assigns the term חשמל to the upper half, thereby providing a link with what was first glimpsed in v. 4.[42] V. 28a briefly moves away from the figure on the throne to describe the surrounding brilliance (נגה). In the service of this description we find the longest simile in the narrative, 'like the appearance of the bow that is in the cloud on a rainy day'. The storm imagery returns the reader to the framework of the thunderstorm-theophany suggested by v. 4, but intertextual connections lead in other directions as well. While the

38. Even at the departure of the chariot in 3.12–13, the prophet records only the sound of the departure, and not the visual representation.

39. E.g. Greenberg, 'plane', and Zimmerli, 'fixed platform'. Cf. Exod. 39.3, Num. 17.4; for the sense of 'beaten out', and Ps. 136.6, Isa. 42.5 for the sense of heavens spread out.

40. So also Allen, *Ezekiel 1–19*, p. 34.

41. Block, *Ezekiel 1–24*, p. 107, suggests that one of the primary functions of the רקיע is to describe a complete separation between the Deity and the rest of the vision. At the same time the description of YHWH as 'like the appearance of a man' points to an identification with the human world.

42. On the meaning of חשמל cf. Akk. *elmešu* as discussed in G.R. Driver, 'Ezekiel's Inaugural Vision', *VT* 1 (1951), pp. 60–62; Greenberg, *Ezekiel 1–20* p. 43, and *CAD* Vol. 4, pp. 107–108. At the same time, this should not be taken to negate the process of gradual unfolding of the vision which we have described. Cf. Pedaya, 'Seeing, Falling', p. 246.

cloud (ענן) is closely associated with theophany in Exodus,[43] the use of the term together with קשת in relation to the divine immediately recalls Gen. 9.13–16, YHWH's promise of non-belligerency to Noah following the flood. But while in Gen. 9 YHWH's promise came after the great deluge, here the devastation is yet to come. The only other references to a divine bow are found in Lam. 2.4 and 3.12, where it is an instrument of Israel's destruction.[44] Thus the most extended figure in Ezekiel's quiver is a double edged image. As a rainbow the קשת should appear at the end of the storm, when all destructive energy is spent; as an allusion to Gen. 9 it should conjure up the idea of covenant and divine protection. Yet it occurs here in the midst of the storm theophany, whose destructive power is only beginning.[45]

Ezekiel's vision remains focused throughout, and offers the most detailed depiction of the divine to be found in the Bible.[46] In this sense Ezekiel defies the biblical norm of presenting only a limited description of the divine. But this great specificity, with attention to both static and dynamic elements, is offset by the extensive use of analogy and approximation in the chapter. Ezekiel mitigates and limits his description with an exceptional number of qualifying elements. The comparative kaph, either standing alone (Ezek. 1. 7, 13, 14, 24, 26, 27, 28) or in the form כעין (vv. 4, 7, 16, 22, 27,) is used to indicate coloration or similitude.[47] The term מראה (vv. 5, 13, 14, 16, 26, 27, 28) serves to approximate a visual likeness. The term דמות in vv. 5, 10, 13, 16, 22, 26, 28 has the general sense of 'likeness' but its meaning changes throughout; it may also be used as an indication of the structure of the vision.[48] While these devices are not unique to Ezekiel, they appear no fewer than 40 times in this vision. The total effect is a simultaneous presentation of detail and qualification, as if the precision of every detail is qualified by ambiguation.[49] Greenberg aptly

43. Exod. 13.21–22; 14.19–20; 16.10; 19.9,16; 24.15–16,18; 33.9–10; 40.34–38.

44. While קשת occurs rarely as a divine weapon, the use of divine arrows is a frequent element in descriptions of YHWH appearing as a man of war; cf. Deut. 32.23,42; Ezek. 5.16; Hab. 3.11; Zech. 9.14; Pss. 18.15; 38.3; 45.6; 64.8; 77.18; 144.6; Job 6.4. Cf. further Allen, 'Ezekiel I', pp. 155–7, who sees the imagery of the storm theophany tied to bellicose traditions in the Bible and in Assyria.

45. In this light, one might attribute an ominous sense to the phrase 'the heavens were opened' in v. 1, given the parallel in the flood narrative in Gen. 7.11. Cf. also Isa. 24.18.

46. B. Uffenheimer, *Classical Prophecy* (Jerusalem: Magnes Press, 2001) (Hebrew), p. 168, sees Ezekiel's daring anthropomorphism in v. 26, 'the appearance of a human being', as an expression which is 'corrected' in v. 28 by 'the appearance of the *kavod* of YHWH'. Cf. *TDOT* vol. 4, pp. 257–9.

47. Cf. *TDOT* vol. 7, p. 5.

48. So J. Muilenburg, 'Form Criticism and Beyond', *JBL* 88 (1969), pp. 1–18 (18), but see the qualifications of Allen, 'Ezekiel I', pp. 147–9.

49. Cf. Block, 'Text and Emotion', pp. 429–30.

suggests that these terms signify 'unwillingness to commit oneself to the substantial identity of the seen with the compared', and refers to this language with the useful expression 'buffer terms'.[50] Beyond this the proliferation of analogies and qualifications indicate the inability of the prophet to find adequate terms for what he sees, suggesting a sense of dissatisfaction with the specificity of his descriptions.

The concentration of these terms increases dramatically from Ezek. 1.26 onwards, as Ezekiel describes the figure above the firmament. In these final three verses the above-mentioned figures are deployed 18 times. When, in v. 28 he finally defines the object of his vision as the *kavod* of YHWH, it is doubly qualified with the unique combination מראה דמות, 'the appearance of the likeness'.[51] This fuzziness is contrary to the expected process of seeing; the progression of the vision has led the reader to believe that the prophet is able to discern the vision more clearly as the object draws closer. Yet in inverse relationship to this increasing proximity is the proliferation of qualifying terms. The multiplication of fiery images in vv. 27–28 adds further to the lack of clarity of what Ezekiel sees.[52] On the one hand the repetition of the phrases כעין החשמל and נגה לו סביב from v. 4 might indicate that what he sees in v. 27 is identical with what he saw earlier. But the description of upper and lower elements of the vision, and the use of the term 'loins' to indicate a more defined human figure, indicate that he sees something different here.[53] Ezekiel is unflinching in his determination to tell the reader everything he sees, yet unable to go beyond

50. Greenberg also claims that 'there is no ground for supposing that he had any reservations respecting the visual likeness in these comparisons', and compares two dream reports (A.L. Oppenheim, *The Interpretation of Dreams*, pp. 204, 251) in which the dreamer uses similar language to describe certain visions. But in these cases the exact likeness (the queen's father, the god Ptah) were known to the dreamer, whereas Ezekiel is describing something that is new to him. Despite the similarities with both Israelite and Mesopotamian temple iconography, the chariot vision does not conform precisely to any of these models. At least part of the reason for the qualification and approximation in Ezekiel's language is that he is attempting to describe something that he has never seen before, and whose full import is not clear to him until the final part of the vision in v. 28. On the parallels with ancient Near Eastern iconography see Uffenheimer, 'Ma'asei Merkavah', pp. 199–200; idem, *Classical Prophecy*, pp. 169–75; Greenberg, *Ezekiel 1–20*, p. 53.

51. Cf. also 1.26 – דמות כמראה אדם. On the relationship of the verse to Gen. 1.26 cf. Smith, *Biblical Monotheism*, p. 171; J.F. Kutsko, 'Ezekiel's Anthropology and its Ethical Implications', in Odell and Strong (eds.), *The Book of Ezekiel. Theological and Anthropological Perspectives*, pp. 119–41.

52. Cf. Allen, *Ezekiel 1–19*, p. 36. Though they may represent different phenomena, we have no way of distinguishing חשמל from אש or from נגה.

53. Note the comment of R. Eliezer of Beaugency on 1.28. 'Ezekiel only saw the divine Glory at the end [of his vision] . . . he saw these things consecutively in the order in which they are written. Even though he saw the *hashmal* in v. 4, he did not see the human likeness [of v. 28 until now], and therefore he fell on his face [at this point]'.

the bounds of his own experience and his own imagination. Since this description emphasizes the process of approach, an experience growing ever more intense as it continues, Ezekiel's mention of his fainting in 1.28 is the natural continuation of the intensity of his gaze.[54]

ii. *Genesis 28.12–13a.* A different type of gradual revelation is found in Jacob's dream in Gen. 28.10–22, in which there is also a progressive unfolding of the meaning of the vision. Here the aspect of motion is present only minimally in the vision itself, which consists of a series of successive static images. In contrast to Ezekiel's vision, there is no attempt to describe the divine, and we see none of the ambiguation and approximation which categorized his narrative. Moreover, this visual apprehension takes place in a dream,[55] after Jacob has lain down his head by or on a stone, whose significance becomes apparent only in the continuation of the narrative.

Behold: A ladder was set on the ground and its top reached to the sky.	(A)	והנה סלם מצב ארצה וראשו מגיע השמימה
Behold: Angels of God were ascending and descending on it.	(B)	והנה מלאכי אלהים עלים וירדים בו
Behold: YHWH was stationed beside him.	(C)	והנה ה' נצב עליו

The visual aspect of Jacob's dream is described in three consecutive clauses, each of which begins with the term הנה. Beyond its function as an organizing factor in the dream,[56] the term itself indicates visual perception, usually serving as syntactic shorthand for a fuller clause with a verb of seeing.[57] While הנה has a specific function in dream

---

54. See the discussion of Ezekiel's reaction in chapter 4.

55. On the discussion of the type of dream represented in the story cf. J-M Husser, *Dreams and Dream Narratives in the Biblical World*, pp. 128–32; I. Peleg, 'Going Up and Going Down', pp. 2–12, 133–43; Fidler, 'Dream Theophany', pp. 152–7; M. Lichtenstein, 'Dream Theophany and the E Document', *JANES* 1 (1969), pp. 45–54.

56. Its further occurrence in 28.15 helps tie together the visual and audial sections of the dream.

57. Kogut, 'הנה in Biblical Hebrew', pp. 144–52, argues that the locus of the term is to be found in conjunction with a verb of seeing, as in Gen. 24.63, 31.10.

narratives,[58] it may also serve to indicate a shift in point of view.[59] In this case the second function is particularly relevant, not as a change in perspective from one character to another, but as an indication of three different stages of visual perception on Jacob's part.[60] The first image (A) is the mysterious *sullam*, which is both grounded in the earth and reaching heavenward. Whether understood as temple, tower, or stair-case, the *sullam* functions here as a symbolic joining of heaven and earth.[61] Visually speaking this segment of the dream must include both extremities of the *sullam*, and as such demands a focus wide enough to encompass the whole scope of the image. One might contrast this with the presentation of the tower of Babel, which focuses primarily on the upper part of the image, as in Gen. 11.4.[62] The two participial forms (מצב, מגיע) which mark the location of the *sullam* lend a continuous present aspect to the vision, as is particularly appropriate to dreams.[63]

The second הנה clause (B) continues in the present tense, but zeros in on the movement upon the *sullam*. It is as if the lens which first viewed the entire *sullam* from a distance now refocuses, capturing both specific shapes and movement. This closer focus on the *sullam* gives some further clues as to its nature. The presence of a number of angels on it makes the idea of a ladder less likely and supports Houtman's idea of a ramp on which Jacob is sleeping.[64] The order of the verbs, first ascending and then descending, is not necessarily significant, Rashi's interpretation notwithstanding.[65] Rather, it is the bi-directionality of the motion that is noteworthy,

---

58. Cf. Gen. 41.7 and F.I. Anderson, *The Sentence in Biblical Hebrew* (The Hague: Mouton, 1974), p. 95.

59. Berlin, *Poetics and Interpretation* pp. 62–7; S. Kogut, 'הנה in Biblical Hebrew', pp. 137–8.

60. Cf. Fokkelmann, *Narrative Art in Genesis*, p. 52. Note the succession of הנה clauses by the same speaker which involve a similar shift in focus. Gen. 41.1–3; 5–6; 22–23; Judg. 9.36–37; 2 Sam. 1.6; 1 Kgs 3.21; Isa. 65.13–14; Jer. 4.24–26; Ezek. 37.2; 7–8; Amos 7.1.

61. On the *sullam* see C. Houtman, 'What Did Jacob See in His Dream at Bethel?', *VT* 27 (1977), pp. 337–51; D. Lipton, *Revisions of the Night* (Sheffield: Sheffield Academic Press, 1999), pp. 64, 83–92; C. Cohen, 'The Literary Motif of Jacob's Ladder (Gen. 28:12)', in Ben-Tulilah (ed.), *Shai Lehadasah – Studies in Hebrew Language and Jewish Languages*, pp. 15–26. Most recently M. Oblath ('"To Sleep, Perchance to Dream". What Jacob Saw at Bethel', *JSOT* 95 (2001), pp. 117–26) has suggested that סולם should be understood as a Near Eastern gate, in keeping with Jacob's own comment in Gen. 28.17.

62. Also YHWH's gaze in Gen. 11.5 is on the upper part as well. On the contrast between Genesis 28 and the tower of Babel see Y. Zakovitch, *Through the Looking Glass* (Tel Aviv: Hakibbutz Hameuchad, 1995) (Hebrew), pp. 60–62; Peleg, 'Going Up and Going Down', pp. 278–87; Fokkelmann, *Narrative Art in Genesis*, p. 53 n. 22; Lipton, *Revisions*, pp. 99–104.

63. Cf. Fokkelmann, *Narrative Art in Genesis*, pp. 51–2.

64. Cf. Houtman, 'What Did Jacob See', p. 345. On the possible connection between *sullam* and Akk. *simmiltu* cf. Cohen, 'Literary Motif', pp. 22–5.

65. Cf. Rashi *ad loc.*

indicating the possibility of mutual communication between heaven and earth, and foreshadowing the continuation of the dream. These two verbs of movement develop the implications of the use of the two participles in clause (A) – ארצה מצב is focussed on the ground, corresponding to the sense of descent, and ראשו מגיע השמימה can be seen as a reflection of ascent.

There are additional ways in which clause (B) builds upon the previous image and clarifies it. The use of the same word (ראש) for Jacob's head and for the top of the *sullam* in the heavens suggests a certain identification between the two, making it particularly appropriate for a dream theophany. Like the tower of Babel, the *sullam*, too, is potentially a means of human ascent. But in portraying the image more precisely, clause (B) also indicates that the *sullam* is meant for non-humans, for angels. And since Jacob is not equivalent to the angels, it is unclear where he fits into the vision. Is the vision meant to convey a message about Jacob's departure from Canaan, which is mentioned in the verbal message in Gen. 28.15?[66] Or is the image a foreshadowing of Jacob's angelic visitors in Gen. 32? The fact that Jacob's head has come into close contact with the ground (his head is by/on the stone) suggests that the ladder's resting on the ground is not just about divine-human communication in general, but about liaison with Jacob directly. As the head of the ladder reaches toward the sky, so Jacob's head looks heavenward in the dream.

The dual focus on heaven and earth (A), developed through the ascending and descending of the angels in (B), finds its resolution in (C) with the appearance of the divine. The third, climactic הנה clause focuses Jacob's vision further, bringing the series of clauses to its conclusion.[67] The *sullam* 'falls away' as YHWH appears, there being no further use for the initial image. In fact, it is a noticeable characteristic of theophany narratives that the introductory image fades as soon as YHWH appears.[68]

---

66. Y. Peleg has developed the suggestive idea that the movement on the ladder should be read allegorically, representing Jacob's journeys out of the land of Canaan and back to it ('Going up and Going Down', pp. 186–236). This interpretation finds support in other theophanies involving Jacob. In Gen. 32.1–2 angels accompany Jacob on his return from Aram, and in Gen. 46.4 YHWH promises to accompany Jacob into Egypt and to bring him up from there. At the same time the applicability of the interpretation to Gen. 28 seems forced. While עלה and ירד can have positive and negative valences (Gen. 38.1, Exod. 32, 2 Kgs 2, Jon. 1.3–5, Amos 9.2; Ps. 30.4; etc.), (Peleg, pp. 45–54), the present context does not offer a contrasting sense of ascent versus descent, but rather a merismus representing vertical motion in both directions. In contrast to the examples brought by Peleg, the use of the verbs IN Gen. 28.13 is closer to its usage in Pss. 104.8, 107.26.

67. Fokkelmann (*Narrative Art in Genesis*, p. 54) notes how the subjects of the three clauses move from 'non-qualified' (the *sullam*) to 'maximally qualified' (YHWH). In a not dissimilar fashion the triple repetition of מקום in v. 12 narrowed the focus from an undefined 'place' to במקום ההוא, 'that place'.

68. Fokkelman, *Narrative Art in Genesis*, p. 54. See, for example, the bush in Exod. 3.

Once YHWH's presence is announced the introductory aspect of the visual imagery, so prominent in clauses (A) and (B), becomes apparent. The only term describing the presence of the divine is the verb נצב, which is used elsewhere precisely for this purpose.[69] The text here reflects a significant ambiguity. Since the term נצב in theophany narratives often implies the presence of the Deity in an immanent, often visible, sense,[70] and since the word עליו can refer either to the *sullam* or to Jacob, the question posed by *Genesis Rabbah* is relevant for our understanding of the text: Is God above Jacob's head or above the *sullam*?[71] Is YHWH present and immanent for Jacob, or is he perceived at a distance? On the one hand, the emphasis on the scope of the *sullam* emphasizes distance – YHWH is high above, at the top of the *sullam*, and the movement of the angels suggests that only by mediated contact can there be communication between YHWH and the earth below. But if we follow the progressive refocusing that the sequence of הנה clauses has indicated thus far, a closer picture of YHWH emerges, one which emphasizes his proximity to Jacob. We would argue that the deliberate ambiguity of the phrase collapses the immanent / transcendent distinction, signalling Jacob's entry into a liminal space. It is here, in this realm, that the contact between the human and the divine takes place. The *sullam* disappears because the connection between heaven and earth has been rendered actual by the appearance of YHWH. This appearance signals the end of the visual sequence of the dream, which enters its second stage as YHWH speaks.

Further cementing this sense of the immediacy of the divine presence is the repetition of the root נצב for both the *sullam* and for YHWH. This repetition helps to frame the vision, describing stationary elements at the beginning (A – the *sullam*) and the end (C – YHWH) with movement up and down connecting the two (B – the angels). But the sense of נצב goes beyond the merely stationary. It is a term used repeatedly in narratives about revelation,[72] and YHWH's 'standing' will be reflected subsequently in Jacob's setting up the מצבה in v. 18 as a replication of the theophany.

The strategy reflected in this text enables the reader to see as the protagonist sees, but, at the climactic moment, the narrator refrains from any description of the divine other than the visually oriented term נצב. The reader is thus included in the theophanic experience, yet is prevented from

---

69. E.g., Exod. 34.5.

70. *TDOT* vol. 9, p. 528.

71. *Gen. Rab* 69.3; cf. also 68.12.

72. Cf. Abraham's visitors in Gen. 18.2, the revelation to Moses and Israel in Exod. 34.5, the angel who visits Balaam in Num. 22.22–35, and the revelation to Samuel in 1 Sam. 3.10. Note also the use of the term for God being stationed in the heavens in Pss. 82.1; 119.89, and for God 'standing' in a vision of judgment in Amos 7.7; 9.1. Cf. Barr, 'Theophany and Anthropomorphism', p. 32.

direct visual contact with the divine. In place of this the speech of YHWH
stands at the center of the narrative as the longest single element therein. In
contrast to Ezekiel's vision, where the prophet's vision was as long as the
entire commissioning narrative in Ezek. 2.1–3.15, here the message
delivered by YHWH upstages the *sullam*. What was primary as a means
of initial contact is relegated to a position of lesser significance, a mere
introduction to YHWH's message to Jacob in 28.13–15.

iii. *Moses – Exodus 3.2*. A third instance of the gradual approach can be
seen in the account of the call to Moses in Exodus 3.1–6.[73] Here, however,
it is the protagonist himself who physically approaches the divine, and who
reveals to the reader the various stages of his perception in direct
description. Even more unusual, we have in 3.4 a glimpse into the
considerations of YHWH as to the process of revelation.

A *malakh* of *YHWH* appeared to him,	(A)	וירא מלאך ה' אליו
In a flame of fire from within the bush.		בלבת אש מתוך הסנה
And he saw:	(B)	וירא
Behold: the bush was all aflame,		והנה הסנה בער באש
Yet the bush was not consumed.		והסנה איננו אכל

While the text places him on 'the mountain of God' in v. 1, as noted above
there is no indication that Moses is aware of the potential significance of
the place. This tension between the narrator's knowledge and Moses'
perception is brought out more directly in v. 2. The verse emphasizes
seeing, both in the appearance of a divine manifestation and in Moses'
perception of it. The complementary use of passive and active forms of ראה
encourages the expectation that what Moses sees (וירא) is identical with
what is revealed to him (וירא אליו מלאך ה'). While this passive construction
is not uncommon in other cases of revelation,[74] there is often a tension
between what is revealed by the narrator and what is seen by the
protagonist.[75] And indeed, what is revealed in (A) is not identical with
what Moses sees in (B). If the former represents an objective, authoritative
description of the spectacle, then the latter is a subjective understanding of
that sight by Moses.

---

73. The larger call narrative stretches from 3.1 to 4.17, with much dialog between Moses
and YHWH. The visual element, however, is present only in 3.1–6.

74. E.g. Gen. 12.7, 17.1, 18.1; 26.2,24, 35.9, etc.

75. In Gen. 18.1, for example, the phrase וירא אליו ה' באלני ממרא could conceivably
indicate that Abraham recognizes the presence of YHWH immediately. But it is more likely a
general introduction to the story in Gen. 18.1–15, indicating that at some time during it
YHWH revealed himself to Abraham, though it is unclear precisely when Abraham comes to
that realization. Cf. the discussion of this text in the previous chapter pp. 47–8.

The narrator uses the term *malakh YHWH* to describe what is revealed here, but the text lacks any of the usual signs of angelic presence. While this expression is also found in Judg. 6.12 and 13.3, in those texts an active *malakh* figure is present in the story. Usually the term indicates a manifestation of the divine in anthropomorphic form, who may come in place of YHWH (e.g. Gen. 16.9–12; Num. 22; Judg. 13) or may alternate with YHWH as in Gen. 22 and Judg. 6.[76] Here there is no indication that the term represents a distinct angelic figure. While one is tempted to appeal to von Rad's interpretation of the term as reflecting subjective human perception,[77] the expression is here part of the narrator's statement, and does not reflect Moses' point of view.[78] Childs suggests that we understand it as 'an interpretive superscription for the entire description', not unlike Gen. 18.1,[79] but as this is not the beginning verse of the section, it is unclear why a chapter heading should appear in verse 2. It seems best, therefore, to understand *malakh* here as the bush itself, in which 'the manifestation [of YHWH] is not anthropomorphic, but fiery'.[80] This solution is necessitated by Moses' response – if it were a recognizable angelic figure, one would expect a reaction other than his observation about the bush in v. 3.[81] Supporting this interpretation is Childs' understanding of the *bet* of

76. In most other places *malakh YHWH* is an 'associate' of the divine, sometimes as one who precedes or performs a task, sometimes as a figure who interchanges freely with God. See the discussions in A. Rofe, *The Belief in Angels in the Bible and in Early Israel* (Hebrew) (Jerusalem. Makor, 1979), pp. 1–10; J. Licht, 'Malakh, Malakhim', *EM* Vol. 4, pp. 975–90 (Hebrew); D. Irvin, *Mytharion*, (Neukirchen-Vluyn: Neukirchner Verlag, 1978), pp. 91–104; Westermann, *Genesis 12–36*, pp. 242–44; *TDOT*, vol. 8, pp. 317–23; F. Polak, 'The Messenger of God and the Dialectic of Revelation', in Hoffmann and Polak (eds.), *Or Leya'akov*, (Jerusalem: Mossad Bialik, 1997), pp. 14*-30*; A. Reinhartz, *Why Ask My Name?*, (N.Y., Oxford University Press, 1998), pp. 154–77; Newsom, 'Angels', pp. 248–53; Propp, *Exodus 1–18*, pp. 198–9.

77. G. von Rad, *Old Testament Theology* (2 vols.; trans. D.M.G. Stalker; San Francisco: Harper, 1962), vol. 1, p. 287, n. 13.

78. Various attempts to explain the *malakh* by appeal to levels of textual editing fail to explain the present form of the text. Cf. *TDOT* vol 8, p. 320.

79. So Childs, *Exodus*, p. 72; idem, 'Anticipatory Titles in Hebrew Narrative', in Rofe and Zakovitch (eds.), *Isaac Leo Seeligmann Volume* vol. 3, pp. 57–65 (58–9).

80. Greenberg, *Understanding Exodus*, p. 70. Cf. also Cassuto, *A Commentary on Exodus*, (Jerusalem: Magnes Press, 1967), p. 31; B. Jacob, *The Second Book of the Bible. Exodus* (trans. W. Jacob; Hoboken, NJ: Ktav, 1992), p. 51. This, however, would be the only biblical instance of such a use of מלאך.

81. In this sense the use of the term heightens the tension between what is shown and what is seen. Newsom suggests that 'the unresolved ambiguity [between YHWH and *malakh YHWH*] allows the reader to experience the paradox' involved in the process of theophany ('Angels', p. 250). Similarly, B.P. Robinson understands the מלאך as stressing 'the transcendence of the Deity while preserving his personality' ('Moses at the Burning Bush', *JSOT* 75 (1997), p. 112).

בלבת אש as a *bet essentiae*,[82] to be understood here as something like 'namely'.[83] As the *malakh* elsewhere serves the function of introducing, or acting as a temporary go-between for YHWH, here the vision of the fire in the bush serves as an introduction to the divine presence.[84]

The vision contains within it a number of unusual locutions. Only here do we find the phrase בלבת אש, which could be understood as a form of the phrase לב אש: the center of the flame, or a core of flame (so Rashi and Ibn Ezra). More plausible is the suggestion that להבה=להבת=לבת, as in flame.[85] סנה occurs only here and in Deut. 33.16, where it refers to YHWH as the 'dweller in the bush'. While that reference might well be taken as a comment in our verse,[86] it may equally point to an original connection between YHWH and Sinai (סיני), which is further played upon with the word סנה.[87] The use of the phrase מתוך הסנה indicates that the source of the flame is within the bush, explaining Moses' subsequent astonishment as to why the bush burns without being consumed. The phrase is intended to point out the singular nature of what Moses sees: bringing together natural elements in an unusual manner, it is arresting and leads Moses to 'turn aside'.[88] Rather than use a single *hapax legomenon* to describe the phenomenon, this depiction of the divine employs a combination of unusual words: not simply fire, but בלבת אש; not the more common עשב, but the rarer סנה. And not as a long construct phrase, but as one within the

---

82. Cf. GKC #119i. In other locations where the same phrase occurs the *bet* is the *bet* of location (Gen. 18.1, 48.3) or of time (Gen. 26.24, 35.9). A similar sense may be found in the context of revelation in Exod. 6.3 וארא...באל שדי (cf. Greenberg *Understanding Exodus*, p. 70 n.2) and in the use of בחלום in 1 Kgs 3.5. In both cases the *bet* indicates more nearly 'how' rather than 'where'.

83. Childs, *Exodus*, p. 50; cf. also Greenberg, *Understanding Exodus*, p. 70. One might also appeal to the notion of the elements as messengers of YHWH as reflected in Ps. 104.3 – 'who makes the winds his messengers (מלאכיו) and the flaming fire his servants'.

84. F. Polak, *Biblical Narrative*, p. 105 sees in the alternation of divine names an expression of the tension between direct visual revelation (the *malakh*) and direct non-visual revelation of God in 3.6. Cf also idem, 'The Messenger of God', p. 25, where he explains the *malakh* as the visual part of the theophany, which is prefatory to the divine voice.

85. Cf. Targ., Sam.; note also Deut. 4.11 – עד לב השמים. Greenberg suggests that לבה in Ezek. 16.30 may also combine the two senses of flame (or passion) and heart (*Ezekiel 1–20*, p. 283). Propp (*Exodus 1–18*, p. 199) also suggests a root לבב and notes the Akkadian *lababu* 'to rage' used in conjunction with *išatu* fire = fever. T. Hiebert (*The Yahwist's Landscape* (N.Y.: Oxford University Press, 1996), p. 132 suggests that the term refers to lightning which has set the bush aflame; cf. Ps. 29.7; 105.32; Isa. 29.6; 30.30.

86. G. von Rad, *Deuteronomy*, p. 207.

87. Note Luzzato's comment here 'God is called after the bush (*sene*) which is Sinai' [*Pentateuch*, p. 270].

88. Propp, *Exodus 1–18*, p. 199, notes that בער usually occurs with אכל, as in Num. 11.1; 2 Sam. 22.9 (= Ps. 18.9); Isa. 9.17; 10.17; Job 1.6; Lam. 2.3.

other.[89] Together they point to something that cannot be reduced to a single image, but demands further contemplation.[90]

Attempts at decoding the image of the burning bush tend to read it in terms of its component parts. The most obvious candidate for the fire is YHWH, who is often compared to fire in both positive and negative images.[91] The bush, however, has been interpreted variously as Sinai,[92] as Egypt,[93] as Israel caught in Egypt but containing the spark of the divine within, or as a figure of the natural world.[94] But one may equally well read the bush in positive terms. It could represent Moses, who is 'burning' but not consumed, by a fire which enlightens and inspires, but does not destroy.[95] This would make the vision serve as an introduction to Moses' revelation in a much more personal sense. In a communal sense the bush could be similar to the seven-branched lampstand in representing a stylized fire-tree, an 'arborescent deity', itself a symbolic representation of perpetual theophany.[96] Whereas Jeremiah in his most powerful confession represents the prophetic voice as a fire which devours him from within (Jer.

---

89. The expression מתוך הסנה seems to indicate some type of separation between the fire and the bush, perhaps as container and emanation. (Note also Ezek. 28.18, where fire comes out of the midst of the sanctuary to destroy the king of Tyre.) In this sense the phrase and its repetition in Exod. 34 indicate not a normal situation of fire in the midst of the burning object, but fire *emerging* from the bush. The sense of one element within another (מתוך) calls to mind the use of the term in Ezek. 1.4,5,16; 10.10. Most other usages of מתוך have to do with taking one thing *out* of another – Lot out of Sodom (Gen. 19.29); Israel out of Egypt, (Exod. 7.5); the Levites from the rest of Israel (Exod. 28.1); etc. The major exception to this is the series of Deuteronomic usages of the phrase to describe what the people perceived at the Sinai theophany (Deut. 4.12,15,33,36, 5.4,22–26; 9.10; 10.14). See I. Wilson, *Out of the Midst of the Fire: Divine Presence in Deuteronomy* (Atlanta: Scholars Press, 1995), pp. 53–76.

90. It is striking that these three theophany texts all employ rare words to describe the visual depiction of the divine – חשמל (Ezek. 1), סולם (Gen. 28), and בלבת אש מתוך הסנה (Exod. 3).

91. In addition to being a general term for representing the divine presence (Isa. 4.5; Ps. 29.7), Greenberg [*Understanding Exodus*, p. 71] notes both positive and negative valences. fury (Jer. 4.4; Ps. 79.5), a consuming fire (Deut. 4.24; 9.31), purity (Num. 31.23; Mal. 3.2), illumination (Exod. 13.21), and guidance (Exod. 13.21).

92. According to *Exod. Rab.* 2.5, the bush was preparation for the subsequent revelation to Israel at Sinai, in order to familiarize Moses with the experience of fiery revelation.

93. Cf. the comments by R. Eliezer and R. Yose in *Exod. Rab.* 2.5; Robinson, 'Moses at the Burning Bush', p. 115. Egypt is referred to as a blast furnace in Deut. 4.20; 2 Kgs 8.51; Jer. 11.4.

94. See further *Exod. Rab.* 2.5.

95. Note the use of תוך to describe the fire in the bush and Moses' basket among the reeds (Exod. 2.5).

96. N. Wyatt, 'The Significance of the Burning Bush', *VT* 36 (1986), pp. 361–5. Robinson, 'Moses at the Burning Bush' p. 120, suggests a connection between the מראה that Moses examines in Exod. 3.3 and the מראה of the lampstand in Num. 8.4. Cf. also C.L. Meyers, *The Tabernacle Menorah*, (Missoula: Scholars Press, 1976), pp. 176–7.

20.9), for Moses the fire is the spark of revelation which empowers without frightening.[97] Propp suggests that the bush marks a shift in YHWH's relation to nature, and foreshadows the unnatural use of nature for YHWH's own ends in the plagues.[98] What stands out in all these readings is the atypical aspect of the combination, suggesting either a radical transformation of the self (Moses called, inspired), or an unstable admixture (Israel/Egypt or YHWH/Egypt) which cannot hold together for very long.

As mentioned above, the double use of ראה points to a clear distinction between the narrator's point of view and the perspective of Moses, which is introduced with הנה. Moses' eye focuses on the quality of the flame, rather than on its source or its essence. The term סנה is also repeated twice, describing first the admixture of flame and bush, and then its not being consumed. The description focuses on Moses' watching, using present tense markers (בער, אכל) to emphasize ongoing observation. By presenting the reader with a contrasting focalization, we are able to focus on the quality of the flame from a dual perspective, the narrator's identification of the flame with the divine presence (מלאך ה'), and Moses' lingering, uncomprehending gaze. The two perspectives might be seen to complement the two types of interpretations of the bush suggested above. The reading of the bush as Israel (or as Sinai) would correspond to the narrator's perspective, and the personal reading to Moses' perspective. The initial image is not frightening to Moses, nor is it necessarily fraught with meaning for him beyond the present moment. At the same time, like Jacob's *sullam*, it offers a symbolic representation of the paradoxical nature of the theophanic experience. It combines contradictory, potentially hostile forces – bush and flame – in an apparently symbiotic relationship in which both are kept alive. In this it defies normal explanation, and demands a closer look.

Whatever the interpretation given to the bush, the phenomenon itself doesn't necessarily 'say' anything to Moses, but is intended primarily to attract his attention. In this sense we must distinguish between different levels of understanding in the relationship between the visual image of the theophany and the accompanying voice. Weiss is correct in maintaining that there is an interpretative relationship between 'voice' and 'image', but this relationship is available to the reader before it is understood by the character.[99] This is essential for developing the transformative character of

---

97. In this sense אש בלבת night be taken from the root לבב, to encourage Moses. Cf. also Rashi *ad loc.*

98. Propp. *Exodus 1–18*, p. 222.

99. M. Weiss, 'Image and Voice', pp. 91–9. This point is revealed to Moses by YHWH's interpretive remark in v. 12, 'This shall be a sign for you', interpreting 'this' to refer back to the bush, which is here understood as a precursor to the Sinai theophany.

the theophany narrative. The potential for communication with YHWH would be there without the visual sign, but its presence heightens both Moses' fascination with the revealed image, as well as the tentativeness involved in not fully comprehending what he sees. If the listener isn't aware, then the experience is in danger of being lost. Thus the continuation of the narrative in vv. 3–4 will emphasize the visual aspect of Moses' experience – 'I will turn aside to *see* this great *sight*' – as well as the visual aspect of YHWH's dependent response – 'When YHWH *saw* that he turned aside to *see*'. To the reader, however, who sees from a wider perspective, the contextual reading of the bush is essential to the reading experience. The presence of a dual perspective in (A) and (B) insures that the reader is aware of both the private experience of Moses as well as its larger meaning in the context of the story.[100]

2. *Sudden Appearance*

A second strategy is the sudden emergence of a full unqualified view of the Deity, presented with no foreshadowing or with any prefatory vision or address. The protagonists recognize the divine immediately, but their view is then deflected, either by the protagonist himself or by the narrator, in order to qualify and limit the reader's perception of what has been seen. In both cases to be discussed below, the seeing is immediate and direct, comprising the first element in the visual representation.

i. *Isaiah 6.1–4.*

1 In the year King Uzziah died,   בשנת־מות המלך עזיהו
    I saw the Lord sitting on a   ואראה את־אדני ישב על־כסא רם ונשא
    throne, high and exalted,
    And his train filled the temple.   ושוליו מלאים את־ההיכל
2 *Seraphim* stood above it;   שרפים עמדים ממעל לו
    Each had six wings: שש כנפים שש כנפים לאחד
    With two he covered his face,   בשתים יכסה פניו ובשתים יכסה רגליו
    with two he covered his legs, and   ובשתים יעופף
    with two he flew.
3 And one called to another,   וקרא זה אל־זה ואמר
    saying:

---

100. This is brought out clearly by the continuation of the commission in 3.7–10 as well as in Moses' objections in 3.11–4.17.; cf. the discussion in chapter 4.

    'Holy, holy, holy is the Lord of
    Hosts; The entire earth is full of
    his glory'.

    קדוש קדוש קדוש ה' צבאות
    מלא כל־הארץ כבודו

4   The doorposts shook at the sound
    of their calling, And the house
    was filled with smoke.

    וינעו אמות הספים מקול הקורא
    והבית ימלא עשן

Isaiah's throne vision is marked by an unusual degree of fullness, both in the detail with which it describes the heavenly scene, and in the triple repetition of מלא in vv. 1,3, and 4.[101] In contrast to the theophanies of Moses and Jacob, where there is no sound until the Deity speaks, here we find a mixing of sight and sound from the earliest stages of the vision.[102] The scene begins boldly with a depiction of YHWH enthroned, moves to a detailed description of his retinue of seraphim praising him, and concludes with the impact of their worship on the temple itself. The structure of the vision draws attention to the relationship between the enthroned Lord (1) and these physical effects (4), both verses referring to the temple itself (בית, היכל) being filled (מלא). The description of the seraphic movements and song in vv. 2–3 receives a fuller explication than the vision of the Deity, which is the first and most important element reported. The centrality of the *seraphim* is emphasized further by their actions. YHWH sits, but the *seraphim* move about, protecting the Deity and singing praises. Indeed, the trembling felt in v. 4 is not seen as the result of the approach of the Deity as in other theophanies,[103] but is a response to the intensity of the angelic praise. The significance of this emphasis on the *seraphim* only becomes clear in the second part of the theophany in vv. 5–13, in which Isaiah is inducted into the heavenly retinue as a messenger on behalf of YHWH. The relative weight given to the description of the *seraphim* recalls Ezek. 1, though there the order is reversed, the vision of the Deity being the final scene reported by Ezek. As opposed to the successively closer foci which we described in Gen. 28.12–13, here the description begins up close and moves farther away. from throne, to retinue, to palace.

---

    101. J. Magonet, 'The Structure of Isaiah 6', *WCJS* 9 (1986), pp. 91–7 (92); Pedaya, 'Seeing, Falling', p. 243.

    102. In the case of Ezekiel, the audial element did not appear until Ezek. 1.25. M. Weiss, ('Image and Voice', pp. 91–9), argues that the visual (Isa. 6.1–4) and the audial (vv. 5–13) components of Isaiah's call are closely interrelated.

    103. Cf. S.E. Loewenstamm, 'The Upheaval of Nature During Theophany', *Oz Ledavid* (Jerusalem: Society for Biblical Study, 1964), pp. 508–20 (Hebrew); Hiebert, 'Theophany', p. 509; cf. Judg. 5.4–5; Pss. 18.8–16.; 77.19; etc.

What Isaiah actually sees is marked by a most remarkable ambiguity, at once describing everything, and yet disclosing nothing. In order to clarify the question of the prophet's point of view we must first try to determine the place where Isaiah is standing.[104] If we envision him in the divine throne room, the inner sanctum of the tripartite temple which corresponds to the דביר in Solomon's temple, he would have visual access to the enthroned Deity.[105] But verse 1c describes YHWH's שוליו, here understood as the hem of his garment, as filling the, היכל leaving no room for Isaiah. The divine presence is so overwhelming, so huge, that the hem of the divine robe flows out of the throne room even to fill the middle chamber.[106] If היכל is metonymic for the entire temple structure, as U. Simon suggests in explanation of Samuel's presence in the היכל in 1 Sam. 3.3,[107] then Isaiah would be situated at some distance from the Deity. The prophet cannot take in the immensity of the Deity, and immediately following the daring statement 'I saw the Lord of Hosts enthroned', he qualifies what he saw, mentioning only the distant border of his robe.[108]

This distancing process is introduced by the initial image of enthronement and by the phrase רם ונשא, emphasizing not immanence, but transcendence. Instead of the zoom-in technique that we saw in the triple stages of Jacob's ladder vision in Gen. 28, here the virtual camera moves *away* from the vision. Since he is privy to this remarkable sight, we expect Isaiah to describe this vision of YHWH in greater detail, but instead he describes only the outmost fringe, that most distant part of the vision.

---

104. S.D. Luzzato suggests that Isaiah was standing outside the temple, and saw the edges of the robe from the rear, since YHWH was facing away from him [*Commentary to The Book of Isaiah* (Tel Aviv: Dvir, 1856) p. 62]. B. Uffenheimer ('The Commission of Isaiah', pp. 34–5) also sees Isaiah recounting an actual experience within the Temple. While most details fit well within the context of the Jerusalem temple – smoke, the altar, the burning coal – the image of the *seraphim* combines the *cherubim* and the bronze serpent (cf. Isa. 14.29–30 for שרף/נחש). Cf. also K. Joines, 'Winged Serpents in Isaiah's Inaugural Vision', *JBL* 86 (1967), pp. 410–15. S. Geller, however, points out the difference between the mythic space represented in the chapter and the actual temple in Jerusalem. 'Isaiah as a human and a layman could enter the Presence only in a vision' *Sacred Enigmas*, p. 118.

105. On the structure of Solomon's temple cf. C. Meyers, 'Temple, Jerusalem', *ABD* vol. 6, pp. 355–8. Magonet, 'Structure', p. 95, sees the chapter reflecting the tripartite structure of the Solomonic temple. Vv. 1–4 take place in the Holy of Holies, vv. 5–10 in the היכל, and vv. 11–13 focus on the courtyard as representative of the earthly domain.

106. M.C.A. Korpel, *A Rift in the Clouds*, p. 95; M.S. Smith, 'Divine Form and Size in Ugarit and Pre-Israelite Religion', *ZAW* 100 (1988), pp. 424–7; idem, *Biblical Monotheism*, pp. 83–6; J. Blenkinsopp, *Isaiah 1–39* (N.Y.: Doubleday, 2000) p. 225, compares the pictorial representation of Assyrian kings as immensely larger than their enemies. Weiss, 'Image and Voice', p. 95, sees the presence of YHWH extending beyond the Temple itself.

107. Simon, *Prophetic Narratives*, p. 64.

108. Ibn Ezra understands שוליו to relate to the throne, though elsewhere the term is applied only to clothes or to humans.

Understanding שוליו as 'the hem of his garment' would indicate the inadequacy of human vision to encompass the divine, both in sight and in description.[109]

Against this traditional reading, G.R. Driver[110] and, more recently, L. Eslinger,[111] have suggested that שוליו here implies not distance, but a glimpse of utmost intimacy. They note that שול as 'hem' appears only in the circumscribed context of the priestly garments (Exod. 38.33–34; 39.24–26), while in all other contexts it relates to the female genitalia (Isa. 47.2; Jer. 13.22, 26; Nah. 3.4; Lam. 1.9). Eslinger maintains that the basic meaning of the term is the physical one, and the meaning 'robe' is to be understood as metonomy for the body part being concealed.[112] The purpose of such graphic anthropomorphism is not to depict the anatomy of the Deity, nor indeed to assign sexual identity, but rather to convey a sense of 'a sacred nakedness, unshielded by the usual cultic prophylactic'.[113] Eslinger suggests that the purpose of the unusual attribution to YHWH is to approximate the sense of the shock felt by the prophet in beholding the essence of the Deity. According to this reading, then, Isaiah does not turn his face aside at the crucial moment, but penetrates to the very substance of the Deity in the manner of the close-up we described in Gen. 28. This is more in keeping with what we might expect from a first-person account (like Ezekiel 1), in contrast with the limitations of the third person omniscient narrator as in Ex. 24.9–11.[114]

A similar tension can be seen in the question of the function of the *seraphim*.[115] The traditional 'hem' reading sees the angelic chorus as part of the normative royal retinue, stationed in close proximity to the Deity, yet shielding themselves from YHWH. All the actions performed by the

109. F. Landy, ['Strategies of Concentration and Diffusion in Isaiah 6', *Biblical Interpretation* 7 (1999) pp. 58–86 (64)], describes this as 'a centrifugal movement from the vision of God to his attributes and effects'.

110. G.R. Driver, '"Isaiah 6.1 'His Train Filled the Temple"'', in H. Goedicke, ed., *Near Eastern Studies in Honor of W.F. Albright* (Baltimore and London, 1971), pp. 87–96.

111. L. Eslinger, 'The Infinite in a Finite Organical Perception', *VT* 45 (1995), pp. 145–173.

112. Eslinger, 'The Infinite', pp. 170.

113. Eslinger, 'The Infinite', pp. 158–9. This is not done to ascribe male sexuality (or androgyny) to YHWH, as does H. Eilberg-Schwartz, *God's Phallus and Other Problems for Men and Monotheism* (Boston: Beacon Press, 1994). This reading of שול is rather intended to serve as a metaphor for what is normally hidden from display. Cf. the critical remarks of Smith, *Biblical Monotheism*, pp. 91–2.

114. On the narrator's depiction of YHWH in biblical narrative see Sternberg, *Poetics*, pp. 322–5; F. Polak, *Biblical Narrative*, pp. 244–8.

115. On the nature of the seraphim see Landy, 'Strategies of Concentration', p. 63; Joines, 'Winged Serpents ', pp. 410–415; Weiss, 'Image and Voice', p. 95.

seraphim reflect their relationship with YHWH.[116] Thus the phrase בשתים יכסה refers to the faces of the *seraphim*, which are in need of protective shielding from exposure to the Deity, the lethal aspect of visual exposure to the Deity being extended to the angels as well.[117] The 'legs' they are covering are likewise their own, (a euphemism for their genitalia) presumably to avoid giving offense to the Deity.[118] As the Deity is enthroned (ישב), so the *seraphim* are attendant (עמדים), the imperfect verbs in v. 3 describing their habitual actions. The description of the *seraphim* is thus intended to complete the picture of YHWH, describing his trappings rather than describing the essence of the Deity itself.[119] This description is an essential part of the visual strategy envisioned by the first four verses, moving outward from the Deity, to his train, to the retinue and their incantation, ending with a depiction of the smoke-filled temple and the trembling door posts to complete the picture.

Eslinger however, develops the idea that Isaiah is perceived as an interloper, and argues that the response of the *seraphim* is to block this inadvertent view of the revealed Deity, and to prevent the prophet from seeing any more.[120] The legs which are covered are the *Deity's* 'nakedness', in the sense of his essence being obscured from Isaiah's sight;[121] the 'face' which is covered is YHWH's face, which cannot be viewed by any human (Exod. 33.20). This covering is not merely physical, but multidimensional, as the masking of YHWH takes place on a number of levels. Even the litany 'Holy, Holy, Holy' is seen as a deliberate substitute for the actual presence of the Deity, exchanging attribute for essence. The progression thus described is reflected in the triple use of מלא in vv. 1–4, in which the 'fullness' is more and more externalized. The theophany begins with the fullness of the Deity's שׁול, moves to the liturgical celebration of this

---

116. Weiss, 'Image and Voice', p. 95, connects the 'burning' aspect of the *seraphim* with the notion of an incandescent revelation, the *seraphim* representing a sort of 'outer shell' of the Deity. For further discussion of the *seraphim*, see the literature cited by Landy, 'Strategies of Concentration', p. 63 n. 17.

117. Landy, 'Strategies of Concentration', p. 63, notes that despite Isaiah's seeing, the *seraphim* must cover their faces, reinforcing the sense that even they cannot look upon the Deity.

118. So Rashi, Radak. O. Keel, C. Euhlinger, *Gods, Goddesses and Images of God* (Minneapolis: Fortress, 1998), p. 273, support this interpretation, though they raise questions as to just how human the form of the *seraphim* may have been.

119. H. Marks, 'On Prophetic Stammering', p. 67, suggests the complexity of the *seraphim*'s wings and the redundancy of language in their litany create a sense of confusion in the reader and thus enhance the awareness of the divine. Uffenheimer, 'Isaiah 6', p. 34 sees this as a reflection of actual Temple liturgy as reflected in Pss. 29.1; 89.6–9; 99.3,5,9.

120. Eslinger, 'The Infinite', p. 163.

121. Indeed the very mention of YHWH's legs would imply that they were visible, not covered by a robe.

fullness in the Trishagion and the כבוד as the externally visible representation of YHWH, and concludes with the 'filling' of the house with smoke.[122] This reading strategy highlights the role of the *seraphim* as protectors of the Deity, a role usually ascribed in cultic terms to inanimate objects like the veil,[123] or, in literary terms, to the narrator's deliberate avoidance of descriptions of the divine. But here it is not only language which veils the appearance of the divine, but the wings of the *seraphim* themselves.

While one could make an argument in favor of one reading or the other, both interpretations are plausible.[124] But instead of creating an impossible reading gap which paralyzes the reader, the sense of the text is better served by maintaining both possibilities. Is שול that which is revealed, or that which conceals? The use of the term here reflects a deliberate ambiguity, representing both the covering *and* the thing which is covered. Isaiah is at once an interloper seeing something which is forbidden to him ('No man may see my face and live'), and at the same time the very model of the biblical visionary, who, despite what he actually sees, limits his descriptions of the Deity to external attributes, to euphemisms, and to the drama surrounding the Deity. This sense of YHWH as both veiled and unveiled, seen and unseen, represented both literally *and* figuratively, presents in its most heightened form a dynamic about the representation of the Deity found throughout the Bible. YHWH is simultaneously displayed and hidden in many texts, whether by locutions such as קול דממה דקה (1 Kgs 19.12), by the view of Moses and Aaron in Exod. 24.9–11 and the immediate change of focus to 'below his feet', or by the mysterious מלאך which seems to represent both the Deity and his go-between at the same time. This bringing together of the immanence and transcendence of the Deity is reflected as well in the seraphic litany, announcing both the separate, distant aspect of holiness, and the immanence of the כבוד as the

---

122.   Eslinger, 'The Infinite', p. 165. Eslinger himself notes the connection between smoke and Sinai, but one could go further. In both texts there is an unusual mixing of sound and sight, the site of the theophany trembles and is filled with smoke, and there is an explicit fear of dying.

123.   Cf. Haran, *Temples and Temple Service*, pp. 152, 164.

124.   The weakness of the traditional reading (שול = hem of garment) is in the ascription of a robe to YHWH, either on the basis of similarity with the priests, or in light of royal iconography from the ancient Near East – nowhere else in the Bible does such an image of divine clothing occur, with the possible exception of Dan. 7.9 (Korpel, *Rift in the Clouds*, p. 367). The weakness of the 'sexual' reading is both in its daring imagery, and in the fact that שול always refers to the female sexual organs, and always in a context of disgrace. See the comments by Smith, *Biblical Monotheism*, p. 246 n. 37, and by Landy, 'Strategies of Concentration', p. 62 n. 10.

visible presence of the Deity with which he comes into contact with the world, and the very filling of that world as well.[125]

In both of these scenarios, the effect on the prophet is the same. he is forced out of his immediate contact with the divine. This may be due to the protective actions of the *seraphim*, or due to his sense of his own foreignness in this context, as he defines it in Isa. 6.5.[126] But there is no mistaking the movement in the description of the divine from inside to out, from YHWH, to his retinue, to his temple. The purpose is, on the one hand, to obscure the Deity, as does the incense cloud in the sanctuary in Lev. 16, but this smoke also indicates the fullness of the presence of the Deity. So too the presence of the cloud containing the *K'vod YHWH* in Exod 40.34–35 makes it impossible for Moses to inhabit the same space as the Deity. As in Exod. 40.34, וכבוד ה' מלא את המשכן, so in Isa. 6.2, את ההיכל ושוליו מלאים, As Moses was unable to enter the tabernacle, so Isaiah would be forced out of the sanctuary. Immanence is desirable to make contact with the Deity, but transcendence is essential to make room for human autonomy.[127] The function of v. 4 is to point out this shift in sacred geography, but also to show us the perceptions of the prophet, as he becomes aware of himself and his surroundings. The trembling is simply not a 'sympathetic reaction' of the Temple to the chant of the *seraphim*,[128] but an indication that the prophet, like the people at Sinai, became aware at a certain moment of the frightening nature of their surroundings.[129] It is this awareness that leads directly into the prophet's anxious reaction in v. 5.

ii. *Exodus 24.9–11*. Less elaborate in its description but employing a similar technique is the theophany to Moses, Aaron, Nadav, Abihu and the seventy elders in Exod. 24.1–2, 9–11. The story is usually seen as a continuation of the narrative from Exod. 19.20–25, which, when taken together with 24.3–8, is understood as part of a covenant ceremony.[130] The

---

125. Magonet, 'Structure', p. 92; Buber, *Prophetic Faith*, p. 128; Blenkinsopp, *Isaiah 1–39*, p. 225.

126. Cf. Pedaya, 'Seeing, Falling', p. 42.

127. On the development of transcendence as a reaction to theophany narratives see Geller, *Sacred Enigmas*, pp. 168–80.

128. So Eslinger, 'The Infinite', p. 173. It is possible that the repetition of קדוש קדוש קדוש is meant to surpass the קדש קדשים in which the ark is housed, thereby declaring the supreme holiness of the Deity above all else.

129. Cf. the verb נוע in the reaction to theophany in Exod. 20.18 and in Dan. 10.10 in relation to revelation and fear. Weiss, 'Image and Voice', p. 97, sees the trembling in Isa. 6:4 as closely related to the shaking of the mountain in Exod. 19.18.

130. For discussions of Exod. 24 cf. Toeg, *Lawgiving at Sinai*, pp. 37ff.; Mann, *Divine Presence and Guidance*, pp. 154–6; E.W. Nicholson, 'The Antiquity of the Tradition in Exodus XXIV 9–11', *VT* 25 (1975), pp. 69–79; idem, 'The Interpretation of Exodus XXIV 9–11', *VT*

theophany is unusual both in its contextual setting and in terms of its significance. In the context of the Sinaitic revelation we have no expectation of any further direct contact between God and the people after Moses' empowerment to act as go-between in Exod. 20.15–18.[131] That Moses will return to the mountain for further consultation with YHWH is clear from of 24.1–2, which emphasize a hierarchical separation. Moses alone is to 'approach', Aaron, his sons, and the 70 elders are to 'ascend', and the people remain below. Moreover, the approach of the select group is qualified by the injunction that they will 'worship from afar'; only Moses is to approach further.[132] Thus it is all the more surprising that, at the moment of the theophany (24.9–11), there is no separation between Moses and the rest of the group which ascends with him, as one finds in Exod. 19–20.[133] The 'content' of the theophany also stands apart. Even though the account in 24.9–11 is likely to be read in conjunction with 24.3–8 as part of the covenant ceremony reflected therein, the theophany itself is purely visual, and offers no explanation in terms of initiation, divine promise, or covenantal act.[134]

What is important for our purposes is the contrast between the suddenness and the intensity of the experience – 'seeing' the God of Israel[135] and the use of the verb חזה which is common for prophetic vision[136] – and the absence of any description of the Deity. Exod. 24.10a recalls the

---

24 (1974), pp. 77–94; idem, 'The Origin of the Tradition in Exodus XXIV 9–11', *VT* 26 (1976), pp. 148–60. Cf also Th. C. Vriezen, 'The Exegesis of Exodus xxiv 9–11', *OTS* 17 (1972), pp. 100–33; Dozeman, *God on the Mountain*, pp. 106ff.; C. Houtman, *Exodus* Vol. 3, (Leuven: Peeters, 2000), pp. 281ff.

131.   Rashi and Nachmanides, however, see this episode as occurring prior to the events of Exod. 20.

132.   Dozeman, *God on the Mountain*, p. 108, distinguishes between redactional levels in Exod. 24.1a and 24.1b-2 in order to develop Moses' exclusive role as covenant mediator.

133.   A hierarchical distinction between Moses, the priests, and people is found in Exod. 19.21–24, but the presence of the 70 elders in 24.1,9 introduces a non-priestly category of leadership, as we see also in Num. 11.16–25. Dozeman, *God on the Mountain*, pp. 180–92, interprets the presence of this group in light of his understanding of the late provenance of this level of redaction, which reflects tensions about leadership during the exilic period and their resolution in the figure of Ezra.

134.   Dozeman, *God on the Mountain*, p. 113, sees the eating and drinking not as part of a covenantal meal, but indicating a 'worship service on the cosmic mountain'. Smith, *Pilgrimage Pattern*, p. 241, understands the experience to reflect theophany associated with pilgrimage on the basis of Pss. 42.3 and 84.8. However, insofar as fasting was seen as preparation for an encounter with the Deity (Exod. 34:28; Deut. 9:9,18), the eating and drinking in Exod. 24:11 might be understood as the end of their fast after the conclusion of the theophany.

135.   LXX qualifies the experience – 'they saw the place where the God of Israel; stood'; cf. also Cassuto, *Commentary on Exodus*, p. 314, and *Targum Onkelos* to Exod. 24:11.

136.   Cf. the verb in Num. 24.4, 16; Isa. 1.1; 2.1, 30.10; Amos. 1.1; Lam. 2.14, etc.; the noun מחזה for prophetic vision in Gen. 15.1; Num. 24.4, 16; חוזה as seer in 2 Kgs 17.13; Isa. 29.10; 30.10; and the experience of seeing God in Pss. 11.7; 17.5; 27.4; 63.3.

directness of experience of Isa. 6.1 in suggesting an uncompromised view of the Deity. But instead of drawing closer to describe the vision in detail, the narrative focus immediately pulls back, describing only what is 'beneath his feet' (10b). In a sense this is not dissimilar to Isaiah's description of the Deity enthroned and the glimpse of שוליו as a royal robe. The mention of lapis lazuli is reminiscent of throne descriptions in the ancient Near East, and the word טהר conjures similar associations.[137] Moreover, the double use of the *kaph* of approximation recalls Ezek. 1 in its use of the same figure to qualify his descriptions of the divine.[138]

Similar to what we saw regarding Isaiah, the text is ambiguous about the reason for this deflection of vision. On the one hand, it could reflect a limitation of the participants' sight, as suggested by Houtman. In his view the description of the throne reflects the prostration of the participants; what they describe is all they can see.[139] While the command to bow occurs only in v. 2, and does not necessarily indicate that they were prostrate at the time of the theophany, this possibility cannot be ruled out. At the same time, the sequence of verbs in vv. 9–10 moves directly from ascent to vision, and the repetition of the visual contact in v. 11 implies a direct connection between seeing, eating and drinking, with no mention of their physical posture. Moreover, the note that those present were not harmed despite having beheld the Deity strengthens the sense of an intensive and direct encounter.[140] Verse 11, however, returns to the hierarchal distinction noted earlier, as the phrase אצילי בני ישראל most likely refers only to the elders, and not to Moses, for whom contact with the divine was not considered as threatening.[141] Once again it remains unclear if the narrator wishes to signal that the instinctive human response to theophany is a

---

137. Cf. *BT* Sotah 17a, Hullin 89a; note the parallel כסא//טהר in Ps. 89.45; Childs, *Exodus*, p. 509 points out the likely parallel with Ugaritic text 51.5.80–81 which describes the building of Baal's palace. Cf. further Vriezen, 'The Exegesis of Exodus xxiv: 9–11', pp. 100–33; Nicholson, 'Interpretation of Exodus XXIV 9–11', pp. 77–97; Houtman, *Exodus* vol. 3, pp. 292–4; Dozeman, *God on the Mountain*, p. 114, n. 74.

138. Dozeman, *God on the Mountain*, p. 113.

139. Houtman, *Exodus*, vol. 3, p. 294.

140. Elsewhere such danger is described in relation to face-to-face encounters with the Deity. Cf. Gen. 32, Exod. 33.

141. Given that their lives were endangered by proximity to the Deity, Houtman may be correct in suggesting that the phrase has a sense of the restoration of one's spirits after a brush with death, as in 1 Kgs 19.6,8; cf. also Gen. 25.34. (*Exodus*, vol. 3, p. 296). The contrast between the physicality of the covenant ceremony with the people in 24.3–8 (only here is blood sprinkled on the people), and the spiritual nature of the experience in 9–11 highlights both the hierarchical sense of the text – such an experience is only for the select few, and not for the rest of the people – as well as the complementary relationship between the two sections – the one elevated, visual, heavenly, the other earthly, bloody, and tied to written obligations. Both elements are essential to the Sinaitic covenant.

deflection of one's sight, or if he considers it inappropriate (or impossible) to describe the presence of the Deity in other than figurative terms.

3. *Sudden Revelation Followed by Gradual Recognition*

In contrast to Isa. 6 and Exod. 24, in a number of texts a *malakh YHWH* appears with no warning to deliver a message. While the *malakh* seems to be entirely visible from the outset, the initial response of the protagonist reflects not a gradual revelation, but a slower process of recognition than we find in the above cases. Kugel has aptly termed this a 'moment of confusion', but the process of realization seems to take somewhat longer; it is usually not until the end of the theophany narrative that this 'click' takes place.[142] While the identifying characteristics of the divine emissary are never made clear in the text, in all these cases the *malakh YHWH* is apparently indistinguishable from a human. In Judg. 6 and 13 the *malakh* is introduced by the narrator with the standard phrase 'The angel of the Lord appeared to ...' with no further elaboration, but in both cases it takes some time for the protagonists to become aware of the nature of the visitor. The *malakh* who comes to Gideon assumes a sitting posture like a human, and Gideon responds with a comment which directly challenges the notion of divine presence; it seems obvious that he takes the angel for a passerby.[143] The *malakh* who appears to Manoah's wife in Judg. 13.3 also has a human form, though she has suspicions as to the divine nature of the 'man of God', as she calls him in 13.6. These doubts arise from his unusual form (13.6 – 'his appearance was that of an angel of God') as well as from the message he delivers in 13.3–5.[144] In both cases the *malakh* appears twice to the protagonist (6.12,20; 13.3,9), emphasizing the absence of chance in the encounter, and giving further support to the idea of gradual recognition. In addition, both Gideon and Manoah require convincing by means of a sign (6.17; 13.19–21). Only after this are both convinced about the nature of the theophany.

In the case of Hagar a similar phrase of introduction is used.[145] As above, Hagar's initial response, 'I am fleeing from Sara, my mistress', gives no indication that she sees her interlocutor as anything out of the ordinary.

---

142. Kugel, *The God of Old*, pp. 5–36. While the gradual recognition process also occurs in theophany accounts where there is no *malakh*, it would seem that the presence of the *malakh* serves as a signal that there will be a delay in recognition. The *malakh* functions not only as an indication of how the Deity reveals himself, but also of how that revelation is perceived.

143. Cf. Abravanel *ad loc.*, Amit, *Judges*, p. 236.

144. Polak, 'Messenger of God', p. 20.

145. 'An angel of YHWH found her' – Gen. 16.7.

However, in the subsequent speech of the *malakh* in Gen. 16.9–12 the narrator repeats the introductory phrase 'The angel of YHWH said to her' three times. Most likely this indicates a series of pauses between comments, indicating the passage of time until Hagar responds with a note of recognition in Gen. 16.13.[146] Only the third speech of the *malakh* in 16:11–12 gives clear indication – the mention of YHWH in connection with the name of the child – that the speaker is not human but divine. Thus is each of the cases where a *malakh* appears the pattern is the same – the visitor is visually unexceptional, and the recognition process is triggered by something in the words of the *malakh*.

As discussed in the previous chapter, the situation of Abraham in Gen. 18 is more complex. The introductory phrase used in Gen. 18.1, 'The Lord appeared to Abraham' leaves it unclear whether the phrase indicates immediate appearance by YHWH,[147] or if it is to be read as a topical introduction to the chapter, during which YHWH appears to Abraham.[148] The latter interpretation seems preferable, for if recognition were present in v. 1 it would be hard to explain Abraham's subsequent reactions to his guests. There are a number of points along the way at which Abraham's speech might indicate awareness of the divine, but it is not until v. 13 that YHWH is named explicitly by the narrator.[149] Since the narrator gives no indication of any visible change that takes place in the speaker(s), here too the text seems to indicate gradual recognition rather than gradual revelation.

Joshua's recognition of the divine emissary in Josh. 5.13–15, who identifies himself as 'chief of the armies of YHWH', is likewise gradual. The text describes the posture and the drawn sword of the 'man' in v. 13, yet Joshua's recognition requires verbal identification before he responds by falling to the ground.[150] The reader's sense of the unusual nature of the figure may arise from the drawn sword, as the phrase is used only of heavenly emissaries.[151] The expression עתה באתי may indicate the suddenness of his appearance – 'I have just arrived'[152] – and reflects more upon Joshua's perception of the emissary rather than upon his

146. Cf. M. Shiloah, 'Vayyo'mer…Vayyo'mer', in Weiser and Luria (eds.), *Sefer Korngrin*, pp. 251–67. See, however, the discussion of this phenomenon in S. Meier, *Speaking of Speaking* (Leiden: Brill, 1992), pp. 73–81.

147. So Rashi, Ibn Ezra.

148. Following Nachmanides and Hizquni.

149. Curiously, אדוני in v. 3 can be understood either as 'my lords' (NJPS) or as 'my Lord' (KJV). The switch from plural to singular voice in v. 10 may also indicate the emergence of a divine voice, as might the content of the annunciation speech itself in 18.10.

150. See the discussion of the text in R.D. Nelson, *Joshua* (OTL; Louisville, KY: Westminster, 1997), pp. 80–3.

151. Cf. Num. 22.23, 31; 1 Chron. 21.16.

152. See Abravanel *ad loc.*

appearance to the reader. In all these cases, there are no clear visual clues
as to the identity of emissary, but the response of the protagonist is slower
than that of the reader, is aware of the divine nature of the visitor only
because the narrator has revealed it.

4. *Transformations of the Visual Motif*

Having established the basic dynamics of the visual appearance of the
divine in theophany narratives, we now turn to a number of texts in which
the visual presentation is muted or transformed.

a. *Minimization*
i. *1 Samuel 3*. In a few texts, at the point where we expect a visual element
to appear it has been purposefully avoided or diminished. Thus, for
example, while Samuel's theophany in 1 Sam. 3.1–21 speaks of prophetic
vision in 3.1, we are not told anything of what Samuel has seen.[153] Yet the
term מראה in v. 15 is clear evidence that there was a visual aspect to this
theophany, though it has not been developed. Likewise, YHWH's
continued revelation to Samuel is referred in visual terms (להראה) in
3.21. While Simon notes that ראה can have an auditory sense, as in 2 Kgs
8.10,13,[154] Amit's observation that the verb ידע is often tied to visual
revelation serves as a convincing counter argument.[155] In keeping with her
interpretation that 1 Sam. 3. speaks about auditory prophecy (דבר ה') as
well as visual revelation (חזון), v. 7 could also indicate both visual (ידע את ה')
and verbal (דבר ה') revelation. Yet there seems to be a deliberate effort to play
down the significance of sighted theophany. The expression מהגיד את המראה
indicates both verbal and visual revelation,[156] but the use of the verb 'to
tell' undercuts the visual element. Samuel is addressed three times by
YHWH in purely verbal terms, and Samuel's climactic response in 3.10 is
'*Speak*, for your servant is *listening*'. The oracle itself in vv. 11–14 lacks
visual elements and stresses the auditory aspect – דברתי, הגדתי לו,
כל שמעו, תצלנה שתי אזניו. On the one hand, this diminution of the visual
reflects the text's emphasis on darkness and the absence of vision, but there
is also a larger reason: the clear preference for the verbal over the visual in
prophetic literature.[157] This tendency is particularly noticeable in 1 Samuel,

---

153. See the discussion of the chapter in Simon, *Prophetic Narratives*, pp. 58–72.
154. Simon, *Prophetic Narratives*, p. 285 n. 35.
155. Y. Amit, 'Samuel's Commission', p. 32, esp. n. 11.
156. This recalls the formulation in Exod 20.18 וכל העם ראים את הקולת, which M. Carasik,
('To See a Sound: A Deuteronomic Rereading of Exodus 20.18', *Prooftexts* 19 (1999), pp.
257–65) understands as both verbal and visual revelation.
157. J.P. Fokkelmann suggests that this tendency is used to emphasize the diminution of
Eli. 'The visual element was dominant in the past to the detriment of Eli, the auditive begins to

where no visual revelations are reported. Rather, we note the change in terminology from רואה to נביא in 1 Sam. 9.9, and the critique of visual recognition in 1 Sam. 16. When a visual element does appear, as in the episode at En Dor in 1 Sam. 28, it does not serve to elevate the significance of visual revelation.[158]

ii. *Jeremiah 1*. Jeremiah's call differs sharply from theophany narratives in general (and call narratives specifically) in that there is no initial visual component presented either by the narrator or by Jeremiah. Neither is there the sort of gradual approach to the call as found with Samuel, despite the fact that he, too, is a נער. It would seem that YHWH's claim to have known Jeremiah (ידעתיך) from birth (or before!) obviates the need for any introduction. Jer. 1.4 describes a relationship which, surprisingly, *begins* with the unusual degree of intimacy. In all other cases the verb ידע, when used to describe relations between the human and the divine, expresses a degree of intimacy that is reflective of a later stage of relationship, rather than the beginning of such relations.[159] Yet here YHWH's attachment to Jeremiah is full-blown from the first moment. As in all theophany narratives, the question implied here is, in what way and to what extent can Jeremiah come to 'know' YHWH? In not prefacing YHWH's address to Jeremiah in vv. 4–5 with any visual component the text has minimized the dual perspective present in other theophany narratives. Indeed, Jeremiah's immediate response to the call in Jer. 1.6 – לא ידעתי – contrasts sharply with YHWH's claim – ידעתיך.

The central act of YHWH's response to Jeremiah is the touching of Jeremiah's mouth in Jer. 1.9. While we find touching as a means of

assume power in favour of Samuel' (*Narrative Art and Poetry in the Books of Samuel*, vol. 4, p. 169). By the same token, if the criterion for exclusion of sight was purely contrastive, one would have expected a corresponding emphasis on Samuel's seeing in order to emphasize his superiority to Eli. Rather, in keeping with the tendency of the text to depict a complex relationship between Samuel and Eli which is not exclusively contrastive, the narrator limits the revelation to the verbal sphere in order to maintain a basic similarity between Samuel and Eli, which is essential for the next scene. Samuel is depicted as superior to Eli in prophecy, but he remains his apprentice, at least for the moment.

158. Note the parallel of מראה to חלום in Num. 12.6, and the relationship of מראה to different types of dreams as suggested by Fidler, 'Dream Theophany', p. 52–5. At the same time we agree with Fidler's rejection of the claim that Samuel's revelation was a dream theophany on the basis of Samuel's responses in 1 Sam. 3.5–10. Given the parallels with Num. 12.6, the absence of the term חלום in our text cannot be accidental ('Dream Theophany', p. 104).

159. The verb ידע carries with it a sense of profound intimacy in divine-human relations – cf. Hos. 2.22, Exod. 33.12–17, and Gen. 18.19. One might contrast this with the chain of verbs in Exod. 2.22–25, which begins with external awareness (שמע), moves to more internal understanding (זכר) and finally progresses to 'knowing' (ידע) as the highest level of divine awareness, describing YHWH's response to Israel's plight.

contact with the divine in Isa. 6.6–7, there it is an act of purification
rather a means of conveying knowledge. Most significant, Isaiah's
contact is mediated by the angel, by the coal, and by the tongs, while in
Jeremiah's case the contact is unmediated, involving YHWH's hand
coming into direct contact with Jeremiah's mouth. Such unmediated
physical contact between human and divine is highly unusual in
theophany narratives[160] and bespeaks intimacy of the highest level, a
physical gesture equivalent to YHWH's 'knowing' Jeremiah. Here we
find the remnant of a visual element. The description of the movement of
YHWH's hand to Jeremiah's mouth only makes sense as the description
of an observed phenomenon.[161] This is accompanied by an explanation of
the contact preceded by the term הנה, which is most frequently a visual
marker in narrative, and especially so in theophany narratives. Moreover,
1.10 begins with the visual command ראה, which should be taken with
the previous הנה as a further visual marker.[162] The confluence of tactile
and visual elements in 1.9 heightens its centrality, as it confirms the
statement of divine intentions in v. 5 and answers Jeremiah's complaint
in v. 6. At the same time the visual aspect is only hinted at, focusing
instead on placing the words in Jeremiah's mouth and on the words he is
to speak. As above, we would offer two possible explanations for the
diminution of seeing, one directed at the narrative itself, and a second,
more global, concern. In keeping with the sense of 'knowing' in v. 5, the
inward focus of the text includes touching but rejects seeing. It embraces
an immanent contact with YHWH in which the sense of touch is
heightened by the absence of sight. As in Gen. 32, touching expresses a
closeness which transcends the visual. On a larger ideological level it also
reflects the strong influence of Deuteronomy, where visual contact with
YHWH at Sinai is replaced with the commanding voice from heaven,

---

160.   In Exod. 33.20 YHWH's use of his hand to protect Moses does not necessarily imply
contact, but even if we assume such proximity, it is of a very different nature. There is direct
prohibition against physical contact (נגע) with the numinous as represented by Mt. Sinai
(Exod. 19.12–13) and by the tabernacle (Num. 4.15). Angelic figures touch Elijah (1 Kgs
19.5,7) and Daniel (Dan. 10.10,16); touching by Gideon's angel in Judg. 6.21 and by YHWH
in Pss. 104.32 and 144.5 creates fire and smoke. The 'touching' of Jacob by the angel in Gen.
32.25 is somewhat less gentle and results in physical injury to Jacob. Thus physical contact
with a divine emissary is possible, but only in Jeremiah's case does YHWH's hand come into
contact with a human being.

161.   Cf. Lundbom, *Jeremiah 1–20*, p. 234; W. McKane, *Jeremiah* (ICC; 2 vols.;
Edinburgh: T and T Clark, 1986), p. 9; note also the comments (and reservations) of
Abravanel, Kimchi, and Metsudat David.

162.   Cf. Kogut, 'הנה in Biblical Hebrew', p. 149: 'The meaning of הנה(ו) is the same as the
root ראה'.

and in which there is an exclusive focus on the spoken oracle as the sole bearer of contact with the divine.[163]

A further point to be taken into account is the representation of the visual in the two vision reports in 1.11–16. While vision reports abound in the prophetic literature, the joining of symbolic vision with a commission narrative is unique to Jer. 1.[164] We would suggest that the vision reports here can be seen as a replacement for the visual appearance of the Deity.[165] Jeremiah's call, however, reverses the usual order; here the address by YHWH is *followed* by seeing, and the visual aspect serves a different function. Rather than serve as an introduction to the appearance of the Deity, its role is didactic, instructing the prophet 'how' to see.[166] The model of prophecy presented here serves as an illustration of the process of prophetic interpretation of everyday reality. The prophet makes an observation about an unexceptional aspect of this reality (an almond branch, a bubbling pot),[167] and is then instructed as to how to interpret this as a symbolic reflection of a deeper truth. If vv. 4–10 have explored the nature of his relationship to YHWH, now Jeremiah is shown what the content of his prophecy will be. Jeremiah has been told that words have been placed in his mouth, yet there is a delicate balance at work in prophecy, between the prophet as a mouthpiece for a previously determined divine word, and prophecy as a reflection of the prophet's own interpretations of his empirical observations. YHWH's statement that Jeremiah has 'seen well' refers not to the emergence of the divine in the theophanic moment, but to the prophet's ability to discern the traces of divine intention in everyday reality.[168]

163. On Jeremiah and Deuteronomy cf. W. Holladay, *Jeremiah 1–2*, (Minneapolis. Fortress Press, 1989), vol. 2, pp. 53–63, and the bibliographic references on pp. 451–2. On Deuteronomy's rereading of Sinai see Toeg, *Lawgiving at Sinai*, pp. 117–44; Weinfeld, *Deuteronomy and the Deuteronomic School*, pp. 191–209, esp. p. 206; Geller, *Sacred Enigmas*, pp. 38–51; M. Carasik, 'To See a Sound', pp. 257–65. On the centrality of the prophetic voice in Deruteronomy cf. Polzin, *Moses and the Deuteronomist*, pp. 57–62.

164. On prophetic vision reports in general see B.O. Long, 'Reports of Visions among the Prophets', *JBL* 95 (1976), pp. 353–65, and note the typology set out by S. Niditch, *The Symbolic Vision in Biblical Tradition* (Chico, CA: Scholars Press, 1983). On Jeremiah's visions see W. Zimmerli, 'Visionary Experience in Jeremiah', in Coggins, Phillips, and Knibb (eds.), *Israel's Prophetic Tradition*, pp. 95–118.

165. Cf. Holladay, *Jeremiah 1–2*, vol. 1, pp. 30–1.

166. J. Lindblom ties this to wisdom traditions; cf. 'Wisdom in the OT Prophets', *VTS* 3 (1955), pp. 192–204 (202).

167. On the details of these visions cf. Holladay, *Jeremiah 1*, pp. 37–40; Lundbom, *Jeremiah 1–20*, pp. 236, 241–242.

168. Y. Hoffman, *Jeremiah* (Tel Aviv: Am Oved, 2001) (Hebrew), vol. 1, p. 117.

iii. *Genesis 32.24–32*. In Gen. 32.24–32 a certain fogginess pervades the entire visual encounter. Jacob's assailant comes upon him at night, and their entire interaction is shrouded in darkness. The confusion as to which character is which is conveyed to the reader by the lack of definite antecedents in v. 25. 'When he saw he could not defeat him, he grasped at the hollow of his thigh'. Up to this point we do not know who is winning and who is losing; only subsequently do we learn that it is Jacob's thigh which was dislocated. Likewise, in the dialogue of vv. 26–29, no names are supplied, leaving us without a clear sense of who asks to be released and who demands a blessing, at least until Jacob speaks his own name in v. 27. This lack of clarity is further reflected in the generic designation of Jacob's opponent as איש, 'a man', which indicates only that he has a human form.[169] After v. 24 his presence is registered only by pronouns, and it is only in hindsight that we realize that he is a divine emissary. The upshot of all this is that the reader is left in the dark together with the combatants. Yet vision finally asserts itself, as the darkness of the first section (vv. 24–25) gives way to the dawning of the third section, vv. 30–32.[170] Most strikingly, Jacob describes the experience in terms as a visual encounter – 'I have seen God face to face and remained alive'. Thus, while there is no visual component to the encounter with the angel, there is certainly a sense of 'seeing' which follows it.

The scene is startlingly physical, if not actually pagan in origin.[171] Its 'face to face' aspect is augmented by a degree of corporeal contact between the adversaries which is wholly exceptional. What limited physical contact there is in theophany narratives can be seen in the call narratives of Isaiah and Jeremiah discussed above.[172] Not only does the physical contact highlight the lack of distance between the two figures at this point, but Jacob's wrestling with the angel bespeaks an unprecedented degree of physical intimacy with the divine. This is emphasized by the repeated use of the expression האבק עמו in vv. 24–25 with reference to the act of wrestling, as well as by the immediacy with which the contact is described. Instead of the gradual approach of human and divine by means of an incremental and intensifying process of recognition, this story begins with immediate bodily contact between Jacob and the divine emissary. There is no vision or speech which leads to the contact with the divine. Indeed, the

---

169. Cf. the use of the term to reflect a similarly enigmatic (divine?) figure in Gen. 37.15. Cf. also Josh. 5.13.

170. Cf. Geller, *Sacred Enigmas*, pp. 9–29 on the structure of the narrative and on parallels between the first and third sections.

171. C. Westermann, *Genesis 12–36*, p. 515; S. Talmon, 'Hatan Damim', *EI* 3 (1954), pp. 93–6 (93).

172. In 1 Kgs 19.5,7 Elijah is touched by an angelic figure, but here the contact seems to involve rousing the prophet from sleep.

use of וירא in v. 25 ironically underlines the absence of the visual element, for Jacob actually sees nothing here. As in Jer. 1, the minimization of the visual element serves to heighten the effect of physical proximity, the tactile sense of the theophany compensating for the absence of vision.

In all the above cases, seeing marks a recognition of the *difference* between the seer and the seen. Yet in Gen. 32 the narrator is interested in undercutting such differentiation, at least in the first part of the story. A similar appeal to senses other than seeing can be found in Gen. 27, where most of Isaac's senses are invoked – touch, taste, smell, hearing – but not sight. The effect there is to heighten the tension as to whether or not Isaac will recognize Jacob and uncover the deceit. Here the absence of sight comes to heighten the intimacy and immediacy of the encounter, making Jacob and the angel virtually inseparable. This is alluded to further by the angel's blessing in 32.28, 'You have struggled with God and man and have prevailed', which develops the temporary lack of separation between the human and the divine.[173] Paradoxically, vision plays a role in this theophany only after the fact, at the conclusion of the fight when Jacob is alone again and when he interprets the experience: 'I have seen God face to face'.[174]

b. *Seeing and Not Seeing – Balaam*
In the previous texts the diminution of seeing is subtle, but in the case of Balaam it is overt and even comic. On the one hand, the structure of Balaam's theophany in Num. 22.22–35 recalls Samuel's experience at the temple in Shiloh in 1 Sam. 3. In both cases the intended person is accosted three times but makes a mistaken assessment of the situation. Samuel is convinced that Eli is calling him, while Balaam acts is if the ass is being deliberately contrary. It is only by means of the intervention of a third party – here Eli, there the ass – that contact with the divine is actualized. But here the similarity ends. It is one thing to have an older priest for a mentor, and quite another to be contrasted (negatively!) with a beast of burden. Moreover, Balaam's violent response to the behavior of the she-ass is diametrically opposed to Samuel's obedient response to Eli's words. Earlier, there was no visual element in Balaam's initial conversations with YHWH in 22.9–12,20, but the subsequent theophany in 22.22–35 utilizes seeing in order to point up Balaam's inferiority as a seer.[175]

173. Cf. Geller, *Sacred Enigmas*, pp. 22–23 on the significance of this blessing.
174. The contextual reading of the story, in which the 'man' is a representative of Esau, only adds to this sense of the inseparability of the two characters. Cf. Fokkelmann, *Narrative Art in Genesis*, pp. 220–1.
175. On the use of the pattern of 3 + 1 in both 1 Sam. 3 and Num. 22 see Y. Zakovitch, *'For Three, and for Four'*, (Jerusalem: Makor, 1979), pp. 93–109.

The theophany here occurs within the context of Balaam's journey to Moab on behalf of Balak,[176] a journey for which he has received hesitant permission from YHWH.[177] Three times in Num. 22.22–27 Balaam's ass encounters an angel of YHWH in his path, attempts an evasive manoeuver, and is beaten by Balaam. While the ass's visual perception of the angel is emphasized by the verb ראה (22.23, 25, 27) and by her consistent attempts to avoid the deadly angel with the sword,[178] Balaam's lack of visual perception is made apparent by the intensification of his violent reactions to the ass' evasive manoeuvers.[179] It is clear in each case that he sees nothing out of the ordinary. These repetitions lead to the climactic interchange in 22.28–35, which breaks the above pattern in accordance with a recognized schema.[180] Most significantly, Balaam's eyes are opened to a different perception of his reality. The initial minimization of the visual element in the first section of the narrative includes a reversal of the usual theophanic pattern of visual revelation as a prelude to verbal revelation. Balaam's initial conversations with YHWH prior to his encounter with the *malakh* take place at night, with no indication of vision.[181] The visual element is introduced into the narrative not in order to attract Balaam's attention, but to highlight his limitations as a seer when contrasted with other recipients of theophany.

c. *Frustrated Expectations*

Two final examples of minimization of seeing the divine occur in midlife theophanies – Moses in Exod. 33 and Elijah in 1 Kgs 19. In both cases, the theophany is initiated by the human protagonist and not by YHWH, yet in both the expectations of the protagonist are deflected, particularly as regards the visual appearance of the Deity. Neither receives the precise revelation he expected, albeit in very different ways.[182]

176. On Balaam's roles as diviner and as one who curses, cf. Levine, *Numbers 22–36*, pp. 212ff.; M.S. Moore, *The Balaam Traditions: Their Character and Development* (Atlanta: Scholars Press, 1990), pp. 87ff.

177. See the attempts of Nachmanides and Malbim to explain the difficulty between YHWH's refusal in Num. 22.12 and his subsequent accession in 22.20.

178. The image of the angel with the sword invites a comparison with Jos. 5.13–15 and 1 Chron. 21.16. In contrast to Balaam and David, to whom the *malakh* was immediately recognizable as a divine emissary, Joshua's question, 'Are you for us or for our enemies?', indicates his confusion about the angel, who is referred to as איש.

179. See Savran, 'Beastly Speech', p. 35.

180. On the X + 1 pattern see Zakovitch, *'For Three, and for Four'*; Savran, 'Beastly Speech', p. 35, n. 5.

181. Fidler describes this as a 'feeble theophany' which is characteristic of the Bible's portrayal of revelation to non-Israelites such as Abimelech (Gen. 20) and Laban (Gen. 31). See Fidler, 'Dream Theophany', pp. 98, 123.

182. On the relationship of these two texts cf. below, chapter 7.

Elijah's experience in 1 Kgs 19 follows a pattern noted above in Judg. 6.11–24, where the appearance of an angel precedes the theophany by YHWH himself. But in Elijah's case, instead of the usual visual formula וירא אליו מלאך ה', the angel(s) in vv. 5 and 7 physically awaken the sleeping prophet, the term הנה being the only indication of visual perception.[183] YHWH speaks to Elijah with no introductory revelation in v. 9, in language which is more characteristic of the reception of a prophetic oracle than of theophany.[184] The initial phrase of the theophany in 19.11, הנה ה' עבר, leads one to expect a visual encounter, as in the use of the verb in Moses' theophany in Exod. 33.19 and 34.6.[185] The text describes a series of natural phenomena which involve seeing and other senses, but we are told repeatedly that YHWH was not to be located in the fire or the earthquake. The fullness of the revelation comes rather in the enigmatic phrase קול דממה דקה, which, whatever its literal sense, implies an audial revelation rather than a visual one.[186] On the one hand this follows the usual pattern of visual manifestation followed by verbal revelation, as described above. Yet there is something categorically different about this revelation, both in the denial of YHWH's presence in the wind, earthquake and fire, as well as in YHWH's repetition of his question to Elijah in v. 13. That Elijah expects a further visual revelation seems to be reflected by his covering his face with his cloak in v. 13. But, as Zakovitch points out, while his expectation is of seeing, the text suggests Elijah's failure to understand correctly.[187]

The suppression of the visual here can be understood on two levels. From a theological perspective, the text polemically rejects any similarity between YHWH's presence and the appearance of Baal in natural phenomena, perhaps as a corrective to the Sinai theophany in Exodus.[188] Here, as throughout the book of Kings, the text is careful to separate between natural phenomena associated with divine intervention and the appearance of the Deity on any level other than that of prophetic

---

183. Cf. above. n.57. The word functions here primarily to indicate a change in point of view from the narrator to Elijah. One may also see here a negative comment on the sleeping prophet, in contrast to all others who are addressed by angelic messengers. Cf. also Jon. 1.6.

184. Cf. Meier, *Speaking of Speaking*, pp. 314–19; Simon, *Prophetic Narratives* p. 214.

185. Cf. *TDOT*, vol. 10, p. 420.

186. Note Elijah's reaction to the theophany in 1 Kgs 19.13 – 'When Elijah *heard* ...'. On קול דממה דקה see Simon, *Prophetic Texts*, p. 213; J. Lust, 'A Gentle Breeze (I Kings 19),' *VT* 25 (1975), pp. 110–15; B.P. Robinson, 'Elijah at Horeb', (522–3, esp. n. 6); Y. Zakovitch, 'A Still Small Voice', p. 340, and the discussion in chapter 7.

187. Zakovitch, 'A Still Small Voice', p. 341; cf. also Robinson, 'Elijah at Horeb', pp. 528–9.

188. Cf. Jeremias, *Theophanie*, p. 65; F.M. Cross, *Canaanite Myth and Israelite Epic*, pp. 192–4.

oracle.[189] Within the story itself the narrative deliberately denies Elijah a visual theophany, at least of the sort that he expects. The reason for this holding back is understood as YHWH's critique of Elijah's presumption, demonstrating his failure at his prophetic task.[190] From Elijah's standpoint the absence of a visual theophany is a sign of incompleteness, yet from YHWH's vantage point, Elijah has completed his prophetic task, and is told to anoint his successor.[191] Here deprivation of the visual is a form of criticism, an experience of 'not-seeing'. While it is less critical than that which is reflected in the Balaam account, it nonetheless indicates divine displeasure.

Much more complex is the visual element in Exod. 33.18–23. Not only is the theophany initiated by Moses, but he makes an explicit request for an unprecedented degree of visual revelation of YHWH in 33.18. Prior to this the contact between Moses and YHWH in 33.12–17 has been entirely verbal, with an emphasis on audial elements – דבר, שם, הודיע, אמר.[192] Moses' request for a direct view of the divine glory is refused, but YHWH's qualification suggests a much richer experience than simply seeing or not seeing. YHWH's response in vv. 19–23 contains three separate locutions which, taken together, answer both 'yes' and 'no' to Moses' request. It is possible to read the three statements consecutively. I will pass before you and call upon my name, and I will forgive Israel's sin (19). BUT SINCE no man can see me and live (20), THEREFORE I will allow you a partial revelation (21–23).[193] This reading has the advantage of explaining the difference between the speeches as parts of a single argument, displaying the concern for Moses which YHWH mentions in 33.17, and emphasizing the centrality of divine control as well as the exceptional intimacy between YHWH and Moses. Moses is to see not the divine *kavod* but 'all my goodness', which may be connected with forgiveness, or with a lesser form of theophanic revelation.[194] In exchange for this limitation of visual revelation, Moses receives an intimation of divine forgiveness for Israel with the formula 'I will show grace to who I will show grace'. And instead

189. E.g. the fire from heaven in 1 Kgs 18.38. On the centrality of the prophetic word in Kings cf. G. von Rad, 'The Deuteronomistic Theology of History in the Book of Kings', *Studies in Deuteronomy* (London, 1953), pp. 74–91; A. Rofe, *The Prophetical Stories* (Jerusalem. Magnes, 1988), pp. 99–105.

190. Cf. Zakovitch, 'A Still Small Voice', pp. 342–3; Robinson, 'Elijah at Horeb', pp. 528–30.

191. Cf. Zakovitch, 'A Still Small Voice', p. 344; Robinson, 'Elijah at Horeb', p. 530.

192. There is visual imagery also in vv. 12–17. 'To find favor in one's eyes' occurs 4 times, YHWH's 'face' accompanies Israel in vv. 14–15 (cf. 2 Sam. 17.11), and the imperative form ראה is used twice by Moses in vv. 12–13.

193. See the discussion of this section in R.W.L. Moberly, *At the Mountain of God*, pp. 30, 79–83.

194. Childs, *The Book of Exodus*, p. 596; Polak, 'Theophany and Mediator', p. 144.

of seeing YHWH's 'face', he receives special treatment: YHWH places him in the cleft of the rock, and covers him with his hand.

If the images do not speak of actual physical contact between YHWH and Moses, then at very least the attention to Moses' welfare at the moment of revelation shows both an unprecedented concern for Moses and an awareness of the limits of human perception. The visual aspect of what Moses actually sees in the subsequent revelation in 34.1–8 is not spelled out, but the dialogue in 33.18–23 describes a transformation of the visual motif. Nowhere else is the recipient of the theophany prepared for the event by YHWH, and nowhere else does the protagonist make an explicit request to see the divine essence. Whereas elsewhere the protagonist or the narrator describes what can and cannot be seen, here YHWH himself explains the limits of human visual perception of the divine.

Chapter 4

HUMAN RESPONSES TO THEOPHANY

The human response to theophany is perhaps the most complex and most varied of all the components of the theophany type-scene. It is at this point in the theophany that we see the first direct interaction between the protagonist and YHWH, and in most cases the beginnings of what will be an ongoing relationship between the two. While such a response is always forthcoming in the texts under discussion, it may take place during the theophany itself, after the Deity has departed, and, in certain cases, at both times. These responses combine the verbal and the non-verbal, and may include physical reactions such as prostration, hiding the face, and movement towards and away from the numinous.[1] While we see this as a discrete element in the theophany type scene, there is a certain degree of continuity with the final phase of the theophany, the stage of externalization, which will be considered in the next chapter.

We can distinguish between two fundamentally different types of responses. The first is an expression of *mysterium fascinans et tremendum* in the presence of the divine, denoting a pair of complementary reactions in which the protagonist is drawn closer to the numinous, while at the same time is struck with fear and inadequacy in the presence of the divine. R. Otto's classic formulation of this phenomenon emphasizes the sense of 'awefulness' before the divine, of being completely overpowered and overcome by the 'absolute unapproachability' of the divine.[2] At the same time, in a 'strange harmony of contrasts', Otto describes an element of fascination that entrances the individual, a response which seeks out a certain closeness with the mysterium despite the sense of it being 'wholly other'.[3] In certain cases the two reactions are set side by side, as our discussion of Gen. 28.16–17 will demonstrate. In other cases they are indicated separately. Thus in Exod. 19 the people and Moses set out to approach the mountain in v. 17, and explicit limitations are placed upon

---

1. The latter reactions can be seen in Exod. 3.5, Josh. 5.14 (towards) and Exod. 20:15 (away); cf. chapter 1, pp. 18–19.
2. Otto, *The Idea of the Holy*, pp. 13–24.
3. Otto, *The Idea of the Holy*, p. 31.

them in vv. 12–13, 21–22, anticipating the people's desire to draw closer to the presence of the numinous. The contrasting sense of fear is mentioned briefly in 19.16, but is made most explicit only in 20.15–18.[4] In a number of cases – Exod. 20; Isa. 6; Ezek. 1 – the text describes genuine anxiety about the ability of the protagonist(s) to survive proximity to the divine. Here the fear is not of failure to perform adequately (as in the following category of response), but a real existential fear of death. The expression indicates the life-threatening nature of proximity to the divine. While both reactions are present in most of the texts we will explore, the biblical tendency is to emphasize the *tremendum* over the *fascinans*.[5]

The second type of response is characterized by an expression of doubt in response to the theophany. This may reflect apprehension about the protagonist's ability to perform the task at hand, or indicate skepticism about the nature of the divine promise which has just been stated. These reactions can be divided into two different groups:

1. Cases of doubt/questioning about the task (e.g. Exod. 3 and Judg. 6). These correspond to the category of doubt in the schema of Habel and others.[6] In the midst of the theophanic experience, the protagonist reveals a sense of inadequacy about the task to be performed. This reaction is fundamentally different from the expression of creature consciousness mentioned above. In those cases, the individual appears to have lost all sense of self in the face of the divine, whereas here the response reflects his self-evaluation in the face of the task. The protagonist questions his ability to perform the assignment, and in some cases YHWH's reliability as well. The purpose of these expressions of self-doubt may be to indicate the difficulty of the mission, the modesty of the individual, or the lack of training or preparedness of the initiate. They further indicate the essential conflict between human desire and divine choice. Here, in contrast with the usual biblical model of free will, the latter overrides the former absolutely. In all cases YHWH responds to the expression of self doubt with a message

---

4. In certain cases only one or the other response is described – as in the sense of fear expressed in Judg. 6, in Num. 22, or the desire for intimacy with YHWH expressed by Moses in Exod. 33.18. See B. Uffenheimer, 'The Method of Rudolf Otto and Prophetic Consciousness', *BM* 38 (1993), pp. 1–13 (7–9) (Hebrew).

5. There are also texts in which a more limited reaction is described. For example, in Gen. 16.13 Hagar's response to the appearance of the *malakh* is אתה אל ראי, 'You are the God who sees me', a reaction of thanksgiving for YHWH's response to her dilemma. The continuation of the verse may also contain an indication of her fear of death from the theophany, but the expression הגם ראיתי אחרי ראי is less than clear (see Westermann, *Genesis 12–36*, p. 247). In Josh 5.13 Joshua responds to the appearance of the captain of the army of YHWH by prostrating himself and declaring complete obedience to the divine messenger. Both of these cases contain elements of fear and fascination, but they are much less developed than in the texts which will be discussed below.

6. Cf. above, chapter 1.

of support and encouragement. We will term this phenomenon the 'response to the response', in which YHWH attempts to answer the objection voiced by the protagonist, or to quell the anxiety which has been voiced. On the one hand this shows the presence of a certain degree of human independence even during the theophany, as well as a sense of divine responsiveness to these concerns. At the same time, YHWH's autonomy is not compromised by attempts to refuse, and the decision of the Deity in all these texts is absolute.[7]

2. Skepticism countered by theophany (e.g. Gen. 18 and Judg. 13). Here the protagonist, not fully aware of the presence of the numinous, expresses some degree of doubt directly or indirectly, and the theophany comes to correct this misperception. An indication of the success of the correction is indicated by a further response by the protagonist: an admission of sin (Num. 22.34), a transparent attempt at denial (Gen. 18.15), an insightful corrective statement (Judg. 13.23). In these cases the psychological state of mind of the protagonist is emphasized in order to indicate the transformative aspect of the theophany. Incredulity is replaced by belief, pride is turned to shame, and confident self-assertion is turned to denial. In all cases the reaction allows us to glimpse the human element in the theophany in its different dimensions. The individual may object, but cannot refuse; he/she may express skepticism, but must ultimately accept divine authority. The protagonist may be scared even to death, but is compelled to complete the divine–human transaction.[8]

As with other type scene elements we will also examine a few texts which display significant transformations of these two patterns. In the first, 1 Sam. 3, the expected reaction to the divine is overshadowed by Samuel's sense of anxiety in anticipation of his post-theophany encounter with Eli. In the second, 1 Kg. 19, Elijah shows an identical verbal response both before and after the theophany, indicating the failure of the theophany to bring about any change in his attitude. In both cases, the significance of these unusual reactions is brought out more fully by understanding the place of human response to the divine.

---

7. See the remarks by Glazov, *The Bridling of the Tongue*, pp. 52–3, on the dialogical character of the objection and YHWH's response.

8. As noted above, Glazov, *The Bridling of the Tongue*, also sees two types of objections along lines similar to those elaborated upon here, the first related to the protagonist's self-assessment in the face of the divine, and the second with regard to the people (pp. 51–3). Glazov's model for this are the objections of Moses and Isaiah, both of which contain multiple objections of this sort. However, his attempt to apply this model to the call narratives of Jeremiah and Ezekiel is less convincing, and involves positing the editorial omission of the second objection from Jer. 1 (pp. 164–219), and a similar form of acrobatic interpretation to explain the absence of any voiced objection in Ezekiel (pp. 232–4). The attempt to include all objections under this rubric creates a structure too rigid to incorporate the wide variety of responses which we find in theophany narratives.

1. *Fear and Fascination*

In each of the following texts we find a different balance between the elements of fear and fascination. These variations may reflect a difference in focus on one or the other element, a juxtaposition of the temporal relationship of the two elements, as well as a contrast with the behavior of the protagonist in other sections of the theophany. Further, YHWH's 'response to the response' of the protagonist lends insight into the nature of the experience.

i. *Genesis 28.*

16	And Jacob awoke from his sleep and said:	וייקץ יעקב משנתו ויאמר
	Surely YHWH is in this place	אכן יש ה' במקום הזה
	And I was unaware.	ואנכי לא ידעתי
17	And he was afraid, and he said:	ויירא ויאמר
	How awesome is this place;	מה נורא המקום הזה
	This is surely the house of God,	אין זה כי אם בית אלהים
	And this is the gateway to heaven.	וזה שער השמים

Jacob's reactions to the dream vision of the *sullam* and to YHWH's promise in Gen. 28.12–15 are described in two verses which are not infrequently seen as redundant, perhaps indicating the presence of multiple sources in our text.[9] In our reading, however, this double reaction reflects two distinct aspects of the human response to the divine. Both verses mention the specific מקום where he is located, and both record Jacob's awareness of the divine presence therein.[10] But here the similarity ends, for the ostensibly repetitive language represents a complex emotional response containing contradictory feelings which exist side by side, if not consecutively. Verse 16 first relates the initial reaction of waking: the dreamer remains temporarily in the dream state, without being fully cognizant of his external reality.[11] Jacob's initial verbal response shows both a further identification of the מקום with the presence of God

---

9.   See, for example, E.A. Speiser, *Genesis* (AB; Garden City, N.Y.: Doubleday, 1964), p. 219; Von Rad, *Genesis*, p. 283; Peleg, 'Going Up and Going Down', p. 94; Fidler, 'Dream Theophany', pp. 157–161.

10.   Cf. the parallels between the two verses drawn by R. Rentdorff, 'Jakob in Bethel', in Rofe and Y. Zakovitch (eds.), *Isaac Leo Seeligmann Volume*, vol. 3, pp. 115–27 (124), and Fidler, 'Dream Theophany', p. 172.

11.   Waking from a dream state in the Bible is often accompanied by a realization that the person had been dreaming. Thus Pharaoh in Gen. 41.4,7: 'And he awoke, and behold, it was a dream'; or, similarly, Solomon in 1 Kg. 3.15. See the discussion in Lichtenstein, 'Dream Theophany and the "E" Document', pp. 42–3, and the comparative examples cited by him.

(יש ה' במקום הזה), and a contrast with his previous lack of awareness (ואנכי לא ידעתי). His reaction is one of amazement in a positive sense; the מקום is utterly different from what he had thought, and beyond that, he himself is now different as a result of the experience. His remark 'I *didn't* know' indicates that he now understands what he had not grasped formerly.[12]

Despite the fact that the dream has ended, the use of יש here underlines Jacob's sense that the divine is somehow still present. When used elsewhere in speaking of YHWH the term יש regularly expresses a conviction on the part of the speaker that YHWH is present and active.[13] At the same time Jacob's use of the first person singular pronoun emphasizes the gulf between his own 'אנכי' and YHWH's 'אני', which has been revealed to him in v. 13. His reaction underscores his amazement that he and YHWH can be present in the same place. This is precisely the paradox encoded in the visual part of the dream, and in the very notion of biblical theophany: how can the Deity be both transcendent and immanent in the same moment?[14] Jacob's reaction shows him waking from the liminal dream state but still within the orbit of the theophany itself, aware of the 'something more' which Otto describes as characteristic of the experience of *fascinans*.[15] The formulation יש ה' indicates that there is still a divine residue remaining in Jacob's awareness, a 'vapour trail' of the numinous. At the same time, the continuation of vs. 16 – ואנכי לא ידעתי – shows this new awareness of self, which indicates the beginning of Jacob's emergence from his dream state.

By contrast, Jacob's second statement, in v. 17, reflects a different set of emotions, centering around his awareness of the numinous as terrifying phenomenon. As in v. 16, Jacob's comment refers to the specific place (המקום הזה), and emphasizes the difference between his prior perception (which showed no awareness of the divine) and his present understanding. This is brought out by the repetition of ידא to describe both the place and

---

12. This phenomenon, recognizing the presence of the numinous only after the departure of the divine, is also reflected in Manoah's awareness of the angel of YHWH after he no longer appears (Judg. 13.21).

13. See 1 Sam. 17.46; Ps. 58.12; 2 Chron. 25.29, and the references to the cloud signifying YHWH's presence in Num. 9.20–21; by contrast note the skeptical responses about YHWH's presence in Exod. 17.7 and Judg. 6.13 which use the interrogative form היש.

14. I refer here to the ambiguity of YHWH נצב עליו in v. 13 – implying divine presence both at the top of the ladder and in close proximity to Jacob. The vision of the *sullam* indicates that YHWH is entirely transcendent and accessible only through angelic mediation, yet YHWH's direct address to Jacob is unmediated. Cf. the discussion in Fidler, 'Dream Theophany', p. 176, n. 240.

15. Otto, p. 35; D. Merkur, 'The Numinous as a Category of Values', in Idinopolus and Yonan (eds.) *The Sacred and its Scholars*, Brill: Leiden, 1996, p. 104–23 (106).

Jacob's own reactions.[16] But there is no mention of a change in Jacob's self-awareness in his comment here, only an overwhelming sense of anxiety. If the 'place' in v. 16 was described as containing within it the presence of the Deity, v. 17 expresses fear and awe in the face of that presence, what Otto refers to as 'religious dread'.[17] The term נורא in relation to YHWH occurs elsewhere primarily with the sense of greatness and fear,[18] though there is no explicit mention of the fear of death as in other theophany texts. In contrast to the use of יש in v. 16 to describe the divine presence from a positive standpoint, אין in v. 17 reflects this other perspective. Indeed, the formulation אין זה כי אם – 'this can be nothing else except' – leaves no room for Jacob's presence in the place where the YHWH dwells.[19]

The sense of distance from the divine which accompanies his fear is brought out by the relationship between בית אלהים and שער השמים. Both are introduced by זה in a deictic sense, and both are ostensibly about the vision and the place in which Jacob finds himself. They are often taken as referring to the same 'place', meaning 'this is a temple of God *which is* the gateway to heaven', or 'this is not simply a temple of God, but an actual gateway to heaven'.[20] But it is not clear why the narrator would use two separate expressions to describe the same holy place. It seems more appropriate to understand Jacob as referring to what is represented by the two ends of the *sullam*: בית אלהים is on the ground, but שער השמים is in the heavens.[21] The use of שמים here recalls the first section of Jacob's dream-vision in v. 12a, in which the separation between heaven and earth is

---

16. E. Fox, *The Five Books of Moses* (N.Y.: Schocken, 1995), p. 131 translates 'He was awestruck and said, "How awe-inspiring is this place"'.

17. Otto, *The Idea of the Holy*, p. 14.

18. Cf. Exod. 15.11; Deut. 7.21; 10.17; 1 Chron. 16.25; Neh. 1.5; 4.8; 9.32; Pss. 47.3; 76.8; 89.8; 96.4; 99.3.

19. C. Westermann's comment on the gate of heaven is apt here: 'The gate does not invite but prohibits entrance; one may not enter the place where God dwells'. The very notion of the gate must be understood as a reflection of 'the dividing line between the divine and the human, the line where awe begins'. (*Genesis 12–36*, p. 457).

20. The phrase is most often read as an aetiology of the temple at Bethel; cf. Peleg, 'Going up and Going Down', p. 96; Fidler, 'Dream Theophany', p. 176; Sarna, *Understanding Genesis*, p. 194.

21. Lipton, *Revisions of the Night*, p. 90 n. 66 notes that '...זה ...וזה occasionally has the same point of reference, as in Exod. 3.15...More often, though, it is used in the sense of "this...and that", as in Job. 1.16... or I Kg. 22.20'. She also concludes that the two pronouns refer to the extremities of the ladder. Further support for this is the fact that בית אלהים always refers to a physical temple in the Bible, never to a heavenly dwelling (Judg. 18.31; 1 Chron. 6.33, 9.11, etc.). שער השמים occurs only here, but the heavenly association of the term is strengthened by the only other reference to שמים in the chapter in v. 12, where the top of the ladder is located in the heavens. Cf. also A. Ehrlich, *Randglossen zur hebräischen Bibel* (7 vols.; Leipzig: Hinrichs, 1908–14) vol. I, p. 136.

clearly delineated by the span of the *sullam*.[22] As that image indicated the beginning of the theophany, Jacob's reaction in v. 17 points to the end of the actual encounter with the divine and the return to human consciousness. The immanent/transcendent distinction which was temporarily overcome by the vision of the *sullam*[23] has now been restored by pointing to heaven and earth ('this . . . this') as separate, and distant, points.[24]

Taken together, these two verses reflect the complex reaction to the holy which Otto describes as *mysterium fascinans et tremendum*.[25] In v. 16 Jacob expresses his fascination with the newly found source of power, a desire to draw closer, an awareness of the positive power of the 'wholly other'. Verse 17, on the other hand, describes his apprehension of the numinous in all its frightening power, evoking his awareness of human limitation, and of his nature as a created being standing before the Creator. (Elsewhere, as in Isa. 6, the reactions also may include an awareness of sin or guilt, but here there is no suggestion of this). The transcendent character of the Deity is emphasized further in v. 17 by the double reference זה . . . זה. YHWH is no longer seen as immediately present; YHWH's presence is in the heavens, and Jacob is at the site of a future earthly sanctuary. The proximity of the two verses, the similarity of language, and relatively equal length of the descriptions indicate a balance between the two types of reaction. The liminal moment of the theophany has ended, and with it comes Jacob's startling realization that his understanding of the world and of himself has changed.[26] The final stage of the theophany which will follow will mark that change in a ritualized, external manner.

ii. *Moses – Exodus 3.3–6.*

3	And Moses said:	ויאמר משה
	I will turn aside	אסרה נא
	And look at this great sight.	ואראה את המראה הגדל הזה
	Why isn't the bush consumed?	מדוע לא יבער הסנה

22. Cf. the midrash from *Gen. Rab.* 69.7 cited by Rashi, which reads the phrases as referring respectively to an earthly and a heavenly temple. By contrast, Sforno *ad loc.* sees the gate of heaven as a reference to the ladder in the dream. Peleg, 'Going Up and Going Down', p. 96, understands זה as a shortened form of the phrase זה פתרנו in Gen. 40.12.

23. Cf. chapter 3, p. 62.

24. Fidler, 'Dream Theophany', p. 172, following Rendtorff ('Jakob in Bethel', p. 124) draws a parallel between the three elements of the dream and the language of Jacob's reaction in vv. 16–17. On the relationship between Jacob's reaction and the content of his dream see also the discussion in Peleg, 'Going Up and Going Down', pp. 91–104.

25. Otto, *The Idea of the Holy*, pp. 12–30; Uffenheimer 'Method of Rudolf Otto', pp. 7–9.

26. In contrast with the impenetrability of Jacob's character before and after (there is no mention of his thoughts or emotions), in vv. 16–17 the reader is privy to Jacob's thoughts, revealing the change which has taken place.

The revelation to Moses at the bush is perhaps the most dynamic of all theophany narratives, for in it Moses reacts a number of times to YHWH's indirect and direct overtures. Moses' response to the sight of the bush aflame in 3.3 is unusual in its use of direct speech/thought to describe intention, as Moses speaks only to himself in what appears to be an unself-conscious manner. Interior monologue is often used to offer an explanation for behaviour, but here the effect goes beyond clarifying an element of the plot (what will Moses do next?) to present a snapshot of the character's mind at that moment. Usually such interior monologue is limited to the protagonist (and the reader), but here, where YHWH is aware of the thoughts of the characters, it effectively begins a dialogue about which Moses himself is as yet unaware. In contrast to the minimalistic representation of thoughts common in biblical narrative, we are given a clear verbal (or mental) indication of Moses' decision making process.[27]

A decision has been made by Moses, but there is more to the process of turning aside than mere physical motion.[28] As in the previous verse we find a double occurrence of the root ראה, but here it emphasizes a significant change in Moses' vision. The description of the bush as המראה הגדל indicates a growing awareness of its significance which is marked by distinct stages. Initially, in 3.2a, the unusual nature of the flame within the bush is described by the narrator without any attendant temporal indication. This is appropriate to a glimpse of the bush as a shrub set on fire, perhaps by lightning. It would be noted momentarily and then forgotten, as the flame burns itself out and the bush disappears from sight. The second stage, v. 2b, marks Moses' initial awareness of temporal significance: the bush is not simply aflame, but continues to burn without consuming itself. While סנה indicates an ordinary shrub, it disobeys the laws of nature by continuing to burn. As Moses continues to peruse the phenomenon (as indicated by the durative sense of בער and אכל), he is led to the third stage of perception in v. 3, marked by a decision to turn off the path and investigate.[29] The characterization of the sight as המראה הגדל הזה

27. Polak, *Biblical Narrative*, pp. 264–5.

28. Turning aside in the Bible most often has a willful quality to it, whether as Israel's turning from God (e.g. Exod. 32.8, Deut. 9.12) or God's turning away from individuals (e.g. 1 Sam. 16.14). Turning aside often requires persuasion, as in Gen. 19.2–3 or Judg. 19.11–15, and thus indicates a decision not taken lightly. The cohortative may be significant here as a further indication of intention; cf. S.R. Driver, *A Treatise on the Use of the Tenses in Hebrew* (London: Oxford University Press, 1892), p. 53.

29. The sense of ראה here is more than simply 'see', but carries the sense of 'observe at length', 'investigate' as in 1 Sam. 6.9,16.

gives it a new specificity and uniqueness. While the entire phrase is found only here, מראה occurs frequently with theophany or with the visions associated with theophany, as in the phrase מראה אש to describe the appearance of the divine presence in Num. 9.15–16 and Ezek. 1.13–16,27; 8.2.[30] Moses' statement is thus more than a casual indication of curiosity, but suggests his growing awareness that something truly unique is present here.

In posing the question at the end of this thought/speech, מדוע לא יבער הסנה, Moses returns to the formulation about the burning of the bush associated with his point of view in v. 2 – הסנה בער. The verb changes from a participal to an imperfect form, indicating a shift from simply gazing at the flame (הסנה בער באש) to an expectation that the flame will burn itself out.[31] The question further emphasizes the extent of Moses' involvement with what he sees. The language of turning aside, the growing interest in the bush, and YHWH's command to halt in v. 5 are clear indications of Moses' fascination with what he sees, reflecting his intention to draw closer with no attendant fear. As Otto suggests, there is 'something more' here which draws Moses closer.[32]

4	When YHWH saw that he had turned aside,	וירא ה' כי סר לראות
	God called to him from out of the bush	ויקרא אליו אלהים מתוך הסנה
	And said:	ויאמר
	'Moses, Moses'.	משה משה
	And he said:	ויאמר
	'Here I am'.	הנני
5	And He said:	ויאמר
	'Don't approach further;	אל תקרב הלם
	Remove your shoes from your feet,	של נעליך מעל רגליך

30. מראה in the context of theophany is found in Exod. 24.17; Num. 9.15–16; 12.8; Judg. 13.6; Ezek. 1.5–28. (7 times); 8.4; 10.1; 11.14; cf. Job 4.16. Of particular significance is the occurence of the term in the context of fire or brightness: Ezek. 1.14 – מראה בזק; 1.28 – מראה ברק; Dan. 10.6 – מראה זהר; 8.2 – מראה הננה.

31. בער here carries the sense of 'burn out', 'consume', as opposed to the sense of 'burn' in v. 2; cf. Judg. 15.14; 2 Sam. 22.9; 1 Kgs. 14.10; Isa. 10.17; Nah. 2.14. It is also possible that בער may have this sense of 'consume' already in Moses' perception in v. 2. In any case, the range of meaning of the verb is wide enough to render unnecessary the suggested emendations discussed by Propp, *Exodus 1–18*, p. 200.

32. Otto, *The Idea of the Holy*, p. 35.

For you are standing on holy ground'.	כי המקום אשר אתה עומד עליו אדמת קדש הוא

6 And he said:
'I am the God of your father,
The God of Abraham, Isaac
and Jacob'.

ויאמר
אנכי אלהי אביך
ואלהי יעקב
ואלהי יצחק
אלהי אברהם

And Moses hid his face,
For he was afraid to look
upon God.

ויסתר משה פניו
כי ירא מהביט אל האלהים

Verse 4 marks the beginning of a complex interchange between YHWH and Moses, in which the initiative which Moses displayed in vv. 2b-3 is returned to YHWH, and all his responses are more fully reactive. Like v. 3 it also contains a double use of the verb ראה as a 'response to the response'. Most striking in this verse is YHWH's reflection upon Moses' turning aside to see.[33] There is not, to my knowledge, an equivalent passage in the Bible in which YHWH's verbal response in theophany is conditioned by a human response. In all other cases YHWH's response is portrayed as unequivocal. The only text that suggests something remotely similar is YHWH being compelled to call to Samuel three times in 1 Sam. 3. There YHWH makes the initial verbal overture and then waits for Samuel to notice that he is being addressed. In Exod. 3.2 YHWH makes an initial visual overture, and waits for Moses' response. However in Exod. 3 the situation is all the more surprising in that YHWH's speech in 3.4 is described as entirely contingent upon Moses' actions. The use of a relative clause ('When YHWH saw...') implies clearly that had Moses not turned aside, YHWH would not necessarily have spoken. Given that the Bible is adamant about YHWH's freedom to respond (or not to respond) according to his own intentions,[34] the linking of YHWH's speech to Moses' turning aside points out another exceptional aspect of this theophany. For all the careful planning evident in the narrative construction of Moses' origins and identity, there is a profound sense of

---

33. The MT here uses both *Elohim* and YHWH in this verse; whatever the redaction history of the text (see Childs, *The Book of Exodus*, pp. 53–6; Greenberg, *Understanding Exodus*, p. 103–5; Propp, *Exodus 1–18*, pp. 190–7), we proceed from the understanding the present redacted text is a unity, and the different names for the Deity are not significant for the understanding of the narrative here.

34. Nowhere is this more apparent than in YHWH's declaration of his identity as אהיה אשר אהיה immediately following in Exod. 3.14, especially if read in light of the *idem per idem* construction in Exod. 33.19 (Greenberg, *Understanding Exodus*, p. 82). See further J. Lundbom, 'God's use of *Idem per Idem* to Terminate Debate', *HTR* 71 (1978), pp. 193–201.

tentativeness about this encounter. The text contains the possibility that Moses could notice the bush and decide *not* to turn aside. Moses' movement from the second to the third stage as outlined above is crucial to YHWH's decision to address him, and to the movement of the story of his call and Israel's redemption from Egypt. It could be argued that YHWH is testing Moses' obedience here, but I think it has much more to do with how the recipient of revelation moves beyond an everyday perception of reality to a readiness for an encounter with the divine. The implications of this text seem to be that the actualization of revelation is dependent to a great extent upon human reactions to the divine. It is by no means assured that a call from the divine (however that might be construed) is automatically perceived as such. Thus while all the theophany narratives conform to the basic pattern of divine initiative followed by human response, Exod. 3 demonstrates that the nature of that response is indicative of the complexity of the divine–human encounter.[35]

The repetition of YHWH addressing Moses מתוך הסנה (v. 2) returns the reader to YHWH's perspective about the bush, but now we move from vision to voice. Whatever the nature of the *malakh* in v. 2, this location within the bush is now clearly identified with YHWH himself.[36] The repetition of Moses' name need not indicate a sense of urgency, as it follows a convention of theophany scenes seen in Gen. 46.2 and 1 Sam. 3.10.[37] These same texts also show Moses' response of הנני to be similarly conventional.[38] The term is a characteristic statement of obedience from son to father, from servant to king, and from humans to YHWH. Speiser's translation of הנני in Gen. 22.1 as 'ready' or 'at your service' is much more appropriate than the LXX 'What is it?'.[39] In this sense the use of הנני here emphasizes yet another stage in Moses' understanding, as the statement indicates a sense of closeness and presence, in contrast with Moses' initial הנה of perception in v. 2. There it emphasized the distance between himself and what was seen, but here (prefatory to the warning in v. 5 not to

---

35. The tentativeness of this encounter may be seen as a reflection of the great distance between YHWH and Israel as depicted in Exod. 1–2. There is no indication here that the Israelites felt a close connection with the God of their fathers, or that they recognized a divine hand in the thwarting of Pharaoh's plans to decimate them. Even their crying out in 2.23 is not directed explicitly to YHWH (though it does reach him). While 2.23–25 heightens our expectation that this particular call will be decisive, it offers contextual support for YHWH's attentiveness to Moses' responses in Exod. 3.

36. Cf. the discussion of *malakh* in chap. 3, p. 78.

37. In contrast to the greater sense of urgency attached to the double name in YHWH's second address to Abraham in Gen. 22.11, as the voice attempts to stop Abraham from killing his son; cf. Greenberg, *Understanding Exodus*, p. 71.

38. Cf. also Gen. 31.11.

39. Speiser, *Genesis*, p. 162. Cf also the comments on the term by E. Auerbach, *Mimesis* (trans. W.R. Trask; Princeton: Princeton University Press, 1953), p. 9.

approach further) it indicates Moses' greater physical proximity and obedience, a sense of presentness which differs from his earlier reaction.

Unlike initial divine speech in other theophany narratives, YHWH begins not with a self-introduction (as in Gen. 28.13), but with a command to Moses to stop moving forward, reinforcing the impression that Moses has been approaching the entire time. This would indicate that Moses, like Jacob in Gen. 28.16, is in a state of fascination with the miraculous sight before him, sensing its power and uniqueness, but thus far with no sense of self consciousness. Following Moses' single word of recognition (הנני), all speech is left to YHWH. The command not to tread on holy ground indicates that a threshold has been crossed, and that Moses has entered a liminal space.[40] The setting of limits regarding the extent and nature of approach to the divine is common in priestly texts dealing with the tabernacle, but also is prominent in the narrative of the Sinai revelation in Exod. 19.12–13, 21–23. The command to remove his sandals may also be associated with priestly worship[41] or simply with a separation from the everyday.[42] The fact that physical limitation of approach is given such prominence in the theophany indicates its significance here, in contrast with Gen. 28, where the dream state precluded actual approach to the divine.[43] The definition of the place as קדש and therefore forbidden reflects the sense of the holy as apart and protected from normal human contact.[44] Finally, while there is no statement of compliance regarding Moses, the cessation of movement is implicit in the participial עומד to describe Moses' physical posture at this moment. The absence of movement further implies

40. הלם is a general term indicating place (e.g. Judg. 18.3; 20.7; 1 Sam. 10.22), but it has a connection with theophany in Gen. 16.13.

41. Exod. 30.19 ordains washing the feet before entering the sanctuary, and may indicate that being barefoot was part of temple worship (Nachmanides *ad loc.*). 2 Sam. 15.30 connects bare feet with self-abasement, and Ezek. 24.17,23 with mourning. Cf. T.N.D. Mettinger, *No Graven Image?* (Stockholm, 1995), p. 193 n. 225. Sarna, *Exploring Exodus*, p. 40 and Propp, *Exodus 1–18*, p. 200, mention an Egyptian custom of going barefoot in the presence of the king. On the removal of shoes in worship in Second Temple times cf. *BT* Rosh Hashanah 31b; Berachot 62b; *Mish.* Megillah 4.8; Berachot 9.5; and the discussion in U. Ehrlich, *The Non-Verbal Language of Jewish Prayer* (Jerusalem: Magnes, 2003) pp. 148–63 (Hebrew).

42. The identical command to Joshua in Josh. 5.15 is clearly built on our text. However, M. Greenberg (*Understanding Exodus*, p. 72 n. 1) notes the biblical propensity for covering the body when approaching the divine in worship, and the association of going barefoot with mourning (2 Sam. 15.30; Isa. 20.2–4) and with suffering (Jer. 2.15).

43. This limitation serves as another means of foreshadowing the theophany on Mt. Sinai in Exod. 19, where the setting of bounds for the people is given a central focus.

44. Further indication of the liminal quality of the place is provided first by the redefinition of the 'sight' (מראה) as a מקום, a term used frequently to describe a place of divine presence, as in Gen. 22, Exod. 33.21, and Hos. 5.15. The term also indicates a movement away from visual phenomenon, intimating that further contact with the divine will be audial.

a relinquishing of that sense of activity which has characterized Moses'
responses to this point.

YHWH continues his speech here with a second ויאמר, which may
indicate a pause in speech, allowing for Moses' compliance with the
instruction of v. 5.[45] YHWH's self-introduction emphasizes both
immediacy ('God of your father') and historical continuity ('God of
Abraham').[46] The question of Moses' response here is no less critical than
was his turning aside in v. 3. If that earlier turning indicated a willingness
to explore further, this 'turning aside', this hiding of the face,[47] indicates a
recognition of the power of the God who has appeared to him. The motif
of hiding one's face or refraining from seeing is found elsewhere in
theophany narratives, as in 1 Kgs. 19.13, and often accompanies a change
from seeing to fearing. In Exod. 3.6 this shift includes a very noticeable
change from the repeated verb ראה to ירא, using instead a different verb of
seeing. Here, as with Jacob and others, Moses' reactions follow Otto's
model of *fascinans et tremendum*, the fascination present in Moses'
approaching the bush, and the fear explicit in hiding his face. This covering
of the face underscores the fact that there will be no further visual
revelation during this theophany, even in the long interchange between
YHWH and Moses which follows in 3.11–4.17. This dual reaction offers a
clear sign of the character's understanding of the nature of this encounter;
after this the narrative moves to the next stage, which is the conveying of
the message by the divine in 3.7–10.

On balance, we seem to see here a greater emphasis on fascination than
on fear. Moses' averred intention to turn aside, his characterization of the
bush as 'this great sight', and his physical approach to the bush coupled

---

45. Following Shiloah, 'Vayyo'mer...vayyo'mer', pp. 251–67; cf. Meier, *Speaking of
Speaking*, pp. 73–81.

46. 'God of your father' (in the singular) seems to refer to Moses' biological father, but
given that the continuation of the speech mentions his forefathers, it could be taken as
referring to both. See the discussion and bibliography in Childs, *The Book of Exodus*, p. 80;
Sarna, *Exploring Exodus*, pp. 42–3; Propp, *Exodus 1–18*, p. 201. An interesting perspective on
the Rabbinic sensitivity to this moment of revelation is suggested in *Exod. Rab.* 3.1:

R. Joshua the priest said in the name of R. Nehemiah: When the Holy One Blessed be He
revealed himself Moses was but a novice in prophecy. God said: If I reveal myself to him in
a loud voice I'll frighten him; if I speak in a small voice, he may show disdain.' What did he
do? He revealed Himself to him in the voice of his father.

The voice of revelation here is profoundly human – the voice of a parent, not the thunder of
Sinai. Its purpose here is to enable meeting between YHWH and Moses by overcoming
distance.

47. On the expression cf. R. Friedman, 'The Biblical Expression *Mastir Panim*', *HAR* 1
(1977), pp. 139–47.

with a divine directive to stop advancing, are hardly balanced by Moses hiding his face in v. 6.[48] The text records Moses' fear of seeing YHWH's face, but without the attendant fear of death found in other theophany narratives. Clearly this is not sufficient information on which to judge Moses' fear in comparison to others, but it is striking that nowhere in Moses' career does he give expression to such a sense of anxiety in the face of the divine. This is all the more noticeable given his *sang-froid* in the face of the people's anxiety in Exod. 20.15–18, and in response to YHWH's anger at the people in Exod. 32. Most telling is the fact that it is YHWH who raises this fear in Exod. 33.19, where Moses expresses only his desire to see YHWH's *kavod*.

Moses' hiding his face is usually understood as a positive response indicating humility, and displaying a genuine awareness of the nature of the voice which is speaking to him. A midrashic response in *Exodus Rabbah* saw in this a connection with subsequent theophanies, suggesting that, because of not looking on YHWH here, Moses was rewarded by actually seeing YHWH face to face, as in Num. 12.8 – ותמונת ה' יביט, and Exod. 33.11 – ודבר ה' אל משה פנים אל פנים. But another midrash emphasizes the tentativeness of this meeting, that even here Moses' unwillingness to look represented a failure of nerve at a crucial moment:

> R. Joshua b. Qorha said: 'What is meant by the verse "You cannot see my face" (Exod. 33.20)? YHWH said to Moses: "When I wanted to, you didn't wish to see. Now that you want to, I don't want to." '[49]

In this understanding of theophany, for neither YHWH nor for Moses is the face always looking forward and engaging the other directly. Revelation as described in Exod. 3.1–6 involves a process of mutual groping towards a meeting, both partners eager for contact, yet both hesitant. And even after the first meeting, there is still a great deal of uncertainty expressed in Exod. 3.11–4.17, moving closer and moving apart. Particularly for Moses and YHWH, revelation is not a one-time meeting, but a process of interaction, as is brought out very clearly in the elaborate negotiation between the two which follows.

---

48. Note also that the verb הביט in v. 6 can have the sense of intensive looking or staring, as in Isa. 42.18; Hab. 1.5; Ps. 91.8; Lam. 1.12; cf. *TDOT* vol. 9, pp. 126–8.

49. *Exod. Rab.* 3.1; 45.5.

iii. *Isaiah 6.*

And I said 'Woe is me for I am undone.	(A)	ואמר אוי לי כי נדמיתי
For I am a man of unclean lips,	(B)	כי איש טמא שפתים אנכי
And I dwell among an unclean people;	(B')	ובתוך עם טמא שפתים אנכי ישב
For my eyes have seen the king, the Lord of hosts.'	(A')	כי את המלך ה' צבאות ראו עיני

In contrast with Moses' experience at the bush, Isaiah's response reflects a more severe internal reaction to the encounter with the divine. If Isaiah's description of what he sees in Isa. 6.1–4 reflects his fascination with the upper worlds, then his reaction in v. 5 discloses the tremendous anxiety evoked by this vision, with no less *tremendum* than *fascinans*. This section is generally seen as a subsequent reaction to the vision of vv. 1–4, in keeping with the increased sense of distance from the divine reflected in v. 4.[50] After witnessing the sight of YHWH enthroned, the angels declaring the overwhelming holiness of the Deity, and the attendant smoke and tremors in the temple, Isaiah is overcome with feelings of inadequacy and a sense of impurity.[51] While this diachronic reading flows naturally from the narrative sequence, it will also be seen that the responses described in vv. 5–7 are in many respects complementary to the vision of 1–4. If vv. 1–4 move to exclude Isaiah from the heavenly realm, then vv. 5–7 describe the process of his aggregation into this world, moving from impure to pure, from association with the human world to communing with the angels. As in the previous cases, both aspects are an integral part of the human response to the divine.

In both vv. 1 and 5 Isaiah describes seeing God (ראה), but from different perspectives. In v. 1 this seeing is the first part of a vision which uplifts him, but in v. 5 it is explained as the cause of the prophet's dread.[52] Verse 1 began with an earthly orientation, the death of the human king, a marked contrast to the exalted Deity in vv. 1–4. But in v. 5 he is returned to this human situation, mired in the impurity of the people. The gap between human and divine is pointed out very clearly: YHWH sits (ישב) upon his throne and Isaiah dwells (ישב) among his impure people.[53] The structure of 6.5 supports this negative reaction to sight of the Deity. Verse 6.1 only

---

50. See the discussion of 6.1–4 in chapter 3.

51. Cf. Otto, *The Idea of the Holy*, pp. 75–6.

52. Landy, 'Strategies of Concentration', p. 66, notes that both sections utilize synecdoche rather than focus on the the totality of the divine or of the prophet. The focus on Isaiah's eyes and mouth serves as a strategy of intensification rather than one of diffusion.

53. Cf. Magonet, 'Structure', p. 93; Landy, 'Strategies of Concentration', p. 61.

hints at this impurity by mentioning the death of Uzziah,[54] developing instead in vv. 1–4 the vision of YHWH enthroned as the antithesis of human kingship. Verse 5, however, emphasizes human impurity (שפתים טמא) and mentions seeing YHWH only at the end of the verse. While (B) and (B') clearly parallel one another, (A) and (A') are sharply contrastive.

Instead of the sight of the Deity uplifting Isaiah from the human sphere, in v. 5 it is a cause for anxiety about his own mortality. נדמיתי should be understood in a double sense here. On the one hand Isaiah fears he is 'finished', dead, for having had the audacity to see YHWH.[55] This lethal sense of נדמיתי is supported by the final clause of the verse reflecting the general sense of the danger inherent in direct vision of the Deity.[56] At the same time the verb also means 'I am struck dumb'.[57] Isaiah is reacting to the overwhelming power of the seraphic litany of v. 3, but also to the aspect of impure speech which is alluded to by clauses (B) and (B'). These unclean lips must be purged of their impurity prior to speaking with YHWH. While the phrase איש טמא שפתים may refer to a specific sin (so Rashi, Targum), it is more likely an indication of a general sense of unworthiness associated with the human condition.[58] What is of greater interest here is the fact that the same malady or impurity afflicts both the prophet and the people, whose presence acts as a counterweight to Isaiah's heavenly vision. Indeed, the striking repetition of the phrase declaring Isaiah's identity with the people is an 'unholy' echoing of the more powerful repetition of 'Holy, Holy, Holy' in v. 3.[59] Where YHWH has his retinue of *seraphim* around him to support and protect him, Isaiah has only his impure people around him to undermine him. It is precisely this connection with the people which will become decisive for the continuation

---

54. On the relationship of Uzziah's death to Isaiah's vision cf. Buber, *Prophetic Faith*, p. 127; Landy, 'Strategies of Concentration', p. 60, n. 6 and the literature cited there; Uffenheimer, 'Commission of Isaiah', pp. 18–23.

55. Cf. Blenkinsopp, *Isaiah 1–39*, p. 223. On the difficulty of distinguishing between the two roots cf. *TDOT* vol. 3, p. 261. Similar ambiguity about the meaning of דמה can be seen in the interpretation of texts like Pss. 49.13,21; 62.5. Cf. J.J.M. Roberts, 'Double Entendre in First Isaiah', *CBQ* 54, pp. 39–48 (44–6).

56. Exod. 33.20; Judg. 6; Gen. 32.30; Pedayah, 'Seeing, Falling', p. 242; see the discussion of the lethal nature of contact with the Deity in chap. 6.

57. So the Vulgate and Aquila; cf. M. Weiss, *The Bible From Within* (Jerusalem: Magnes Press, 1984), p. 127, n. 2. For Isaiah's desire to participate in the praise of the divine see *Pesiqta Rabbati* 33. Cf. the discussion in Glazov, *The Bridling of the Tongue*, pp. 130–6.

58. V.A. Hurowitz, 'Isaiah's Impure Lips and Their Purification in Light of Akkadian Sources', *HUCA* 60 (1990), pp. 39–89 (39–50, 73–9). Hurowitz's review of the Mesopotamian literature indicates that the mouth could serve as a symbol for the entire person, *pars pro toto*, and need not relate exclusively to that organ.

59. Eslinger, 'The Infinite', p. 167; Weiss, 'Image and Voice', p. 97. On the opposition between impurity and holiness cf. Milgrom, *Leviticus 1–16*, pp. 686, 732.

of the call narrative. It is logical that Isaiah assumes that his own
purification anticipates a subsequent cleansing of the people, that this
experience will prefigure Israel's transformation.[60] However, the details of
the commission in vv. 8–10. create an even greater tension between Isaiah's
connection to the divine pantheon and his attachment to the community of
Israel.[61]

   The 'response to the response' of the prophet is described in cultic
terms. Contained within the biblical concept of impurity is the assumption
that it can be ritually removed, that the impure person can be cleansed
and returned to a proper relationship with YHWH and with his
community.[62] In v. 6 the appearance of one of the *seraphim* with the
verb ויעף recalls the use of the same verb to describe their activity in v. 3.
As the *seraph* attended to YHWH in vv. 1–4 now it attends to Isaiah. But
the use of the verb here also accentuates the distance between Isaiah and
the angels.[63] In contrast with the absolute holiness of the Deity and his
retinue, Isaiah's unclean lips betray his human identity and his need of
purification. The *seraph* here acts like a cultic functionary, making
determinations of purity and impurity and performing the necessary
rituals.[64] While this act bears linguistic similarity to YHWH touching
Jeremiah's mouth in Jer. 1.9 (ויגע על פי), the two acts are functionally
different. In Jeremiah's case, as with Moses, it is an act of divine support
essential to the task of prophesying to Israel. For Isaiah, however, the act
of purification has more to do with the ability to draw near to, and
perhaps to speak within, the divine council. The final stage of this process
is the *seraph's* speech in 6.7, structurally parallel to the litany of 'Holy,
Holy, Holy' in v. 3. The threefold repetition of שפתים in this section

   60. Cf. Glazov, *The Bridling of the Tongue*, p. 126.
   61. Weiss, *The Bible From Within*, pp. 123–6 understands the relationship between the
clauses to indicate that Isaiah's impurity is a reflection of the people's impurity, and that the
mention of the people shows the extent of Isaiah's sense of sin. Weiss dismisses the existential
sense of inadequacy emphasized by Otto and prefers a moral reading. This interpretation may
have validity in the prophet's *own* conception of his imagined relationship to the people, but it
is sharply refuted by the terms of his commission in vv. 8–10. He himself is purified, but this
only serves to magnify the people's guilt.
   62. On the removal of ritual impurity see Milgrom, *Leviticus 1–16*, pp. 254–61; 269–78.
   63. A.L.H.M. Wieringen, *The Implied Reader in Isaiah 6–12* (Leiden: Brill, 1998), p. 43.
   64. Cf. the role of the priest in Lev. 13–15. It is striking that the angel must use tongs to
handle the coal, implying both intense heat, and also an inability to 'handle' the divine, similar
to the reading of v. 3 in which the angel cannot look directly at the divine. As Landy notes
('Strategies of Concentration', p. 67) the use of the tongs and the mention of the hand further
indicates the distance between the human and the divine. Isaiah is not brought closer, but the
mediation establishes the possibility of his participation. In addition to the Mesopotamian
background of the purifying of the mouth discussed by Hurowitz, 'Isaiah's Unclean Lips',
Glazov, *The Bridling of the Tongue*, p. 121 sees a connection with the Egyptian rite of the
opening of the mouth.

parallels the Trishagion; Isaiah doesn't begin to approximate the holiness of YHWH, but the process allows him to stand in the presence of the divine. The text doesn't record Isaiah's reaction to being 'purified' with a burning coal, and while it is obviously metaphorical, the imagery reflects the same sense of *tremendum*.[65] If vv. 1–4 record the prophet's fascination with the encounter with the divine, vv. 5–7 describe the fear and anxiety that goes hand in hand with it. What may have earlier been perceived as a source of joy now serves to terrify the prophet.[66] As with Jacob and Moses, the sequence of attraction followed by fear appears to be the standard way of representing this complex set of feelings. In both sections the visual is the dominant element, with verbal elements having additional significance as well.[67]

<u>1–4</u>	<u>5–7</u>
YHWH seen – ראה	YHWH seen – ראה
Seraph flies around YHWH – יעופף	*Seraph* flies to Isaiah – ויעף
Seraph speaks – קדוש	*Seraph* speaks – sin atoned for – וחטאתך תכפר

These parallels also clarify the role of 6.4 as a distancing element, marking the shift in the prophet's consciousness from a heavenly to an earthly perspective, from a concentration upon angels, holiness and the divine presence, to a focus on impurity, death, and the people. It is not accidental that the beginning of the vision focuses on the inner sanctum, while v. 4 moves outward to the doorposts and the 'house'.

While certain aspects of the two sections are complementary, they do not reflect the same sort of experience or even the same sense of movement. Vv. 1–4 move from close proximity to the divine in v. 1 to a growing sense of distance in v. 4. Verses 5–7, on the other hand, begin by describing the immense gap between Isaiah and the heavenly realm in v. 5, but move to a point of greater closeness to the world of the numinous by the purification of his lips in v. 7. Both sections begin with an existential

---

65. Hurowitz notes that the use of fire for purification is rare in the Bible (Num. 31.23; Mal. 3.2–3 only in regard to metal), but better known in Mesopotamia ('Isaiah's Impure Lips', p. 79, n. 112). Uffenheimer, 'Isaiah 6', p. 40, points to the cleansing power of fire in Num. 17.11. Perhaps the violence of this method of purgation (purification by water is the norm) is meant to foreshadow the violent means by which the sin of the people will be expunged, as alluded to in vv. 11–12.

66. Landy, 'Strategies of Concentration', p. 65, suggests that the references to distinct body parts found here – eyes, lips, mouth – indicates the fragmentation of the prophet's self.

67. Note also the presence of smell (smoke) and of touch (v. 7), contributing to the totality of the experience described.

description of theophany and conclude with a report of cultic contact between the human and the divine. But whereas the trembling of the temple and the filling up with smoke are the external manifestations of cultic experience, the purgation with the coal and the removal of sin reflect the internal change inherent in that process. Our overall sense of the relationship between these two sections is that they are cumulative in their representation of the process of transformation, but complementary in portraying the duality of human response to the encounter with the divine. There is a sense in which the purifying of Isaiah's mouth could be understood to temporarily overcome the sense of *tremendum* present in v. 5, in allowing him entry into the heavenly sphere. But despite Isaiah's willingness to serve as an emissary in v. 8 ('Here I am; send me') this proves to be merely a foil for the prophet's dismay at the description of his task in v. 11 ('How long?'), showing him to be more fully identified with the human sphere. The prophet is alone in his shocked reaction to YHWH's instructions; as in vv. 1–4, he is again shown to be an interloper in the house of the Lord.

iv. *Exodus 19–20*. The very phenomenon of group theophany, as well as the complex role of Moses in the narrative, complicate our understanding of the responses of the Israelites in the Sinai pericope.[68] Throughout Exodus 19 Moses' actions are stressed more than the those of Israelites, to the end that we hear less of the people's actual responses, and more of Moses' movement back and forth between YHWH and the people. The reactions of the people described by the narrator consist of their statement of acceptance of the terms of the covenant in 19.8, washing their clothes in 19.14, stationing themselves at the bottom of the mountain in 19.17 and their attendant trembling in v. 16,[69] and their address to Moses in 20.18–20. Of these only the last two are relevant for our concerns, in that they describe actual fearful reactions to the approach of the divine. Alongside the emphasis on the people's fear which finds particular expression in 20.18–20, we find an strong undercurrent of popular desire to make contact with the numinous in a visceral or visual manner. This, however, is described only indirectly in the instructions to Moses to limit

---

68. The difficulties in reading this text are detailed in the source critical and tradition critical analyses of Exod. 19–20 in Dozeman, *God on the Mountain*; Childs, *The Book of Exodus*, pp. 344–64; Toeg, *Lawgiving at Sinai*, pp. 32–59. We will restrict our analysis primarily to a discussion of Exod. 20.18–20, about which there is a wide consensus that it is a unified section.

69. The trembling of the mountain in v. 18, may be taken as a metaphor for the increased fear of the people.

the people's approach to the mountain in 19.12–13,21–24.[70] Most revealing in this light is YHWH's concern lest the people break through 'to see' (21) or 'to ascend to YHWH' (24).[71] In contrast with other theophany texts, this desire is held in check by the physical limitations placed upon the people.[72]

However, it is the element of *tremendum* which is emphasized most strongly in the Sinai traditions. The reaction recorded in 20.15–18 underscores the people's sensory experience of the theophany – sound, sight, and smell are all invoked to heighten the experiential nature of the event.[73] The items mentioned in 20.18 are all recalled from the description of the theophany in 19.16 (thunder, lightning, and ram's horn) and in 19.18 (smoke), implying a clear connection with 19.16–18. The description of these natural phenomena in 19.16–18 is designed to accentuate their frightening quality by describing a gradual increase in intensity.[74] The piling up of these descriptions one after another in 20.18 creates a cumulative effect of intensification which leads to the people's reaction in 20.19.[75] The connection between the immediacy of the experience in 20.18 and the people's subsequent reaction is effected by the repetition of ראה. In 18a a participial form is used to denote ongoing experience, while in 18b the verb occurs in the perfect, and is tied to the people's movement away from the divine. No other theophany narrative has such an extreme

---

70. J. Licht ('The Revelation of God's Presence at Sinai', p. 265) would add 19.13 to this list, understanding the verse to refer not to the conclusion of the theophany (so LXX, Rashi), but to the willing ascent of the people during the theophany. Contra, cf. Dozeman, *God on the Mountain*, pp. 23–4.

71. While the restatement of this concern in vv. 20–25 is likely the result of a complex redactional process, the effect of the repetition is to emphasize the desire of the people to 'break through'. See the discussion in Childs, *The Book of Exodus*, pp. 361–4; Dozeman, *God on the Mountain*, pp. 103–6.

72. Polak, 'Theophany and Mediator', p. 135, notes a suggestive parallel with Moses' attraction to the fire in the bush and YHWH's command not to approach further in Exod. 3.2–5.

73. Ibn Ezra suggests that all sensory experience is processed by a single place in the brain, hence the use of unusual expressions such as 'behold, the smell of my son' (Gen. 27.27) or 'the light is sweet' (Qoh. 11.7). Alternately, U.M. Cassuto suggests we understand ראה not simply as 'to see' but as a general term of perception [*Exodus*, p. 252].

74. Thus the ram's horn gets louder between 19.16 – 'the sound of the ram's horn was very loud' – and 19.19 – 'the sound of the ram's horn grew progressively louder'. Likewise the intensity of the smoke increases from 19.18a – 'Mount Sinai was all in smoke' – to 19.18b – 'the smoke arose as from a kiln', with the attendant reaction of the mountain attached – 'the entire mountain trembled violently'. The LXX on this verse – 'all the people trembled violently' – reflects an intensification of the description in 19.16 – 'all the people who were in the camp trembled'.

75. So NJPS 20.15: 'and when the people saw it, they fell back and stood at a distance'. Cf. Polak, 'Theophany and Mediator', p. 137.

physical movement in reaction to contact with the numinous; while other texts record prostration or an emotional distancing, there is no attempt to create a physical distance from the divine.[76]

18	And all the people saw the voices and the lightning,	וכל העם ראים את הקולת ואת הלפידם
	The sound of the ram's horn and the smoking mountain.	ואת קול השפר ואת ההר עשן
	The people saw it, moved away and stood at a distance.	וירא העם וינעו ויעמדו מרחק
19	They said to Moses: 'You speak to us and we will listen,	ויאמרו אל משה דבר אתה עמנו ונשמעה
	But let God not speak to us lest we die'.	ואל ידבר עמנו אלהים פן נמות
20	Moses said to the people: 'Don't be afraid;	ויאמר משה אל העם אל תיראו
	For God has come in order to test you,	כי לבעבור נסות אתכם בא האלהים
	And in order that his fear will be with you so that you do not sin'.	ובעבור תהיה יראתו על פניכם לבלתי תחטאו

There are many questions which surround this response in Exod. 20.18–20. First of all, it is not clear precisely when during the theophany this reaction occurred. Did it follow the narrative flow of the story, occurring after YHWH's speech of the Ten Commandments in 20.1–17? Or, given that the people are deathly afraid of hearing YHWH's voice, do they object in anticipation of the divine voice? Second, despite the upheaval of nature which is emphasized in 20.18, the people state that the reason for their anxiety is the dread of hearing YHWH speak. In all other theophany texts the fear is explicitly that of seeing YHWH;[77] why here (and in the Deuteronomic reworking of this tradition in Deut. 5) is there an explicit

---

76. Exod. 20.18 records a one-time retreat; the stage of *fascinans* took place before YHWH spoke, and once he did, the people moved away and stood at a distance. The midrash (Mekhilta Bahodesh, 9), however, was unwilling to give up on the people's attraction to the numinous throughout the theophany, and understood the term וינעו to describe the people moving back and forth (12 miles!) at each commandment. They move forward in anticipation of each commandment, and backward in reaction to the *tremendum* of the divine voice.

77. E.g. Gen. 32.30, Exod. 3.6; 33.19; Judg. 6.22; 13.22.

fear of hearing? Finally, Moses' 'response to the response' in 20.20 is not clear. In what sense is לבעבור נסות אתכם to be understood as a trial for the people, and what is the purpose of the double mention of ירא in his response in 20.20?

Regarding the place of this response within the story, we have at least three possible explanations, none of which is completely satisfactory. While the simplest solution would be to understand the chronology of events according to the order of the text in its present form, it is difficult to explain the people's fear of hearing YHWH speak. For if they have already heard YHWH's words in 20.1–17, why are they afraid of further discourse? Moreover, the sense of 19.19 seems to be that, in contrast with the קולת mentioned earlier, the people hear YHWH answer Moses בקול, that is, in a speaking voice.[78] Alternately, the entire section might be taken as referring to an earlier point in the narrative. One could follow the suggestion of Nachmanides, who sees the proper place for this section *before* YHWH speaks (before or after Exod. 19.19), following the appearance of the thunder, the fire, and the smoke.[79] A variation on this idea is offered by Hizkuni, according to whom the people's reaction comes *in the midst* of the speaking of the Ten Commandments.[80] Any of these readings could with fit the participial form of the verb ראה in v. 15, which can indicate simultaneity with YHWH speaking, a simple perfect, or a past perfect sense, 'All the people had seen . . .'.[81]

As interesting as these last two solutions may be, there is no narrative indication that the people responded with anything but trembling in chapter 19, and no indication that YHWH spoke only some of the commandments to the people. The earliest commentary on Exod. 19–20, which is found in Deut. 5, clearly understands that the people's expression of fear follows YHWH's speech. In order to accommodate this, Deut. 5.22 states explicitly that the people heard YHWH *speak* to them, and to clarify the issue adds the phrase ' . . . if we hear the voice of the Lord our God *any longer* . . . ' (Deut. 5.24). Moreover, in all the theophany narratives we have examined, the reaction of dread always comes after YHWH appears *and*

---

78. Cf. Sommer, 'Revelation at Sinai', p. 428; Childs, *The Book of Exodus*, p. 343. Contra, cf. J. Van Seters, 'Comparing Scripture with Scripture: Some Observations on the Sinai Pericope in Exod. 19–24', in Tucker, Petersen, and Wilson (eds.), *Canon, Theology, and Old Testament Interpretation*, p. 119.

79. Nachmanides on Exod. 20.18.

80. Hizkuni on 20.18; *Song of Songs Rabbah* 1.2. This position is ostensibly supported by the change in language between the second and third commandments. See, however, the discussion of the midrashic sources of this view in B. Schwartz, ' "I am the Lord" and "You Shall Have no Other Gods" Were Heard from the Mouth of the Almighty: On the Evolution of an Interpretation', in Japhet (ed.), *The Bible in Light of its Interpreters: The Sarah Kamin Memorial Volume*, pp. 170–197 (Hebrew).

81. Sommer, 'Revelation at Sinai', pp. 429–31.

speaks. Thus it is highly unlikely that YHWH would refrain entirely from speaking to the people because of their fear.[82] At the same time, the reaction of the people should be understood to be ongoing, as indicated by the participial form of ראה in 20.18. This, coupled with the fearful reactions of the people in 19.16–25, would seem to indicate a growing sense of fear which begins with the disturbance of nature, increases as YHWH descends and 'speaks' with Moses in 19.19,[83] and reaches its climax in their reaction to divine speech in 20.18.[84] The people's anxiety in Exod. 20.19 is not a reaction which has been fixed at a single moment in time, but is the culmination of a series of responses which grow in intensity as the theophany proceeds.[85]

The second issue, the people's fear of hearing, is tied to another unique aspect of the Sinai revelation, Moses' role as mediator of the covenant. Dozeman ties this motif (and this section) to what he refers to as the Deuteronomistic redaction of the text, which focuses upon the inclusion of legal material within what was originally an independent theophanic tradition.[86] F. Polak finds in this motif a tension between seeing, which draws one close, and hearing, which keeps the people at a distance. This is similar to Moses at the burning bush, who is drawn to approach what he sees until an auditory warning tells him not to come any closer. Thus in Polak's reading the visual element is that which draws the protagonist closer, and the verbal element is that which compels him to remain at a distance.[87] While this may be the case in Exod. 3, it does not seem to apply to texts such as Isa. 6 and Ezek. 1, in which the spoken element is used to help overcome the prophet's anxiety about seeing the divine. A more satisfying answer to the question begins with the position taken by A. Toeg, which posits that the unique emphasis on the lethal nature of the audial element is tied to the centrality of Moses' role in the text.[88] The motif serves to highlight Moses' reception of the revelation in contrast to the limited perceptions of the people, an interpretation which is used to help establish Moses' role as covenant mediator. To this we would add the idea that it is only as a speaker that Moses can represent YHWH's presence to the people, and thus overcome their fear. The same message

82. Sommer's argument that 1 Kgs. 19.11–12 could be used to support the idea of a non-verbal revelation is certainly supported by the other texts he brings. But in and of itself this idea does not comfirm Nachmanides' interpretation of Exod. 19–20.

83. See the discussion of this verse in Dozeman, *God on the Mountain*, pp. 47–9; Childs, *The Book of Exodus*, p. 343.

84. Cf. Childs, *The Book of Exodus*, p. 371; Sommer, 'Revelation at Sinai', p. 429.

85. Cf. above n. 74.

86. Dozeman, *God on the Mountain*, p. 38.

87. Polak, 'Theophany and Mediator', p. 137; idem, *Biblical Narrative*, pp. 104–5.

88. Toeg, *Lawgiving at Sinai*, p. 53.

will be transmitted, but it is filtered through a different voice. Contrary to Dozeman, this is not a Deuteronomic idea which has been interpolated into the Exodus text, but rather an early tradition of group revelation. The narrative traditions in the Bible do not admit to the possibility of group revelation without a mediating figure.[89] At the same time, while this motif is not dependent upon Deuteronomic editing, it certainly opens the way for the extensive reworking of this tradition in Deuteronomy which will give speaking and hearing an exclusive role in this theophany.[90]

Moses' response to the people in 20.20 also serves to emphasize the centrality of his position. He presents himself as someone experienced in matters of theophany and therefore able to comfort the people. But at the same time he warns them that fear is to remain a central part of their experience of YHWH, though not quite in the way that they presently conceive of it. First, Moses states that God has come 'to try you', but exactly what the trial is here is far from clear. M. Greenberg has proposed understanding נסות here as 'to give you experience of him', which is in keeping with the experiential nature of theophany experiences.[91] This particular aspect of theophany narratives emphasizes that there is something about the meeting between the divine and the human which is irreducible and essential in and of itself, regardless of the message to be passed on.[92] Accordingly, Israel undergoes this experience at Sinai not simply to understand the requirements which are placed upon the people, but to gain experience: to acquire some sense of this Deity, how he is to be perceived, and, mostly, how he is to be feared. In this sense we should note the paradoxical nature of Moses' statement in v. 17: 'Do not fear' and yet, 'so that the fear of him will be upon you'. Gaining experience is about learning to be 'appropriately afraid'. This would seem to be a corrective to the notion of fascination, of approaching the divine without a sense of the danger involved as we saw in Exod. 19.[93] 'To gain experience' in texts like Deut. 28.56, Judg. 3.1–3, and 1 Sam. 17.39 means to gain knowledge as a corrective to a naive state in which one is unprepared for the trials at

89. E.g. Moses and Aaron in Lev. 9, or Elijah in 1 Kgs. 18.

90. Cf. S. Geller, *Sacred Enigmas*, pp. 38–51; Polak, 'Theophany and Mediator', p. 133 n. 56. At the same time, the description of Moses' veiled face in Exod. 34.29–35 is an attempt to have Moses symbolically represent the presence of YHWH in a physical fashion. See the discussion in chap. 5.

91. M. Greenberg, 'נסה in Exod. 20.20', *JBL* 79 (1960), pp. 273–6.

92. Otto, *Idea of the Holy*, p. 7, Merkur, 'The Numinous as a Category of Values', p. 107.

93. Polak, 'Theophany and Mediator', p. 137 n. 71 suggests understanding לבעבור נסות אתכם as 'in order to initiate you', which would convey a much more positive sense, and would fit Moses' initial comment 'Don't be afraid'. Cf. further Otto, *The Idea of the Holy*, pp. 13–19.

hand.[94] The second part of his statement, 'so that his fear be upon you so that you won't sin' refers to the *tremendum* as an overwhelming fear, but also points towards something beyond the theophanic experience. 'Not sinning' may refer to abiding by the rules of the encounter which Moses has laid out for the people, but more likely it is oriented towards the future, indicating that the content of the theophany (the commandments) is to serve as an ongoing guide for the people. Moses' response here suggests a degree of externalization of the experience of the theophany, an attempt to instruct them in the implications of the theophanic experience for their future lives.[95]

The emphasis in this theophany is clearly oriented more towards *tremendum* than to *fascinans*, though both are present in the text. This is primarily a reflection of the empowering of Moses as a central aspect of the theophany. Moses is legitimated in the eyes of the people, as is anticipated in Exod. 19.9, ratified in 19.19, and reinforced by 20.20.[96] However, in elevating Moses' position as the one who approaches YHWH, the text necessarily distances the people from direct contact with YHWH.[97] Thus there remains a good deal of ambiguity about the people's position in this theophanic encounter, particularly as regards the extent of their contact with YHWH. On the one hand, they are fully present in their fear; but on the other, they are kept back and are not allowed to approach. Despite the power and uniqueness of the revelation at Sinai the question of just how transformative this theophany is for the people looms large here, for the narrative continuation of the story leads inevitably to the apostasy of the Golden Calf, which threatens to undo all that has been accomplished in Exod. 19–20.

The differences in the Sinai account between Exodus and Deuteronomy have been described at length in a number of studies.[98] Not only is the idea of seeing the Deity ruled out completely, but the entire notion of *fascinans*

94. Abravanel and Sforno *ad loc.* understand this as an attempt to get Israel used to the experience of prophecy.

95. J. Van Seters, *The Life of Moses: The Yahwist as Historian in Exodus-Numbers* (Kampen: Kok Pharos, 1994), pp. 267–8, points out a striking parallel between Exod. 20.20 and late Babylonian texts from the time of Nabonidus which draw a connection between the people's fear of the god and not sinning.

96. This legitimation is demonstrated by the ability of the leader to stand firm in the face of the appearance of the divine as represented by the upheaval of nature. Thus the popular reaction to the splitting of the sea in Exod. 14.31 is the people's belief in both God and Moses, and the exceptional storm in 1 Sam. 12.18 leads to people's fear of both God and Samuel. On the latter text see Elat, *Samuel and the Foundation of Kingship in Israel*, p. 139.

97. Abravanel, *ad loc.*: '...it is said 'and the people stood far off' to contrast them with Moses, about whom it says "And Moses approached the deep darkness"'.

98. Sommer, 'Revelation at Sinai', pp. 432–5; Childs, *The Book of Exodus*, p. 343; Von Rad, *Deuteronomy*, pp. 55–61; M. Weinfeld, *Deuteronomy 1–11* (AB; New York: Doubleday,

has no place here, for there is no immanent presence, 'only a voice'.[99] Accordingly, Deut. 5.20–27 presents us with a rather different version of the people's response in Exod. 20.18–20. First, in this section Deuteronomy is more expansive than Exodus. Where Exodus devotes much more space to describing the events leading up to the commandments, Deuteronomy gives more attention to the aftermath.[100] As a rule, Deuteronomy is less concerned with the experience of the event being described than with its significance for future generations. Second, the nature of the response has changed. The approach to Moses is not made *en masse* by 'all the people' as in Exod. 20.18, but only by 'the heads of your tribes and your elders' (Deut. 5.23), who have organized themselves into a representative body. Moreover, these are not the words of a frightened throng of Israelites who fear YHWH's speech 'lest we die'. Rather, the speech in Deut. 5.24–27 is a long, well-crafted theological deliberation on the meaning of divine revelation. Included in the rhetorical flourishes of the speech are not just a commission of Moses as the covenant mediator, but the covenantal promise 'we will hear and we will obey' which in Exodus precedes the theophany. Gone is the sense of immediate anxiety and dread; it has been replaced by a meditation on the distinctiveness of this theophanic experience and on the nature of the Deity. Third, while in Exod. 20.20 Moses responds to the people with an explanation of the reason for the theophany, in Deut. 5.28–30 YHWH himself responds at length, ratifying the people's choice of Moses. Most significantly YHWH's concern is with the long term implications of the act; he addresses not just their immediate fear of the presence of the divine, but his wish that they will 'fear me and do all my commandments'. It is not the anxiety of the moment which concerns YHWH, but rather how the Israelites will comport themselves in the future, and the implications for subsequent generations as well.[101] These tendencies are characteristic of Deuteronomy's focus on Israel's future and on obedience to the divine commandments. Thus the immediate terrifying experience of theophany is transformed from encountering the divine to the performance of the

---

1991), pp. 241–2; 323–6; idem, *Deuteronomy and the Deuteronomic School*, pp. 206–8; Toeg, *Lawgiving at Sinai*, pp. 55–9; 117–20; Van Seters, 'Comparing Scripture with Scripture', pp. 111–30; Wilson, *Out of Midst of the Fire*, pp. 45–104.

99. Carasik, 'To See a Sound', pp. 257–265; Geller, *Sacred Enigmas*, pp. 30–61; contra cf. Wilson, *Out of the Midst of the Fire*, pp. 89–97.

100. Von Rad, *Deuteronomy*, p. 60.

101. See also the use of this quote in Deut. 18 to support the idea of future prophetic leadership as discussed in Polzin, *Moses and the Deuteronomist*, pp. 59–62; Toeg, *Lawgiving at Sinai*, pp. 135–6; Savran, *Telling and Retelling*, pp. 114–15. and below, chapter 5.

commandments.[102] Scholem's distinction between revelation and tradition as reflecting primary and mediated religious experience is quite appropriate to Deuteronomy:

> In Judaism tradition becomes the reflective impulse that intervenes between the absoluteness of the divine word – revelation – and its receiver... Every religious experience after revelation is a mediated one. It is the experience of the voice of God rather than the experience of God.[103]

For Deuteronomy, the voice of God is primarily the voice of the commandments.

v. *Ezekiel 1.* Ezekiel's reactions to his call are characterized by total compliance and passivity on the part of the prophet. Ezekiel says not a single word and does precisely as he is told throughout this entire theophany. This passivity is even more noticeable given the fact that the narrative is told in the first person. Insofar as Ezekiel controls the narrative voice, his lack of control of the situation is all the more striking. There is first person narration also in Isaiah 6, but without the same degree of absence of response.

This passivity is linked with a description of physical collapse in the face of the numinous unlike any other text we have studied. Ezekiel's response to the totality of the vision (or to the figure of כבוד ה') is 'falling on his face' in 1.28. While elsewhere the phrase has connotations of prayer, or dismay, here it indicates physical breakdown. Only with the assistance of the spirit of 2.2 is Ezekiel able to rise and be attentive to the divine voice. H. Pedaya has described this collapse as fainting, of a type which prefigures the collapse of the individual in later mystical revelations such as are found in *Enoch* and the *Hekhalot* literature. She maintains that Ezekiel is 'emptied out', that his ego dissolves entirely in the face of the divine. His passivity and the fact that he is filled with the spirit that uplifts him indicates an ecstatic experience something like the *unio mystica* known in later texts.[104] The prophet is near death in 1.28 as a result of the lethal nature of seeing

---

102. This can be seen as a stage along the path that leads to the substitution of Torah for the experience of the divine as reflected in Psalm 119; see the discussion of this in chapter 8. At the same time, Wilson (*Out of the Midst of the Fire*, pp. 45–83) argues strongly for an intense experience of the divine in Deut. 4–5 on the basis of phrases such as 'stand before YHWH' and 'gather the people to me' (4.10), 'the midst of the fire' (4.15,33,36; 5.24,26), and 'face to face' (5.4). This, however, does not gainsay Deuteronomy's extensive focus on the commandments as the central focus of theophany.

103. G. Scholem, 'Revelation and Tradition as Religious Categories in Judaism', *The Messianic Ideal in Judaism*, (N.Y.: Schocken, 1971), pp. 282–303 (292).

104. Pedayah, 'Seeing, Falling', p. 246.

the divine. While there is no explicit mention of the fear of death, or of the danger of seeing, the revival of the prophet here recalls the actions of the angel(s) who nurse Elijah back to life in 1 Kgs. 19. There Elijah's wish to die is explicit, and his sleeping is a clear reflection of this. Here, Ezekiel is revived not by food, but by a mysterious spirit, as is appropriate to one who has left the realm of the human world.[105]

While we agree with much of Pedaya's understanding of Ezekiel as straddling the gap between classical prophecy and apocalyptic,[106] her reading of the prophet's reaction in 1.28 is extreme, and fails to take into account the range of meaning inherent in 'falling on one's face' in the Bible. The phrase may reflect an immediate response to the presence of the Deity without the same sense that Pedaya projects upon it.[107] While it can express a reaction of dismay,[108] it can just as easily express a sense a thanksgiving[109] or introduce a statement of entreaty before God.[110] That Ezekiel is overwhelmed by the vision he sees is understandable, and a sense of shock and bewilderment falls within the semantic spectrum of the expression,[111] but to say that an absence of reflectivity on the part of the prophet indicates a loss of his sense of self goes too far.[112] Moreover, the role of the spirit here seems to be different from the role that Pedaya assigns to it. Nowhere does the text suggest that this spirit fills him as a *pneuma*, but rather assists and enables him to attend to the voice which addresses him.[113] Although no verb of fearing is used, his reaction is certainly one of experiencing the *tremendum* of the numinous, in contrast with the sense of fascination which is evident throughout Ezekiel's

---

105. Greenberg understands this spirit as something internal to the prophet (*Ezekiel 1–20*, p. 62), while Pedayah ('Seeing, Falling', p. 245) sees it as an external force. Zimmerli, (*Ezekiel 1–2*, vol. 2, pp. 566–8), however, offers an extended discussion of the meanings of רוח in Ezekiel, the results of which indicate uncertainty as to whether the term 'is to be understood simply in anthropological terms, or whether it is not also theological'.

106. Pedaya, 'Seeing, Falling', p. 242.

107. E.g. Lev. 9.24; Josh. 5.14; Judg. 13.20; 1 Kgs. 18.39; Ezek. 3.23; 43.3, 44.4; Dan. 8.17. There may be an element of fear involved as well, that falling on the face is a way of avoiding looking directly at the divine. (R. Yosef Karo, Isaiah of Trani *ad loc.*)

108. E.g. Gen. 17.17; Num. 16.4; Num. 20.6; cf. also Gen. 50.1 and Num. 17.10.

109. E.g. Gen. 17.3; Ruth 2.10; 2 Sam. 14.22 (אל פניו).

110. E.g. Num. 14.5; 16.22; Josh. 7.6; 1 Sam. 25.23; 2 Sam. 9.6; Ezek. 9.8; 11.13; cf. also Gen. 44.14 (לפניו).

111. One might draw a connection with Ezekiel's more explicit reaction of anger and confusion in 3.14 at the end of the entire theophanic experience. Glazov's claim that this falling constitutes a non-verbal objection to the call ignores the fact that he has not yet been addressed by YHWH [*The Bridling of the Tongue*, p. 232].

112. Pedaya, 'Seeing, Falling', p. 248. Cf. also Uffenheimer, 'Method of Rudolph Otto', pp. 10–13, on the absence of a desire for *unio mystica* as characteristic of biblical prophecy.

113. Cf. above n. 105 on רוח. One finds a more elaborate description of this phenomenon in Dan. 8.18 and Dan. 10.8–12. In the latter text the prophet's fainting is also tied to having

prolonged gazing at the vision in 1.4–28a. His sense of disorientation can be seen in the last phrase in 1.28, מדבר קול ואשמע, in which the speaker is not named, nor is the voice described as emerging from the image on the throne. This reflects the confusion of Ezekiel, who does not necessarily recognize the voice at this time. The Septuagint reading, 'the voice of one speaking here', captures the sense of the unknown in the voice he hears.[114] After he is revived by the spirit which restores his strength in 2.2c the speaker still remains unidentified. But at this point Ezekiel seems to recognize the speaker, insofar as he identifies the voice to be directed at him (מדבר אלי).[115]

Ezekiel's subdued reactions throughout the narrative support the idea that the prophet is in a trance – he sees, hears, and registers what is around him, but he is physically so passive that even standing on his feet and eating are activities which require divine assistance. This is nowhere more apparent than in the episode of the eating of the scroll, which evokes disgust and fright on the part of the reader, but leaves a sweet taste in Ezekiel's mouth. The episode is clearly of great significance, since the concentric structure of the commission narrative finds its center in the eating of the scroll.[116] The episode recalls YHWH touching Jeremiah's mouth and placing his words within him, but here the highly concrete aspect of the scene runs counter to the more straightforward symbolism in Jeremiah. For Jeremiah the divine touch signifies a moment of great intimacy with the divine. But, even though a divine hand proffers the scroll, and there is something of the mother–child relationship in the image of YHWH feeding the prophet, for Ezekiel there is much less intimacy. The hand which offers the scroll is the same hand which possesses and compels

fasted – J.J. Collins (*Daniel* (Hermeneia; Minneapolis: Fortress Press, 1993), p. 374) points to a parallel with Saul in 1 Sam. 28.20. While the source of the enabling רוח in Ezek. 1.28 is unclear, in Daniel the power that invigorates him is clearly angelic.

114. See Greenberg, *Ezekiel 1–20*, p. 61, Zimmerli, *Ezekiel*, p. 131; both note how the formulation preserves the mystery of the Deity, but neither comments on the confusion of the prophet reflected by the expression.

115. Zimmerli suggests adopting the LXX here to read מדבר אתו instead of the awkward MT מדבר את. (p. 89). Greenberg sees the hitpa'el pointing of the verb *middabber* as an indication that Ezekiel here identifies the speaking voice with YHWH, as this form is found in reference to divine speech in Num. 7.19 (and again in Ezek. 43.6), 'the Shekinah speaks in its majesty to itself; its messengers only overhear it' (Rashi). Both Greenberg and Zimmerli see this as a reflection of later theological sensibilities about divine speech, but it is very likely that this is a way of indicating that Ezekiel has identified the voice at this point, and is aware that YHWH is addressing him.

116. Cf. B. Schwartz, 'The Concentric Structure of Ezekiel 2.1–3.15', *WCJS* 10 (1990), pp. 107–14; Greenberg, *Ezekiel 1–20*, pp. 77–8; Zimmerli, *Ezekiel I*, pp. 135–6; Glazov, *The Bridling of the Tongue*, pp. 226–34.

the prophet, as he describes in 1.3 and 3.14.[117] And the physical repulsiveness and indigestibility of a parchment scroll, and the devastating content of its message – קנים והגה והי – undercut the sense of tender nourishment. Ezekiel's bizarre statement about the sweetness of the scroll can only be understandable if we assume him to be in a state of trance possession. Moreover, what precedes and follows the episode of the scroll in 2.3–7 and 3.4–9 are statements which emphasize the rebelliousness of Israel, and these give the eating of the scroll a larger significance in terms of Ezekiel's identity as a prophet. In contradistinction to the rest of Israel, Ezekiel is to be the very model of obedience. He is commanded to eat whatever YHWH gives him in 2.8 and 3.1. Ezekiel is to speak only what he is told, and nothing more, a fact which is emphasized by the episode of his dumbness in 3.22–27.[118] Thus the lack of active response on the part of the prophet describes not just the nature of Ezekiel's encounter with the divine, but also the essence of his prophetic persona.[119]

2. *Doubt*

a. *Doubt About Performance*

The responses discussed in the previous section occur entirely within the liminal world of the theophanic encounter, and describe the relationship between the human and the divine along the spectrum of fear and fascination. This response is focused solely upon the immediacy of the encounter, with no relation to the external world. By contrast, the expressions of doubt we will now discuss reflect a degree of self-assessment, not only with respect to the divine, but with respect to the world as well. When Jeremiah says 'I don't know how to speak' he is not referring to his inability to respond verbally to YHWH, but to the performance of his prophetic task before the people. As a consequence of this relation to the world beyond the framework of the theophany these reactions to the divine contain within them an element of externalization (which will be discussed primarily in the next chapter), representing a halfway position between being completely enveloped within the sphere of the divine, and the reintegration into the human community which marks the end of the theophany. The responses of Moses and Jeremiah in particular reflect a concern, on the one hand, with how the self sees itself over against the

---

117. The use of the 'hand of God' here is similar to its use in preclassical prophecy, particular with Elisha in 2 Kgs. 3.15. Cf. Greenberg, *Ezekiel 1–20* pp. 41–2; Zimmerli, *Ezekiel I*, pp. 117–18; J.J.M. Roberts, 'The Hand of Yahweh', *VT* 21 (1971), pp. 244–51.

118. Cf. Greenberg, *Ezekiel 1–20*, pp. 121–2.

119. Cf. Ellen F. Davis, *Swallowing The Scroll* (Sheffield: Almond Press, 1989, esp. pp. 47–71; M.S. Odell, 'You Are What You Eat: Ezekiel and the Scroll', *JBL* 117 (1998), pp. 229–48.

divine, as well as how that self asserts itself in the social world to which they will return.

i. *Exodus 3.11–4.17.* This text is the most elaborate and developed of all the instances of doubt we will discuss. After YHWH states the terms of Moses' commission in 3.7-10, Moses brings forward no fewer than five objections to his commission. While these focus primarily on questions of self-doubt, there is also an undertone (and sometimes an overtone) of disbelief in Moses' protestations. Just who is this God? Can he perform as promised? Each objection is answered in turn by YHWH, at first in an even-handed manner, then less patiently, and even angrily towards the end. Where the complaints are realistic and to the point in the beginning (Who am I to do this? Who are you to send me? How can I convince the people?), the tone of the last two complaints reveals a more skeptical attitude. The fourth complaint, that Moses can't speak well (4.10), is undercut by being delivered in a high rhetorical style which shows, if anything, Moses' ability to express himself quite well. And the last complaint, שלח נא ביד תשלח, usually translated as 'Send someone else!' (4.13), belies Moses' powerful desire to avoid the commission at all costs. What kind of process is being described here, and how does the entire series of objections fit into the schema of the theophany narrative?[120] Buber notes that the beginning and the end of this section focus on Moses' sense of inadequacy,[121] but there is also a significant change in the way this inadequacy is assessed.

Moses' first objection has much in common with the type of response which is found not only among in the call narratives of Jeremiah and Gideon, but also in the reluctance to accept a position of leadership expressed by Saul (1 Sam. 9.21; 10.21–22), by David (1 Sam. 18.18; 2 Sam. 7.18) and by Solomon (1 Kgs. 3.7).[122] While this is often seen as a stereotyped response which ascribes to the candidate a sense of modesty in the face of the commission, the formulation of the question in Exod. 3.11 reflects a double reservation on Moses' part, concerning both his sense of self as well as his public persona. The beginning phrase 'who am I' bespeaks a degree of self-denigration in the face of the divine, not unlike

---

120. For a fuller discussion of the redactional issues which lie behind the text cf. the discussion in Propp, *Exodus 1–18*, pp. 190–7; Childs, *Exodus*, pp. 51–71; Greenberg, *Understanding Exodus*, pp. 101–7.

121. Buber, *Moses*, p. 46.

122. Cf. Habel, 'Call Narratives', pp. 297–323; Simon, *Prophetic Narratives*, pp. 53–5; Glazov, *Bridling of the Tongue*, pp. 30–53.

the negative self-assessment discussed above.[123] Here Moses finds his own voice (אנכי) for the first time since YHWH spoke (אנכי) in v. 6.[124] At the same time the rest of the verse, 'that I should go to Pharaoh and bring out the children of Israel', reflects self-evaluation in the face of public circumstances – first Pharaoh, then the Israelites. We can see in this formulation a midway position between the complete self-involvement of responses to the divine in the previous category, and the entirely external reflection of the theophany in what we will describe in the next chapter. If our earlier analysis of Exod. 3.1–6 reflected his gradual approach to the numinous, we find in 3.11–13. the beginnings of Moses' disengagement from the encounter.

YHWH's response also reflects this two-sided aspect in the ambiguous expression וזה לך האות.[125] The point at issue is whether זה points to an antecedent or to subsequent point in the text. If we follow Ibn Ezra and take זה as referring to the bush, then the referential sign is the private theophanic experience which Moses has just experienced. The bush as the sign of YHWH's presence serves as a guarantee to Moses of YHWH's support for him. The phrase 'I will be with you' expresses the sense of continuity with the theophany of 3.1–6, in which the Deity and Moses are brought together.[126] On the other hand if זה refers to the latter half of the sentence,[127] the reference is to future public events: the Exodus of the Israelites from Egypt and the future revelation at Sinai, both of which are at a remove from the private concerns of the theophany. If this is the case YHWH would be referring to Moses' role in the future as the one who takes Israel out of Egypt, and the one who leads Israel to the group theophany at Mt. Sinai.[128] While a case can be made for one or the other referent, the ambiguity here may well be deliberate, focusing YHWH's response on both the private and the public aspects of the theophany.

---

123. Note the comment of N. Leibowitz (*Studies in Shemot* (Jerusalem: Jewish Agency, 1976) (Hebrew), p. 70) comparing the approach of Rashi to that of Rashbam: 'In these first moments of prophecy, in the atmosphere of Divine immanence, he recoils at His transcendence, sensing the nothingness of man, dust and ashes'. Cf. further Hizkuni *ad loc.*

124. R.P. Carroll, 'Strange Fire', *JSOT* 61 (1994), pp. 39–58 (44).

125. See the extended discussion of the verse in Childs, *Exodus*, pp. 56–60; Greenberg, *Understanding Exodus*, pp. 74–8. On the formula itself see M. Fishbane, 'The Biblical OT', *Shnaton* 1 (1975), pp. 213–34 (216–17) (Hebrew).

126. A similar idea is reflected by Ehrlich, (*Mikra Ki-Pheshuto*, Vol. 1, p. 138), who takes זה as referring to the clause which immediately precedes it: 'I will be with you'. Cf. also *Exod. Rab.* 4:5.

127. So Cassuto, *Exodus*, p. 36.

128. Cf. Buber's comment on the connection between the sign and the theophany at Sinai: 'Then Moses will experience the mission of this God as an expression of His being' (*Moses*, p. 47).

Moses' second and third objections are focused more fully on the question of Moses' reception by the people. His question about YHWH's name (3.13) is phrased not in terms of his own knowledge (though this may also be in question),[129] but in terms of what to tell the people.[130] The concern for the impression made on the people is also reflected in YHWH's response(s)[131] 'Thus shall you say to the children of Israel' in 3.14–15. Likewise, the complaint 'They won't believe me' in 4.1 results in external signs whose exclusive function is to demonstrate Moses' credibility to the people.[132] The relationship between Moses and YHWH in this section (4.1–9) is characterized by a didactic style with constant give and take, with YHWH speaking and Moses reacting physically. In contrast to the previous cases where we have little idea of how Moses reacts to YHWH's answers, here Moses' reactions give the impression that the graphic nature of the signs is convincing.[133] Yet with the last two reactions in 4.10 and 4.13 we see that the reverse is true. There is no mention of the Israelites at all; the text returns us to Moses the person, but with a noticeable change. Beyond the obviousness of the excuse, the rhetoric of Moses' protestations about his inability to speak in 4.10 reflects a sense of self-assessment which is more extensive than his earlier statements, including a temporal perspective on the past.[134] YHWH's response in 4.11–12 repeats his promise 'to be' with Moses, but with a significant difference. 'I will be with your mouth' is the language of prophetic speech, and indicates a greater distance from the divine than the earlier 'I will be with you'.[135]

Moses' final objection in 4.13 reflects with an even greater sense of distance from the numinous; the expression שלח נא ביד תשלח shows no sense of personal relationship to the divine. 'Send someone else' (other than me) indicates that Moses is now far from the thrall of the theophanic experience, and is measuring himself entirely by his own preferences. The

---

129. Cf. Cassuto, *Exodus*, pp. 16, 37.

130. Cf. Childs, *Exodus*, pp. 60–70, and Greenberg *Understanding Exodus*, pp. 78–84 on this objection and the traditions which lie behind it.

131. Most commentators see two different responses in 3.14 and 3.15 – cf. Childs, *Exodus*, pp. 68–70; Propp, *Exodus 1–18*, pp. 224–6.

132. On the nature of these signs see Childs, *Exodus*, pp. 77–8; Greenberg, *Understanding Exodus*, pp. 87–8; Propp, *Exodus 1–18*, pp. 209–10; 226–7.

133. In 4.3 Moses is frightened by the serpent, and in 4.6–7 the term הנה indicates Moses' observation of the leprosy and its disappearance.

134. Greenberg [*Understanding Exodus*, p. 89] hears an 'accusatory or complaining overtone in Moses' statement that his ineloquence persists even "now that you have spoken to your servant"...'. On the meaning of 'heavy of mouth and tongue' see Propp, *Exodus 1–18* pp. 210–11, and the literature cited there.

135. Cf. Propp, *Exodus 1–18*, p. 212, and passages like Deut. 18.18 and Isa. 51.16. On the question of Moses' speech impediment cf. the discussion in Glazov, *The Bridling of the Tongue*, pp. 69–88.

literal sense of the phrase 'send by the hand of', to send by means of a messenger,[136] certainly expresses greater distance from the divine. Propp may be correct in detecting a hostile tone here, in keeping with the *idem per idem* formulation as a means of cutting short further conversation.[137] Up to this point YHWH has taken everything Moses has said with great seriousness, but the emergence of YHWH's anger in 4.14 reveals an element of the divine which is common enough in the Bible, but is highly unusual in theophany narratives. The intimacy which was present earlier is completely absent here, as YHWH concedes the role of Aaron but commands Moses in no uncertain terms. The prophetic language of being 'with your mouth' which we encountered in 4.12 is expanded here to include Aaron as well. The time for discussion has passed, and with it the sense of dialogue which characterized the earlier stages of the theophany. YHWH's anger, coupled with the instruction that Aaron will accompany Moses, indicates most clearly that the solitary liminal element of the theophany has ended, and Moses will now return to the public sphere. The mention of Aaron in the last objection undercuts the exclusive nature of the relationship between YHWH and Moses by bringing in another human figure. The image of Moses as a god and Aaron as his prophet indicates the diminishing presence of YHWH – on the theophanic stage there is not room for two gods at the same time.

This set of responses is unique to Moses. It reflects the unparalleled relationship between YHWH and Moses, but one is hard pressed to say that it sets a model for other prophetic objections. The extent of the negotiations, the number of questions and answers, the sense of divine anger, and the emergence of Moses' ego reflect, even at first meeting, something of the complexity of their relationship, and their unusual intimacy. As we will see later, the dialogue in Exod. 33 reflects this as well, albeit from another perspective.

ii. *Jeremiah 1*. On the surface Jeremiah's response in Jer. 1.6, 'I can't speak', appears to be simply a more concise version of Moses' fourth objection in Exod. 4.10. But an examination of the response in context of Jeremiah's call shows it to be somewhat different. It does not exhibit the same degree of reluctance as Moses' comment, but rather is an essential part of the process of becoming a prophet which is described in Jer. 1.4–10.[138] In order to understand its function it shall be read as a response to the initial part of Jeremiah's call in 1.5:

---

136. E.g. Gen. 38.20; 2 Sam. 11.16; 15.36; 1 Kgs 2.25; 2 Kgs 17.13.
137. Propp, *Exodus 1–18*, p. 213, correctly notes the contrast between the acquiescence of 'Send someone else' and the complaining tone of בי אדני.
138. Cf. W. McKane, *Jeremiah*, vol. 1, p. 7.

בטרם אצורך בבטן ידעתיך	(A)	Before I created you in the womb I knew you.
ובטרם תצא מרחם הקדשתיך	(B)	And before you emerged from the womb I sanctified you;
נביא לגוים נתתיך	(C)	I appointed you a prophet to the nations.

As we noted in the previous chapter, Jeremiah's call narrative is unusual in that it starts from a position of intimacy, and not with a description of gradual approach of the divine. The account begins with a poetic oracle of three parallel stychs, which addresses Jeremiah's situation in a graduated way. In the context of the call narrative the series of verbs are arranged in a pattern of 3 + 1: נתתיך, הקדשתיך, ידעתיך, are all in the past, gradually moving into the present with הפקדתיך in v. 10.[139] The similar form of the three verbs in v. 5, together with their placement in the final position of each clause, links them together as they describe the change in Jeremiah's status. The first two clauses describe divine intentions or actions which predate the prophet's existence, while the verb in the third stych, נתתיך, can be taken as past ('I made you') or as present ('I hereby make you').[140] Taken together, the clauses describe a three stage process: knowing, setting aside/sanctifying, and appointing. While there are biblical and royal ancient Near Eastern models for preordination,[141] Jer. 1.5 speaks not only of foreordination of the chosen individual's task, but of an intimate prenatal relationship as well.

The relationship described by these three verbs begins with a designation of the most intimate sort of divine–human bond, reflected in the verb ידע. The use of this language in the theophany in Exod. 33.12–17 to describe YHWH's relationship with Moses attests to the exceptional

---

139. Lundbom, *Jeremiah 1–20*, p. 228. Though the perfect form is used, the addition of the modifier היום clarifies the immediate force of the verb here.

140. Holladay, *Jeremiah*, vol 1, p. 20, favors Dahood's suggestion of 'I summoned you', following the *ktiv* אצורך in light of the parallelism in Ps. 77.3, and therefore divides the verse differently:

'Before I summoned you, in the belly I knew you; Before you came forth, from the womb I dedicated you'.

141. E.g. Samson in Judg. 13, the servant in Isa. 49.1, and implicitly the promised child in most annunciation stories. For ancient Near Eastern examples see Lundbom, *Jeremiah 1–20*, p. 231; S. Paul, 'Deutero-Isaiah and Cuneiform Royal Inscriptions', *JAOS* 88 (1968), pp. 180–6 (184–5).

closeness implied by the term.[142] The intimacy of knowing is also bound up with YHWH's involvement in Jeremiah's own creation (אצורך).[143] The sense of election associated with the verb in texts like Amos 3.2 and 2 Sam. 7.20 points ahead to the next verb in the chain, הקדשתיך 'I have consecrated you'. While there is some degree of synonymy between ידע and קדש,[144] the latter implies a sense of distance as well; if knowing is all inclusive, then sanctifying places limits upon the object of consecration. Like a holy object Jeremiah is consecrated to YHWH, but is set apart from the rest of the people.[145] While Jeremiah's emergence from the womb is syntactically parallel to his being formed in the womb in (A),[146] it also points to a greater degree of autonomy than the previous stych. In (A) Jeremiah is the passive object of creation, but (B) states 'before *you went forth* from the womb'. In contrast to the two previous verbs, the third verb, נתתיך is the most general, appropriate to the widest variety of contexts, and the phrase 'to the nations'[147] creates an even sharper contrast with the intimacy and circumscribed nature of the previous phrases. The parallel temporal elements of (A) and (B) underscore this distinction even more clearly. The knowing and sanctifying were 'before', but the appointing in (C) has no temporal marker attached to it. It has rather a sense of immediacy, a present tense orientation which is enhanced by the parallel phrase in 1.10 הפקדתיך, which itself is modified by the term היום. When taken together with the three verbs, the parallelism between all three nouns with their attached prepositions – '*in* the belly', '*from* the womb', '*to* the nations' – describes a movement from inside to outside, with ידעתיך representing the point of greatest intimacy, and נתתיך the most externally focused action.

---

142. Cf. also Gen. 18.19, Hos. 2.2; 13.5. On the use of this language in Exod. 33 cf. J. Muilenburg, 'The Intercession of the Covenant Mediator,' in Ackroyd and Lindars (eds.), *Words and Meanings: Essays Presented to David Winton Thomas*, pp. 159–81; N.M. Waldman, 'God's Ways – A Comparative Note', *JQR* 70 (1979–80), pp. 67–72.

143. In addition to this sense of intimacy there are treaty connections associated with ידע which Holladay sees as reflecting Jeremiah's subservient status in this relationship. Cf. Holladay, *Jeremiah 1–2*, vol. 1, p. 33; Lundbom, *Jeremiah 1–20*, p. 231; H. Huffmon, 'The Treaty Background of the Hebrew ידע' *BASOR* 181 (1966), pp. 31–7.

144. The verbs ידע and קדש appear in proximity to one another three times in the book of Ezekiel (20.20; 36.23; 38.23). In each case the order of the verbs indicates sanctifying as a preparatory act for 'knowing' God, though in Ezekiel this implies recognition rather than intimate knowledge.

145. Israel is also described as 'holy to YHWH' in Jer. 2.3. Note Num. 8.16–17 on the dedication of the first born to God. Carroll, *Jeremiah*, p. 93, understands the phrase as 'ritually prepare' in 6.4; 22.7; 51.27,28. The Rabbis understood this to indicate that Jeremiah was born circumcised (*ARN* 2, *Mid. Teh.* 9).

146. Holladay, *Jeremiah*, vol. 1, p. 33.

147. See the discussion in Holladay, *Jeremiah*, vol. 1, p. 34. Carroll, *Jeremiah*, p. 95, suggests that this refers to the period of dominance of nations over Israel, against whom Jeremiah acts in 51.59–60.

Instead of describing a detachment from the world in order to encounter the divine, followed by a subsequent process of aggregation into human society, 1.5 describes an orientation which begins with YHWH and his creation of the prophet, and ends with a sending forth, out of the womb, to the nations.

We are now are in a better position to understand Jeremiah's objection in 1.6. When we examine Jeremiah's only verbal response in this section, we are made aware of a significant incongruity: YHWH 'has known' Jeremiah, but in v. 6 Jeremiah 'knows not' how to speak until YHWH places the words in his mouth. These words shift the point of view of the text more clearly to that of Jeremiah in both an imitative and an ironic sense. It is imitative in that Jeremiah now knows something about himself, as a result of YHWH's 'knowing' him, but ironic in the sense that the knowledge is not mutual. Jeremiah will not come to 'know' YHWH as YHWH knows him, and the text offers only a minimal sense of the prophet's perceptions at this moment. While in other cases the human protagonist sees something of the divine, Jeremiah will come to know YHWH only by His words. Jeremiah's first word, אהה, is commonly taken as an indication of his reluctance to accept his commission.[148] But it is hardly clear that this fits the context in Jer. 1.6. Rather, Gideon's use of the same expression in Judg. 6.22 as a reaction to the theophany he experiences seems more appropriate here – it is simply an expression of anxiety about encountering the numinous. Jeremiah's subsequent objection is not that he doesn't know YHWH, but that he doesn't know how to speak, the term נער indicating inexperience rather than age.[149] While this is crucial for the prophet, whose whole endeavour is to translate the divine word into human terms, the absence of the possibility of a deeper sort of knowing is very noticeable.

The 'response to the response', the touching of Jeremiah's mouth, contains within it both an act of intimacy – touch between the human and the divine is extremely rare in the Bible – and an act of distancing. For the

---

148. Muffs, 'Who Will Stand in the Breach?', p. 29, notes that אהה can have the force of an objection by the prophet to a divine decree, as in Jer. 4.10 and Ezek. 9.8.

149. On נער see Lundbom, *Jeremiah 1–20*, p. 233; Holladay, *Jeremiah*, p. 34; Carroll, *Jeremiah*, pp. 98–9. Holladay ['The Background of Jeremiah's Self-Understanding: Moses, Samuel, and Psalm 22', *JBL* 83 (1964), pp. 153–164; 'Jeremiah and Moses: Further Observations', *JBL* 85 (1966), pp. 17–27] makes a great deal of the theological significance of the similarities with Moses' call, yet here the difference is starkly apparent. Moses, who is also 'known by name' by YHWH (Exod. 33) achieves a deeper understanding of the nature of YHWH that eludes Jeremiah. The breadth of Moses' objections in Exod. 3.11–4.17. opens up a range of possibilities for Moses that do not seem to be present for Jeremiah. C. Seitz ('The Prophet Moses and the Canonical Shape of Jeremiah', *ZAW* 101 (1989), pp. 3–27) develops a significant difference between the two around the theme of Jeremiah's loss of the intercessory role.

purpose of the contact is not 'knowing' YHWH, but knowing the words in
order to speak, which addresses only the question of the specific message
he is to deliver. Where the contact between Jeremiah and YHWH was
from the inside out in v. 5, here it continues the focus on its external
manifestation. A connection is made between the act of forming Jeremiah's
body in the womb and the formation of his prophetic consciousness, but
while the former was a reflection of the relation between Jeremiah and
YHWH, the second focuses on the relationship between Jeremiah and the
people. Immediately following this contact the appointment of the prophet
is complete; in the same breath that declares 'Behold I have placed my
words in your mouth' (1.9) the fourth and final verb of Jeremiah's
appointment is uttered. Not only is he 'appointed' (הפקדתיך), but he is now
placed over 'nations *and* kingdoms' (compare 1.5). If the verb נתתי carried
a sense of the present tense with it in verse 5, the appointing in verse 10 is
even more immediate – 'I appoint you *this day*'.

The progression of Jeremiah's growth which is developed in these verses
moves from an unborn child in v. 5, to a נער in v. 6,[150] to a prophet in v.
7.[151] The total effect is one of 'becoming', moving from the notion of
conception and birth in v. 5 to a full-blown definition of the mature
prophet.[152] The parental overtones here are unmistakable: YHWH acts as
both mother and father, giving comfort, protection and instruction to the
impressionable Jeremiah. The vagueness of Jeremiah's definition as a
prophet is fleshed out by the words being placed in his mouth; the
uncertainty of when he is appointed is given specificity by the 'today' of v.
10, and the unclear sense of 'knowing' Jeremiah is given immediacy and
currency by the touching of his mouth. At the same time, very little room is
left for the human responses of the prophet as we saw them expressed with
Samuel, Moses, and even Isaiah.

iii. *Judges 6*. Gideon's responses to the theophany in Judg. 6.11–24. display
a double aspect. On the one hand, they fit the pattern of the reversal of
skepticism which we will discuss in the next section, as reflected in
Gideon's concluding statement in Judg. 6.22 'I have seen an angel of the
Lord face to face'. At the same time this is not a sudden reversal, but the
result of a gradual process of realization, in which Gideon's initial
expression of doubt is similar to what we saw with Moses' objections. In

150. Lundbom, *Jeremiah 1–20*, p. 233, feels that an age between twelve and fifteen is
appropriate here. However, the term in this context has more to do with experience than with
age.

151. YHWH's statement of 5c, appointing Jeremiah a prophet (נביא לגוים נתתיך) is
expanded by YHWH's placing his words in Jeremiah's mouth (נתתי דברי בפיך).

152. Similarly, Samuel is referred to as a נער before his call (1 Sam. 2.11,18,21, etc.) but
not afterwards.

response to the angelic overture in 6.12 Gideon is skeptical about divine involvement in Israel's life in general, and by extension his own in particular. He contrasts YHWH's previous concern for Israel with his present disregard for their fate.[153] Gideon seems to have no idea that he is speaking with a divine emissary. The dual sense of 'YHWH is with you' is duly noted by Abarbanel; in saying 'YHWH is with you' the angel hints at the present tense sense of the theophany, but Gideon's response is future oriented – '*Will* YHWH be with us'?[154] The Masoretic vocalization of אדני in v. 13 as 'my lord', the references to YHWH in the third person, and the absence of any sign of reaction to the divine at this point all indicate that Gideon remains ignorant of the identity of his interlocutor.[155]

The next stage in this dialog is marked by the assignation of speech to YHWH in v. 14 and by the unusual verb ויפן to describe the divine presence. Polak, among others, understands ויפן as indicating the presence of YHWH as distinct from the *malakh*, but this is unlikely given the continuation of the narrative.[156] In the narrative theophany traditions, when YHWH and the *malakh* appear in the same text, there is no essential difference between them. The malakh functions as a substitute for YHWH in a number of texts, and may represent a different level of revelation.[157] But when the two appear in the same scene there appears to be no essential distinction between them.[158] While they may have originally represented different redactional layers of the text, at this point they function identically. The verb ויפן seems to have more to do with the beginning of

---

153. Gideon seems to take 'YHWH is with you' as referring to the nation and not to himself individually, thereby misconstruing the personal element of the initial address by the *malakh*.

154. Abarbanel *ad loc.*

155. The phrase בי אדני is used as frequently of contact with YHWH, (Exod. 4.10,13; Num. 12.11; Josh. 7.8; Judg. 6.15; 13.8) as it is of human contact (Gen. 43.20; 44.18; 1 Sam. 1.26; 1 Kg. 3.17, 26).

156. F. Polak, 'The Messenger of God', pp. 14*-30*, suggests that the manifestation of the divine here is divided between vision (*malakh*) and voice (YHWH). But this results in a much more complex reading of the story. We follow Amit, *Book of Judges*, p. 238, who holds that the *malakh* is present throughout the narrative. Cf. also the LXX reading of v. 14 'the *angel* of the Lord turned to him'. Y. Kaufmann (*The Book of Judges* (Kiryat Sepher: Jerusalem, 1973) (Hebrew) p. 159) understands ויפן to indicate a shift in the tone of the speaker to a more commanding voice. It is also possible to read this as a shift in Gideon's point of view, indicating a change in the way he relates to his interlocutor, who up to now has been simply an anonymous stranger, but becomes identified as a numinous entity in v. 14.

157. There is a certain logic to such a position, but often YHWH and the *malakh* are interchangeable, as in Gen. 21–22.

158. In a similar fashion, in Gen. 18.1–15 אנשים appear prior to YHWH with no indication that there is any difference between them and the Deity. In Exod. 3 *malakh YHWH* and the Deity appear together, but here the *malakh* functions not as an angelic figure but as a fiery manifestation of the divine.

Gideon's awareness that he is being addressed by the Deity and not by some unknown stranger. Masoretic tradition ascribes to Gideon the words 'please, my Lord' in v. 15, but his comment here focuses not on YHWH, but rather on his own sense of inadequacy for the task.[159] A demurral of this type is common to other leaders upon hearing of their appointment (Moses, Saul, David, etc.), but here there is no sense of false modesty, but only a genuine sense of self-doubt. Gideon may understand something more about his interlocutor at this point, but he still remains unconvinced. As Y. Amit suggests, Gideon's skeptical comment is at least in part a response to the unclarity of the angel's words לך בכחך זה – by what strength can he succeed, when he is inexperienced and lacking in soldiers?[160] YHWH's statement in v. 16 'I will be with you' indicates both presence and future assistance, and gives Gideon a clearer sense that YHWH is speaking with him.

The final phase of Gideon's reaction leads into the response as will be outlined below. It begins with Gideon's request for a sign in 6.17, and concludes with his statement of conviction in v. 22, which is the final indication that he fully accepts what the reader had known all along, namely that YHWH has been speaking with him. A further indication that Gideon is moving in this direction can be seen in the shift in balance in the speeches from v. 17 on. Although Gideon is the one to request a sign, we see significant changes in the style and content of his speech in 6.17: The phrase 'If I have found favor in your eyes', the promise of an offering, and his concern that the speaker will disappear before he can bring the sacrifice. There is no further expression of skepticism of the sort that he voiced in vv. 13 and 15. One sees a certain balance between Gideon's actions in preparing the offering in v. 19 and the angel's actions in v. 21. It is the angel who controls the scene and Gideon who simply obeys, most noticeably with the compliance formula ויעש כן, indicating that all resistance from Gideon has evaporated. The conclusive act is the angel's disappearance, which is set off against Gideon's disappearance and return in v. 18. Gideon goes and returns to the angel, but the angel simply disappears. The combination of the fire and the departure of the *malakh* lead Gideon to reach the proper conclusion in v. 22. Gideon's concluding statement marks the point at which he is convinced, presenting a gradual move from outright skepticism, to gradual conviction, to genuine fear that the experience will prove to be fatal. YHWH's final words 'you will not die' remain after the disappearance of the divine to answer this anxiety. As in Gen. 18.15, it is YHWH who has the final word.

---

159. Cf. Radak on 6.15; Amit, *The Book of Judges*, p. 237.
160. Cf. Amit, *The Book of Judges*, pp. 236–7, and n. 42.

iv. *Genesis 32.*

26	And he said:	ויאמר
	'Release me, for the dawn is coming'.	(A) שלחני כי עלה השחר
	And he said:	ויאמר
	'I won't release until you have blessed me'.	לא אשלחך כי אם ברכתני
27	And he said to him:	(B) ויאמר אליו
	'What is your name?'	מה שמך
	And he said:	ויאמר
	'Jacob'.	יעקב
28	And he said:	ויאמר
	'Your name will no longer be Jacob,	לא יעקב יאמר עוד שמך
	But rather Israel,	כי אם ישראל
	For you have struggled with divine beings	כי שרית עם אלהים
	and with humans and have prevailed'.	ועם אנשים ותוכל
29	And Jacob asked and said:	(C) וישאל יעקב ויאמר
	'Tell me your name'.	הגידה נא שמך
	And he said:	ויאמר
	'Why do you ask my name?'	למה זה תשאל לשמי
	And he blessed him there.	ויברך אתו שם
30	And Jacob named the place Peniel.	ויקרא יעקב שם המקום פניאל
	'For I have seen God face to face	כי ראיתי אלהים פנים אל פנים
	And my life was spared'.	ותנצל נפשי

In contrast to Judg. 6 there is no indication of skepticism in Gen. 32, but Jacob's response to his opponent in 32.26–29 also betrays a gradual sense of understanding, culminating in his statement about a face-to-face encounter with the divine. Similar to 32.24–25, the beginning of the dialogue mentions no names, sustaining the sense of confusion which accompanies the darkness and the wrestling. There is a sudden transition from physical to verbal interaction in Gen. 32.26, but the threat of physical danger is carried over from the previous two verses by the angel's request to be released, following the physical pressure on Jacob to let him go.[161] Whatever the cause of the conflict may have been, the inability to defeat Jacob leads to the dialogue in 32.26–29.

The dialogue consists of three parts. (A) (v. 26) and (C) (v. 29), each contain a question and a refusal, whereas (B) (vv. 27–28) contains a question, an affirmative answer, and a blessing. In (A) the angel asks to be released, and Jacob refuses; in (C) Jacob asks to know the angel's name, and the angel refuses. Both sections involve the repetition of a key word, in (A) שלח and in (C) שם.[162] Both involve a refusal to 'let go' of something which is considered precious. At the same time there is an imbalance of power between the two, for though Jacob will ultimately liberate the angel, the latter remains anonymous to Jacob. Offsetting the refusals in (A) and (C) is the granting of Jacob's demand: in (A) he asks for a blessing, and in (C) he receives it. Thus the synchronic ABA structure created by the parallel refusals is balanced by a movement from (A) to (C) which proceeds diachronically from request to blessing.

As opposed to the profound distance and difference between the human and the divine common to most theophany narratives, there is in Gen. 32.24–32 a surprising lack of separation between the two. This is also reflected in the lack of clarity about Jacob's awareness of the nature of his adversary. On the one hand, since he asks for a blessing, one might assume that Jacob is aware that he is dealing with a numinous being who has the power to bless. Thus Westermann concludes that 'bless' here contains the sense of 'transfer of strength' and implies a superhuman opponent.[163] At the same time the range of the term is broad enough to include a variety of nuances related to humans as well.[164] Moreover, in v. 30 Jacob's request to know the name of his adversary could well indicate that, like Manoah in Judg. 13, he is unaware that this is a divine being with no name. If this is the case, these verses also display a change in Jacob's awareness about the nature of this encounter, a change which is marked finally by his clear expression of comprehension in 32.30.

At the center of this dialogue is Jacob's blessing, the change of name which bespeaks a change in identity. The meaning of the name is similar to other West Semitic names, having a theophoric focus and declaring that 'El rules'.[165] But the aetiological explanation of the name has to do with the

---

161. Westermann, *Genesis 12–36*, p. 517.
162. Note also the play on שם as 'name' and 'there' in 32.29.
163. Westermann, *Genesis 12–36*, p. 518.
164. *TDOT* vol 2, pp. 300–8.
165. Cf. R. Coote, 'The Meaning of the Name Israel', *HTR* 65 (1972), pp. 137–46. Coote attempts to derive this meaning as related to the sense of 'cutting' as ruling by analogy with the root חתך 'to cut' and 'to judge' in Ugaritic. But the internal biblical evidence is sufficient to understand שרר as 'to rule' based on Judg. 9.22 and Isa. 9.5–6.

nature of human interaction with this 'ruling' God. Two alternate readings
of the verse present themselves. If v. 28 is read as a prose sentence, and the
phrase עם אלהים ועם אנשים is taken together to mean 'everyone',[166] then
human and divine are brought together as those with whom Jacob
struggles and whom he defeats. This reading emphasizes the heroic aspect
of Jacob's character and heightens the absence of a clear distinction
between the human and the divine in this narrative. Strikingly, Jacob's
adversary is referred to as both איש (32.24) and אלהים (32.30). On the other
hand, the structure of the verse suggests that it may have originally been
intended to be read as a poetic couplet:[167]

כי שרית עם אלהים
ועם אנשים תוכל

In this case we should understand it as 'You struggle with divine beings,
you overcome humans', and the linkage between the two stychoi is left
unclear[168]. The parallelism suggests similarity between אלהים and אנשים
(they are both adversaries of Jacob), but not equality. While Jacob may
defeat his human opponents, he may struggle with divine forces but cannot
defeat them. He cannot overpower the angel just as he cannot cross the
divine–human barrier. Read in this manner the blessing understands
Jacob's new name as a reflection of his human identity.

Reading the verse the first way, as an indication of Jacob's 'divine'
status, Jacob appears to be on the same level as the angel. His demand for
a blessing bears a certain similarity to Moses' request in Exod. 33.18.
Having received concessions from God regarding his exceptional status in
YHWH's eyes (33.12–17), Moses presses ahead and asks to see YHWH's
kavod. In Gen. 32, after Jacob has already received the sought after
blessing from the angel, he too pushes further and asks to know his name.
The question seems geared to elevate Jacob to a status equal to his
opponent. Since the angel cannot defeat him, Jacob is in a sense victorious,
and thus emboldened to ask the angel's name (just as the angel asked
Jacob for his). But the answer he receives, the refusal, is in keeping with the
second reading, emphasizing Jacob's human status. This too recalls
YHWH's response to Moses in Exod. 33.19, in which Moses is not allowed
this level of intimacy with the divine. For Jacob, struggle is an insufficient
indication of superiority to or of victory over divine forces. As a human

166.   As in Judg. 9.9,13; Prov. 3.4; cf. Geller, 'Struggle at the Jabbok', p. 47; Westermann,
Genesis 12–36, p. 518.

167.   Cf. Coote, 'The Meaning of the Name', p. 137, omitting the *waw* in ותוכל.

168.   It can be read variously 'Though you struggle with divine beings you can (only)
overcome humans', or 'Because you struggle with with divine beings you can overcome
humans'.

Jacob cannot know the identity of the angel, and his request is rejected. The repeated mention of the blessing in v. 29 further emphasizes this limitation, understanding ויברך אתו שם as 'he blessed him at that point'. The blessing both confirms Jacob's power and his subservience.[169]

Gen. 32.30 combines an aetiological explanation of Peniel with Jacob's realization of the danger involved in the encounter. Jacob showed no sign of fear in his dialogue with the angel in 32.26–29, indicating a closeness, if not an intimacy, with this representative of the divine. If Jacob's request for a blessing in v. 26 indicated his closeness with the angel, perhaps even a reflection of *fascinans* in the face of the divine, then 32.30 represents the other side of the coin. After receiving the blessing in v. 29 Jacob gives voice to the danger of having been so close to the numinous. This realization comes at the very end of the theophany, after the angel has departed and Jacob is alone again.[170] The naming of the place on the basis of the experience bespeaks distance from the event, leading into the final stage of externalization of the theophanic experience.

b. *Skepticism Reversed*
Each of the three texts to be discussed below contains a dramatic reversal in the perception of one of the protagonists, from complete lack of awareness to a sudden realization of the presence of the numinous. The term skepticism is most appropriate in the case of Sarah in Gen. 18, but the other two cases also display more than a simple failure of perception, an almost willful refusal to recognize that something extraordinary is taking place. Also common to all three texts is the unusual situation of a second figure who is also privy to the theophany. The two characters are not equal in their awareness of the divine, and this difference is used to heighten the sudden awareness of the main figure.

i. *Genesis 18.1–15.* The use of a dual protagonist is reflected in the centrality of Abraham in the first part of the story (vv. 1–9) and the focus on Sarah in the second part (vv. 10–15). In the first section Abraham is initially the active protagonist, welcoming his guests and feeding them with great energy and attentiveness, but he subsequently displays passivity in showing no reaction to the annunciation itself. Apart from the reference in v. 2 to Abraham's 'lifting up his eyes' and seeing them standing before him the text makes no further reference to Abraham's perceptions, and, as

---

169. Cf. Geller, 'Struggle at the Jabbok', p. 56.

170. This follows Geller's division of the pericope into three parts according to structure and style; part 2 is vv. 26–29 (all dialogue), and part 3 in vv. 30–32 (two aetiologies). This division indicates that the encounter with the angel has been concluded with the words ויברך אתו שם at the end of v. 29. V. 30 begins a new section in which the angel is not present. See 'Struggle at the Jabbok', pp. 39–41.

mentioned in the previous chapters, we have no indication precisely when he understands the divine nature of his visitor. The moment of revelation is made clearer to the reader by the use of a singular verb for the visitors to introduce the annunciation in 18.10 (prior to this they had spoken in the plural). Yet here too Abraham doesn't react, whether out of shock or because of prior knowledge of the message;[171] only Sarah's reaction is of subsequent interest to the narrator. Abraham's basic passivity in the face of this encounter, when read in light of the frequent contact between Abraham and YHWH, reflects acceptance and belief.

Sarah is clearly treated as a secondary figure in her remaining 'within the tent', and in not being featured as part of the welcoming party. Yet, in the second part of the story, she is the more responsive of the two, with her skeptical laughter in 18.12 and her denial in 18.15. While the narrator offers some justification for her skepticism with a direct comment in v. 11, the import of the verb צחק here definitely implies disbelief.[172] Such skepticism is hardly surprising, both because of Sarah's awareness of her biological limitations[173] and her inability to see the mysterious visitors.[174] YHWH's 'response to the response', catalyzes the reversal of Sarah's disbelief. This is accomplished by the quotation of her private thoughts, and by the change in the content of the quotation in order to heighten the effect upon Sarah. The revealing of her most private thoughts is deeply disturbing to her. First, her sense of privacy is shattered by the quotation. Uttered not only in the privacy of the tent but within the recesses of her own mind, these words are suddenly made public. Moreover, what is quoted is not precisely what she had said. Her remark in 18.12 referred to both herself and Abraham as being advanced in years, while YHWH's

---

171.   The question of the relationship of Abraham's laughter in Gen. 17.16 to Sarah's laugh in 18.12 is complex. From the standpoint of source criticism, the two chapters represent two variant traditions in which laughter is the central element as a foreshadowing of Isaac (יצחק) (cf. Van Seters, *Abraham in History and Tradition*, p. 284). If 17 and 18 are read as a continuous story, the rebuke of Sarah is explained alternately as a difference in the nature of the two laughs (Rashi) or a continuing skepticism on Sarah's part even after Abraham had informed her of YHWH's promise (Abarbanel).

172.   Compare Abraham's laughter in 17.17 – also internal, but less clearly skeptical. Falling on one's face can indicate dismay (Num. 16.14), but it can just as easily signal thanksgiving (Ruth 2.10), entreaty (Num. 14.5; 1 Sam. 25.23), or an immediate response to the appearance of the divine (Lev. 9.24; Num. 20.6; Judg. 13.20; 1 Kgs. 18.39; Ezek. 1.28). Moreover, while the phrase לו ישמעאל יחיה לפניך can be taken as an indication of disbelief (so Rashi and Kimchi), it can also indicate belief on Abraham's part, and a concern for Ishmael's fate when he is replaced by Isaac (so Nachmanides).

173.   Note the poignant comment in *Midrash Tanhuma*: Sarah looks at the reality of her own body and declares 'Can these loins bear a child, and can these dried-up breasts give milk?' (Shofetim 18).

174.   See Nachmanides on Gen. 18.15.

quote in 18.13 refers only to Sarah. While Rashi maintains that YHWH does this out of consideration for Abraham's feelings, the focus of this section is entirely upon Sarah's reactions, and in this light the 'corrected' quote of her private words has a unique purpose. Only she (and YHWH) are aware of the change, but this awareness brings with it a complete realization of just who the speaker is. Her words have been changed in order to impress upon her that the speaker can penetrate her innermost thoughts and make them public. The quotation brings home to Sarah the disparity between human and divine speakers.[175] The difference between the public world of Abraham – outside the tent, with the guests – and the private world of Sarah – in the tent, within her self, within her own body – is overcome by the quotation.

Her laugh is also the occasion for the single moment of direct revelation between her and YHWH. YHWH's speech in v. 14 – 'היפלא דבר מה – makes a further connection between knowledge and performance: omniscience – the ability to discern hidden thoughts (v. 13) – is tied to omnipotence – here the ability to bestow fertility upon a post-menopausal woman. Sarah's further response, her denial of her laughter in v. 15, may also be a private admission, but most likely it indicates the emergence of Sarah into the sphere of activity outside the tent, in the presence of YHWH and Abraham. This moment of Sarah's fear shows the dramatic change in her understanding in a most revealing way. We have seen her innermost feelings laid bare twice, first in her skepticism, and now again in her embarrassment. Her denial that she had laughed is an example of what M. Bal calls the retrospective fallacy.[176] Now that she has reached a new level of understanding and belief she would deny her previous reaction, disavow that she had ever laughed at the idea of birthing a child at her advanced age. YHWH's statement לא כי צחקת – 'No, you *did* laugh' – makes it clear to her and to the reader the nature of the transformation that has occurred. This moment of realization is portrayed through Sarah's reactions, not through Abraham's. His lack of response only serves to highlight the significance of the change that Sarah undergoes.

ii. *Judges 13*. In Judg. 13 husband and wife again seem to reflect contrasting sides of the theophany experience, though here it is Manoah who acts the role of the skeptic, and his wife who is the primary recipient of the theophany. While it is not certain that Manoah's wife initially guesses the identity of her interlocutor in vv. 2–5, she seems to have an instinctive understanding that the man of God who spoke to her was no ordinary human messenger. In 13.6 she describes his appearance as

---

175. Cf. Savran, *Telling and Retelling*, pp. 92–3; Sternberg, *Poetics*, pp. 91–2.
176. M. Bal, *Lethal Love* (Bloomington, IN: Indiana University Press, 1987), p. 108.

equivalent to a מלאך אלהים and as נורא, a term which nearly always implies divinity.[177] Her reticence about asking the name of the angel may also bespeak an intuitive sense of the nature of the messenger, especially in light of Jacob's inquiry and rebuff by the angel in Gen. 32.29, and Manoah's subsequent refusal later in the chapter. Adele Reinharz has argued that these elements, as well as the anonymity of both the angel and the woman, are indicative of a basic similarity between the two figures.[178] Strikingly, though Manoah appeals to YHWH for a return visit, the angel reappears once again to the woman, who must then fetch her husband.[179] The claim in v. 11 that 'Manoah followed after his wife' is very significant in establishing the primacy of her experience over his.[180] All the crucial information about the nature of the child and the restrictions surrounding him are transmitted to the woman. Her superior knowledge is reflected in the fact that she withholds information from Manoah when she relates this in 13.7. And when Manoah asks for further clarification about the fate of the boy, the angel answers that his wife is the proper channel for information – 'Everything I commanded the woman she shall do' (13.14). He repeats nothing more than what had been reported by Manoah's wife, withholding the same information about cutting the boy's hair.[181]

Manoah, on the other hand, displays none of this sensitivity. His wish to hear the messenger himself is not surprising in and of itself,[182] but he seems unable to decode the message implicit in the angel's evasive responses. In 13.11–17 he asks repeatedly and is continuously rebuffed or not answered. In no other theophany narrative do we find such a lengthy dialogue which does not advance the plot, but serves primarily to establish what the protagonist does *not* perceive. When Manoah asks about the identity of the

---

177. E.g. Exod. 34.10; Pss. 66.3; 68.36; 76.8; 96.4, etc. Elat (*Samuel and the Foundation of Kingship*, p. 34. n. 103) suggests a connection between נורא and the *melammu*, the shining aura which is often a sign of divinity in Mesopotamia.

178. She is responsible for the fate of the child by her attention to the angel's restrictions, and like the angel she is superior to her husband in perception. Cf. Reinharz, 'Samson's Mother', pp. 25–37.

179. In both this story and in Gideon's theophany in Judg. 6, the angel/YHWH is asked to wait while the protagonist temporarily leaves the stage to perform an activity. Here the woman goes to fetch her husband, and in Judg. 6 Gideon enters his house to bring out the sacrifice.

180. Cf. Amit, '"Manoah Promptly Followed his Wife"', pp. 146–56.

181. While the meaning of this omission is unclear in the context of Judg. 13, it may well have larger significance in the context of the Samson story as a whole. See the discussion in Savran, *Telling and Retelling*, pp. 83–85, and the literature cited there.

182. Whether this is a function of jealousy (see Josephus, *Antiquities* V:277–284), male prerogative, or of genuine concern, the notion of intercession by the husband for the wife was an accepted custom, as seen in Gen. 25.21. However, in contrast to Rebecca's situation, it is not clear that Manoah's wife is in need of such intercession.

speaker (13.11) he receives a simple אני, not unlike Jacob's evasive reply to Isaac's question in Gen. 27.24. To the second question about the fate[183] of the boy (13.12), the angel's response pertains only to the woman's behaviour; nothing is offered regarding Samson's future. Manoah's third remark about preparing a meal (13.15) is rebuffed, and is followed by the narrator's direct statement about Manoah's lack of understanding at this point (13.16).

The climactic moment of this frustrated interrogation begins with Manoah asking the precise question which his wife refused to ask earlier, about the name of the mysterious guest (13.17). The request for the name of the angel is, as in Gen. 32, a signal for the imminent separation of the divine from the human sphere, which is accomplished by the angel's disappearance in the flame of the sacrifice. Only then, when the angel is no longer present, is Manoah said to understand. The contrast between Manoah and his wife is brought out here as well. While in vv. 18–20 the repetition of the phrase ומנוח ואשתו רואים emphasizes the mutuality of the visual experience, the reactions to the disappearance of the angel separate them once again. Once he realizes that this was an encounter with a divine messenger Manoah is filled with anxiety, fearing death. While this sense of dread is common to a number of other theophany narratives, in most other cases there is a real indication of danger. But here his fears are dismissed by his wife with a series of logical arguments in which she again asserts her superior understanding of what has just transpired. This discrepancy between husband and wife heightens the sense of Manoah's move from lack of understanding to a fuller cognizance of the meaning of the encounter with the angel.

iii. *Numbers 22*. Balaam's reaction to the appearance of the *malakh YHWH* in 22.31–34 reflects a complete about-face for the seer. Unlike the skepticism described above in the annunciation stories, no promise is made by the *malakh*; nor does Balaam express a sense of doubt, as with Moses and Gideon, for there is no indication that Balaam questions his own ability to perform. Rather, the opposite may be the case. Balaam seems to be possessed of an overweening sense of his own abilities, and the purpose of the theophanic encounter is to cut him down to size, to clarify to him who leads and who follows.

Balaam's theophany in Num. 22.22–35 is unusual in that it follows two earlier audial revelations to him by YHWH, night-time encounters which have no visual component to them.[184] In the first half of the chapter

---

183. On משפט here cf. Zakovitch, *The Life of Samson*, p. 51, n. 103.

184. These revelations in 22.9–12 and 22.20 are sometimes understood as dreams, though they lack the visual component common to many dream narratives. In contrast to this

Balaam is approached by Balak's messengers and offered a substantial reward for cursing the Israelites. Balaam is of two minds; after receiving clear instructions from YHWH he rejects the offer in 22.13, but his ambivalence is brought out in his response to the second request. Though he replies that he 'cannot defy the word of YHWH' (22.18), he asks the messengers to stay the night so he can have a further consultation with YHWH (22.19). This conflicted response reflects Balaam's dilemma within the story: to what extent does Balaam's power stem from his ability to call down curse and blessing, and to what extent is he a mere conduit for the intentions of the divine?

This human uncertainty is mirrored by a corresponding degree of divine ambivalence as reflected in YHWH's responses in 22.12 and 22.20. Balaam's first request is met with an absolute refusal: 'You shall not go with them'. But YHWH's second response seems to reverse this: 'If the men have come to invite you, go with them'. This ambivalence towards Balaam is played out further in the theophany which follows in 22.22–35.[185] YHWH's anger at Balaam and the attendant threat to his life posed by the angel appear to reinforce the absolute refusal of v. 12. Yet when Balaam offers to return home, he is ordered to keep on towards his destination, with the caveat that he is to speak only as YHWH instructs him (22.35). However we understand the origins of the inconsistency of YHWH's responses,[186] the change in the message reinforces the point that Balaam is entirely dependent upon YHWH's decision for his actions. Since Balak is so insistent about hiring him, and Balaam is sorely tempted by his offer, the narrator takes advantage of an opportunity to 'reeducate' both king and seer at the same time. Balak will be taught that Israel's blessedness is of a different sort from what he imagines, and Balaam will be taught a lesson about the limits of his prophetic powers.

---

position, R. Fidler has described them as 'feeble theophanies', a category of revelation common to non-Israelites in the Bible such as Abimelech (Gen. 20) and Laban (Gen. 31). See the discussion in Fidler, 'Dream Theophany', pp. 98, 123–30 and the literature cited therein.

185.   On the place of the ass narrative within the larger context of the chapter cf. Rofe, *Sefer Balaam*, pp. 40–9, 52–4; Fidler, 'Dream Theophany', p. 123 n. 94.

186.   Cf. the discussion of the question of sources in Rofe, *Sefer Balaam*, pp. 10–26, 37–45. In addition to the contradiction between vv. 20 and 22, scholars have suggested the presence of conflicting or unnecessary doublets in vv. 3a and 3b, v. 5 (the location of Balaam's home), and the repetition of the details of the envoy to Balaam in quoted direct speech in vv. 5–6 and 10–11. See further M. Noth, *Numbers* (Philadelphia: Westminster Press, 1968), pp. 171–8; G.B. Gray, *A Critical and Exegetical Commentary on the Book of Numbers* (Edinburgh: T. & T. Clark, 1903), pp. 308–13; P.L. Day, *An Adversary in Heaven: 'Satan' in the Hebrew Bible* (Atlanta: Scholars Press, 1988), pp. 45–67. For attempts at harmonizing some of these difficulties cf. Rashi, Ibn Ezra, Ramban, and Abarbanel on Num. 22.30; A.B. Ehrlich, *Mikra Ke-Pheshuto*, vol. 1, p. 283; Moberly, 'On Learning to Be a True Prophet', pp. 5–8.

The theophany itself has been characterized by Rofe as a 'burlesque' because of its satirical style.[187] Three times in 22.22–27 Balaam's she-ass turns aside to avoid the angel in his path, upsets her master and suffers a beating. These repetitions lead to the climactic interchange in 22.28–30, in which the she-ass is transformed from a dumb beast of burden to an articulate respondent capable of confronting her master. She displays understanding, perspective, and even the ability to count in her statement in 22.28. The contrast with Samuel's inability to perceive the divine in 1 Sam. 3 noted earlier heightens the irony of the situation.[188] Where Samuel needs only a brief explanation from Eli in order to comprehend the nature of the divine call, Balaam is not so quick to understand. Balaam does not react to the speaking of the ass as something out of the ordinary.[189] His response in 22.29 reflects only his anger, and this in an ever intensifying fashion, moving from the actual striking in 22–27 to the threat of killing, from thrashing with a staff to smiting with a sword. His use of the verb התעלל to imply physical and emotional suffering of an extreme kind is a clear exaggeration of his situation.[190] Yet it is noticeable that the ass doesn't explain her behavior in terms of the appearance of the angel,[191] as if the fact of the revelation is not hers to reveal.[192] The second remark of the she-ass goes beyond this to display a temporal perspective on the nature of their relationship.[193] Balaam's response here is a monosyllabic לא, indicating that he accepts the reasoning of the ass; the discrepancy between the length of her question and the brevity of his answer may indicate that his perception of the situation has begun to change. Perhaps he has become aware of the oddness of the fact of a talking animal, or he has been persuaded by the logic of her argument.

---

187. Rofe, *Sefer Balaam*, pp. 49–52.

188. Cf. Chapter 3, p. 85.

189. On the phenomenon of the ass's speech cf. Savran, 'Beastly Speech', pp. 36–41.

190. Exod. 10.2; Judg. 19.25; cf. J. Licht, *A Commentary on the Book of Numbers* (Jerusalem: Magnes Press, 1995), vol. 3, p. 23 (Hebrew).

191. B. Levine, *Numbers 21–36*, p. 157. Ramban, however, suggests that the ass only perceived something frightening, but did not identify it as a divine emissary, and hence did not mention it to Balaam.

192. Beyond the statement that 'YHWH opened the mouth of the she-ass' (22.28) the extent of divine involvement in this process is left unclear. Abravanel assumes that Balaam was prevented from seeing the angel by divine intervention, since the text does not say that YHWH opened the eyes of the ass. This seems unlikely, as the accompanying servants (v. 22) also see nothing unusual. By contrast Nachmanides maintains that the revelation to the ass included both seeing and speaking. Levine [*Numbers 21–36*, p. 158] suggests that the unusual term רגלים (instead of פעמים) is indicative a divinely ordained journey such as the pilgrimage festivals (Exod. 23.14).

193. The use of the phrase עד היום הזה brings this out even more humorously. Levine, (*Numbers 21–36*, p. 158), argues that הסכן הסכנתי should be understood as 'to gain advantage', as the verb has the sense of controlling another; cf. esp. Ps. 139.3.

This sets the stage for the revelation of the angel in 22.31, which is the final stage in an unusual gradated revelation – from the opening of the ass's eyes, to her speaking, to Balaam's seeing of the angel. Balaam's response to this sight differs from the ass's efforts to avoid the wrath of the angel, as his actions reflecting a posture of prayer and obeisance: 'And he bowed low to the ground' (22.31). Here we see no element of *fascinans*, only the sense of *mysterium tremendum*. Balaam's abject acceptance of divine authority, even to the point of saying 'I have sinned' in v. 34, highlights the change which has overtaken him, from complete confidence in himself and his own perceptions to a new awareness of his relationship to YHWH. This level of understanding will be expanded upon in Num. 23–24, particularly in 24.1, where Balaam achieves further insight in such a way as to change the nature of his self-definition, and thereby completing his inner transformation.[194] The 'response to the response' in 22.35 comes to sharpen the central point of the theophany. As with all prophetic figures, Balaam's free will is limited; he may 'go with the people' who have summoned him, but he can speak 'only that which I speak to you'.[195]

3. *Transformations of the Motif*

i. *1 Samuel 3*. In a text where the absence of emotional reaction exceeds even the laconic norms of biblical narrative, this section of Samuel's theophany offers a surprising variation on the patterns of response described above. On the one hand, there is no direct mention of Samuel's reaction to the experience he has just undergone. Unlike Jacob and Moses, we see no response to the divine, no mixture of *fascinans et tremendum*, no expression of creature consciousness. This omission should not necessarily be taken to imply that such a response by Samuel was not forthcoming, but that the narrator's concern lies elsewhere.[196] As in the earlier sections of the narrative the focus is placed more intensively upon Samuel's relationship with Eli than upon his relationship with YHWH. Given the ferocity of YHWH's condemnation of Eli in the preceding oracle, one might assume that just as YHWH has rejected Eli, Samuel would also turn

194. Savran, 'Beastly Speech', p. 36. See also the discussion of the stages of Balaam's awareness in T. Wolf-Monson, '"Nofel Vegalu'i Einayim"', *BM* 47 (2002), pp. 237–56 (Hebrew).

195. In this sense the entire episode of the ass can be seen as an attempt to clarify the double message of 22.20.

196. Simon, *Prophetic Narratives*, p. 69, nonetheless finds such a reaction to be present in Samuel's reluctance to mention the name of YHWH in v. 10. Fokkelmann, *Narrative Art and Poetry in the Books of Samuel* (p. 171), however, raises the possibility that this is simply an ellipsis which need not indicate anything about Samuel's state of mind at this point. On the other hand, LXX[L] includes the name YHWH in both vv. 9 and 10.

his back on the priest. Yet Samuel's reaction to Eli displays an emotional complexity which reflects the depth of his relationship with Eli as his mentor and surrogate father.

The reaction as described in v. 15 begins with Samuel lying in place passively. The continuation of the verse shows him physically active, opening the gates of the temple[197] as a way of avoiding facing Eli, and as an attempt to evade the implications of the theophany for his own future.[198] This is brought out by the structure of v. 15. The verse begins with two consecutive imperfect converted clauses, describing continuity of action in Samuel's external behavior. The third clause, however, reverses the order of subject and verb and has a different temporal force. Rather than continuing the narrative sequence, it relates to the previous sections of the verse in an explanatory manner, indicating that Samuel's actions to this point have been by way of putting off the confrontation with Eli. This is the only moment in the narrative in which the narrator gives us an inside view of Samuel's thoughts, and at that moment we see that Eli is foremost in his mind. Thus while we cannot know what Samuel is thinking anywhere else in the narrative, here the nature of his anxiety is absolutely clear. How can he possibly tell his mentor/father figure of the terrible end prophesied for him?[199]

16	And Eli called to Samuel and said:	ויקרא עלי את שמואל ויאמר
	'Samuel, my son'.	שמואל בני
	And he said:	ויאמר
	'Here I am'.	הנני

The post-revelation conversation between Eli and Samuel in v. 16 follows the pattern of call and response described in 3.4–8, only here it is Eli and not YHWH who is addressing him. As before, Eli calls Samuel 'my son', and Samuel's answer consists of הנני. While the term is used more often than not for divine–human encounters,[200] here it has been established as the phrase of choice between Eli and Samuel.[201] Earlier, in vv. 5–8, Samuel responded three times with the term הנני precisely because he thought Eli was calling him. But in v. 16 the tension is much greater because Eli

197. On the significance of this act see chapter 5.
198. Simon, *Prophetic Narratives*, p. 68.
199. Simon, *Prophetic Narratives*, p. 68, sees in Samuel's response a reflection of the idea of the reluctant prophet.
200. Gen. 22.1,11; 31.11; 46.2; Exod. 3.4; Isa. 6.8; cf. also Isa. 52.6; 58.9; 65.1; in contact between humans it appears in Gen. 22.7; 27.1,18; 1 Sam. 22.12. Fidler, 'Dream Theophany', p. 107, suggests that the term originally reflects a spontaneous response to a command, but it becomes a stylized response in preparation for receiving a divine oracle.
201. With YHWH Samuel uses other words, as we see in v. 10.

actually *is* calling him; this time Samuel knows exactly what he has to say, and does not want to say it.[202]

Eli's speech to Samuel in v. 17 encapsulates Samuel's dilemma very plainly. If he is to be a prophet, then revelation cannot remain a private matter, and it is incumbent upon him to reveal what has been spoken to him. It reflects that moment of truth in the relationship between mentor and apprentice where the trainee has surpassed his teacher in ability and in knowledge. How can the teacher convince the student to demonstrate his knowledge without betraying his teacher? The mentor, too, is put to the test: can he live up to the demand of the moment and accept the difficult new reality placed before him? Eli's speech allows Samuel no room for compromise. Neither YHWH's oracle nor Eli's adjuration has within it any message of comfort or support which are the standard fare of prophetic call narratives.[203] YHWH's speech was perfectly clear in its condemnation of Eli's house, including a divine oath (v. 14) to impress upon Samuel the seriousness of the matter. The chiastic structure clearly highlights the oath formula in (C) as the center of the chiasm, paralleling the severity of the oath in YHWH's speech in 14.[204] Eli's words are equally clear in emphasizing to Samuel the nature of his responsibility, repeating in (B) and (B') the injunction not to keep anything back.

17

What did He say to you?	(A)	ויאמר מה הדבר אשר דבר אליך
Don't hide anything from me.	(B)	אל נא תכחד ממני
Thus and more may God do to you	(C)	כה יעשה לך אלהים וכה יוסיף
If you hide a single thing from me	(B')	אם תכחד ממני דבר
of all that He said to you.	(A')	מכל הדבר אשר דבר אליך

Both speeches focus upon a דבר, essentially upon the same divine oracle; YHWH's speech anticipates that many will hear it – כל שמעו תצילנה שתי אזניו – and Eli states twice that the oracle is not to be kept secret. As YHWH promises in v. 11 to perform (עשה) a certain action against the house of Eli, so Eli's oath assumes that this precise fate will devolve upon Samuel (עשה) should he not deliver the message as required.[205]

202. One cannot but sense the similarity between this dialogue and the interchange between Abraham and Isaac in Gen. 22.6–8, where הנני and בני are also pregnant with unspoken meaning.

203. E.g. Exod. 3.12; Judg. 6.16; Jer. 1.8.

204. Hurowitz, 'Eli's Adjuration', pp. 487–8; cf. Simon, *Prophetic Narratives*, p. 285, n. 37.

205. Simon, *Prophetic Narratives*, p. 70, goes so far as to describe this conversation with Eli as the equivalent of the sign in other prophetic calls, as it provides confirmation of the prophet's commission. While this is an attractive idea, it should be noted that the sign is

The responses of both Eli and Samuel in v. 18 solidify the roles which have been projected for them. Samuel, obedient to both YHWH and Eli, tells Eli 'everything' and conceals nothing, underscored by the use of the verb ויגד as the enactment of the command והגדתי לו from v. 13.[206] The triple emphasis on כחד in vv. 17–18 heightens the impossibility of denial or avoidance.[207] Eli is well aware of Samuel's attachment to him and of the boy's uncomfortable position. Yet he does not attempt to take advantage of Samuel's feelings, appealing instead to Samuel's absolute obedience to him. As Samuel followed all of Eli's commands to the letter during the call, now the phrase of compliance ולא כחד ממנו in v.18 echoes precisely Eli's command to him in v. 17. Eli's stoic acceptance of his fate – 'It is YHWH. He does what is good in his eyes' – completes the process of self-denial which has characterized Eli throughout the narrative.[208] The further repetition of עשה pulls together YHWH's promise in the oracle (אנכי עשה הנה), Eli's words to Samuel in v. 17 (כה יעשה לך) and Eli's acceptance of his fate in v. 18 (הטוב בעינו יעשה).[209] In all three cases YHWH is the subject, the doer. The statement further emphasizes the change that has taken place regarding different levels of seeing: From the darkness of night time, the blindness of Eli, and the absence of vision (חזון), to Samuel describing the theophany in terms of vision in v. 15 (מראה), to YHWH's active seeing (and doing), to the final stage in v. 21 – בשלה כי נגלה ה' אל שמואל בשלו ויסף ה' להראה – 'YHWH continued to appear in Shiloh; YHWH revealed himself to Samuel at Shiloh'.

The withholding of any information about Samuel's response to YHWH is compensated for by the extended presentation of Samuel's reactions to Eli. As Samuel mistook YHWH's voice for Eli's in the earlier section of

---

always a positive element forecasting the success of the prophet, and only here would it have an ironic sense. Hurowitz, 'Eli's Adjuration', p. 494, suggests that Eli is 'authoritatively reminding Samuel of his legal obligations as a prophet'.

206. The form והגדתי in v. 13 is often taken as a regular perfect, referring to YHWH's oracle of 2.26–36. (so M.H. Segal, *The Books of Samuel* (Jerusalem: Kiryat Sefer, 1968), p. 35; H.W. Hertzberg, *I and II Samuel* (OTL; Philadelphia: Westminster Press, 1960), p. 40, with Targum, LXX and Vulgate) However, reading the verb as a converted perfect, 'I will tell him', places the emphasis upon Samuel's act of revealing the prophecy to Eli in v. 18. See the discussion in Simon, *Prophetic Narratives*, p. 68.

207. Cf. Josh. 7.19; Isa. 3.9; Pss. 40.11; 78.4; Job 15.18; note also the usage in Jer. 38.14, 25, to answer truthfully to a prophet; cf. also Simon, *Prophetic Narratives*, p. 285, n. 36.

208. Jantzen notes the contrast with Hannah in 1.18,23 – 'What is good in His eyes'. The statement begins the process of reversing the anarchic situation described by the phrase in Judg. 17–21.

209. Eslinger, *Kingship of God*, p. 155, finds in Eli's words an admixture of piety and despair which highlights Eli's aloneness. This reading is highly suggestive, offering as it does an unusual glimpse into the heart of the rejected priest, who remains a deeply sympathetic figure at this point.

the narrative, here the narrator's description of Samuel's 'fear and trembling' before Eli shows the continuation of Samuel's relation to his mentor. It is almost as if Samuel prizes his relationship with Eli above his relationship to YHWH, and it falls to Eli to clarify to Samuel the proper order of things in v. 18.

ii. *1 Kings 19*[210]. Like other texts in which the protagonist has had prior contact with YHWH, Elijah here displays a number of different reactions, first to the appearance of the *malakh* in the desert in vv. 5–8, and then to the unusual theophany of YHWH in vv. 9–13. While Elijah shows an appropriate sense of surprise at the initial appearance of the divine[211] – הנה זה מלאך – he is not as obedient as one might expect. Told to 'rise and eat', he follows the command to eat, but does not arise. Instead, he returns to sleep – surely a unique reaction to the appearance of a *malakh*! This is usually taken as an indication of Elijah's exhaustion and despair, for he has been fleeing from Jezebel and in v. 4 asked YHWH to take his life. However, given the extent of his anxiety about Jezebel's pursuit we might expect some indication of relief at YHWH's positive response.[212] When compared with other responses to the divine in which an individual is saved from death, such as that of Hagar in Gen. 16.13, Elijah's reaction seems minimal at best. His reaction to the second appearance of the *malakh* in v. 8 is more obedient, this time rising as well as eating. This fuller response may reflect Elijah's understanding of the nature of the *malakh*[213] – but the text leaves open the question of why Elijah decides to go to Horeb. The absence of an explicit divine command allows for the possibility that the trek to Horeb is entirely his own idea, and is not a response to a divine command.[214] Indeed, there is something odd in both of these responses, wavering between passivity (returning to sleep in v. 6) and exceptional eagerness (traveling to Horeb with a 40-day fast). Moreover, the very fact of being addressed twice by the *malakh* calls for further comment. Robinson suggests that the double appearance of the *malakh* can be understood as a parallel to Elijah's being fed twice

210. A fuller analysis of this text can be found in chapter 7. The present discussion is limited to Elijah's reactions.

211. Cf. Zakovitch, 'A Still Small Voice', p. 333.

212. Throughout the chapter we are given very few inside views of Elijah's thoughts or feelings. The exceptions to this are Elijah's desire to die in v. 4, and support for the reading 'he was afraid' in v. 3 (LXX, Peshitta, and some Hebrew mss.); cf. M. Cogan, *I Kings* (AB; N.Y.: Doubleday, 2000), p. 450; Zakovitch, 'A Still Small Voice', p. 331.

213. So Simon, *Prophetic Narratives*, p. 203.

214. Cf. Robinson, 'Elijah at Horeb', p. 518. Contra, Simon, *Prophetic Narratives*, p. 204, esp. n. 123.

miraculously in 1 Kgs. 17.[215] Abarbanel understands the first eating as related to Elijah's escape from Jezebel, while the second eating is directed toward his trip to Sinai.[216] But the very fact of the repetition casts aspersions on Elijah – less than obedient, not altogether attentive, he must be called twice, where a single address suffices for most everyone else in the Bible.[217]

The next stage of response comes in v. 10, when Elijah is asked to explain his presence at Sinai. His opening words, קנא קנאתי, could be seen as such an explanation in light of his close identification with the Deity.[218] But the term is also strongly associated with the language of revenge.[219] As Zakovitch points out, Elijah describes the negative behavior of the people in a graduated sense, moving from general disobedience to more specific sins, and culminating in their desire to remove him as well.[220] The verse presents a dramatic portrait of Elijah's sense of frustration and isolation, but it is not clear what he is asking for. While the most frequent explanations suggest that Elijah is seeking protection[221] or asking YHWH to punish the people,[222] he may be presenting further justification for his earlier request to die in v. 4. The striking similarity of קח נפשי in v. 4 and his present words ויבקשו את נפשי לקחתה suggests a renewal of this request – the people are so mired in sin that he has lost all hope of their repentance.[223] The picture of Elijah which emerges is very bleak; despairing of all hope, Elijah seeks to die but YHWH revives him, not once, but twice. He proceeds to Horeb to renew his request for death, or at very least to explain himself further. In light of this his earlier comment, 'I am no better than my ancestors', indicates that he has not

215. Robinson, 'Elijah at Horeb', p. 518; B.O. Long, *I Kings, with an Introduction to Historical Literature* (FOTL; Grand Rapids, MI: Eerdmans, 1984), p. 199; Simon, *Prophetic Narratives*, p. 204.

216. Abarbanel *ad loc.* Zakovitch, 'A Still Small Voice', p. 334, balances the double appearance of the *malakh* against the double appearance in YHWH in vv. 9–12 and 13–18.

217. The parallel with the sleeping Jonah in Jon. 1.5 is striking, and adds to this negative picture of a prophet who is less than fully responsive to what everyone else understands to be a message from the divine. Cf. J. Magonet, *Form and Meaning: Studies in Literary Techniques in the Book of Jonah* (Bern: Herbert Lang, 1976), pp. 67–9.

218. In Song 8.6 it is parallel to אהבה, and is often used to describe YHWH, as in Exod. 20.5; 34.14; Deut. 4.24; 6.15.

219. 2 Kgs. 10.16–28; cf. also Exod. 20.2; Num. 25.11,13; Ps. 78.58.

220. Zakovitch, 'A Still Small Voice', p. 336.

221. Rashi, Radak, Abarbanel *ad loc*; Robinson, 'Elijah at Horeb', p. 519.

222. Gersonides *ad loc.*; Zakovitch, 'A Still Small Voice', p. 336.

223. Simon, *Prophetic Narratives* p. 206, suggests a variation on this idea: Elijah seeks to understand 'what task can remain for him in Israel?'

succeeded in changing the people's attitudes about worshipping YHWH.[224]

Thus far YHWH has not succeeded in relieving Elijah's despair. At this point the exceptional theophany of vv. 11–12, with its reversal of the usual pattern of the storm theophany, is intended to bring about just such a change in Elijah. In all the texts we have discussed this process of change stands at the forefront of the experience, and the protagonist emerges from the experience significantly transformed, whether as newly blessed or as a leader of the people. In light of this expectation, Elijah's word-for-word repetition of same speech after the theophany in v. 14 comes as a complete surprise. On the one hand Elijah has displayed the external signs of humility associated with theophany by hiding his face in his cloak in v. 13. But YHWH's question to him, while phrased in the same language as in v. 9, clearly has a different sense after the dramatic revelation of the still small voice, as if to say 'NOW, Elijah, why are you here?'.[225] At this point we expect a new response by the prophet, one which reflects his understanding in light of the theophanic experience. But the unusual use of literal repetition, rare in biblical narrative speech, reflects a lack of change in Elijah, an inability to respond to the theophany with a different perspective than what he described earlier.[226] While YHWH's question has changed in meaning as a result of the theophany, Elijah's explanation has not. Whatever the precise import of the theophany itself – whether it is to be understood as a rejection of Baal,[227] as a repudiation of the idea of violent struggle advocated by Elijah,[228] or as a foreshadowing of Jehu, Hazael and Elisha[229] – its essential message is one of change, of recognizing that YHWH does not necessarily perform according to human expectations. Elijah fails to achieve this realization for emotional or theological reasons, as pointed out by Gersonides: 'Because of his great anger over Israel's sins, he was unable to understand the meaning of this spectacle, and thus spoke

224.   Simon, *Prophetic Narratives* p. 202 suggests that a comparison with one's ancestors is often used to indicate continuity over generations, as in Gen. 46.34; Pss. 116.16; 139.13. Read in this way the phrase expresses the idea that the situation which obtained before his actions is still current among the people, and all his actions have made no difference whatsoever.

225.   Zakovitch ('A Still Small Voice', p. 341) notes a slight but significant variation between 9b and 13b, where the latter records not a דבר ה' but a קול. The variation indicates that YHWH's speech is 13b is of a different order than his previous address to Elijah, and highlights the lack of change in Elijah's response.

226.   On literal repetition see Sternberg, *Poetics*, pp. 387ff.; Savran, *Telling and Retelling*, p. 29.

227.   B. Uffenheimer, *Ancient Prophecy in Israel* (Jerusalem: Magnes Press, 1973) (Hebrew), p. 233; Cross, *Canaanite Myth and Israelite Epic*, p. 194.

228.   R.B. Coote, 'Yahweh Recalls Elijah,' in Halpern and Levenson (eds.), *Traditions in Transformation*, pp. 115–20.

229.   Zakovitch, 'A Still Small Voice', p. 343.

(to YHWH) exactly as he had earlier.'[230] Contrary to those who see this narrative as a recommissioning of the prophet,[231] YHWH's subsequent speech in vv. 15–18 effective relieves him of his prophetic commission by having him anoint his successor.[232]

---

230. Gersonides on 1 Kg. 19.13–14; Simon, *Prophetic Narratives*, p. 214. Abarbanel offers an explanation of the difference in light of Elijah's placement within the cave (v. 10) and on the rock (v. 14), but the result is unconvincing.

231. Simon, *Prophetic Narratives*, p. 209.

232. Robinson, 'Elijah at Horeb', p. 528; Cogan, *I Kings*, p. 457.

Chapter 5

TRANSFORMATION AND EXTERNALIZATION

Just as the theophany type-scene begins with a clearly marked separation from the world of normal social interaction, so its conclusion signals a return to society and to societal concerns. But the protagonist who returns is not the same person as before, nor is the world to which he returns the same as it had been. The protagonist has undergone a major change – in identity, in awareness, and in relation to the divine. The world which now receives him must also adjust itself to this change. What had been to this point primarily a private encounter must now address the outside world as well. The theophany type-scene concludes with an externalized reflection of this private moment of contact between the human and the divine, which attempts to convey some remnant of this encounter to the larger societal framework in which the protagonist functions.[1]

All theophany narratives contain at least one element of externalization of the theophany, which moves beyond personal experience to address a larger issue: the appointment of the prophet, the birth of a child, the establishment of a sacred place, or the origin of a ritual act. In all the cases to be discussed here the evanescence of the theophany is recrystallized into something that can be passed on, ritualized, or physically sensed by others who have not directly experienced the encounter with the divine. Jacob anoints a stone and vows to build a temple at the site of the theophany. Moses dons a mask to hide his shining face. Hagar bears a son who is the very embodiment of the promise spoken in the theophany. Samuel acts out the role of the prophet in the public arena. In all these cases the externalization has a dual focus. On the one hand, it carries within it a remnant or a residue of the transient experience of the divine. For the community to which the protagonist returns the externalization is evidence of the reality of that theophanic experience, and in most cases, the closest they will come to actual contact with the divine. At the same time, the externalized element signals detachment from the divine, reflecting the

---

1. On the interplay between external description and inner states see Sternberg, *Poetics*, pp. 342–64.

needs and desires of the human community, and, as such, it is a clear marker of the end of the theophanic experience.

While in many cases the externalization is focused on a single action, it may also reflect a process which takes place in stages, moving from the private to the public in a graduated fashion. In Gen. 28.18–22 Jacob's first externalized action upon waking is the setting up of the stone by his head as a מצבה, which can be visualized as repositioning the stone associated with the dream in v. 11. In so doing Jacob draws a direct line between the experience of the theophanic dream – focused in his head – and the focus of subsequent worship, the stone on which he lay his head. The next stage, the naming of the place as בית אל, recapitulates Jacob's response upon waking in vv. 16–17. The place now takes on a new identity which is to be associated with Jacob's experience, distinguishing it from its previous name, Luz. The final stage is Jacob's vow in vv. 20–22. Here Jacob consciously recalls YHWH's promise to him in the dream to accompany him and bring him home safely, offering a vow of his own: To transform the place known as בית אל into a בית אלהים where he will offer a tithe, thereby filling out the process of externalization.

In contrast to the other elements of the theophany type-scene, which are limited to the theophany narrative itself, externalization has its beginning in the theophany account but may continue beyond the narrative pericope. Indeed, one of the primary ways that the theophany narrative is contextualized within a larger narrative is by means of ever-enlarging circles of externalization. Thus, for example, Jacob's consecration of Bethel is extended in Gen. 35 to include the construction of an altar, emphasizing the narrative focus of the larger narrative around the themes of theophany, promise and fulfillment.[2] Likewise the construction of the tabernacle in Exod. 35–40 serves as the final phase of the establishment of the divine presence in the camp, more permanent than the periodic encounters with the divine reflected in the tent of meeting in 33.7–11 or in Moses' shining face in Exod. 34.39–35.[3] In the case of prophetic call narratives like Exod. 3–4. the subsequent interaction between the people and the prophet serves to anchor the theophany in the experience of the people.

Insofar as externalization serves as a reflection of the relationship between the theophany and its societal function, it will be useful to explore this phenomenon from a double point of view. From a vertical standpoint, the perspective of relations between the human and the divine, we must ask how the externalization relates to the theophany itself. Can one discern in

---

2. Cf. Fishbane, 'Composition and Structure', p. 23; von Rad, *Genesis*, pp. 337–9.

3. Polak, 'Theophany and Mediator', p. 147, suggests out that the tabernacle serves as the culmination of a process which began with Moses at the bush in Exod. 3.

the externalization something of the visual aspect of the revelation, or does it relate primarily to the verbal content of the theophany? Does the externalized element embody some other element of the theophany, albeit in a modified form? In what ways does the externalization reflect the transformation of the protagonist, and will the relationship with the divine continue past the moment of the theophany? At the same time, this element must also be examined from the horizontal perspective of the relationship between the protagonist and the human community. How does the externalizing phenomenon reflect the social framework to which the protagonist returns and in which he/she will continue to dwell? What is the nature of the new relationship between the protagonist and the community? In cases where there was a skeptical human response to the divine, the externalization reflects both axes: The externalizing element establishes the separation from the numinous, and also forges a new relationship with the human community.

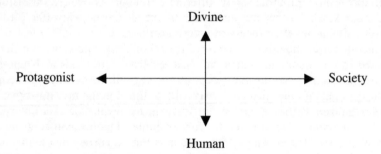

While there is, generally speaking, a preference for one or the other of these two perspectives, in certain texts there is a balance between private theophany and public experience. In Exod. 34.29–35 Moses descends from Mt. Sinai with a shining face, reflecting the fiery revelation to which he has just been privy together with this visual component, he carries with him a concrete manifestation of the tablets of the covenant, for the express purpose of passing them on to the people. The people who were too frightened to hear the divine voice in Exod. 20.18–20 are here allowed a reduced glimpse of divine glory in the form of Moses' radiant face, and a figurative representation of that voice in the words on the tablets. In this sense the externalization is a diluted version of the fiery theophany of YHWH.[4] Yet in addition to these representations of theophany, Moses also establishes a ritual framework for speaking to the people. His donning

---

4. On the ancient Near Eastern connection to the *melammu*, the aura which surrounded the head of kings and gods, cf. M. Haran, 'The Shining of Moses' Face: A Case Study in Ancient Near Eastern Iconography', in Barrick *et al.* (eds.), *In the Shelter of Elyon*, pp. 150–73 (167–8).

a veil at regular intervals establishes his authority before the people and routinizes what was a singular experience. In contrast to their fearful response to the singular experience of the divine at Sinai,[5] Moses' shining face appears before them on a regular basis, allowing them a taste of the visual aspect of revelation coupled with the words of the verbal revelation. The result is a successful means of mediating between the exclusivity of private experience of Moses before the divine (Exod. 33.18–23), and the public 'face' or mask which Moses must put on for the people.[6]

The organization of this discussion of externalization will move between these vertical and horizontal axes, oscillating between a divine–human orientation and a societal perspective. The first grouping of texts reflects a particularly close interaction with the numinous, describing how a direct theophanic encounter can result in and life or death. One positive result of this contact with the numinous is reflected in the annunciation by the Deity of the birth of a child, and in the fulfillment of the promise in its subsequent birth. In the cases of Sarah and Manoah's wife the intervention of the divine is essential to the pregnancy, for both women are described as barren. An exceptional degree of closeness to the Deity is reflected in YHWH's responsibility for the conception of the barren woman;[7] the externalization takes the form of the actual birth of the child and his naming by his parents. Diametrically opposed to this process of giving life is the account of the death of Nadav and Avihu. Fire from YHWH is the direct cause of the death of Aaron's sons, and the externalization takes place in a series of stages describing the human reactions to that death: Moses' interpretation of the event in Lev. 10.3, Aaron's reaction, the removal of the bodies, and the subsequent prohibitions against priestly drinking.[8]

In a second cluster of texts the externalization involves the appointment of a prophetic figure who is to speak on behalf of YHWH. The idea of the prophet reflected here is approximated by the LXX understanding of the

---

5. Cf. the discussion of Exod. 20.18–20 in chapter 4.

6. Cf. the discussion in T.B. Dozeman, 'Masking Moses and Mosaic Authority', pp. 21–45.

7. In both of these texts the women are explicitly described as barren, and in both cases sexual relations between the couple is not mentioned. The stories do not argue expressly for divine impregnation, but the matter is left deliberately unclear. For more on this cf. Zakovitch, *The Life of Samson*, pp. 74–83.

8. Most commentators see these prohibitions in Lev. 10.8–10. as belonging to a subsequent pericope, but their adjacency here supports another level of interpretation of the death and Nadab and Avihu; cf. the discussion in Milgrom, *Leviticus 1–16*, pp. 633–5; E. Gerstenberger, *Leviticus* (Louisville, KY: John Knox, 1996), pp. 115–27.

term נביא as προφητης, one who speaks on behalf of another,[9] as described
by Exod. 7.1 – 'I place you in the role of God to Pharaoh, with your
brother Aaron as your prophet'.[10] The authority and inspiration for this
role come from YHWH in the form of a theophanic commissioning of the
prophet (Moses, Samuel, Isaiah, Jeremiah, Ezekiel), but its externalization
is reflected in the protagonist himself taking on the public mantle of the
role of prophecy. This direct connection between theophany and
externalization is present regardless of whether the role is actually
undertaken within the narrative pericope (Samuel) or assumed by the
placement of the call narrative at the beginning of the prophet's literary
record (Jeremiah, Ezekiel). The very idea of being a spokesperson for the
Deity would seem to imply that the vertical axis would stand at the center
of the prophetic book. However, insofar as the prophet's reception (or
rejection) by the people is no less central than his relationship to the Deity,
the horizontal axis is of great significance here, more so than in the
annunciation narratives. In many instances involving the classical prophets
there is a marked tension between the horizontal and the vertical axes, as
reflected in the conflict between the demands of prophetic oracle and the
people's perception of its own best interests.[11]

   In the third grouping, the texts conclude with the establishing of a ritual
or cultic framework. The externalization in these texts is characterized by a
lack of direct contact with the Deity, and focuses primarily on the
horizontal, societal axis. The encounter with the divine is carried over only
by association: A newly (re-)established sacred place (Bethel, Peniel), a
cultic role (Moses and the mask in Exod. 34.29–35), or a ritual prohibition
(גיד הנשה in Gen. 32). While there is some degree of continuity between the
theophany and the externalization, here the latter generally results from
the protagonist's initiative, and not the bidding of YHWH. For example,
Gideon's establishing the altar *YHWH Shalom* in Judg. 6.24 has a double
focus. As a reflection of the vertical axis it is a direct response to YHWH's
message of wellbeing to Gideon in 6.23: שלום לך. The fact that Gideon
remains alive after the theophany is concretized by the naming of the altar.
At the same time the altar is established at Gideon's own volition, and it
becomes a public site with an ongoing existence (עד היום הזה). The offering
which was made at that spot by the *malakh* in 6.21 as the culmination of
the theophany becomes externalized as a site for other offerings as well.

---

   9. See S.M. Paul, 'Prophets and Prophecy', *EJ* vol. 13 col. 1150–75 (1153); B.
Uffenheimer, 'Nevu'ah, Navi', *EM* vol. 5, 690–731 (691) (Hebrew) .
   10. Cf. also Exod. 4.16.
   11. As has been often noted, Gideon's appointment as judge/deliverer in Judg. 6 also
bears some resemblance to these prophetic calls. However the externalization of that
theophany within the narrative itself consists of building an altar in 6.24. His assumption of
the role of deliverer of the people takes place only in the subsequent chapter.

While ritual itself may carry with it a sense of the recovery of the divine,[12] it also serves as a clear point of delineation between the human and the divine, between 'then' and 'now'.[13] For all these reasons, the examples to be discussed in this last section are primarily a reflection of the relationship between the protagonist and the human community.

1. *Life and Death*

A. The births of the foretold sons Isaac and Samson are the actualization of the promise made to their mothers and fathers. In the case of Samson, his birth in Judg. 13.24 is an integral part of the story, following immediately upon the disappearance of the angel and the reactions of Manoah and his wife.[14] In this sense the birth can be seen as a direct outcome of the theophany which Manoah and his wife have experienced, and therefore an externalization of it.[15] The statement that the spirit of the Lord 'began' (ותחל) to move him in 13.25 recalls the promise given to his mother in 13.5, that he will 'begin' (יחל) to deliver the Israelites. Indeed, the very notion that it is a divine spirit which arouses and impels Samson suggests a further connection between the theophanic experience of the parents and the behaviour of the son, as if this spirit is an indirect continuation of the encounter with the divine, albeit on a very different level.[16] At the same time the birth also indicates a clear break with the

---

12.   Cf. R. Rappaport, 'The Obvious Meaning of Ritual', *Ecology, Meaning and Religion* (North Atlantic Books: Richmond, Cal., 1979), pp. 173–221; C. Bell, *Ritual: Perspectives and Dimensions* (New York: Oxford University Press, 1997), pp. 8–12. M. Eliade, *The Sacred and the Profane* (N.Y., 1961), pp. 99–100, speaks of ritual as a human re-enactment of the acts of the gods; our understanding of ritual here is not so much a re-enactment of the theophany as an extension of it in a diluted fashion.

13.   Cf. J.Z. Smith, *To Take Place: Toward Theory in Ritual* (Chicago: University of Chicago Press, 1987), pp. 96–117. 'Then' is understood in Eliade's sense of *in illo tempore*, the time of divine activity represented in the mythos, while 'now' reflects human, everyday time.

14.   While most commentators see this as an integral part of the narrative, Amit, *Judges*, p. 227 sees 13.24b-25 as a sequel to the main story.

15.   The nature of YHWH's role in the woman's conception is left deliberately vague by in the text. However, the narrator's focus on the exclusivity of the relationship between the woman and the *malakh* (in contrast to her superiority in her relationship with her husband) lends support to the idea of the Deity's immanent involvement in the conception of the child. Cf. Zakovitch, *Life of Samson*, pp. 74–83; Amit, ' "Manoah Promptly Followed his Wife" ', pp. 146–56.

16.   Zakovitch (*Life of Samson* p. 72) also points out the importance of the phrase ויברכהו ה' in 13.24 to emphasize the connection between the blessing and the subsequent divine spirit in 13.25. At the same time it should be noted that Samson's personal contact with YHWH is limited to two short prayers in 15.18 and 16.28, and most commentators see Samson as more focused on his own abilities than upon YHWH. Cf. Amit, *Judges* p. 242; Josephus *Antiquities* Book 5, 8–9; Zakovitch, *Life of Samson* p. 203. A more positive view of

theophany which preceded it, for once the child is born the story proceeds exclusively on the human plane. The name Samson shows no direct connection with the preceding theophany,[17] and the divine spirit impels him toward contact with the Philistines, not with YHWH.

In the case of the birth of Isaac, the externalized conclusion to the story comes only in Gen. 21.1–2, after a break of two and one-half chapters. Sarah's astonished response and denial in Gen. 18.12–15 should be followed directly by Gen. 21.1–7. This gap is likely the result of an editorial process which omitted the original ending to make room for the subsequent narrative about Sodom and Gomorrah. A new ending for the annunciation story, the account in 21.1–7, was subsequently appended.[18] In this way the promise which stands at the center of this theophany finds its ultimate conclusion in the birth of the announced child. YHWH's direct involvement on behalf of Sarah is recalled by the pair of terms עשה/פקד in 21.1. Moreover, the name יצחק ties the externalized event closely to the theophany itself, where 'laughing' is central to the experience. The societal dimension of the externalization emerges more clearly with the development of the narrative. While the focus upon Sarah's laughter in 21.6 may have originally been part of a separate 'laughter' tradition,[19] the resulting text reveals a progression from Sarah's internal laughter in 18.12, to the exposing of that laughter by YHWH in 18.13, to a more externalized laughter by others in 21.6. In this light Sarah's comment in 21.6 that 'all who hear about it will laugh at me' serves as a 'measure for measure' response to her laughter in 18.12–15. The convoluted syntax of Gen. 21.3 emphasizes the relationship of Abraham to the birth, as well as additional

Samson's relationship to YHWH is offered by J.C. Exum, 'The Theological Dimensions of the Samson Saga' *VT* 33 (1983), pp. 30–45, and by E. Greenstein, 'The Riddle of Samson', *Prooftexts* 1 (1981), pp. 237–60 (252).

17. On the meaning of the name see Zakovitch, *Life of Samson*, p. 70; Amit, *Judges*, p. 226.

18. Westermann, *Genesis 12–36*, p. 332; T.D. Alexander, 'The Hagar Traditions in Genesis XVI and XXI', in Emerton (ed.), *Studies in the Pentateuch*, pp. 131–48 (142). Van Seters (*Abraham in History and Tradition*, pp. 202–6) follows Neff in basing the connection between 18.1–5 and 21.2 on form-critical grounds, comparing the structure of the annunciation story in 2 Kgs 4.14–17 ('The Birth and Election of Isaac in the Priestly Tradition', *Biblical Research* 15 (1970), pp. 5–18). On the reasons for the separation of Gen. 18.1–15 from 21.1–7 see Rudin-O'Brasky, *The Patriarchs in Hebron and Sodom*, pp. 61–3; Westermann, *Genesis 12–36*, p. 274.

19. E.g., a tradition in which people other than Sarah laugh at her miraculous conception and birth. Cf. Westermann, *Genesis 12–36*, pp. 333–4; the discussion of sources in Gen. 21 in Alexander, 'Hagar Traditions', pp. 141–4; Van Seters, *Abraham in History and Tradition*, p. 206. While 21.6 is usually assigned by critics to the E source, Van Seters sees 21.6 as a direct response to Sarah's question in 18.12, suggesting a closer literary relationship between the two stories.

stages of externalization reflected by the naming of the child (21.3) and his circumcision (21.4).

The third annunciation narrative, that of Hagar in Gen. 16, also has a double focus for the externalization, but of a somewhat different sort. Like the stories of Sarah and Manoah's wife, the birth of the child is the final stage of externalization of the promise given in 16.11–12. The child is promised by the *malakh*, borne by Hagar (15a), then named by Abraham (15b) as the final stage in the narrative. Since Hagar was not barren, divine intervention was not necessary to bring about conception, but it is used to enable the birth of the child under Abraham's roof. As such, the birth of the child does not reflect the same degree of divine involvement as in the previous two cases. There is, however, an additional externalized focus of the theophany in the naming of the well which is the site of the theophany in 16.14.[20] Hagar's naming of the site makes no mention of her expected birth, but only recalls the miraculous fact of 'seeing'. If we understand Hagar's words ראי אל אתה ראי as indicating Hagar's seeing of YHWH, then the aetiology refers to the *malakh* who she has seen and with whom she has conversed. On the other hand, if her words are indicative of YHWH seeing her, then the focus of her words is more properly upon YHWH's promise to provide for her and her son.[21] If the birth of the son in this case is indicative of the societal, horizontal axis, then the naming of the well relates directly to the vertical axis of Hagar's relationship with YHWH.

These three annunciation stories are also notable in that they are the only cases where a woman has direct contact with YHWH in the context of theophany.[22] While there are positive aspects to the woman's involvement in all cases, it is hard to escape the conclusion that, as in many other areas of biblical life, the woman's subservient relationship to a superior male figure qualifies the nature of the experience.[23] What men can experience

20. The location of the well on the road to שור, another term for seeing, points to this understanding of her words. Given the additional significance of seeing and the well in Gen. 21, it would seem that the confluence of *malakh*, well, and seeing/hearing in both stories is intended to emphasize the aetiological element.

21. See the discussions of Hagar's seeing in T. Booij, 'Hagar's Words in Gen. xvi.13', *VT* 30 (1980), pp. 1–7; K. Koenen, 'Wer sieht wen? Zur Textgeschichte von Gen. xvi.13', *VT* 38 (1988), pp. 468–74. Van Seters, *Abraham in History and Tradition*, p. 193, sees the well aetiology as an addition to the story.

22. See the discussion of the annunciation stories in E. Fuchs, 'The Literary Characterization of Mothers and Sexual Politics in the Hebrew Bible', *Semeia* 46 (1989), pp. 151–66; R. Alter, 'How Convention Helps us Read', pp. 115–30; Zakovitch, *The Life of Samson*, pp. 74–84; M. Calloway, *Sing, O Barren One*, (Decatur, GA: Scholars Press, 1986), pp. 12–33.

23. While a number of biblical women are recipients of messages from the divine, in no other cases are they the subjects of theophany in the way we have defined it. For example, in Num. 12, Miriam is not singled out for an individual theophany, but is treated together with

alone, women (with the exception of Hagar) must experience in the company of their husbands. And where theophany directed at men tends to reveal to them a new and different future role, one not dictated by biological concerns, theophany to women is limited to granting divine approval for childbirth, which, in the cases of Sarah and Manoah's wife, has been withheld for unclear reasons. The relative freedom of the male protagonist is contrasted with the woman's more limited, biologically dictated role. Moreover, the responses of the women are more restricted, and the theophany does not establish an ongoing relationship with YHWH.

B. The inverse of this equation between theophany and life can be seen in the direct intervention of YHWH to bring about the death of Nadab and Avihu in Lev. 10.[24] This is the diametrical opposite of the annunciation stories, not only in the actions of YHWH, but in the externalization of these deaths in a series of human responses in 10.3–7.[25] The two priests are guilty of encroachment, of coming too close to the divine precincts, and are killed by YHWH.[26] The process of externalization begins in Lev. 10.3, where Moses interprets and explains YHWH's actions to Aaron. The unusual formula הוא אשר דבר in 10.3 ('This is as he said'), may indicate an adapted quotation of an earlier speech by YHWH,[27] but is better understood as a new revelation to Moses in conjunction with the deaths of Nadab and Avihu.[28] Whether the verse is understood as justification for

Moses and Aaron throughout the theophany. She is singled out only for exceptional censorship by the punishment of leprosy. Rebecca appeals to YHWH and receives an oracle in Gen. 25.22, but the language indicates the request for an oracle, which is different from theophany. Zipporah is involved in the attempt by YHWH to kill Moses (or his son) in Exod. 4.24–26, but her involvement is limited to her saving actions; there is no oracle directed at her, and her perceptions of the divine are not recorded.

24.   This theophany differs from others we have discussed in that the divine is manifest only in the form of a lethal fire, and there is no direct verbal message from YHWH. The narrative nonetheless conforms to the structure we have seen in the other theophany texts: 1) preparation/separation (the incense offering in 10.1); 2) the appearance of the divine in fire (10.2); 3) human response (death of Nadab and Avihu); 4) externalization in the elements to be discussed below.

25.   These are responses to the death of Nadab and Avihu rather than reactions to the appearance of the divine as in other theophany narratives. Moses' explanation of the events in v. 3 is the closest the narrative comes to a response as discussed in the previous chapter.

26.   Cf. Milgrom, *Leviticus 1–16*, p. 1012.

27.   Rashi discerns a paraphrase of Exod. 29.43, Bahya hears an echo of Exod. 19.22, and Abravanel finds a reference here to Lev. 8.33–45, but none of these approximates the language of Lev. 10.3.

28.   This is suggested by Luzzato, *Commentary on the Pentateuch, ad loc.* and by Ehrlich (*Mikra Kipheshuto*, vol. 1, p. 221), and reinforced by Milgrom, *Leviticus 1–16*, p. 600, who

the punishment of the priests for their actions,[29] or as an indication of their esteem in YHWH's eyes,[30] Moses' words emphasize the vulnerable position of the priesthood as the first line of defense between YHWH and the community of Israel. Because they stand in greater proximity to the numinous, they are in greater danger. To the extent that these are YHWH's words they can be seen as part of the theophany itself; YHWH takes the life of the two priests, then explains himself through Moses' speech. The use of קרב in 10.3 recalls the description of the actions of Nadab and Avihu in 10.2 with the same verb.[31] Insofar as their death is seen as a sacrifice, it can be understood as an act which bridges the distance between the human and the divine, even merging the two spheres temporarily.[32] But if their death is understood as punishment for encroachment upon the divine, then Nadab and Avihu serve as a buffer between the human and the divine, absorbing punishment which would otherwise devolve upon the people. Read this way, their death points to the enormous gulf between the human and the divine. Moses' words in 10.3, in offering an explanation of the death of Nadab and Avihu, serve to mediate between seeing their death as an indication of closeness with the Deity and understanding it as a necessary sacrifice for the ongoing life of the people.

The process of externalization begins more properly with Aaron's response in 10.3, וידם אהרן. This has been understood variously as silent acceptance of Moses' justification, or as a strangled moan of despair.[33] In either case we see Aaron caught between the human need to mourn his sons, and the divine imperative to forego the mourning rites and to continue to officiate in the Tabernacle. Here too we see the liminal position of the priest reflected in Aaron's own behavior, as he is caught between the

---

understands דבר here as 'decree' in the present tense. If this is read as a new immediate revelation to Moses, then the content of 10.3 may be understood as a verbal revelation which accompanies the visual aspect, as in other theophany texts. However, since the place and timing of the lethal fire are far from clear, it cannot be determined whether or not Moses was present in the tabernacle when Nadab and Avihu were killed, and would have been privy to this sight. On the uncertainty of time and place in the narrative cf. E. Greenstein, 'Deconstruction and Biblical Narrative', *Prooftexts* 9 (1989), pp. 43–71.

29. Cf. the discussion in Milgrom, *Leviticus 1–16*, pp. 600–604, and in P. Segal, 'The Divine Verdict of Leviticus 10.3', *VT* 39 (1989), pp. 90–5.

30. So Philo, *Special Laws*, 2:57–58; Milgrom, *Leviticus 1–16*, pp. 634–5.

31. Note the use of the same verb as a leitmotiv in the references to this event in Lev. 16.1 (cf. LXX), Num. 43.4; 26.61. Peretz Segal suggests that the term should be read בקרבי in order to emphasize the connection with Nadav and Avihu ['The Divine Verdict of Leviticus 10.3', p. 92].

32. Cf. Philo, *Special Laws*, 2.57–58; *On Dreams*, 2.6–7.

33. Cf. *LXX* 'stupefied', and Milgrom, *Leviticus 1–16*, p. 604; B.H. Levine, 'Silence, Sound, and the Phenomenology of Mourning in Ancient Israel', *JANES* 22 (1993), pp. 89–106.

human and divine spheres. The next level of externalization, the removal of the corpses in 10.4–5, returns to the key word קרב to describe the approach to the sanctuary by Mishael and Elzaphan. In contrast to Nadab and Avihu, they approach for the purpose of removing the impurity from the sanctuary; the bodies are carried out of the camp, which means they are borne through the camp in the sight of all the people, and the death of the priests receives public recognition. In contrast to 10.3, their death is now completely exposed and externalized in the separation from the camp and the burial of the bodies.

The third phase of externalization draws a physical and psychological line between the public response of the community to death and the expected priestly response. The people may undertake a full mourning process with all the attendant rituals, but according to Lev. 10.6–7 the priests themselves are to refrain from this.[34] The death of Aaron's sons is referred to by Moses with the impersonal term השרפה אשר שרף ה', 'the burning which YHWH has burned', perhaps to distance himself from the death of his nephews, or possibly to indicate that the real focus of the priests' concern should be the sanctity of the Tabernacle, and not the death of family members.[35] The establishment of cultic instructions for priestly mourning represents the final stage of externalization, moving beyond Aaron's personal response in 10.3 (וידם אהרן) to define a code of behavior for all priests. Societal order is re-established, and the ritual guidelines reinforce the distance between the human and the divine.

If the birthing of live bodies externalizes the annunciation theophany, then the removal of the corpses of the victims concretizes the lethal theophany. The two images are brought together in Aaron's gruesome comparison of Miriam's leprosy to a stillborn in Num. 12.12.[36] Though not fatal, Miriam's affliction is similar to death, a connection which can be supported by the similar means of purification for the leper and for corpse-contamination and by the comparison made between death and leprosy in Job 18.13.[37] The drama of her being stricken with leprosy and Aaron's plea

---

34. Cf. also Lev. 21.1–4. While Milgrom sees this as an integral part of the narrative, Gerstenberger (*Leviticus*, pp. 115–16) understands the rules for priestly behavior in the continuation of the chapter as separate from the narrative.

35. Cf. Ehrlich, *Mikra Kephushuto* on 10.6. Note how אחיכם is used here to describe not Nadab and Avihu, but 'all the house of Israel'. The priests' true allegiance must be to their community, not to their family.

36. On Miriam in Num. 12 see J. Milgrom, *Numbers* (Philadelphia: Jewish Publication Society, 1990), pp. 93–9; Licht, *Numbers*, vol. 1, pp. 35–41; B.P. Robinson, 'The Jealousy of Miriam: A Note on Num. 12', *ZAW* 101 (1981), pp. 428–32; D. Schinkel, 'Mirjam als Aussätzige? Zwei Bemerkungen zu Num. 12', *ZAW* 115 (2003), pp. 94–101; P. Trible, 'Bringing Miriam out of the Shadows', *Bible Review* 5,1 (1989), pp. 15–25, 34.

37. Cf. Milgrom, *Leviticus 1–16*, p. 819, who also notes the rabbinic comparison between death and leprosy in *BT* Nedarim 64b and *Gen. Rab.* 1:29.

to Moses is not played out before the people, but is a form of reaction to the theophany reflecting the vertical axis.[38] On the other hand, the societal aspect is made explicit in 12.15, where we hear that the people's journey was delayed until Miriam was healed. While this might be taken as a refusal to travel out of respect for Miriam,[39] it is more likely a punishment of the people, an enforced pause in their progress towards the promised land.[40] The externalization of YHWH's rebuke of Miriam and Aaron in 12.8 is reflected first in Miriam's affliction and quarantine, and is then extended to the larger community by the seven day pause in their journey.

2. *Theophany and Prophetic Leadership*

a. *The Emergence of the Prophet as Externalization.*
In the texts to be discussed here the protagonist emerges as a prophet in the context of the Israelite community.[41] As noted above, the appearance of the prophet in his social role reflects the continuation or extension of the divine presence into the social framework of the community in the form of prophecy. By bringing the words of YHWH before the people the prophet's personal contact with YHWH is transformed into a public role. In this way the prophet is primarily identified with YHWH, reflecting the vertical axis of relationship between the human and the divine. At the same time the prophet's very humanness underscores the disparity between these two worlds. YHWH cannot address the community directly, nor are his words communicable to the people except by one of their own. This is reflected in the prophet's powerlessness as a human being, his vulnerability to danger from the people, as well as his helplessness before YHWH.

In these texts, the process of externalization may begin within the narrative pericope, but in all cases it extends beyond it. On this point the treatment of this element differs from our other discussion of the components of the theophany type-scene. In previous chapters we have taken careful notice of the limits of the specific pericope in order to focus on the dynamics of the theophany itself. However, despite the fact that externalization often extends beyond these limits, the presence of this element outside the bounds of the narrative should not be taken as an indication that the externalization is a secondary or supplementary component. On the contrary, the externalized element is the primary

---

38. In this way it is similar in function (but not in content) to Aaron's response in Lev. 10.3.

39. Licht, *Numbers*, vol. 2, p. 47; Rashi *ad loc.*; *BT* Sotah 9b.

40. Milgrom, *Numbers*, p. 99.

41. On the relationship of the prophet to his society cf. R.R. Wilson, *Prophecy and Society in Ancient Israel*, Philadelphia: Fortress Press, 1980; D.L. Peterson, *The Roles of Israel's Prophets*, Sheffield: JSOT Press, 1980.

connective factor between the theophany and the social world which surrounds it. For the theophany to have significance beyond the private life of the protagonist, the narrative must bridge the gap between the divine and the character's social framework, in order to effect the reintegration of the character within his society. In some cases the externalization is implicit within the narrative, and made explicit only later. Although the prophets Isaiah, Jeremiah and Ezekiel do not actually assume their roles as prophets within the call narrative, this expectation is readily apparent in YHWH's statement of encouragement 'do not fear', as well as in other anticipated reactions.[42] In the form-critical analyses of Habel and others this phenomenon is often interpreted as indicating the prophet's reluctance to undertake the task.[43] While this may be true in certain cases, in our view this phenomenon is equally indicative of the conflicted social role of the prophet, and the tension between the vertical and horizontal axes.

i. *1 Samuel 3*. The opening of the temple doors in 1 Sam. 3.15 ushers in the first level of externalization of Samuel's theophany, extending the experience beyond the immediate moment of revelation to a larger frame of reference. G. Jantzen has suggested a connection between Samuel opening his mother's blocked womb in 1 Sam. 1 and his breaking through the limitation on prophecy mentioned in 3.1.[44] Samuel's opening of the gates is more than just 'business as usual', but a symbolic representation of his new public role as prophet. This theme continues into Samuuel's confrontation with Eli in vv. 16–18. As discussed in the previous chapter, reporting the details of this prophecy to Eli is the first stage in Samuel actualizing his role as prophet, for this demands not only receptivity to the divine message, but also the willingness to transmit it to those who must hear it. In vv. 16–18 Samuel acts under duress, as Eli urges him to disclose what he has been reluctant to reveal. The public aspect of prophecy receives only limited expression in these verses, as the disclosure of the prophecy is thus far limited to Samuel and Eli.

---

42. See the discussion of 'do not fear' in Fishbane, 'The Biblical OT', pp. 217–29.

43. Cf. Chap. 1, n. 13.

44. Jantzen, ' "Samuel Opened the Doors of the House of Yahweh" ' pp. 89–96, sees here a figurative 'opening up' of prophecy which had been closed down. In comparison to 1 Sam. 1 this chapter can be seen as another birth story for Samuel. Where Hannah's womb was closed by God in 1.5–6 but opened by prayer in the temple at Shiloh, so her barrenness has a clear parallel in Israel's lack of contact with YHWH in 1 Sam. 3. In both stories Eli plays the role of 'helper' who is ultimately left out of the experience of the divine. Conversely, Samuel is the פורץ, the opener of his mother's womb, and the opener of the gates of prophecy. Cf. further Gen. 38.29; Mic. 2.13.

The conclusion of the narrative in 3.19–4.1a describes a series of ever-widening circles of externalization which concretize Samuel's new role:

19 Samuel grew up, and YHWH   ויגדל שמואל וה' היה עמו
    was with him; He left none of his   ולא הפיל מכל דבריו ארצה
    prophecies unfulfilled.

20 All Israel from Dan to Beer   וידע כל ישראל מדן ועד באר שבע
    Sheba knew that Samuel was a   כי נאמן שמואל לנביא לה'
    trustworthy prophet of YHWH.

21 And YHWH continued to   ויסף ה' להראה בשלה
    appear at Shiloh, for YHWH   כי נגלה ה' אל שמואל בשלו בדבר ה'
    revealed himself to Samuel with
    the word of YHWH.

4.1a And the word of Samuel went   ויהי דבר שמואל לכל ישראל
    forth to all Israel.

This section details the transformation of Samuel's status, as well as a reversal of the entire situation which was detailed in the introductory three verses of the chapter.[45] Where Samuel was described as a youth (3.1), now he has grown up and matured (3.19).[46] Before Samuel served YHWH through indirect means such as apprenticeship to Eli and tending the lamp in the temple in v. 3, but now YHWH is 'with Samuel' (3.19), implying a closer, more direct relationship. In place of the teacher-student relationship between Eli and Samuel, the term נאמן in v. 20 implies a new intimacy between Samuel and YHWH.[47] In contrast to the prone posture of Eli and Samuel in vv. 2–3, YHWH, who has 'stationed himself' (3.10 – ויתצב)[48] and promised to 'raise up' (אקים – 3.12) his oracle against the house of Eli, does not allow any of his oracles 'to fall to the ground', i.e. to go unfulfilled.[49] Whereas earlier

45. Cf. Simon, *Prophetic Narratives*, pp. 60–1; M. Fishbane, 'I Samuel 3: Historical Narrative and Narrative Poetics', in Gros Louis (ed.), *Literary Interpretations of Biblical Narratives*, vol. 2, pp. 191–203 (193). See also the discussion of 1 Sam. 3.1–3 in chapter 2.

46. The verb גדל can also indicate an increase in authority; cf. Gen. 48.19; 1 Sam. 26.24; 1 Kgs 10.23; Qoh. 2.9. Eslinger, *Kingship of God*, p. 156, notes the contrast with Samuel as נער in 2.21.

47. Eslinger, *Kingship of God*, p. 158, suggests that נאמן here indicates 'a rare closeness between Samuel and God'. Note also the phrase בכל ביתי נאמן הוא in Num. 12.7 to describe the intimate connection between Moses and YHWH.

48. The verb has the connotation of standing; cf. *TDOT* vol. 9, p. 528.

49. The ambiguity about the antecedent of 'his words' (YHWH's words or Samuel's words?) heightens the sense of closeness between YHWH and Samuel. Cf. Eslinger, *Kingship of God*, p. 446 n. 11; Hurowitz, 'Eli's Adjuration of Samuel', p. 486.

prophetic vision was described as a rarity (3.1), now all Israel benefits from the multiplication of oracles (3.20; 4.1a). Samuel had been in a state of incomprehension before the call (ושמואל טרם ידע את ה'); now all Israel 'knows' (וידע) of Samuel's prophetic gift.[50]

The expansion of a singular theophanic experience into a broader pattern of ongoing prophecy in a public context is further reflected in 3.21, where we learn that Samuel continued to have revelatory encounters. The use of the term יסף to mark this ongoing experience recalls Eli's words to Samuel in v. 17 כה יעשה...וכה יוסיף. Whereas Eli's threat was directed at Samuel, should he *fail* to reveal the oracle vouchsafed to him, in v. 21 it implies the opposite – a continuous experience of prophecy. Moreover, he continues to have contact with YHWH through oracular revelation at Shiloh, the site of the first theophanic experience. 1 Sam. 4.1a further expands what had been a private revelation to something that is directed to all Israel.[51] In all these ways the personal transformation implicit in the narrative now receives explicit externalized confirmation.

Despite this triumphant ending, in which Eli is all but forgotten in the flush of Samuel's success, the double mention of Shiloh in v. 21 recalls the fact that the place is deeply associated with Eli, and that Samuel's fame and success as a prophet is built upon the assistance of Eli, both as mentor, and as subject of his first oracle (3.11–14). Indeed, the fullest externalization of this prophetic theophany will come in the fulfillment of that prophecy in 1 Sam. 4, with the capture of the ark and the demise of Shiloh. As 1 Sam. 4 indicates very clearly, the proof of Samuel's prophecy resides in the decline of Eli and his entire house, and ultimately, in the disenfranchising of the place which housed this revelation.[52] Externalization contextualizes the theophany in an ever enlarging framework of texts which continue to focus attention back upon the original divine–human encounter.[53]

---

50. Simon, *Prophetic Narratives*, p. 72. Fokkelmann, *Vow and Desire*, pp. 185–9, uncovers a chiastic structure in vv. 3.19–4.1a which heightens the focus on v. 20 and Samuel's public role in Israel.

51. Note how the formulation 'the word of Samuel' (in place of the more usual 'the oracle of YHWH') emphasizes the prophetic role as one who speaks for YHWH. Fokkelmann, *Vow and Desire*, p. 190 notes the iterative nature of this speech, indicating the continuing nature of Samuel's prophetic function.

52. The rise of Samuel is concomitant with the complete destruction of his predecessor. This is a pattern which will continue in the Book of Samuel, the rise of David being complete only with the complete demise of the house of Saul.

53. See the comments of Fokkelmann, *Vow and Desire*, pp. 190–2, who uses the term 'prolepsis' to describe the relationship between 1 Sam. 3 and Samuel's continuing prophetic role in the book of Samuel. For further discussion of this editorial process and the

ii. *Moses*. The externalization of Moses' appointment as prophet begins to take shape during his objections in Exod. 3.11–4.17.[54] As we have mentioned above, this is particularly noticeable in his third objection (Exod. 4.1–9), where YHWH gives him the rod *cum* snake as a tool to convince the people. Polak aptly points out the movement from the vertical to the horizontal axis as reflected in the shift from the bush, a symbol of divine presence, to the rod, a sign of human authority.[55] Both signs maintain a connection with Moses' physical being (the leprous hand, the rod in his hand), but the ultimate sign mentioned by YHWH in 4.9 is more externalized: the transformation of Nile water to blood. In the response to Moses' fifth objection YHWH announces the appointment of Aaron as Moses' spokesperson (4.14–17). All these elements function proleptically in anticipating Moses' gradual assumption of authority in the subsequent narrative. The rest of the events of Exod. 4.18–31 – the departure from Jethro, the meeting with Aaron – culminate in the fuller externalization of YHWH's promises: The gathering of the elders (cf. 3.16), the performance of the signs (cf. 4.8), and the people's acceptance of Moses' authority (cf. 4.5).[56]

Moses' assumption of his role is played out on a number of additional levels in the Sinai pericope. This is first seen in the description of Moses' role in 19.9, where one of the purposes of the Sinai experience is explained

recontextualization of a narrative in an ever enlarging group of concentric circles see Y. Zakovitch ' "Aleh Qereah, Aleh Qereah" – Circles of Interpretation in Biblical Narrative', *Jerusalem Studies in Hebrew Literature*, vol. 5, (1985), pp. 7–23 (Hebrew).

54. Fishbane, 'The Biblical OT', p. 226, suggests that the first sign in 3.12 is taken by Moses as a personal sign to him, but not as one to the people. This occasions Moses' subsequent request for signs which will impress the people. According to this reading the requesting of signs moves from the personal to the societal, following the pattern of externalization described above.

55. Polak, 'Theophany and Mediator', p. 124: 'What started as a divine revelation is now turning into human action'.

56. Cf. also Greenberg, *Understanding Exodus*, pp. 107–10; Childs, *Exodus*, pp. 101–4. Fishbane, 'The Biblical OT', pp. 226–7, adds to this list the additional sign mentioned in 4.22–23. These two signs, the blood and the death of the firstborn, foreshadow the entire plague cycle and Moses' role therein. Fishbane also points out the proleptic function of all of Exod. 1–4 in foreshadowing the events of Exod. 5–15, where the latter section presents a more public working out of Moses' call and prophetic task as specified in the former.

The curious episode of the bridegroom of blood in Exod. 4.24–26 contains within it certain elements of the theophany narrative, albeit in a truncated fashion (for commentary and bibliography on this section cf. Propp, *Exodus 1–18*, pp. 233–8). Whatever one's understanding of this text as an independent unit, in its present context it mirrors YHWH's threat to kill Pharaoh's first born in 4.23. Moses is saved by the apotropaic effect of the circumcision of his son, the externalization of which can be seen in Exod. 11–12, where Israel will be saved by the placing of blood on the doorposts to ward off the danger of the tenth plague. Cf. Fishbane, 'The Biblical OT', p. 228.

as validating Moses' authority in the eyes of the people: 'So that the people may hear when I speak with you'. Generally Exod. 19.19 – משה ידבר והאלהים יעננו בקול – is seen as the fulfillment of this process, and thus the process of externalization begins with this verse.[57] A second level of externalization comes as a result of the people's anxiety in 20.15–18 and Moses' appointment as their spokesperson. This in turn is reflected further in Moses' separation from the people and approach to Sinai in Exod. 20.18; 24.12–18, and in his descent with the tablets of the law in 31.18; 32.15–16. Yet another concretizing element is reflected in the difficult pericope of Exod. 24.1–11, where vv. 3–8 describe the ceremony of the blood of the covenant which externalizes in ritual fashion the promise of obedience made earlier in 19.8.[58]

An additional level of externalization is reflected by the use of the tradition of the people's response first in Deut. 5.25–27, and then again in Deut. 18. In the latter text we see the appointment of Moses as mediator of the covenant at Sinai as presenting a model of covenant mediator for future generations. According to Deut. 18, the appointment of prophets after Moses is a continuation of the idea of covenant mediator established at Sinai, and a further extension of this role for future generations.[59]

The examples of externalization in the Sinai traditions differ from other cases because of the unique aspects of the Sinai theophany. Since this is a group experience which is mediated by Moses, his social role is played out not only at the end of the experience, but in the midst of the theophany itself. Moreover, because the text in Exod. 19–24 has such a complex redactional history, the sense of 'before' and 'after' is not easily determined, as illustrated, for example, by the question of the place of Exod. 24.1–11 within the larger narrative.[60]

iii. *Balaam.* Balaam does not assume his prophetic role during the theophany narrative in Num. 22.21–35, but only when he arrives at Balak's territory in Num. 22.36. Indeed, the relationship between the theophany

---

57. Much depends here upon the understanding of בקול – does it mean 'in thunder' (NJPS) or 'in a voice' (JPS; KJV)? If the former, then the phrase simply describes YHWH's approach to the people, but if it is the latter, then a dialogue with Moses in the sight of the people is indicated. See. Sommer, 'Revelation at Sinai', p. 428; Childs, *Exodus*, p. 343, 368–9; Dozeman, *God on The Mountain*, pp. 47–9; Ibn Ezra at 19.19. Toeg, *Lawgiving at Sinai*, p. 33, sees 19.9 as secondary addition to the text.

58. Cf. Polak, 'Theophany and Mediator', p. 132. Likewise, the mysterious eating and drinking in 24.11 may be understood as a covenantal meal (Polak, p. 139), or as a return to normal affairs after a life-threatening experience. Cf. above, comments on Exod. 24 in the chapter on visual encounter, and C. Houtman *Exodus* (Leuven: Peeters, 2000), vol. 3, p. 296.

59. See the discussion in Polzin, *Moses and the Deuteronomist*, pp. 59–62; Toeg, *Lawgiving at Sinai*, pp. 135–6; Savran, *Telling and Retelling*, pp. 114–15.

60. Cf. Dozeman, *God on the Mountain*, pp. 106–16.

and this role is brought out only gradually in Num. 23–24.[61] On a structural level this is brought out by the parallel between the 3 + 1 pattern in the theophany, the series of four oracles delivered to Balak in Num. 23–24, and Balaam's fourfold reiteration of the divine warning to speak only what YHWH tells him to say.[62] A still closer connection between the episode of the she-ass and Balaam's role in the rest of the story is made by analogy: Balaam's relationship to Balak is drawn in inverse fashion to Balaam's relationship to the she-ass in the theophany pericope.[63] For example, the opening of Balaam's eyes by YHWH (Num. 22.31) serves as a prelude to the opening of Balaam's mouth by YHWH.[64] Unlike other prophets who undergo prophetic inspiration rather freely, Balaam is constrained to speak only what YHWH allows him to say, much as he has seen only what YHWH has allowed him to see. And as his eyes were opened to the presence of the *malakh* (22.31) only after a number of false starts, so Balaam's understanding of the significance of his prophecy comes upon him gradually, in 24.1.[65] The emergence of Balaam's prophetic voice relates on an inverted level to the motif of the sword. The sword in the hand of the *malakh* (22.23,31), usually a sign of impending violence,[66] is here indicative of the restraint of that power. In the theophany tale Balaam refrains from killing the she-ass and the angel holds back from attacking Balaam. In the larger narrative, too, violence is averted, even to the extent that Balak refrains from killing Balaam and from attacking Israel.[67] And as the *malakh* with the sword – YHWH's hidden power – was not revealed immediately, so Balaam in his oracles reveals the blessing that YHWH has in store for Israel only gradually.

The conflict between the vertical and horizontal axes is noticeable in the Balaam narrative, but it is not central to the development of the story, for there is no tension here between YHWH's plan for Israel and Israel's well-being. On the contrary, Balaam's speeches as sponsored by YHWH

---

61. The observation that there is little narrative connection between the theophany tale (22.21–25) and the rest of the story has led many commentators to conclude that the story of the she-ass has been interpolated into the larger Balaam narrative. See, for example, Rofe, *Sefer Bilaam*, pp. 10–30; Licht, *Commentary on Numbers*, vol 3, pp. 5–15. On the other hand, see the arguments for the literary integrity made by R. Alter, *Biblical Narrative*, pp. 104–7; Savran, 'Beastly Speech', pp. 35–6.

62. Num. 22.38; 23.11; 23.25; 24.10–11. This follows the mention of the same by YHWH (22.20) and by the *malakh* (22.35).

63. Cf. Alter, *Biblical Narrative*, p. 106; Moberly, 'On Learning to be a True Prophet', p. 14.

64. On the focus on seeing in the narrative cf. Rofe, *The Book of Balaam*, pp. 33–4; Savran, 'Beastly Speech', pp. 46–8.

65. Cf. Wolf-Monson, ' "Nofel Vegalu'i Einayim" ', p. 249.

66. Cf. Josh. 5.13–15; 1 Chron. 21.16.

67. Cf. Abravanel, *ad loc.*; Ehrlich, *Mikra Kephshuto*, vol 1, p. 280.

protect Israel from harm by the Moabite king. In contrast to this, the externalization of the theophany found in the call narratives of Isaiah, Jeremiah, and Ezekiel describes a heightened tension between the prophet's connection to the divine and his membership in the community of Israel. In all three cases the theophany narrative has only a limited contextualization in the narrative of the prophet's life, and a more developed intertextual relationship with other segments of the prophet's book.

iv. *Isaiah*. The externalization of Isaiah's prophetic role does not take place immediately in Isa. 6, but it is implicit in the way the narrative develops the changes in the prophet's expectations.[68] While the usual conclusion of the theophany narrative assumes the prophet's return to society, here the prophet is inducted into the heavenly realm. And where the familiar task of the prophet is the imparting of a divine word to the people, here the prophet's role is to confuse and deceive his audience. If Isaiah's theophany to this point has been marked by a sharp contrast between the human and the divine, the holy and the impure, between enchantment and alarm, now the continuation of the call is characterized by equally sharp reversal of expectation. First, Isaiah's purification in 6.5–7 excuses his association with the sinful Israelite community and paves the way for his membership in the community of heavenly retainers. YHWH's double question in 6.8 employs both singular and plural forms: 'Who shall *I* send?' – for decision rests with YHWH – but also 'Who will go on *our* behalf?'. The messenger will represent not just the Deity but the entire pantheon, as in the commissioning of Micaiah ben Yimlah in 1 Kgs 22.20–21.[69] At the same time this double question places YHWH at a certain distance from the rest of the heavenly pantheon, not unlike the way in which Isaiah stands apart from the human community.[70] Landy notes that Isaiah's response to the question in 6.8b discloses a reversal of his earlier speech: אוי לי becomes הנני, and נדמיתי becomes שלחני.[71] To this we might add that seeing has given

---

68. There is still considerable debate on the significance of Isaiah's theophany not occurring at the beginning of his book. See the discussion in Blenkinsopp, *Isaiah 1–39*, pp. 223–4; B.S. Childs, *Isaiah 1–39* (OTL; Louisville, KY: Westminster, 2001), pp. 51–4; Glazov, *The Bridling of the Tongue*, pp. 111–15, and the literature cited therein.

69. Cf. Blenkinsopp, *Isaiah 1–39*, p. 226. The plural form also recalls similar usage in Gen. 1.26, 3.22, and 11.7.

70. Landy, 'Strategies of Concentration', pp. 67–8.

71. Landy, 'Strategies of Concentration', p. 68. On the similarity between Isaiah's willingness to volunteer and the vision of Micaiah in 1 Kgs 22 see M. Tsevat, 'The Throne Vision of Isaiah', *The Meaning of the Book of Job and Other Essays* (New York: Ktav, 1980), pp. 155–76 (162–72).

way to hearing, marking a different kind of perception than that which the prophet had earlier indicated.[72]

Isaiah may expect to receive a commission like that of other prophets, but he is told that his task will be one of deception, not enlightenment.[73] Moreover, both seeing and hearing are to be thwarted by the prophetic directive.[74] The people are to experience the reverse of what Isaiah has just undergone: not seeing but obfuscation; not hearing, but confusion. Their sin will not be forgiven, but will be allowed to fester.[75] The response of the prophet, 'How long?' (6.11),[76] is met by an even harsher judgment upon the people. Magonet has detailed the multiple reversals which take place between the beginning and end of this theophany. YHWH continues to sit on his throne as in v. 1 (ישב), but the land is to be divested of all its inhabitants (ערים מאין ארם). The thrice mentioned fullness (מלא) in the description of the heavenly temple (בית) in 6.1-4 is exchanged for the threat of empty houses in 6.11 (בתים מאין אדם). In place of the depiction of a refined heavenly realm, the language of 6.11-13 presents a series of images of desolation on the earth. If Isaiah experienced a transformation from a state of human impurity to a holier reality, the people and the earth are also to undergo a transformation, but from bad to worse. Only the thinnest remnant of that supreme holiness remains in 6.13, where it has become merely the *seed* of holiness (זרע קדש).[77]

Complementing the ironic reversal of what has come before, there are significant ways in which the prophet's experience in 6.8-13 is analogous to his earlier experience in 6.1-7. For example, as the prophet describes attraction followed by fear in his initial response to the vision of the divine, so in vv. 8-11 his reactions display an initial eagerness to act as a divine

---

72. It is striking that the purification of Isaiah's lips is not necessary for seeing the vision of YHWH enthroned, but only for hearing the message. While this motif is obviously prefatory to the call to prophecy, it nonetheless points out how clearly the verbal is valued over the visual in theophany texts. Cf. V.A. Horowitz, 'Isaiah's Impure Lips', pp. 59-60, who notes that in Akkadian texts 'pure lips are necessary or desireable in order that the gods may approach'.

73. On the interpretation of vv. 9-13 see the discussion and literature cited in McLaughlin, 'Their Hearts Were Hardened', pp. 1-9; Glazov, *The Bridling of the Tongue*, pp. 126-30,

74. Landy, 'Strategies of Concentration', p. 70, perceptively suggests that this disruption of the people's perceptions recapitulates the interruption of the prophet's vision in vv. 1-4.

75. The inclusion of all three organs of understanding – heart, eyes and ears – indicates the completeness of this confusion of the senses.

76. Rather than read this as an indication of Isaiah's reluctance to accept the commission, it is preferable to understand it as a reaction to the message itself, a protest against YHWH's harshness along the lines of Pss. 6.4, 80.5, and 90.13. Cf. the literature cited by Landy, 'Strategies of Concentration', p. 74 n. 47.

77. Magonet, 'Structure', p. 93.

messenger, followed by a sense of revulsion at the nature of the message he is to deliver. Both Landy and Weiss see an essential similarity between Isaiah's experience of the divine and the message to confound human understanding. 'The more closely one listens, the less one understands, the more indefatigably one looks, the more complexity and unfathomability one finds.'[78] While this is true of Isaiah's initial experience of the divine, it is even more pronounced in the definition of his prophetic task, and in the inability of his audience to see and hear clearly. In this way the expected externalization of the prophet's commission receives an unusual twist, for the message that is externalized is one of disruption rather than communication. Vision is to be made opaque, and hearing will only dull the senses, with the result that no understanding can result from this experience. In this sense the externalization is also continuous with the prophet's experience of the divine, for as Isaiah's vision of the divine is blocked by the *seraphim*, so the people's seeing is obstructed by the prophet. Isaiah's impure lips are cleansed by a burning coal, an unusually violent image when compared to the usual means of purification by water (Lev. 15.5–27) or by cedar and hyssop (Lev. 14.2–9). Hurowitz suggests that this is intended to focus upon the intensity of the experience, but one cannot ignore the violent purification by burning (6.13 – לבער) which the people will also undergo.[79] Caught between his desire to align himself with the divine and his obligation to act as a prophet to the people, the prophet remains in limbo, neither associated fully with human world, nor able to join completely with the angelic retinue of the upper realms. The text ends with the prophet in a state of suspension between the human and the divine, exemplifying the liminal situation of the classical prophet.

v. *Jeremiah*. As with Isaiah's call, Jeremiah does not assume the prophetic mantle in Jer. 1, though the placement of the chapter at the beginning of the book and the subsequent reuse of its themes render its function obvious.[80] Here the notion of externalization begins with the image of birth, for when Jeremiah metaphorically emerges from the womb in 1.5ab he proceeds directly to the role of 'a prophet unto the nations' in 1.5c. YHWH's statement here, appointing Jeremiah a prophet (נביא לגוים נתתיך),

---

78. Landy, 'Strategies of Concentration', p. 81; cf. also Weiss, 'Image and Voice', p. 98.

79. Hurowitz, 'Isaiah's Impure Lips', p. 79. Landy, 'Strategies of Concentration', pp. 78–80, claims further that the very opacity of the simile in v. 13 is part of a strategy of obfuscation which could be understood as a further reflection of the prophet's task of obscuring clarity. On the place of this strategy within the whole of Isaiah see F. Landy, 'Vision and Voice in Isaiah', *JSOT* 88 (2000) pp. 19–25. On the reuse of this image of the confusion of seeing and hearing elsewhere in Isaiah cf. McLaughlin, 'Their Hearts Were Hardened', pp. 9–25.

80. See the comments of Carroll, *Jeremiah* p. 100, who emphasizes the public nature of Jer. 1.4–10 in authenticating Jeremiah's position as prophet.

is expanded by YHWH's placing his words in Jeremiah's mouth (נָתַתִּי דְבָרַי בְּפִיךָ).[81] As such the internalizing of the word of YHWH ('Behold I place my words in your mouth') in 1.9 is followed immediately in v. 10 with the external ramifications of the act: Jeremiah's appointment as the speaker of those words to the nations. Implicit in the internalizing of the words is an inner transformation of the prophet, although the text does not linger on this. Rather, the focus in v. 10 is upon Jeremiah's external role and his affect upon those nations and kingdoms to whom he will prophesy. The first two verbs of dedication in v. 5 – יְדַעְתִּיךָ and הִקְדַּשְׁתִּיךָ – are replaced in 1.7 by imperfect forms with a second person suffix – אֶשְׁלָחֲךָ and אֲצַוֶּךָ – which bring out the externalized aspect of this relationship, as well as its coercive nature: After being 'known' and 'sanctified', Jeremiah is now commanded and dispatched. The antecedent of YHWH's speech in v. 8 ('Don't be afraid because of *them*') must likewise refer to the final stych in v. 5, in which Jeremiah's audience, 'the nations', has been named.[82] While Jeremiah's objection in v. 6 made no explicit mention of any fear on his part, such apprehension is implied by YHWH's reply, and by the anticipation of a hostile reception. The encouragement and support implicit in YHWH's words are accompanied by hints of popular resistance to this role, which will be developed further in vv. 17–19.

It is quite noticeable that Jeremiah is given very little chance to speak in 1.4–10, and none whatsoever after his two brief answers in vv. 11 and 13.[83] And instead of hearing of Jeremiah's reaction to this commission towards the end of the narrative, we find only YHWH's words of assurance in vv. 17–19. This reaffirmation, however, goes further in disclosing a number of ominous developments regarding Jeremiah's role. The phrase תֶאְזֹר מָתְנֶיךָ is a term used in preparation for a variety of actions, among them setting out to engage in war (Ezek. 23.15).[84] The prophet's hand is strengthened by YHWH, but at the same time he is threatened: 'Do not break down before them lest I break you before them' (NJPS). The first part of this sentence is a development of the command not to fear in v. 8,[85] but with a much more ominous connotation. Not only are the people threatened, but the prophet

---

81. In a similar fashion, it is not out of the question that YHWH's promise of 'I am with you' in v. 8 should be seen as a development of יְדַעְתִּיךָ from 1.5a.

82. On 'do not fear' in prophetic speech cf. Fishbane, 'The Biblical 'OT', pp. 217ff., who points out the close connection between the statement and the appearance of an 'OT as a sign of encouragement as seen in Jer. 1.8–9.

83. Glazov, *The Bridling of the Tongue*, pp. 166–76, notes that Jeremiah is quite vocal about protesting YHWH's decrees elsewhere, and argues that a similar form of objection has been edited out of Jer. 1.

84. Lundbom, *Jeremiah, 1–20*, p. 244.

85. The parallelism אַל חִירָא // אַל תֵּחַת is a common trope: Deut. 1.21; Josh. 1.25; 8.1; Jer. 30.10; 46.27; Ezek. 3.9; 1 Chron. 22.13; 28.20; 2 Chron. 20.15,17.

is a potential target of YHWH's anger as well. The warlike imagery is
developed further in v. 18, and the very term which was used to appoint
Jeremiah as a prophet in v. 5 (נתתיך) now transforms him into a fortified
city in the face of expected hostile reactions. Likewise the use of היום in v.
18 refocuses the appointment as prophet in v. 10 in terms of battle
imagery. Holladay sees here a salvation oracle, not unlike Isa. 41.8–13, but
the ominous tone is unmistakable.[86] The image of the prophet as an
embattled city reworks the bellicose image of the encampment of the kings
of v. 15 against Jerusalem. While Holladay finds here a contrast between
Jerusalem's vulnerability in v. 15 and the prophet's fortification as a sign of
encouragement to the prophet,[87] the upshot of the image is that, although
Jeremiah will be protected, he will be no less embattled than Jerusalem
itself. The repetition of the verb להצילך, which was first seen in v. 8,
likewise bodes ill for Jeremiah, for now it is repeated in the context of
actual warfare.[88] Carroll correctly notes the ultimate passivity of the
images of the embattled city and the wall of bronze – they will resist attack,
but will not themselves be aggressors.[89] This also reinforces the image of
the prophet as the object of attack by the people, yet one who must remain
passive and absorb their anger.

　　The succession of images in the narrative progresses from the peaceful to
the warlike, reflecting the changes that the prophet will undergo. The first
impressions of the prophet in the womb in 1.5 are succeeded by the more
aggressive image of YHWH touching his mouth (1.9),[90] moving to the
sprouting of the almond branch (1.11–12), (a reflection of the blossoming
of the prophet as well, for he too is identified with the oracle of YHWH).
From here on the images become progressively more threatening and
bellicose, beginning with the boiling pot and the attendant attack on
Jerusalem (1.13–16), and ending with the prophet as embattled city with
reinforced walls (1.17–19). Not only is there a clear movement from inward
to outward, as is appropriate for one called to be a prophet (compare the
images associated with Samuel's call), but we can also discern a movement

86. Holladay, *Jeremiah*, vol. 1, p. 31.

87. Holladay, *Jeremiah*, vol. 1, p. 45; cf. also S. Talmon, 'An Apparently Redundant MT
Reading – Jeremiah 1.18', *Textus* 8 (1973), pp. 160–3. Lundbom, *Jeremiah 1–20*, p. 239, also
notes the connection of הנני in v. 15 and ואני הנה.

88. Lundbom, p. 246, notes the reuse of the phrase to describe Jeremiah's salvation from
the hand of Nebuchadnezzar in 42.11.

89. Carroll, *Jeremiah*, p. 109, also notes the connection with Jer. 15.20. He discounts the
chapter (and the book of Jeremiah as a whole) as a depiction of a real prophetic personality,
and tends to see in the book a reflection of the struggles of various Judean groups in sixth
century Judea, during the exile and afterwards. Cf. most recently C.J. Sharp, 'The Call of
Jeremiah and Diaspora Politics', *JBL* 119 (2000), pp. 421–38.

90. Lundbom, *Jeremiah 1–20*, p. 235, understands 'something more vigorous' here, and
translates '[YHWH] hit upon my mouth'.

from images of growth and development to those associated with destruction and warfare. While YHWH's reassurance addresses the prophet's own physical well-being in vv. 17–19, an unusual type of externalization is reflected here. On the one hand, Jeremiah's struggle will be outward, in conflict with the people. But at the same time, as Jeremiah will spell out in his lament in 20.7–18, his own body will become the battleground between YHWH and the people.[91]

The externalization of the role of the prophet which is anticipated in Jer. 1 finds its actual expression only later within the book. To give but a few examples: Jer. 12.3 plays upon 'knowing' and being sanctified with a plea: If you, YHWH, truly 'know' me, then 'sanctify' my enemies for slaughter. The placing of the words in Jeremiah's mouth is recalled in 5.14 and in 15.16 – נמצאו דבריך ואכלם ('Your words were found and I devoured them').[92] Jeremiah's designation as 'a prophet to the nations' is recalled explicitly in 25.13 as an introduction to Jeremiah's oracle of the cup of wrath in 25.13–38.[93] The series of six infinitives which describe the nature of Jeremiah's message in 1.10 recur throughout the book in a manner which offers a variety of different interpretations.[94] As we become aware of the extent of the intertextual connections of the call narrative with the rest of the Jeremiah book it becomes clear that we are reading not only an account of an inaugural experience, but one which anticipates the expression of Jeremiah's *agon* as a prophet throughout his career.[95]

vi. *Ezekiel.* In contrast to the detached character of the theophany narratives of Jeremiah and Isaiah, Ezekiel's elaborate chariot vision/call narrative in Ezek. 1–3 offers a greater degree of narrative closure on the experience. As the vision of the chariot approached the prophet in vv. 1.4–28, so it departs from him in 3.12–13. Moreover, as a spirit/wind uplifted him in 2.2, so a wind now carries him back to the place where the theophany began (1.1, 3.14–15). In this sense we see both the separation which precedes the revelation, as well as the prophet rejoining the community, albeit in a transformed state of mind. But the expressions of

91. Cf. M. Fishbane, 'A Wretched Thing of Shame, a Mere Belly', in Polzin, *The Biblical Mosaic*, pp. 169–98.

92. In keeping with the sense that Jeremiah's confessions reflect angrily upon his initial call by YHWH, Ellen Davis suggests that the call should be read together with Jer. 20.8 ff, marking the boundaries of the larger rhetorical structure of chapters 1–20. Cf. E. Lewin Davis, 'Arguing for Authority'.

93. Cf. Sharp, 'The Call of Jeremiah', pp. 433–8.

94. Jer. 12.14–17; 18.7,9, 24.6; 31.28,38,40; 42.10; 45.4. Cf. S. Olyan, '"To Uproot and to Pull Down, to Build and to Plant": Jer. 1.10 and its Earliest Interpreters', in Magnes and Gittin (eds.), *Hesed Ve'emet – Studies in Honor of E.S. Freirichs*, pp. 63–72.

95. Cf. Hoffmann, *Jeremiah*, vol. 1, pp. 103, 108–110, who sees in the chapter Jeremiah's own retrospective meditation on his career.

externalization here confound our expectations. The prophet's subsequent response to his experience is not the same fear and fascination which we noted in our discussion of Ezek. 1, but only bitterness and astonishment in 3.14–15.[96] As Greenberg notes, this may be a reaction to the depressing message he has been told to deliver, or an expression of his own anxiety about the rigors of the task he must perform.[97] In either case the first reaction reported in 3.14–15 is primarily an internal one, yet it is closely tied to Ezekiel's performance of his prophetic role within the society of the exiles. A contrast is drawn between the numinous spirit which carries him to and from (3.14)[98] and his own 'angry spirit', that is, his personal reaction to this event.[99] Upon his return to the exilic community in 3.15 he sits where they 'sit', but it is unclear if this sitting 'in their midst' indicates identification with the exiles or emotional distance from them.[100]

Like Isaiah, Ezekiel is compelled to take up a contrary position, forced to speak against the community in which he lives. But Ezekiel's posture is far more extreme. First, there is no mention of any sympathetic feelings for this community, nothing even so brief as Isaiah's 'How long?' The tenuous situation of the prophet regarding his allegiance to the human community is reinforced by three consecutive pericopes which embody the first stages of externalization for the prophet. Each of these defines the prophet's role in relation to the community of exiles while enumerating some unusual limitations.[101] First, in 3.16–21 he is told to be a look-out, yet he is to remain apart from the community that he warns. On the one hand, his title, צופה, is entirely a human task, a sentinel in time of war, as in

---

96.   While Isaiah's theophany is also described in the first person, here we see the protagonist reflecting upon his experience in an explicit manner. This type of response is unique to Ezekiel, and may have served as the model for Daniel's distress in the face of terrifying visions in Dan. 7.28 and 8.27.

97.   Greenberg, *Ezekiel 1–20*, p. 71; cf. the suggested parallel with Jeremiah's withdrawal from the rest of society in Jer. 15.17. Eliezer of Beaugency attributes the anger to the scroll which he has eaten, while Y. Karo sees here a desire to avoid prophesying, in keeping with the Targum's translation of משמים as 'kept silent'. Glazov, *The Bridling of the Tongue*, p. 236, sees the devouring of the scroll as the source of this bitterness.

98.   As is common in Ezekiel's visionary experiences; cf. Ezek. 3.12; 8.3; 11.1; 43.5.

99.   Block, *The Book of Ezekiel: Chapters 1–24*, p. 137.

100.   The term משמים in 3.15 may be meant to distinguish Ezekiel's reaction from that of the rest of the exiles (similar to Jer. 15.17), or to indicate that the entire exilic community shares this reaction to the exile, a reaction of 'desolation'. In Dan. 4.15, 8.27 the same verb is used in the hithpa'el to indicate confusion, but there it is a confusion borne of a lack of understanding. On the meaning of the word cf. Allen, *Ezekiel 1–19*, p. 13; Block, *The Book of Ezekiel*, p. 138.

101.   The difficulties in connecting these various sections are enumerated by Allen, (*Ezekiel 1–19*, pp. 56–7), but M.S. Odell makes a strong argument for reading Ezek. 1–5 as a unified editorial unit ('You Are What You Eat', pp. 229–48). Among the factors which favor this reading are: the absence of introductory formulas in 3.16–5.17, the literary links with 1.1–3.15,

Jer. 6.17.[102] On the other hand, he is responsible primarily to YHWH, and only secondarily to his fellow exiles.[103] Uffenheimer argues that this passage is YHWH's response to Ezekiel's silence of seven days following the theophany. Not unlike Eli's warning to Samuel in 1 Sam. 3.17, Ezekiel is here rebuked and told that he is forbidden to hide the prophecy he receives. Thus the passage reflects both Ezekiel's relationship with YHWH, as well as his essential prophetic role before the community of exiles.[104] What he does may impact upon the fate of his fellow exiles, but he is answerable first and foremost to YHWH.

In 3.22–27, Ezekiel is told to be a reprover to the people (3.27), yet he is to lock himself up within his house, and remain bound and dumb until YHWH tells him to speak. The text has clear links to the theophany described in chapters 1–3,[105] but it is far different from the earlier experience. Here the prophet is told to move from the outdoors to the confines of his own house, thereby emphasizing the limitations placed upon Ezekiel as a member of the exilic community.[106] In this way he is joined to the rest of the exiles, but also kept apart, under YHWH's control.[107] Finally, in 4.1–5.17, he is to act out a range of symbolic actions

and the failure of form criticism to explain either section within the usual form critical categories. Moreover, the narrative flow of chapters 1–5 extends and develops the process of Ezekiel's initiation to prepare him more fully for his prophetic role.

102. Cf. also 2 Sam. 13.34; 18.24–27; 2 Kgs 9.17.

103. This is contrasted with the use of the same image in the parallel passage in Ezek. 33 to bring about the people's repentance. Cf. Greenberg's discussion of the relationship between 3.16–21 and chap. 33, *Ezekiel 1–20*, pp. 90–7.

104. B. Uffenheimer, 'The Commission of Ezekiel and his Early Prophecy', *Dor Ledor*, 1995, p. 38 (Hebrew); cf. also Eliezer of Beaugency on 3.17.

105. Note the reference to the *kavod* (1.28), to the Chebar canal (1.1), to his falling on his face (1.28), and to the spirit entering him and lifting him up (2.2).

106. M.H. Segal, 'Prophet, Look-out, Reprover', in *Masoret Ubiqqoret* (Jerusalem: Kiryat Sepher, 1957), pp. 150–9 (Hebrew), suggests that Ezekiel functioned as a look-out prior to actually assuming his role as prophet. In this sense the role of look-out would be a stage on the way to assuming the vocation of prophet. More likely is Greenberg's understanding of the reprover as a semi-public role in keeping with Lev. 19.17 'You shall reprove your neighbor' (*Ezekiel 1–20*, p. 102). He also points out the connection between Ezekiel's dumbness and confinement to his house, and his subsequent prophesying within his house (8.1; 14.1; 20.1; 33.30) (p. 121). In his reading Ezekiel's bound situation within his house is a reflection of his prophetic role.

107. On the meaning of Ezekiel's dumbness see Greenberg, *Ezekiel 1–20*, pp. 120–1; Allen, *Ezekiel 1–19*, pp. 61–4; Block, *The Book of Ezekiel*, pp. 154–61; Y. Komlosh, 'Ezekiel's Silence at the Beginning of his Prophecy', (Hebrew), *Zer Ligevurot: Shazar Jubilee Volume*, ed. B.Z. Luria, (Jerusalem: Israel Society for Biblical Research, 1973), pp. 279–83 (Hebrew); Glazov, *The Bridling of the Tongue*, pp. 238–61; Davis, *Swallowing the Scroll*, pp. 48–58. If, as Davis claims, Ezekiel's dumbness is preparatory to his being a prophet of the written word, then this would constitute yet a further extension of the externalization of the prophetic role.

before the people to bring home the precise nature of their fate.[108] Taken together these activities make it clear to the people that the prophet is to be actively involved in the determination of their future, yet he is set apart from them. While this liminal aspect is part and parcel of the prophetic role, in Ezekiel's case it is carried to a new level, for, in contrast with other prophets, we do not hear of Ezekiel's identification with the people, nor of any attempt to intercede on their behalf.[109] Ezekiel's unusual situation in these chapters may also illustrate his transition from priest to prophet,[110] but more importantly these sections dramatize the dilemma of betwixt and between that is the prophet's lot.

b. *The Prophet and the Community in Crisis.*

In two noteworthy texts, in order to solve a crisis in the community of Israel, the prophet initiates contact with the divine which results in a theophany. In Exod. 32–34, Moses opens negotiations with YHWH after the episode of the Golden Calf, and the subsequent theophany leads to the renewal of the covenant and the inscribing of a second set of tablets of the law (34.27–28). Here the tablets themselves serve as the clearest example of externalization of the theophany, as the covenantal ideal reflected in the commandments will assume the function of contact with the divine. The lack of clarity as to who wrote the words on the second tablets – YHWH (34.1) or Moses (34.27–28) – lends force to the externalizing idea of the tablets. By their origin they represent a powerful connection to the Deity, yet the ambiguity allows the transition from words spoken by YHWH to a sacred relic which inscribes those words.[111] The actual transmission of the tablets to the Israelites is not recounted, and further externalization of the theophany is reflected in the shining of Moses' face (34.29–35), which will be discussed in the next section.

1 Kgs 19 presents an interesting variation on the process of externalization. If, up to now, the externalization of the prophetic call was reflected in the recipient of the prophetic call becoming a prophet, here Elijah is told to anoint *other* individuals to carry out the divine will. Elijah's failure to understand YHWH's message leads to YHWH's command to anoint Jehu, Hazael and Elisha in vv. 15–18.[112] The three anointings are stated in reverse order, as Zakovitch points out, to highlight

---

108. On the significance of these actions cf. Greenberg, *Ezekiel 1–20*, pp. 122–8; Zimmerli, *Ezekiel I*, pp. 156–78.

109. Cf. Odell, 'You Are What You Eat', p. 245–8, on the liminal quality of binding.

110. So Odell, 'You Are What You Eat', p. 236.

111. See the discussion in Moberly, *At The Mountain of God*, pp. 101–6; Childs, *Exodus*, pp. 615–17.

112. See the discussion of this text in chapter 7.

the idea that Elijah was here commanded to anoint his own successor.[113] Insofar as the only biblical model for prophetic succession is the appointing of Joshua by Moses, this command elevates Elijah to the status of Moses, in keeping with one of the central aspects of the narrative intention of the text.[114] But the analogy is double-edged: it must be remembered that the account of the appointment of Joshua follows an explicit recounting of Moses' failings, and of his punishment by YHWH.[115] Both the narrative context of the appointment of Elisha and the analogy with Moses give the impression that Elijah is to be relieved of his duties.[116] Elijah, rather than being reconfirmed as a prophet, is to be retired, and the appointment of Elisha will serve as the primary form of externalization of this theophany.[117]

This subsequent section, which deals with the anointing of Elisha in 1 Kgs 19.19–21,[118] shows Elijah as extending the process of theophany in a way which recalls Moses' shining face in Exod. 34.29–35. This brief text recapitulates the stages of the theophany type-scene, but with Elijah cast in the role of the divine and Elisha in the role of the recipient of the revelation.[119] Elisha is involved in the mundane activity of plowing until Elijah's appearance, whereupon he is separated from his family and his previous life, and transformed by Elijah casting his cloak over him. The means of this transformation, Elijah's cloak, is the very object which was

---

113. Zakovitch, 'A Still Small Voice', p. 343.

114. See the nuanced discussion of this parallel in J.T. Walsh, *1 Kings* (Berit Olam Collegeville, MN: Liturgical Press, 1996), pp. 284–9.

115. Cf. Num. 27.12–23; Deut. 3.23–28.

116. See the discussion of this text in chapter 7.

117. Despite the command to Elijah to anoint Hazael and Jehu in 19.15–16, it is Elisha who carries this out (2 Kgs 8–9), emphasizing that all further externalization of this theophany will be accomplished not by Elijah but through Elisha.

118. It is not clear if the connection of vv. 19–21 to the first part of the chapter is organic, or if it is the result of an editorial hand. Y. Shemesh, ['From Following the Footsteps of the Oxen to Following the Footsteps of Elijah – The Appointment of Elisha as Elijah's Servant (I Kings 19.19–21)', *Studies in Bible and Exegesis* vol. 5 (Ramat Gan, 2000), pp. 73–93 (73–6) Hebrew)] and Y. Zakovitch, ('Still Small Voice', p. 330) detect significant differences in the depiction of Elisha here and see 19–21 as a separate tradition. By contrast, Simon [*Prophetic Narratives*, p. 219] sees an integral connection between Elijah's rededication to his task and the anointing of Elisha. In either case, the anointing of Elisha becomes a further concretization of the process of externalization described above. See the comments of A.J. Hauser (A.J. Hauser and R. Gregory, *From Carmel to Horeb*, (Sheffield: Almond Press, 1990), p. 78) and R.L. Cohn ('The Literary Logic of I Kings 17–19', *JBL* 101 (1982), pp. 333–50 (349)) on the relationship of 19.19–21 to 1 Kgs 17–19 as a whole.

119. The fuller realization of this process takes place in the narrative of 2 Kgs 2.1–18, which can be seen as the natural continuation of our narrative. Cf. however the remarks of Z. Weismann, 'Elijah's Mantle and Consecration of Elisha', (Hebrew) *Shnaton* 2 (1977), pp. 93–9. On the relationship between 1 Kgs 19.19–21 and the prophetic initiation narrative see Shemesh, 'Footsteps of the Oxen', pp. 76–8.

involved in the theophany in v. 13, protecting Elijah from the presence of the divine.[120] Elisha is singled out by Elijah from among the rest of the workers, as is indicated by the seemingly superfluous detail והוא בשנים העשר in 19.19.[121] As YHWH commanded Elijah 'go, return' in v. 15, so Elijah tells Elisha לך שוב in v. 20.[122] In both cases the verb עבר is used to describe the encounter (19.11,19).[123] Walsh has observed that Elisha's meeting with Elijah parallels the encounter between Elijah and YHWH earlier in the chapter.[124] However, there is an element of reversal here as well, for now it is Elisha who feeds the people, not YHWH.[125] This positive attitude toward family and people continues the critique of Elijah from 19.1–18. Where Elijah only receives food from the *malakh* in 19.5–8, Elisha prepares and dispenses food to the people. Likewise, where Elijah is given to sudden appearances and disappearances (1 Kgs 18.10–12), Elisha asks permission to bid farewell to his family, and his kiss is a clear gesture of affection and respect for those he leaves behind.[126] All this bespeaks a positive relationship with the people which contrasts sharply with Elijah's less than generous attitude in 1 Kgs 17–19.[127] Elisha will serve Elijah (and thereby YHWH), but as a symbol of externalization will remain closely connected with the people.[128]

3. *Ritual/Cultic Demarcation of the Divine*[129]

A number of theophany narratives include within them the mention of ritual behavior which is seen to derive from the theophany. The concept of

---

120.   On the significance of the cloak cf. Simon, *Prophetic Narratives*, pp. 219–20.

121.   Ehrlich, *Mikra Kephshuto*, vol. 2, p. 316 understands Elijah as observing eleven teams of oxen go past him before choosing Elisha with the twelfth pair. Cf. also Shemesh, 'Footsteps of the Oxen', p. 82.

122.   In both cases there is a release from the prophetic task, though Elijah's is permanent and Elisha's is but temporary. Contra, cf. Shemesh, 'Footsteps of the Oxen', p. 86.

123.   Walsh, *1 Kings*, p. 281. The verb is also used in 2 Kgs 2.11,14 regarding the transfer of prophetic authority; cf. W.J. Bergen, *Elisha and the End of Prophetism* (Sheffield: Sheffield Academic Press, 1999), p. 49.

124.   Cf. Walsh, *1 Kings* p. 281.

125.   Hauser, *From Carmel to Horeb*, p. 78.

126.   Shemesh, 'Footsteps of the Oxen', p. 84 draws an interesting parallel with Gen. 2.24: Elisha leaves his parents here not to bind himself to a woman, but to attach himself to Elijah as his new master.

127.   Cf. Shemesh, 'Footsteps of the Oxen', p. 80.

128.   Shemesh, 'Footsteps of the Oxen', p. 89 points out the repetition of Elisha's distribution of food to the people in 2 Kgs 4.42–43.

129.   The application of anthropological theories to biblical theophany narratives is done with full awareness of the serious difficulties inherent in using ritual theory to illuminate narrative texts. Among these problems is the difference between the actual performance of ritual behavior and its literary representation in a narrative framework. Despite this,

ritual which will be employed here is derives from the understanding of the connection between ritual behavior and contact with the numinous as suggested by studies in the phenomenology of religion. M. Eliade has defined ritual activity as a human attempt to re-enact the deeds of the gods in order to create a sense of *in illo tempore*, an attempt to recover the power and energy associated with the ordering of the cosmos in a primordial fashion.[130] The idea of ritual as a means of sanctifying the world stands at the center of Eliade's understanding, and ritual activity is closely linked with a sense of human participation in the divine *mythos*. In order to adapt this idea to the Bible it must be modified, for YHWH is deemed incomparable and his deeds can be mimicked in only a limited fashion. In a religious system where contact with the divine is limited to certain individuals and particular circumstances, one of the functions of ritual/cultic behavior is to extend the idea of such contact with the numinous to a larger audience. Understood in this way, the rituals described here are less an attempt to recover a mythic act of the gods, than a limited replication of the encounter between the human and the divine which is present in the theophany. Ritual activity of this sort is inspired by contact with the numinous, and can be seen as a human response which seeks to transfer some of the power of that encounter to a human audience.[131]

Since the sphere of the numinous cannot be imitated or recovered, ritual in the Bible can serve another, almost paradoxical purpose: to clarify the boundary between the human and the divine.[132] Insofar as ritual serves as a focus for understanding proper relationship to the sacred, its very repetitiveness heightens the awareness of the gap between the idea of contact with the divine and the reality of everyday human existence. On the one hand ritual may function to clarify the limitations of human society, emphasizing human fallibility in the face of the divine.[133] But it may also serve a redemptive function, offering an idealized structure for correct

conceptualizing the relationship between ritual and the sacred can be helpful in understanding the connection between the theophany event and its externalized manifestation in a ritual-like fashion. See the thoughtful comments of M. Odell, 'You Are What You Eat', p. 237, n. 34. On the relationship between ritual-like behavior and rite cf. C. Bell, *Ritual*, pp. 138–69.

130. M. Eliade, *Myth and Reality* (New York: Harper and Row, 1963), pp. 1–20; 39–53; idem, *The Sacred and The Profane*, pp. 68–113, esp. pp. 99–100. See the discussion of Eliade in Bell, *Ritual: Perspectives and Dimensions*, pp. 10–11.

131. Thus J.Z. Smith understands temple rituals as enabling this type of communication between the human and the divine, both by focussing attention on the sacred place and by 'ritual repetition and redundancy' (*Imagining Religion* (Chicago: Univ. of Chicago Press, 1982), p. 54). For a fuller discussion of the place of ritual in the priestly worldview see. F.H. Gorman, Jr., *The Ideology of Ritual* (Sheffield: Sheffield Academic Press, 1990).

132. 'Ritual is a means of performing the way things ought to be in conscious tension to the way things are' (Smith, *To Take Place: Toward Theory in Ritual*, p. 109).

133. Smith, *Imagining Religion*, p. 63.

relations between the human and the divine. This may have the effect of
allowing the society to correct a failed encounter with the divine, to right a
relationship which had gone wrong.[134]

i. *Genesis 28*. Verses 18 and 19 of Gen. 28 describe a series of external
behaviors on Jacob's part which can be seen to correspond to his internal
reactions to the theophany in vv. 16–17.[135] These verses mark the densest
concentration of repeated words in the narrative, recapitulating and
reinterpreting his earlier actions, with the result that the מקום of the
theophany is redefined in a manner which brings together all the threads of
the narrative. At the same time the series of externalizations here occur in a
graduated fashion which proceeds outward from the theophany.

Jacob's waking (וישכם) is to be understood differently from his reactions
in vv. 16–17. The verb as employed here does not refer to waking from
sleep, but to physically rising up from inactivity. It is frequently used
prefatory to some action,[136] and it is this sense which is most appropriate
here.[137] Fokkelmann's insightful analysis of Jacob's anointing of the stone
takes careful note of repeated words from v. 11 – מראשותיו, שם, אבן, and
נצב/מצבה – and of the order of their occurrence in vv. 16–19. Jacob's
actions here – taking, placing, and anointing the stone – mimic the original
act of placing the stone by his head, but now with a very different intent.[138]
They signal the next stage of his response, moving from the wonder and
increased awareness of vv. 16–17 to the performance of actions intended to
symbolize the emergence of the divine into the human world. The marking
of the site as a מצבה has cultic significance – whether for his own personal
recognition when he will return to this spot (Ibn Ezra), or in order to turn
it into an altar at a later time (Kimchi).[139] Fokkelmann suggests that the
anointing of stone is symbolically equivalent to Jacob's 'anointing' the
sullam in the dream.[140] And since Jacob's own head had earlier touched the
stone, the parallels with v. 11 suggest an analogy between the anointing of
the stone and Jacob's dreaming. As the dream reveals the representation of
divine presence in a manner internal to Jacob, so the anointing of the stone
and its establishment as a sacred pillar are the externalization of this

134. Cf. Smith, *To Take Place*, pp. 96–117.
135. See the discussion in chapter 4.
136. E.g. Gen. 19.27; 21.14; 22.3; Num. 14.40.
137. It makes little sense to assume that Jacob returned to sleep after the intensity of his
reactions in vv. 16–17. Fokkelmann notes the unusual occurrence of the root שכם in Gen. 20.8;
21.14; and 28.18 to describe actions undertaken in the wake of contact with YHWH. Cf.
Narrative Art in Genesis, p. 65, n. 41.
138. Fokkelmann, *Narrative Art in Genesis*, pp. 66–73.
139. On the significance of the מצבה in ancient Israel cf. *TDOT*, vol. 9, pp. 483–94.
140. Fokkelmann, *Narrative Art in Genesis*, p. 67.

experience. The confluence of מצבה and מצב (28.12), of stele and *sullam*, implies a connection between the dream and Jacob's response here. As the *sullam* connected heaven and earth in a visionary manner, the stone will bring together heaven and earth in a ritual, cultic fashion.

The next stage of this externalizing process is the naming of the anonymous site, as reflected in the movement from v. 11 (המקום) to vv. 16–17 (המקום הזה) to v. 19 (המקום ההוא).[141] The place that Jacob understood as בית אלהים in v. 17 is now concretized as בית אל; while בית אלהים can be a generic term for a temple,[142] בית אל gives the same idea a specific location. The combination of setting up the stele and announcing the name of the place reflects the dual nature of Jacob's experience of a vision followed by speech. Although he was the passive recipient of both the vision and the speech during the theophany, now his own actions and words are manifestations of the change which has occurred within him. It is precisely in this sense that the theophany experience is understood to be transformative. This may be reflected in the awareness of the nature of the divine in the world, the cognizance of a newly defined task (as in prophetic call narratives), or in the confluence of the two. Jacob's actions here bespeak a new sense of purpose, as well as a new sense of self.

A further development of the meaning of מקום is reflected in the observation that this place did in fact have a name – Luz – but that name is now obsolete. The narrator here makes no direct mention of the venerable cultic history of Bethel, for better or for worse. In his description of Luz the term מקום is not used, but rather העיר, simply 'the city' with no numinous associations.[143] The repetition of the term בית in the place name anticipates the construction of a temple which is promised in v. 22. If

---

141.   While הזה refers to the immediate present, ההוא points to something which has already been mentioned, and as such is at a greater distance from the initial reference to the phenomenon. Cf. *GKC* 136b.

142.   E.g. Josh. 9.23; Judg. 17.5; Dan. 1.2.

143.   S. Ahituv [*Joshua* (Jerusalem: Magnes, 1995) (Hebrew), p. 275] and Y. Kaufmann (*The Book of Joshua* (Jerusalem: Kiryat Sepher, 1976) (Hebrew), p. 200) suggest that Luz may have been the 'secular' name of Bethel, which would explain the distinction drawn between the two names in Gen. 28. N. Ne'eman, 'Bethel and Beth-Aven', *Zion* 50 (1985), pp. 15–25 (Hebrew), maintains that Israelite sanctuaries were often built on the outskirts of existing Canaanite settlements. He further suggests (p. 16) that the original name of the sanctuary was בית אבן, in keeping with the focus of the stone throughout the narrative in Gen. 28. Fokkelmann, *Narrative Art in Genesis*, p. 68, sees here a certain degree of ridicule of Bethel, in contrast with Sarna (*Understanding Genesis*, p. 194), who sees the entire story as a polemical aetiology directed at resacralizing a Canaanite shrine. One should also note the inner-biblical polemic against the Tower of Babel in Gen. 11, where the building of עיר ומגדל is deemed negative by YHWH and therefore destroyed. Cf. Y. Zakovitch, *Through the Looking Glass: Reflection Stories in the Bible*, pp. 60–2; Lipton, *Revisions of the Night*, pp. 99–104. On the history of Bethel cf. H. Brodsky, *ABD* vol. 1, pp. 710–12.

בית אלהים in v. 17 represents the notion of the indwelling of the Deity, and בית אלהים in v. 22 represents a to-be-constructed temple, then בית אל as a place name in v. 19 combines the two. This is entirely appropriate to the naming of the place in light of the symbolic anointing of the מצבה, somewhere between ritual and revelation, intended to ground the theophanic experience in a concrete fashion. Thus the externalization of Jacob's experience moves from his realization of the nature of the experience (16–17), to setting up and anointing the stele (18), to naming the place (19).[144] This latest stage might be termed the most mundane in that it is the most external, employing a standard aetiological formula. But even here מקום continues to have a charged meaning, in keeping with Jacob's remarks about the unique sanctity of the place in vv. 16–17.

20	And Jacob made a vow, saying:	וידר יעקב נדר לאמר
	If God will be with me,	אם יהיה אלהים עמדי
	and protect me on the journey that I am on,	ושמרני בדרך הזה אשר אנכי הולך
	give me food to eat and clothing to wear,	ונתן לי לחם לאכל ובגד ללבש
21	And if I return safely to my father's house,	ושבתי בשלום אל בית אבי
	YHWH shall be my God.	והיה ה' לי לאלהים
22	And this stone, which I set up as a pillar,	והאבן הזאת אשר שמתי מצבה
	will be a house of God,	יהיה בית אלהים
	and I will give a tithe from whatever you give me.	וכל אשר תתן לי עשר אעשרנו לך

The final stage of Jacob's response to the theophany moves beyond the narrative present to address anticipated experiences in the future. If Jacob's actions in 18–19 were the active counterpoint to the visual sequence of the dream, then his vow in vv. 20–22 corresponds point for point to YHWH's promises in v. 15. Recalling the promise of הנה אנכי עמך – (28.15 – 'Behold I am with you') Jacob vows אם יהיה אלהים עמדי – (28.20 – 'If God will be with me'); ושמרני בדרך הזה אשר אנכי הולך (28.20 – 'And protect me on the journey that I am on') looks back to 28.1 ושמרתיך בכל אשר תלך ('And I will protect you wherever you go'); Jacob's

---

144. The graduated process of externalization in this text is strikingly parallel to the graduated presentation of what Jacob sees in his dream in 28.12. See the discussion above, Chapter 3.

anticipated return home (ושבתי בשלום – 'I will return in peace' – 28.21) also recalls YHWH's assurance: והשבתיך אל האדמה הזאת – (28.15 – 'I will return you to this land'). Moreover, if we take Jacob's words והיה ה' לי לאלהים – (28.21 – 'YHWH will be my God') not as the beginning of the apodosis of the oath but as the final line of the protasis,[145] we should see this as parallel to YHWH's promise of v. 15: כי לא אעזבך.[146] Thus far the vow recapitulates YHWH's promises to Jacob, but v. 22 goes further in extending the process of externalization of the theophany. The aspects of temple building and tithing referred to here move Jacob's response from the personal to the ritual level. The building of a temple is a further stage of concretization of his experience, going beyond the transformation of a single stone into a stele. Here Jacob uses the term בית אלהים not in its metaphorical sense as in v. 17, but as a reference to the building of an actual temple which he vows to support by tithing himself. The anointing of the stone may have been a private act, but the building of a temple is an attempt to carry over the private experience of the divine into the public world of ritual worship.

While YHWH repeatedly mentions ארץ (28.13,14) and אדמה (28.14,15) as his points of reference, Jacob continually refers to בית אלהים (28.17,22) and בית אבי (28.21). Whereas YHWH's allusions to the land are absolute – this spot, the entire land – Jacob's references to בית are made in relation to an opposing point, whether horizontal or vertical. Jacob's first reference to בית אלהים in v. 17 is set in opposition to שער השמים, and contrasts the earthly house with the heavenly gate.[147] Correspondingly, בית אבי in v. 21 as the point of return is contrasted with the road he has recently embarked on. These are the poles of Jacob's experience – heaven and earth, home and away. The final reference to בית אלהים redefines the stone he has anointed as 'the first brick' of his temple in progress in response to the experience

---

145. So Fokkelmann, *Narrative Art in Genesis*, pp. 75–7; Kimchi, Nachmanides, *ad loc.*; Lipton, *Revisions of the Night*, p. 76; Peleg, 'Going Up and Going Down', pp. 165–70 and the literature cited therein. See also Fidler's comparison with the vow of King Keret following a vision – ('Dream Theophany', p. 43). Contra, cf. von Rad, *Genesis*, p. 287; T. Cartledge, *Vows in the Hebrew Bible and the Ancient Near East* (Sheffield: Sheffield Academic Press, 1992), pp. 168–75. The reversal of subject and predicate in 28.22 marks the shift in subject and the beginning of the apodosis. In the biblical context it would make little sense for Jacob to be so completely overwhelmed by the theophany and yet to refrain from committing himself to YHWH until his life experience 'proves' this to be the case.

146. Both phrases restate what had been mentioned earlier: אם יהיה אלהים עמדי ('If God will be with me') is recalled in והיה ה' לי לאלהים ('YHWH will be my God'), and כי לא אעזבך ('I will not abandon you') repeats והנה אנכי עמך ('And behold, I will be with you'). The phrase לא אעזבך implies an intimate connection as in Ruth 1.16, where עזב is used in opposition to דבק. Cf. also 2 Kgs 2.2,4.

147. See the discussion of this opposition in Chapter 4.

of the theophany,[148] and as a reflection of what Fokkelmann calls the 'growing' of the stone through the narrative – from stone, to pillar, to temple.[149]

The promise of the tithe at the very end of Jacob's vow has both an external and an internal aspect. On one level, the function of such tithes was to provide for the ongoing functioning of the temple which received the donations, for sacrifices, for donations to the priests, etc.[150] The reference implies not only the extension of the theophany into the sphere of temple worship, but also that the singular, one-time experience Jacob undergoes is to be replaced by an ongoing temple cult of worship to the Deity. In this sense the transformation of stone to stele to temple is paralleled by the change from choosing the stone, to anointing the stone, to tithing. In both sets of examples one moves from an act of relative inconsequence (choosing the stone) to an event of heightened one-time significance (anointing the stone/stele), to an ongoing activity of continuing ritual importance (tithing). But on another level, the promise of the tithe reveals an internal reaction by Jacob, in the manner of *do ut des*. What YHWH promises to give him Jacob vows to return in worship. Ending the pericope in this way signals the completeness of the transformative experience – from stone to pillar to temple; from stone/place to land; from singular experience to routinized worship; and from gift to Jacob to gift for YHWH. Jacob's final expression transforms the sense of intimate connection of the theophany into an ongoing relationship marked by reciprocity. While the rest of his oath refers to YHWH in the third person, in 22c Jacob shifts to the second person to address YHWH directly, the only place in the narrative in which Jacob does this. The language here emphasizes the mutuality of YHWH's gift and Jacob's gift; it is not given to the priests or the temple treasury, but directly to YHWH – עשר אעשרנו לך.

---

148. Lipton, *Revisions of the Night*, pp. 80–92 draws a close connection between Jacob's dream and ancient Near Eastern dreams regarding temple building. See also the discussion of the dream of Gudea in V.A. Hurowitz, *I Have Built You an Exalted House* (*JSOTS*, 115; Sheffield: Sheffield Academic Press, 1992), pp. 31–57.

149. Fokkelmann, *Narrative Art in Genesis*, p. 79.

150. E.g. Deut. 14.22; Neh. 10.38–39. On tithes in the Bible cf. M. Haran, 'Ma'aser', *EM* vol. 5, pp. 204–12; M. Weinfeld, 'Tithe', *EJ* vol. 15, col. 1156–1162; J. Milgrom, *Leviticus 23–27* (AB; N.Y.: Doubleday, 2000), pp. 2421–31.

ii. *Genesis 32.*

30	And Jacob named the place Peniel:	ויקרא יעקב שם המקום פניאל
	'For I have seen God face to face	כי ראיתי אלהים פנים אל פנים
	and my life was spared'.	ותנצל נפשי
31	And the sun rose on him	ויזרח לו השמש
	as he passed by Penuel.	כאשר עבר את פנואל
	And he was limping on his hip.	והוא צלע על ירכו
32	Therefore the Israelites do not eat the thigh muscle	(A)	על כן לא יאכלו בני ישראל את גיד הנשה
	which is on the hip socket	(B)	אשר על כף הירך
	to this day.	(C)	עד היום הזה
	For Jacob's thigh was dislocated	(B′)	כי נגע בכף ירך יעקב
	at the hip socket.	(A′)	בגיד הנשה

The externalization in this episode takes a different form to that which we found in Gen. 28, and its function is different as well. On the one hand Gen. 32.30–32 provide closure to the story by following up on clues given in the first part of the narrative. The sunrise, which was anticipated in 32.24, finally appears in v. 31, where it serves as both a temporal marker and an indicator of a shift in focalization from the character Jacob back to the narrator. The wounding of the thigh first mentioned in v. 25 returns in v. 32. As Jacob was alone in 24a, he is once again alone in v. 31, in contrast to the intense contact with the angel in the rest of the narrative, especially the dialogue and blessing in vv. 26–29.[151] But at the same time these elements are transformed in a number of interpretive moves by which the externalization comes to explain the narrative. The temporal frame also shifts dramatically from עד עלות השחר to עד היום הזה, from story time to the real time of the narrator. The angel's dislocation of Jacob's thigh in v. 25 took advantage of a point of weakness, but in v. 32 it is recalled to indicate discipline and respect for the deeds of the ancestor. From לא יכל in v. 25 –

---

151. On the structure of the story and the relationship of the first and last sections cf. Geller, 'The Struggle at the Jabbok', pp. 37–47.

the angel's inability to defeat Jacob by normal means – we move to
לא יאכלו in v. 32 to describe the behavior of the children of Israel. It will be
noticed that all these moves go from the personal to the public, from the
immediacy of the event to a reflective perspective on its significance.

Verse 30 combines a place aetiology with realization of the danger
involved in the encounter. The transition to this final section is effected by
the sudden mention of place in the last phrase of v. 29, ויברך אתו שָׁם, which
has had no real significance up to this point.[152] However, the naming of the
place in v. 30 is a reflective response to the theophany, both the *fascinans*
(ראיתי אלהים פנים אל פנים) and the *tremendum* (ותנצל נפשי).[153] We noted in
the previous chapter how Jacob's realization that the encounter was
fraught with danger comes only at the end of the encounter, after the
departure of the angel. If, in Gen. 28, Jacob's naming of the location comes
as the culmination of his actions with the stone, here the naming precedes
everything else. The act of naming grows out of the experience of the
theophany; the primacy of the place name is an analogous externalization
of Jacob having received his new name in v. 28. He who struggles with
אלהים is he who sees אלהים face to face, (despite the fact that there has been
no seeing in the narrative to this point). By means of the aetiology we have
emerged from the solitary confines of the theophany and returned to the
world, where naming is a sign of social identity.[154]

The point of focalization of the narrator continues to move further away
from Jacob in v. 31, as he is observed moving past Peniel as the sun rose
upon him. As sunrise and morning in the Bible are not infrequently
associated with a new beginning and an end to suffering,[155] so Jacob has
crossed over the river successfully, having moved from night to daylight.
The verse has the sense of a retrospective glimpse on the scene,[156] the risen

152.   Cf. Westermann, *Genesis 12–36*, p. 519. We might translate it 'then and there' to give
the sense of immediacy in time and place.

153.   Zakovitch argues for a second, more hostile, meaning of ראה פנים connected with
war, as in 2 Kgs 14.8–11; cf. 'Jabbok, Peniel, Mahanaim, Beth-El', p. 192.

154.   The contextualization of the story within the anticipated conflict with Esau in Gen.
32–33 (as discussed in Chapter 2) develops this more fully. The focus on seeing the face of his
adversary in 32.20, and Jacob's comment to Esau in 33.10, 'Seeing your face is like seeing the
face of God', are further externalizations of Jacob's statement 'I have seen God face to face'.
Note also the connection between Jacob's prayer in 32.11 – הצילני נא – and Jacob's reflection
that, as a result of the encounter with the angel ותנצל נפשי – 'my life was saved'.

155.   E.g. Ps. 30.6; 2 Sam. 23.4; Lam. 3.23.

156.   The phrase זרחה לו is unusual, and should be understood as equivalent to זרחה על as
in Exod. 22.1, where it means the sun shines upon him, e.g. illuminates him so that he can be
seen. In both cases the character is viewed by others. Cf. S.M. Paul, *The Laws of the Book of
the Covenant in Light of Cuneiform and Biblical Law* (*VTS*, 18; Leiden: Brill, 1970), p. 86.

sun illuminating him for all to see,[157] in contrast with the darkness which has prevailed since the beginning of the pericope. In addition to the sense of Peniel as the place of the face of God, the remark that Jacob had passed Peniel indicates that the previous experience, the naming and the realization of being saved, is over (Peniel as פנה, ended).[158] The mention of Jacob's limping in 31b is directly connected with this change, for the external limp contrasts with the inner change. Instead of seeing an outward sign of blessing to go with his newly changed name, we see an external indication of injury, or vulnerability. Prior to this point we did not know if the angel's actions had left him wounded, but now, in the light of day, at a distance from the divine, the extent of the injury is made clear.

The final stage of externalization of the experience is seen in the prohibition against eating the thigh muscle in 32.32. The oddness of the connection between the story and the interdiction is even greater because the prohibition is directed at the Israelites as a group, and not at Jacob himself. The connection between the Israelites and Jacob is reinforced through the phrase ירך יעקב, which is an expression for the descendants of Israel in Gen. 46.26 and Exod. 1.5.[159] Jacob, following his name change, now comes to stand for the group identity of the Israelites, who are symbolically represented by the renamed Jacob/Israel.[160] Moreover, it is the 'touching' of the thigh by the angel (mentioned twice in vv. 25, 32), which is of special significance here. The verb נגע has within its semantic range the sense of 'to do harm', as is generally assumed to be the case here.[161] However the verb appears more than a few times in the context of theophany, most specifically regarding a divine touch.[162] In the texts we have studied this is most noticeable in Jer. 1.9 and Isa. 6.7, but one also finds physical contact with an angelic messenger in 1 Kgs 19.5,7, and in Dan. 8.18; 10.10,16,18. In poetic texts YHWH's touch creates cosmic upheaval in Amos 9.5 and Pss. 104.32; 144.5. Given its occurrence in theophany texts, it seems likely that נגע in Gen. 32 is multivocal, implying both injury and divine touch. In light of Jacob's name change to Israel, and in light of the dramatic interpretation of the name which claims the ability

---

157. Rashbam compares this with Gen. 29.25, 'And it came to pass in the morning, Lo, it was Leah'.

158. Jer. 6.4 uses פנה in this sense. One might also understand it as 'God has departed', alluding to the end of the theophany; cf. Westermann, *Genesis 12–36*, p. 520.

159. Cf. also Judg. 8.30. The thigh is symbolic of virility in Gen. 24.2 and Gen. 47.29. Cf. Geller, 'The Struggle at the Jabbok', p. 50.

160. The Israelites as a group do not exist in Genesis, but only come into being in Exod. 1 as the transformed sons of Jacob/Israel. See the comment of M. Greenberg on Exod. 1.9 (*Understanding Exodus*, p. 20).

161. E.g. Gen. 12.17; 26.11; Josh. 9.19; 2 Sam. 6.9.

162. Cf. also the comments by Fishbane, 'The Biblical "OT"', p. 224 n. 38.

to overpower even the divine, Jacob's wound is double-edged. The Israelites are to refrain from eating the thigh muscle because it has become sanctified by divine touch, much as Jacob has been transformed by the touch of the his wrestling partner.[163]

This gloss on Jacob's experience refers twice to the sciatic nerve, at the beginning and end of the verse (A), (A′), surrounding the description of Jacob's injury.[164] Thus the prohibition carries with it essential aspects of Israelite identity – distinctive dietary restriction (ingestion) and a distinctive lineage (progeny).[165] Jacob's limp is a sign of both his vulnerability and his blessedness, and the Israelites partake of both.[166] Israel refrains from eating the sciatic nerve as a way of continuing the 'limp', the state of vulnerability to YHWH reflected by Jacob's new name, Israel.[167] Likewise the phrase 'the children of Israel' refers here to the nascent nation of Israelites, as opposed to the more limited sense of Jacob's sons. Jacob's thigh is both the place of the wound and, paradoxically, the place of blessing. The concentric structure of the verse – ABCB′A′ – highlights the notation עד היום הזה at the center of the verse, redirecting the temporal sense of the story to a present moment. This further externalization of the story brings it into the contemporary experience of the writer and the Israelites. Here the ritual prohibition of eating the thigh muscle is at once a reenactment of Jacob' struggle, and an indication of the difference between the human and the divine.[168]

---

163.   N. Stahl, *Law and Liminality in the Bible* (Sheffield: Sheffield Academic Press, 1995), pp. 75–89, finds ambivalence here about the character of Jacob and his right to the blessing.

164.   On the meaning of גיד הנשה cf. S.E. Loewenstamm, 'Gid Hannasheh', *EM* vol. 2, col. 480–1 (Hebrew). Stahl (*Law and Liminality*, p. 81 n. 17) notes that both כף ירך and גיד הנשה match each other as containing a double metonymy: כף and ירך both refer to the male genitals (cf. S.H. Smith, '"Heel and Thigh": The Concept of Sexuality in the Jacob-Esau Narratives', *VT* 40 (1990), pp. 464–73); גיד connotes the genitals in Job 40.17, and נשה may be a euphemism for זכר in a sexual sense.

165.   H. Eilberg-Schwartz, *The Savage in Judaism* (Indiana University Press: Bloomington, IN, 1990) p. 167, makes a connection between the wound to the thigh and circumcision as a distinctive mark of lineage. Insofar as the dietary laws in Lev. 11 should be understood as reflecting a proper relationship to the Deity (table::altar), the fact that Jacob's wound is divinely caused would be further support for the prohibition against eating the thigh muscle (see the discussion in Milgrom, *Leviticus 1–16*, pp. 718–36). Cf. also the suggestive remarks about the connection between this story and Exod. 4.24–26 in Geller, 'The Struggle at the Jabbok', pp. 57–9.

166.   Cf. Geller, 'The Struggle at the Jabbok', p. 55, on the double sense of the name Israel in the narrative. Cf. also Stahl, *Law and Liminality*, p. 82.

167.   In its literal meaning of 'El rules' (cf. Geller, 'Struggle at the Jabbok', p. 53) or 'El judges' (Coote, 'The Meaning of the Name *Israel*', p. 140).

168.   On ritual as a means of highlighting the difference between the human and the divine cf. Smith, *To Take Place*, p. 110.

iii. *Exodus 33–34*. At the conclusion of the pericope Exod. 32–34,[169] we find
an example of externalization which encapsulates many of the themes we
have examined in this chapter. In Exod. 34.29–35, Moses descends from
the mountain holding a new set of the tablets of the law, and also possessed
of a 'shining face' (קרן אור פניו). This image partakes of the theme of light
associated with divine revelation in the Bible, and owes something to the
concept of the *melammu*, an aura which surrounded gods and kings in
Mesopotamia.[170] The two elements taken together convey a sense of
personal transfiguration on the part of Moses, as well as a concretization
of the theophanic experience. Rarely do we see actual physical relics
related to the theophany, or actual bodily change. The two elements recall,
on the one hand, Moses' use of the staff in Exod. 4.17,20,[171] and on the
other, Jacob's limp after his encounter with the angel in Gen. 32.31. To a
certain extent, Moses' appearance here can be said to recapitulate the
limitation of the experience of revelation at Sinai. In 33.19–23 YHWH
does not allow Moses to see his פנים, and reveals to him something less
than a frontal view. Similarly, in Exod. 34.30 Moses reveals his own פנים to
the people, but they shrink from a direct view of his shining face.[172]

But the change in the people's response in 32.31–32 reveals a significance
difference in ritual function. Earlier, direct contact with the Deity was
compromised by the people's fear (Exod. 20.15–18) or by YHWH's refusal
(Exod. 33.19). But here Moses is able to overcome the people's fear by

---

169. On the redaction of Exod. 32–34 cf. Moberly, *At The Mountain of God*, pp. 182–6;
Smith, *The Pilgrimage Pattern in Exodus*, pp. 248–57.

170. On the language קרן עור cf. Hab. 3.4 and the discussion in R.W.L. Moberly, *At The
Mountain of God*, pp. 106–9; 177–180; B.S. Childs, *The Book of Exodus*, pp. 617–19;
Dozeman, 'Masking Moses and Mosaic Authority', pp. 21–45; W.H. Propp, 'The Skin of
Moses' Face – Transfigured or Disfigured?', *CBQ* 49 (1987), pp. 375–86. J.I. Durham, *Exodus*
(WBC; Waco, Texas: Word, 1987), p. 467 suggests that the verb קרן is used to avoid the more
common verb האיר, in order to indicate that the origin of the shining is from YHWH and not
from Moses. On the *melammu* cf. A.L. Oppenheim, 'Akkadian *pul(u)h(t)u* and *melammu*',
JAOS 63–4 (1943), pp. 31–4; M. Haran, 'The Shining of Moses' Face: A Case Study in
Ancient Near Eastern Iconography', *In the Shelter of Elyon*, p. 168; G. Mendenhall, *The Tenth
Generation* (Baltimore: Johns Hopkins University Press, 1973), pp. 52–6.

171. Cf. Polak, 'Theophany and Mediator', p. 124; Propp, *Exodus 1–18*, pp. 227–9.

172. What is the significance of Moses' not knowing that his face is glowing in v. 29? It
appears to be set off against Moses' deliberate behavior of donning and removing the mask as
a ritual act in vv. 34–35. In this sense it highlights the one-time, spontaneous nature of the
Moses' descent and the people's response in vv. 29–33, and contrasts it with the deliberate,
ritualized nature of his actions in 34–35. B. Jacob, *Exodus*, p. 1006, sees in it an indication of
Moses' attentiveness to the reactions of others, which would also be a sign of Moses' essential
identification with the community of Israel despite his physical transfiguration. Childs,
Exodus, p. 619, sees in Moses' lack of awareness of his transfiguration a reminder of his
human status: he is not transformed into a deity.

calling out and speaking to them in v. 31.[173] The people's reactions here display the dual response to the divine common to theophany narratives: fear in 34.30, followed by a willingness to approach and listen in vv. 31–32. Moreover, what was narrated as a one-time event in vv. 29–33 is described in vv. 34–35 with verbs of habitual behavior, offering 'a paradigm for continual ritual practice'.[174] The encounter between the people and Moses' shining face describes a process which repeats itself in ritual fashion, marked by Moses' donning and removing the veil to signify his unique status in the eyes of the people.[175] This ritual re-enactment of theophany effectively gives the people an opportunity to respond differently to the divine, as is appropriate to the theme of sin and forgiveness in Exod. 32–34.[176] As YHWH has forgiven the people's sin and agreed to renew the covenant with them, so the people are given a new opportunity to respond with an appropriate sense of mutuality.

The use of the veil to hide Moses' shining face acts as a mechanism for reflecting the complex status of Moses in this covenantal relationship, at once the carrier of the divine presence, and also the human leader of the people.[177] One cannot avoid comparing this to the other repeated ritual moment in Exod. 32–34, the establishment of the tent of meeting outside the camp in Exod. 33.7–11, to which Moses goes when he wishes to speak with YHWH in 34.34.[178] Here, too, a ritual framework is established for communication between the human and the divine, with Moses' role as mediator between the two realms central to the text. In both cases there is an secondary figure – Joshua in Exod. 33 and Aaron in Exod. 34 – whose function is not entirely clarified. There is a noticeable emphasis on face-to-face contact between YHWH and Moses. In both cases Moses is, on the one hand, exposed to the people (walking to the tent in 33.8–10; removing the veil in 34.33), and on the other hand hidden from the people (speaking inside the tent in 33.11; donning the veil in 34.33–35).[179] Here the veil

173. Dozeman, 'Masking Moses', p. 27, n. 35, notes how speech is privileged over sight in this section, as is often the case in biblical theophany. We would add that, as he demonstrated in Exod. 20.15–16, here too Moses is able to overcome the people's fear of hearing.

174. Dozeman, 'Masking Moses', p. 21.

175. On the מסוה as mask or veil cf. Dozeman, 'Masking Moses', p. 25; Haran, 'Shining of Moses' Face', pp. 163–5. Dozeman correctly notes that the masked Moses does not function as a 'private citizen'. Rather, the mask serves as an exceptional marker of his authority in the eyes of the people ('Masking Moses', p. 28).

176. Cf. A. Berlin, 'Numinous *Nomos*: On the Relationship Between Law and Narrative', in *'A Wise and Discerning Mind': Essays in Honor of Burke O. Long*, ed. S.M. Olyan, R.C. Culley, (Providence, RI: Brown Judaic Studies, 2000), pp. 25–31.

177. See the discussion in Stahl, *Law and Liminality*, pp. 71–3.

178. Cf. Dozeman, 'Masking Moses'. pp. 31–2.

179. Dozeman, 'Masking Moses', pp. 33–45, maintains that the double masking of Moses in 34.29–35 (he sees the both the veil and Moses' shining face as masks) serves to establish his

functions as an externalizing ritual element which helps to create a non-threatening framework for the encounter between the human and the divine, and through which the concerns of the covenant can be implemented.[180]

The externalization of the theophany through the symbolic embodiment of the divine in the shining of Moses' face in 34.29–24 concretizes the emergence of Moses as the authoritative mediator of the covenant at Sinai.[181] But both the tent of meeting in 33.7–11 and the masking of Moses are only temporary externalizations of the theophany. In the final editing of the book of Exodus both of these are superseded by a fuller, more permanent stage of externalization of the manifestation of the divine presence in the camp: the erection and dedication of the tabernacle in Exod. 40.34–38.[182]

authority as the mediator of the covenant. The appearance of Moses in this role is not unlike the emergence of the role of the prophet as an externalization of the theophany in the texts discussed above.

180.   This use of the veil in conjunction with Moses' shining face illustrates J.Z. Smith's definition of ritual as the construction of a 'controlled environment' for reflecting the tension between the exigencies of reality and 'the way things ought to be'. Cf. *Imagining Religion*, p. 63.

181.   Dozeman, 'Masking Moses', pp. 44–5.

182.   Polak, 'Covenant and Mediator', p. 147. On the relation between the tent of meeting and the Tabernacle see M. Haran, *Temples and Temple Service in Ancient Israel*, pp. 260–75.

Chapter 6

On the Lethal Nature of the Divine Presence

The instructions for the service of the priests in the tabernacle refer on numerous occasions to the danger inherent in approaching the divine.[1] The laws governing the transporting of the tabernacle in Num. 4 make clear reference to the possibility of death resulting from improper contact, whether physical or visual.[2] The guidelines for proper priestly behavior in the tabernacle precincts are punctuated with the warning (ולא ימות(ו) 'so that he (they) shall not die'.[3] The notion of contagious holiness which attaches to all things connected to the tabernacle ascribes a lethal quality to the divine when approached in an improper or unbidden way.[4] In addition to these prescriptions, there are a few narrative texts which make reference to actual death resulting from such contact. The short tale of the death of Aaron's sons in Lev. 10.1–5 offers a practical demonstration of this, their death being explained by the use of two expressions which cast their behavior in a negative light. They offer אש זרה, 'strange fire', which may be understood as an improper mixture of incense (Exod. 30.9), or as implying an improper source of fire for the offering.[5] In addition, their offering is characterized by the phrase אשר לא צוה אתם, 'which he had not commanded them'. This formulation, sharply at odds with the regular priestly formula אשר צוה ה',[6] has been taken to indicate a lack of faith in the divine fire which precedes their offering in 9.23–24,[7] or as a sign of disrespect to Moses and Aaron.[8] But beyond their improper behaviour, most commentators see a connection between their death and their

---

1. See Haran, *Temples and Temple Worship*, pp. 175–88.
2. Cf. Num. 4.15,19–20.
3. E.g. Exod. 28.35; 30.20–21; Lev. 10.6–7,9; 16.2,13.
4. Cf. Haran, *Temples and Temple Service*, pp. 176ff; *TDOT* vol. 12, p. 513; Y. Licht, 'Holy, Holiness', *EM* vol. 7, col. 43–62 (49–50) (Hebrew).
5. Cf. Milgrom, *Leviticus 1–16*, p. 598; Haran, *Temples and Temple Service*, p. 183 n. 18.
6. E.g. Exod. 35.1,10,29; Lev. 7.36; 8.5; 9.6, etc.
7. So Rashbam, who understands ויקחו in 10.1 as 'they had taken', referring to the time before the divine fire consumed the flame on the altar in 9.24.
8. Cf. *Leviticus Rabbah* 20; *Pirkei DeRabbi Eliezer*, 26. See the discussion in E. Greenstein, 'Deconstruction and Biblical Narrative', pp. 43–71.

proximity to the divine. This is reflected quite clearly in the MT of Lev.
16.1, which reads בקרבתם, 'when they drew too close',[9] implying either
entrance in the divine precincts, or 'encroachment'.[10] Thus, whatever
infraction they may be guilty of, their proximity to the divine, either in
physical or professional terms, puts them at great risk and ultimately leads
to their death.[11]

A similar sense of lethal proximity is found in the equally disturbing tale
of the death of Uzzah during the transporting of the ark to Jerusalem in 2
Sam. 6. Here the nature of the infraction is clear – touching the ark – yet in
contrast to Nadav and Avihu the narrator ascribes no contrary intention
to Uzzah. The text reports that he was killed על השל – which most
commentators understand as Aramaic for שלו, 'error',[12] and which the
Chronicler interprets as על אשר שלח ידו, 'because he put forth his hand'.[13]
Yet if anyone is to blame here, it seems that David's words and actions
indicate his own guilt, which is developed further in the self-criticism
voiced in 1 Chron. 15.13.[14] Moreover, the narrator takes care to supply a
motive which in any other context would vindicate Uzzah's behavior. The
explicit mention of the stumbling oxen and the fear of damage to the ark
would seem to be sufficient justification for transgressing the prohibition of
physical contact. However, proximity to the holy once again proves lethal,
regardless of the intentions of the individual.[15] Taken together, these two
texts are of a single mind about the danger of contact with the divine:
death will result from inappropriate encroachment upon the divine
precincts or from even inadvertent contact.[16]

Far more perplexing is YHWH's attempt to kill Moses in Exod. 4.24–26.
No reason for YHWH's actions is given within the pericope itself, and
commentators have generally offered contextual explanations such as
Moses' guilt for killing the Egyptian in Exod. 2.12, his objections to his

9.   This contrasts with the LXX here and with the MT in Num. 3.4 and 26.61, which read
בהקריבם, 'when they sacrificed'.

10.   Cf. Ibn Ezra *ad loc.*; Milgrom, *Leviticus 1–16*, pp. 1011–12; idem, *Numbers*, pp. 423–24.

11.   See Ibn Ezra's interpretation of Lev. 10.3 as well, and the idea of priestly responsibility
described by Segal, 'The Divine Verdict of Leviticus 10.3', pp. 90–5.

12.   So most traditional Jewish commentators following the Targum; cf. esp. Radak on 2
Sam. 6.7

13.   So 1 Chron. 13.10, which McCarter [*II Samuel*, p. 165], following 4QSam, takes to
reflect the original reading.

14.   Cf. S. Gelander, *David and His God* (Jerusalem: Simor, 1991), pp. 42–6; S. Japhet, *I
and II Chronicles* (Louisville: Westminster/John Knox, 1993), p. 301.

15.   Cf. J. Milgrom, *Cult and Conscience* (Leiden: Brill, 1976), p. 43.

16.   In a similar vein, the tale of Korach's rebellion in Num. 16 also describes an improper
offering. See the discussion in Milgrom, *Numbers*, pp. 414–23, and in B. Levine, *Numbers 1–20*, pp. 423–32 and the bibliography cited therein.

prophetic commission in 3.11–4.17, an inappropriate delay in circumcising his son, or as a symbolic representation of the subsequent threat to the Egyptian first born.[17] In this case there is no apparent encroachment upon the precincts of the divine; rather it is YHWH who seeks out (ויבקש) Moses. Moreover, where the previous two texts described the actual death of the protagonists, here Zipporah is successful in foiling the divine intention and in saving Moses' (or his son's) life. It appears that an attack by the Deity need not be lethal, though the precise meaning of Zipporah's heroic behavior here still escapes us.[18]

A few general points emerge from these three texts. First, contact with the divine is at least potentially lethal, if not actually so. In keeping with this there are rules for proper behavior before the divine, any infraction of which may be punishable by death. These are illustrated negatively by the stories of the deaths of Nadav and Avihu on the one hand and of Uzzah on the other. Beyond this, however, it seems that YHWH may strike out even at favoured individuals for reasons that are not necessarily justified by the character's intentions. Conversely, YHWH may refrain from lethal action for reasons that are equally unclear.[19]

These conclusions are generally justified by the idea of YHWH's complete freedom, and the corresponding unpredictability of the divine will.[20] But we would ask, how is this notion of lethal proximity to the divine applied in theophany narratives?[21] Given the priestly notion of a

---

17. See Talmon, 'Hatan Damim', pp. 93–93 (Hebrew); Y. Avishur, 'On the Demonic Nature of the Bridegroom of Blood Story (Exod. 4.24–26)', *Eshel Beer Sheva* 2 (1981), pp. 1–17 (Hebrew); B.P. Robinson, 'Zipporah to the Rescue: A Contextual Study of Exodus 4,24–6', *VT* 36 (1986), pp. 447–61; W.H. Propp, 'That Bloody Bridegroom (Exodus iv:24–26)', *VT* 43 (1993), pp. 495–518.

18. The apotropaic function of blood seems to be central to her actions, an idea which is foreign to the theophany texts we have studied. Moses' passivity is in keeping with the behavior of protagonists in the theophany narratives, and it is precisely here that Zipporah's aggressive behavior is most striking. I. Pardes, *Countertraditions in the Bible* (Cambridge: Harvard University Press, 1992), pp. 79–97, sees signs of female divinity submerged in the text, while S. Ackerman suggests that Zipporah may be acting in a priestly role here. Cf. 'Is Miriam Also among the Prophets (And Is Zipporah Among the Priests?)', *JBL* 121 (2002), pp. 47–80 (71–5).

19. Cf. Haran, *Temples and Temple Service*, p. 187 describes this 'impersonal' reaction as 'one of the outstanding characteristics of holiness in general'.

20. E.g. W. Eichrodt, *Theology*, vol. 1, p. 261.

21. H. Pedaiah, 'Seeing, Falling', p. 239, discerns three distinct levels of connection between seeing YHWH and death: 1) Actually seeing the divine as in Exod. 19.21; 2) seeing a *malakh* as in Judg. 6.22–23 and 13.21–22, and 3) prophetic encounters with the divine, as in Isa. 6. It would seem, however, that this suggested differentiation is based on distinctions in post-biblical literature, and is not inherent to the biblical texts. Thus while post-biblical texts frequently substitute contact with an angel for actual contact with the Deity, the Bible is less than clear about this distinction. Nor is there any way of determining whether the intensity of

lethal aura pertaining to all that surrounds the tabernacle and the divine service, we might therefore assume that theophany itself, which describes actual contact with YHWH, would constitute an even greater source of danger to the protagonist. If handling the appurtenances of the divine is considered to be lethal, how much more so then proximity to divinity itself. In addition to Exod. 4.24, a number of descriptions of biblical theophany give visual expression to this lethal quality by portraying an armed *malakh*. Thus, for example, in Josh. 5.13 a *malakh YHWH* appears girded for war with drawn sword in hand. In this case the intentions of the *malakh* must be clarified by Joshua, but in Num. 22.23,31 and 1 Chron. 21.16 the hostile designs of the *malakh* are immediately apparent to Balaam and to David respectively. One would therefore expect that some awareness of the danger inherent in contact with the divine would be a permanent component in all theophany narratives.

Yet this sense of the danger of approaching (or being approached by) the divine is not made explicit, nor even apparent, in all theophany narratives. First of all, it is rather striking that *no one dies* in any of the theophany narratives we have discussed.[22] Moreover, only in certain cases is the potentially lethal aspect of theophany mentioned.[23] Texts such as the calls of Jeremiah and Samuel make no mention whatever of this belief.[24] In other cases, if the theme is present at all it is understated, limited to the statement that Moses 'feared to look upon God' (Exod. 3.6), or to Ezekiel's falling on his face before the divine (Ezek. 1.28). Given the ban on seeing the divine, this last instance is most surprising, for we would expect Ezekiel, for whom the visual aspect of the theophany is so highly developed, to make some unambiguous mention of this mortal danger. What is the meaning of this lack of consistency about the lethal quality of

the encounter may have been muted by the presence of a divine intermediary. At times the מלאך seems to appear in place of YHWH (e.g. Gen. 16.7–16, 32.24–32; Judg. 13.2–25) but the situation is must less clear in Exod. 3.1–6 and Judg. 6.1–24. Yet in all these cases (excepting Gideon) the protagonist states that he/she has seen God. Moreover there is no clear biblical basis for establishing a categorical difference between prophetic and non-prophetic experience of the divine.

22. Even where the approach of the divine presence is associated with judgment of the people (e.g. Num. 14, 16), the punishment meted out is not associated with contact with the divine, but with other natural or supernatural means such as plague or earthquake. While it might be argued that the danger inherent in YHWH approaching a human protagonist is of a different nature than encounters which are initiated by humans (such as Uzzah, Nadav and Avihu), Exod. 4.24–26 (and perhaps Gen. 32.24–32) argue against this.

23. Explicit mention is made in Gen. 16.13; 32.30; Exod. 20.16; 24.11; 33.20; Deut. 5.22–23; Judg. 6.22; 13.22; Isa. 6.5. In addition, the danger inherent in the armed *malakh* in Num. 22.33 is clear from the context and from Balaam's reaction.

24. This, despite the likelihood of actual physical contact between Jeremiah and YHWH in Jer. 1.9. See above, chapter 3.

theophany? To what extent is the statement about seeing YHWH and remaining alive intended as a theologoumenon concerning all contact with the divine, and to what extent is it to be understood as the subjective response of the protagonist to the experience of theophany?

In order to shed light on this question and to assess these statements it will be useful to pose questions which reflect upon the narrative perspective of the text. We must first ask, who mentions the fear of lethal contact? Is it spoken by the protagonist, by YHWH, or by the narrator? These points will be helpful in identifying the relative authority of the statement, as well of the point of view from which it is expressed. Moreover, we would ask with what intention is it spoken? Is it intended as a warning, as a conclusion reached by the protagonist about the nature of the divine, or as an expression of relief or disbelief? Further, the narrative placement of the statement may also be significant: at what point in the narrative is the statement made? Is it an immediate response to the presence of the divine, or is it a retrospective comment upon the experience of theophany? And is there a response to the comment, or does it stand alone?

1. *Subjectivity and Objectivity*

The tension between objective statement and subjective evaluation is one of the key dynamics in the deployment of expressions of danger in the face of the divine. As we will see, in the majority of cases it is the protagonist who expresses this sentiment as an indication of his or her state of mind following the theophany. Only two cases out of nine diverge from this rule: in Exod. 33.20 YHWH says to Moses 'No man can see me and live', and in Exod. 24.11 the narrator states 'Yet He did not raise his hand against the leaders of the Israelites'. This fact suggests that the primary role of the statement is one of characterization, and that it should be taken as a significant indicator of the state of mind of the protagonist. This is further emphasized by the fact that each occurrence of the expression is a unique formulation, rather than a set formulaic expression.[25] At the same time, the occasional placement of the observation in the mouth of YHWH or the narrator indicates that the danger which is described reflects the biblical understanding that this phenomenon has an objective reality as well.

In the majority of cases, the lethal nature of the encounter is mentioned near the conclusion of the theophany, usually indicating that contact with YHWH has come to an end. In this way it often appears to be a subsequent reaction to the experience of the numinous. Thus Hagar

---

25. Certain phrases do recur, such as פנים אל פנים in Gen. 32.30 and Judg. 6.22. But while the first person plural is found in Exod. 20.15, Deut. 5.22 and Judg. 13.22, in each case a different grammatical construction is used, emphasizing the individuality of each formulation.

reflects upon her experience only after the *malakh* has ceased speaking. In her enigmatic statement in Gen. 16.13 הגם הלם ראיתי אחרי ראי, 'Have I not gone on seeing after He saw me',[26] she seems to be remarking on the quality of her experience, coupled with a realization of the nature of the divine speaker who has addressed her. Her words combine her amazement at seeing and being seen by the divine with her awareness of the danger inherent in the experience. This recognition is apparent in her words אתה אל ראי, which can be taken either as her seeing God or as God seeing her. The double sense of the expression makes it an appropriate substitute for the more usual 'face to face' expression.[27] In this sense 13b, which is correctly understood as an interpretation of 13a,[28] repeats the verb 'to see' in order to emphasize the mutuality of seeing here: she continues to see after she has been seen. As this is Hagar's only response to the triple speech of the angel in 16.9–12, it can be taken to indicate her acceptance of his instructions, and an attendant change in her attitude, since she returns to Abraham and Sarah in 16.15. Rashi's understanding of Hagar's words as a subjunctive expression – 'who would have thought' – emphasizes the subjective aspect of Hagar's observation. As elsewhere, the purpose of this subjective stance is not to cast aspersions on the nature of the experience, but to highlight the impression made upon the speaker.[29]

An even more powerful degree of subjectivity is reflected in Jacob's mention of being saved from death in Gen. 32.30, following his struggle with his unidentified assailant. Here, too, the statement reflects Jacob's realization about the divine nature of his nocturnal visitor, a realization which comes only after the he receives the blessing from his opponent, and after he has departed. Together with this realization is his awareness of his own vulnerability (ותנצל נפשי), of having survived a potentially lethal ordeal. Yet the verb ראיתי here cannot refer to visual seeing, as darkness pervades this entire encounter, and the inability to ascertain identity by

---

26. Following NJPS. The frequently accepted emendation of הלם to אלהים in order to read 'I have seen God after he saw me' is rendered less likely by the temporal sense of אחרי – Hagar's seeing God is not subsequent to Him seeing her, but simultaneous with it. Verse 13b is clearly intended to be an interpretation of 13a, אתה אל ראי, whose ambiguity indicates that seeing and being seen are simultaneous reactions. See the discussion in Westermann, *Genesis 12–36*, p. 248; Th. Booij, 'Hagar's Words', pp. 1–7; Speiser, *Genesis*, p. 117; G. Wenham, *Genesis 16–50* (*WBC*; Waco, TX: Word, 1984), pp. 3,11. Wellhausen's often cited emendation would change אחרי to ואחי, rendering 'Did I really see God, yet remained alive'; but the MT itself yields a similar sense without emendation.

27. See the discussion of the LXX here in Booij, 'Hagar's Words', p. 4.

28. Cf. Westermann, *Genesis 12–36*, pp. 247–8.

29. At the same time Ehrlich, *Mikra Kipheshuto* I, p. 43 suggests that this should not be read as a question, since what the Masoretes took to be an interrogative *heh* in הגם is simply dittography from the end of the previous word. The sense of Hagar's words, then, would be a declarative statement.

means of sight is one of the characteristics of this narrative. Instead we should understand the term as reflecting 'experience' of the divine, just as the verb functions in a number of places to indicate a type of perception which is not limited to a single sense.[30] Similarly 'face to face' should be read here as a term for closeness or intimacy, without necessarily implying visual contact.[31] Jacob's use of the phrase is thus not a simple rehearsal of the more common idea of seeing the divine, but reflects the emotional depth of his encounter. The vulnerability mentioned above is also heightened by the reference to Jacob's limp in 32.31, a visceral reminder of the danger of the situation. This connection also highlights the tension between the objective and the subjective. On the one hand the narrator has continually mentioned the physical nature of the struggle as well as Jacob's injury, emphasizing the real danger inherent in the encounter. At the same time the fact that Jacob's comment has no specific addressee heightens the sense of subjective evaluation in his words.

A number of additional verbal connections in the context of Gen. 32–33 reinforce Jacob's subjective sense of danger and deliverance, albeit in a different sense. The marked similarity between Jacob's words ותנצל נפשי and his earlier prayer for deliverance from Esau in 32.11 – הצילני נא מיד אחי – sharpen the parallel between Jacob's fight with the angel and his anticipated meeting with his brother. But the context also suggests another interpretation: that the encounter with the angel has been protective or encouraging, forecasting the success of his subsequent meeting with Esau. This is reinforced by the multiple mention of appeasing Esau's 'face' in 32.20–21 and 33.10.[32] The comparison between seeing Esau's face to 'seeing the face of God' in 33.10 is perhaps the most compelling element in interpreting Jacob's experience of the divine as a reflection of his anticipated encounter with Esau. As with Jacob's statement in 32.30, all these phrases also occur not in the words of the narrator, but in Jacob's direct speech, heightening their subjective quality. There is thus a degree of tension between the sense of danger in the struggle with the angel and the sense of deliverance suggested by the contextual comments. In this light one could say that while Jacob fears that seeing Esau might lead to death, the encounter with the angel ultimately serves as a source of strength and blessing, despite the sense of his vulnerability which is revealed through it.[33]

30. As in Exod. 20.18, 'All the people saw the sounds', or Ps. 34.8, 'O taste and see that is good'.

31. See the use of the phrase in Exod. 33.11 with regard to speech, in Deut. 34.10 with the verb ידע or in Ezek. 20.35 with the verb שפט. In Deut. 5.4 the phrase פנים בפנים indicates verbal contact. Cf. Wilson, *Out of the Midst of the Fire*, pp. 76–9.

32. Cf. M. Gruber, 'The Many Faces of *Nasa' Panim* "Lift up the Face"' in *The Motherhood of God and Other Studies* (Atlanta: Scholars Press, 1992), pp. 173–83.

33. On the double sense of the blessing and the change in name cf. above, Chapter 4.

A different sort of affective emphasis can be seen in the reaction of Manoah in Judg. 13.22. Like Jacob, his fear of death coincides with the realization that he was in the presence of the divine, an understanding that comes only with absence, rather than with presence.[34] The reactions of Manoah's wife, however, particularly in Judg. 13.23, point out the subjective sense of his statement by undercutting its reliability. Throughout the narrative her interpretation of events is proven correct while that of Manoah is shown to be faulty or incomplete. While she has her suspicions as to the divine character of this visitor (13.6), Manoah himself seems remarkably dense. In 13.11–18 he reveals his ignorance in a series of questions about the visitor's name and purpose, despite the messenger's (and the narrator's) clear indications that these requests are inappropriate. While the mutual reaction of Manoah and his wife are emphasized in vv. 18 and 20, twice mentioning their visual perception of the messenger's ascent in flame (ומנוח ואשתו ראים), only Manoah expresses any fear about dying in 13.22. His wife's level-headed response, that YHWH has no intention of taking their lives after the *malakh*'s message and demonstrative departure, strongly implies that Manoah's fear of death is rather exaggerated. While his statement is an accurate assessment of the nature of divine power, in this specific setting it proves to be incorrect. On the one hand it indicates Manoah's realization of the significance of this encounter with the divine, but it also demonstrates his mistaken perceptions in contrast to those of his wife. Her criticism of Manoah's conclusion comes not to discredit the potentially lethal nature of divine encounters, but to demonstrate her superior powers of discernment.

In addition to the many parallels between Manoah's encounter and Gideon's theophany in Judg. 6, both express a fear of dying at the end of the encounter, and both are graced with a response.[35] Like Manoah, Gideon explains this fear by saying, 'I have seen the angel of the Lord';[36] YHWH, however, replies by declaring 'Do not fear – you shall not die' (Judg. 6.23). While YHWH's response is functionally similar to that of Manoah's wife in offering reassurance,[37] there is a significant difference. Here the response is intended not as a criticism of Gideon's perception, but

---

34. D. Schulman, *The Hungry God* (Chicago: Univ. of Chicago Press, 1993), p. 30.

35. On the parallels between the two episodes see Zakovitch, *Life of Samson*, pp. 54–8; J.A. Cook, 'The Theophanies of Gideon and Manoah', *JTS* 28 (1927), pp. 363–83.

36. Not a few commentators have suggested that the word *malakh* has been added for theological reasons; cf. J.G. Boling, *Judges* (*AB*; Garden City, NY: Doubleday, 1975), p. 134; Amit. *Judges*, p. 239 n. 46.

37. So Zakovitch, *Life of Samson*, p. 55.

as divine reassurance.[38] Where Manoah's wife offers no less than three reasons why YHWH would not want them dead, Gideon is simply told he will not die, with no explanation. The affective aspect of Gideon's statement is brought out by the contrast between Gideon's deeply subjective fear and YHWH's authoritative denial of this. While we only understand the nature of this fear from YHWH's response, it is precisely this statement – שלום לך – which lends to Gideon's perception an objective quality as well. The subsequent building of the altar by Gideon with the name *YHWH shalom* in 6.24 adds to this objectified aspect. As in Judg. 13 the response to Gideon's fear comes not to deny the real possibility of death as a result of encountering the divine, but to highlight YHWH's protection of Gideon.

2. *Fear of the Divine and Prophetic Initiation*

On two occasions where the fear of death is mentioned in the middle of the theophany its subjective function is balanced by a different kind of objective factor. Here we find the appointment of a prophetic figure through whom the theophany will move to a different level of contact. In the previous section the expression of fear was a *result* of the objective danger of being in the presence of the divine. In the following cases this subjective fear points to this moment of realization in a more immediate way, for the numinous is still present and threatening. It is therefore coupled with a wish to escape the danger of the encounter. Instead of marking the end of the theophany and emphasizing the gulf between the human and the divine, it serves to focus the experience in a new way by including the prophet as an associate of YHWH.

The report of the theophany at Sinai in both Exodus and Deuteronomy includes a subjective expression of the people's fear in somewhat similar fashion. Although Exod. 20.19 and Deut. 5.25 express this apprehension as a fear of hearing rather than of seeing, the essence of their words resembles what we have seen in other cases, describing the people's awareness of their proximity to the divine in terms of their anxiety about the lethal nature of the encounter.[39] In both cases there is a response to their statement – Moses in Exod. 20.20 and YHWH in Deut. 5.28. The general purpose of these responses is to verify the people's perceptions and to comfort them. But the practical consequence of this emotional reaction is the emergence

---

38. In light of the interesting parallels between Manoah's wife and the *malakh* this similarity of function between Manoah's wife's response to him in 13.22 and YHWH's response to Gideon in 6.24 reinforces A. Reinhartz's claim as to the sense of spiritual kinship between her and the *malakh*. Cf. 'Samson's Mother', pp. 25–37.

39. Cf. Geller's insights about this tension in Deuteronomy in *Sacred Enigmas*, pp. 47–9.

of Moses as the democratically appointed mediator of the covenant, the figure who will continue the encounter with the divine as the people's representative. Where Israel is afraid Moses is fearless; the people's statement effectively contrasts their trepidation with Moses' courage.[40]

The statement of fear is, however, framed in significantly different ways in the two versions of the Sinai theophany. In Exodus, the narrator has provided much narrative justification for the people's fear, with his description of thunder and lightning (19.16), the trembling of both the people and the mountain (19.16,18), and the warning of death for anyone who trespasses on the mountain during the theophany (19.12–13,21). Moreover, the mention of the people's physical movement away from the site of theophany in 20.18 (וינעו מרחוק) underscores their verbal reaction in 20.19. As noted earlier, it is not at all clear whether this response is to having heard the divine voice speak the Ten Commandments in 20.1–17, or simply to the anticipation of hearing the divine voice amid these intense sensory stimuli.[41] Their statement in Exod. 20.19 is relatively brief, beginning with their suggestion that Moses speak on their behalf and concluding with their fear of death. The unique mention of a fear of hearing rather than of seeing fits well with the idea of Moses' role as prophet and covenant mediator. It would make little sense for Moses to see YHWH on their behalf; in order to conclude the covenant in their stead he must speak and listen where they fear to do so.[42]

The Deuteronomic reworking of this tradition expands the people's speech considerably in 5.25–27, from 10 words in Exodus to 75 words in Deuteronomy. The purpose of this elaboration is to clarify a number of ambiguous issues in the Exodus narrative, regarding what was (or wasn't) seen by the people, and to explain that the people actually did hear YHWH speak to them. In contrast to Exodus, the Deuteronomic insistence on hearing over seeing is elaborated here: The people were shown (הראנו) YHWH's *kavod*,[43] but all that they actually saw (ראינו) was that could hear the divine voice.[44] The rest of their speech mentions hearing no less than five times.[45] The length and rhetorical style of their speech in Deuteronomy

40. On Moses' role as mediator of the covenant see the discussion in Childs, *Book of Exodus*, pp. 351–60, and Dozeman, *God on the Mountain*, pp. 49–65.

41. Cf. the discussion of their reaction in Chapter 4.

42. This focus on speech over seeing is not necessarily the result of Deuteronomistic reaction as argued by Dozeman, (*God on The Mountain*, pp. 45–50), but stems from the inclusion of legal material in the context of revelation. Cf. Toeg, *Lawgiving at Sinai*, esp. pp. 96–108.

43. Weinfeld, *Deuteronomy 1–11*, p. 323, emphasizes the limited understanding of visual revelation here.

44. Cf. Geller, *Sacred Enigmas*, p. 47.

45. Onkelos translates ונשמעה in Exod. 20.16 as ונקביל, 'and we will accept', understanding the term as 'to obey' as in the expression נעשה ונשמע, 'we will do and we will obey' in Exod.

tends to undercut the subjective sense of fear we have seen in other texts and replace it with what sound like theological dicta: 'we have seen this day that man may live though God has spoken to him' (5.24),[46] and 'For what mortal ever heard the voice of the living God speak out of the fire, as we did, and lived?' (5.26). YHWH's response here offers objective affirmation of the people's good sense in being afraid, and summons Moses to approach closer to continue the process of revelation.

Also in the case of Isa. 6 we find a deeply subjective expression of fear of dying in the middle of the theophany, followed by acceptance of the prophetic task. In contrast to Moses at Sinai, however, Isaiah's emotions are laid bare in the text: first he is frightened by his vision of the divine, and then he is appalled at the task which he given to perform. His anxiety here is not limited to his sense of indiscretion for having seen YHWH, but also from a profound sense of sin which is tied to belonging to 'a people of unclean lips'.[47] The choice of the verb דמה accentuates his fear of dying as well as his being struck dumb by the experience.[48] But instead of marking the end of the theophany, his expression of fear provides the occasion for his purification from sin, which in turn prepares the way for his entrance into the presence of YHWH. As with Moses at Sinai, this marks the prophet's separation from the rest of the human community in order to perform the required covenantal task. While his fear of death is intensely affective, the process of purification is more than a subjective impression, and lends a sense of credibility to his perception.[49]

The final two cases to be discussed differ from all the rest in that the lethal aspect of the theophany is expressed by an authoritative speaker. The occurrence of the phrase in Exod. 24.11 marks the only case where the phrase is spoken by the narrator. Here there is no subjective portrayal, as the phrase does not necessarily reflect the point of view of the characters. Equally authoritative is Exod. 33.20, where YHWH himself says כי לא יראני האדם וחי – 'No man can see me and live'. The phrase is part of YHWH's partial rejection of Moses' request to see his *kavod*. YHWH

24.7. Deut. 5, on the other hand, uses שמע primarily in the sense of hearing; only in Deut. 5.27 does שמע have the sense of obedience. The upshot of this is to emphasize the centrality of hearing in the Deut. text, where Exodus describes both the verbal and the visual sense of revelation.

46.   Cf. the discussion of this verse in A. Rofe, 'The Monotheistic Argumentation in Deut. 4.32–40, Contents, Composition and Text', *VT* 35 (1985), pp. 434–45 and M. Weinfeld, *Deuteronomy 1–11*, p. 324.

47.   Cf. Hurowitz, 'Isaiah's Impure Lips', pp. 44–5; Glazov, *The Bridling of the Tongue*, p. 125.

48.   See the discussion of נדמיתי in Chapter 4.

49.   Cf. Hurowitz, 'Isaiah's Impure Lips', pp. 73–9.

begins by agreeing to Moses' request in 33.19, rejects it in a categorical fashion in v. 20, and concludes by offering a compromise in 21–23, allowing Moses to see his 'back'. Here the tables are turned in a dramatic way, for the subjective point of view is not that of Moses, but of YHWH. Not only does Moses voice no fear about seeing the divine presence, but he actually beseeches YHWH to reveal himself to his view. YHWH states the impossibility of seeing Him and living as a simple fact of the reality of the numinous, but then he contradicts the statement by allowing Moses a qualified vision of the divine. Here divine and human roles are reversed. Whereas the human is usually fearful of the divine presence, and must be calmed in the face of this fear of death, here Moses asks for exposure to the fullness of the divine presence. YHWH for his part is not in the position of placating Moses' fear, but of limiting his access in such a way as to indicate concern, and to diffuse the absolute nature of the statement.[50] On the one hand Exod. 33.20 offers an authoritative view of the issue placed in the mouth of YHWH, offering a categorical rejection of Moses' request. But the context, as in all the theophany narratives we have examined, declares the opposite – man may see YHWH and live.[51]

Given the subjective importance of the mention of the lethal quality of the divine in nearly all the texts we have examined, the absence of the phrase in a considerable number of theophany narratives, including the calls of Moses, Samuel, Jeremiah and Ezekiel, is all the more striking.[52] Here we can only argue from silence, and try to explain this absence simply by speculation. In some cases the fear of death may be inappropriate to the nature of the theophany. So Jacob in Gen. 28 sees YHWH in a dream, which by its nature is not life-threatening.[53] Moses, it can be argued, constitutes an exceptional case because of his unusually close and ongoing relationship with YHWH. In this light he may be seen to be more immune to exposure to the divine than other prophets, as demonstrated by his experiences at Sinai.[54] The revelations to Jeremiah

---

50. See the discussion of this process in Wolfson, *Through a Speculum That Shines*, pp. 26–8.

51. Cf. Moberly, *At the Mountain of God*, p. 81: 'Yet the paradox is clear in the fact that it is precisely those passages which say that man cannot see or hear God which affirm that just such has indeed happened'.

52. The phrase is also lacking in Gen. 28.10–22; Num. 12, and 1 Kgs 19.1–19.

53. This may also explain the difference between Balaam's non-threatened reactions to YHWH in Num. 22.2–21 and his awareness of the danger inherent in the appearance of the *malakh* in 22.22–35. On the nature of Balaam's night-time revelations cf. Fidler, 'Dream Theophany', pp. 123–31.

54. In light of this his hiding his face in Exod. 3.6 would be constitute an initial sense of awe before the divine, but need not be an expression of fear of death. Nonetheless the attack by YHWH described in Exod. 4.24–26 indicates that he is not exempt from the lethal aspect of the divine.

and Samuel were distinctly non-visual, or at very least the visual component is understated, as we have seen.[55] Those revelations which are more visual may well entail greater risk, as the prohibition centers around primarily around *seeing* the Deity, Exod. 19–20 notwithstanding. In 1 Sam. 3, although חזון is mentioned and Samuel experiences a מראה, the emphasis is on the verbal message.[56] So too Elijah's experience of the divine is primarily audial, with the emphasis placed on the 'still small voice'.

In still other cases the presence of the lethal quality of the divine may be illustrated by non-verbal gesture, with no explicit mention of the fear of death. Thus Ezekiel's falling on his face could well be indication enough that he was close to death as a result of seeing the chariot vision.[57] And Moses' hiding his face in Exod. 3.6 could also be understood as an expression of a fear of death.[58]

Another factor should also be considered here. In most of the texts in which the lethal quality is mentioned in the narrative, there is no mention of any external source of danger.[59] By contrast, in a number of texts where the lethal quality of meeting the divine is not mentioned (or is undercut by the context) the danger to the protagonist is represented by an outside factor. This is brought out most clearly in the calls of Jeremiah and Ezekiel; in both cases no explicit fear of death is mentioned, and in both cases danger and hostility is located with the people who will be resistant and hostile to the prophet's message.[60] Thus it could be argued that in these texts the mention of future danger from the people takes the place of a focus on the lethal quality of the divine. It may well be that in these texts the sense of cooperation and support by YHWH is primary, and a comment about the potentially lethal quality of the encounter would be out of place. A similar situation could be said to be implicit in Elijah's lack of mention of lethal danger in 1 Kgs 19, where the real threat to his life is identified as Jezebel.

These speculations about the absence of the phrase cannot be proved or disproved. But the variability of how and when the mention of the lethal quality of the divine is deployed, as well as the differences in its formulation, indicate that its use is far from automatic, but is

55. Cf. discussion in Chapter 3.

56. Moreover, we suggested in chapter 4 that the absence of any mention of Samuel's fear is balanced by his anxiety at having to relay the prophecy to Eli. Cf. above p. 143.

57. Cf. Pedaya, 'Seeing, Falling', p. 247. This is likely the way the authors of Enoch 14 and Dan. 10 understood Ezekiel's gesture.

58. E.g. Propp. *Exodus 1–18*, p. 201.

59. E.g. Gen. 16; Exod. 19–20; 24; 33; Isa. 6.

60. Jer. 1.8,17–19; Ezek. 2.3–7; 3.4–9.

governed by a complex poetics of expression. The tension between subjectivity and objectivity underscores the dialogical purpose of the phrase in the context of theophany, and attempts to reduce it to a simple theological statement tend to overlook this nuanced aspect of the encounter.

Chapter 7

SINAI REVISITED: THEOPHANY AND INTERTEXTUALITY

While our discussion of the various aspects of theophany narratives has reflected upon the unique dynamics of each phase of the theophany, there is a good deal more to be said about the larger connections between these texts. Clearly, a more sophisticated intertextual understanding of the subject will add substantially to our appreciation. When read within the context of the larger narrative in which they are embedded, various linkages between the individual theophanies beg to be noticed and remarked upon. These connections describe a wide variety of intertextual relations, ranging from multiple theophanies involving the same person, to the re-use of themes and motifs, to the fashioning of one character after the image of another.[1]

Thus one can hardly ignore the contextual parallels between Jacob's dream upon exiting the land of Canaan in Gen. 28.10–15 and his encounter with the angel upon his re-entry in 32.24–30. Jacob's two encounters with the divine in Gen. 28 and 32 have been contrasted often and well.[2] Both events take place at night, marking Jacob's departure from and return to the land of Canaan, and both hold out the promise of divine blessing. While in the first YHWH offers a general promise of protection, the second affirms that protection in answer to Jacob's prayer to be delivered from Esau (Gen. 32.11), an event which occurs in the very next chapter. If Gen. 28 speaks of an encounter with a house of God (Bethel), then Gen. 32 describes seeing the very face of God. But the relationship between the two goes deeper than this. Whereas Jacob's dream in Gen. 28 is a solitary

---

1. The literature on intertextuality is vast and can only be hinted at here. Exemplary studies include D.N. Fewell, *Reading Between Texts: Intertextuality and the Hebrew Bible* (Louisville: Westminster John Knox, 1992); E. van Wolde, 'Texts in Dialogue with Texts: Intertextuality in the Ruth and Tamar Narratives', *Biblical Interpretation* 5 (1997), pp. 1–28; L. Eslinger, 'Inner-Biblical Exegesis and Inner-Biblical Allusion: The Question of Category', *VT* 42 (1992), pp. 47–58; T.B. Dozeman, 'Inner-Biblical Interpretation of YHWH's Gracious and Compassionate Character', *JBL* 108 (1989), pp. 207–33; Savran, 'Beastly Speech'; Sommer, *A Prophet Reads Scripture*, pp. 6–31; Zakovitch, *Through the Looking Glass*.

2. E.g., see the discussion of the chiastic structure of the Jacob cycle in Fishbane, 'Composition and Structure', pp. 19–32, esp. pp. 28–30.

experience, taking place in a dream without physical contact or dialogue between him and YHWH, his struggle with the 'man' in Gen. 32 is among the most intimate of all human–divine encounters in the Bible, describing a degree of physical contact and closeness which is unknown elsewhere.[3] And if the encounter at Bethel leaves Jacob unmarked and unscathed, ripe in his innocence for both the promise of YHWH and the deceit of Laban, Gen. 32 portrays a wiser, older Jacob, a man who has learned the lessons of conflict, and who comes away wounded from the encounter. In Gen. 28 Jacob's concerns are for his future, while in Gen. 32 he is aware that having an encounter with the divine also implies a close call with death. If the first theophany is about innocence and initiation, as are many initial theophanies, then the second encounter is about the responsibilities of the continuation of his life – the welfare of his family, and his role as the eponymous father of Israel. These two texts define Jacob's relationship with YHWH in both synchronic and diachronic ways – the former describing a phenomenological similarity between the encounters, and the latter detailing growth and development of the character.[4]

Similarly, one might compare Moses' revelation at the bush in Exod. 3 with his subsequent encounters with the Deity at Sinai in Exod. 19–24, and again in Exod. 33. These theophanies help to give shape to our understanding of Moses' development, and play an important role in the structure of Exodus as a book.[5] Moreover, the interrelationship of Moses' encounters with the divine in Exod. 3, Exod. 19–20, 24 and 33–34 offers some insight into the dynamics of public/private revelation. In addition to the presence of the usual phenomena associated with the numinous – fire, fear of seeing, the use of mediating elements to reflect the presence of the divine, a communal focus on Moses' relationship to the Israelites – all three encounters take place at 'the mountain of God' at Sinai, which lend a spatial focus to this cluster of encounters.[6] While Moses is initially afraid to look directly at YHWH (Exod. 3.6), in Exod. 33.19–23 YHWH refuses

---

3.   See, for example, Smith, 'Heel and Thigh' pp. 466–9.

4.   Note also the encounter with angels at Mahanaim in Gen. 32.1–2, and the appearance of YHWH to Jacob in Gen. 46.1–4; cf. Fokkelman, *Narrative Art in Genesis*, pp. 197–200; Peleg, 'Going Up and Going Down', pp. 212–22.

5.   Cf. Polak, 'Theophany and Mediator', p. 113, 144–7. The three main sections of Exodus each feature theophany in a central way: Moses at the bush in Exod. 3 gives shape and direction to the exodus narrative of Exod. 1.1–15.21; the theophany at Sinai is obviously central to the desert/Sinai narrative in Exod. 15.22–24.18; and the theophany in Exod. 33 stands at the center of the tabernacle narrative in Exod. 25–40. In addition, note the significance of the revelation of the name YHWH to Moses in Exod. 6; the appearance of *k'bod YHWH* to the people in Exod. 16; and the construction of the Tabernacle as a locus for the divine presence in Exod. 25–32; 35–40.

6.   Polak, 'Theophany and Mediator', p. 114 sees the triad of 'water/wood/mountain' as an overarching theme unifying the book of Exodus.

to let Moses' look upon his face.[7] And in contrast to Moses' hesitancy in
Exod. 3, he is much more aggressive in the third encounter, using his
relationship with YHWH to persuade him to continue to accompany the
people.[8] In between these two encounters, it is the people's fear (of hearing
YHWH's voice) which stands at the center of the theophany at Sinai.
Taken together, the texts offer a meditation on the impossibility of direct
encounter with the divine, on the need for some restraining element to be
offered by one of the parties involved, and on the development of strategies
for dealing with this indirection.

These texts also present a spectrum of possibilities concerning individual
and group experience. If the first encounter is Moses' private theophany, in
which his aloneness is clear, in Exod. 19–24 the group aspect of the
experience dominates even Moses' private conversations with YHWH. In
Exod. 19.9,19, the very fact of verbal intercourse between Moses and
YHWH serves as a sign of public recognition of Moses' role, rather than
the transmission of any private message. By contrast, the third theophany
in Exod. 33–34 contains both private and public elements. While Moses
begins in 33.12–17 by using his favored status in YHWH's eyes for the
people's benefit, the concern of 33.18–23 is entirely private, focused on
what Moses can and cannot be privy to.[9] The actual theophany in Exod. 34
is private in terms of the experience, but public in terms of what is to be
conveyed – the tablets, the description of YHWH's forgiving nature in
34.6–7, and the covenantal stipulations in 34.10–26. The very final stage of
Moses' descent merges these two once again. On the one hand Moses has
'absorbed' YHWH's presence as reflected by his shining face, but the
wearing of the veil in 34.29–35 emphasizes the public nature of Moses'
role.[10] The constant interplay of communal and individual concerns in
these narratives underscores the complexity of the dynamics between
YHWH, Moses and Israel.

A somewhat different type of intertextual relationship is reflected in the
re-use of a significant motif, such as the repeated approach by YHWH
which is misunderstood by the protagonist. Both Balaam and Samuel are
approached by the numinous a few times before their respective 'helpers'
are able to convey to them the true meaning of what they have been unable

---

7. Cf. *Exod. Rab.* 45.5 – 'When I wanted to show you [my face] you didn't want to see it.
Now that you want to see it, I don't want to show you.'

8. Cf. Polak, 'Theophany and Mediator', p. 145. Polak also notes the similarity between
YHWH proclaiming his name to Moses in Exod. 3.15 and 34.6–7, especially in the *idem per
idem* formulations of אהיה אשר אהיה and אשר אחן חנתי את אשר (33.19). What is most striking here is
how the name is interpreted as implying forgiveness, in contrast to the explanation of the
name in Exod. 20.5.

9. The people are referred to only obliquely here, if at all.

10. See discussion above in Chapter 5.

to comprehend. In both cases we find the formula of three unsuccessful attempts followed by a final successful one.[11] In both there needs to be a third party who is serves as the 'helper', who enables the theophany, and without whom the encounter would not take place. But at the same time, Eli's role is not exactly parallel to the that of the she-ass. For Eli is never privy to the divine, whereas the donkey perceives the *malakh* before Balaam does. Moreover, since Eli has had a prior revelation (1 Sam. 2.27–36.), he should be more immediately aware of the divine voice calling Samuel. Balaam, too, has had such an encounter, twice, in the first part of the chapter, while the she-ass has had no prior experience of the divine. While the Balaam story comes to illustrate that even an experienced seer can be outclassed by a she-ass, the story of Samuel's call shows that even a discredited priest may be essential for opening the path to revelation to Samuel. Both Samuel and Balaam overcome this secondary status and have direct contact with the divine. Balaam's experience of the theophany is ultimately more impressive than the she-ass's fear and attempts at escape, and Samuel's experience of the theophany is ultimately of a superior nature to Eli's prior encounter with the *malakh* in 1 Sam. 2. But while the effect of this misunderstanding is used for satiric effect in the case of Balaam, in Samuel's case it serves to increase the reader's identification with the confusion of the uninitiated prophet-to-be.[12]

1. *Moses at Sinai/Elijah at Horeb*

The type of intertextual relationship to be examined here differs from the above examples in a number of ways. First, the intertexts do not occur in the same book, or even with regard to the same character. Rather, their situations are separated by a temporal distance of hundreds of years, according to biblical chronology. What draws the texts together is a weave of references which go beyond the correspondence of one or two central motifs. First, the location. As we have seen, theophanies occur at a wide variety of locations, and no other named site is the subject of multiple theophanies. Moreover, Sinai functions as a place of theophany for both

---

11. Cf. Zakovitch, *For Three, and for Four*, pp. 93–106.

12. To mention a few more of the many examples of intertextual relationship in theophany narratives: Glazov, *The Bridling of the Tongue*, pp. 317–22, argues for an intertextual reading of the prophetic call narratives, where each one must be read in light of those who precede him in the biblical chronology. In both Judg. 6 and Judg. 13, the fiery ascent heavenward of the *malakh* as a final proof to the protagonist of the presence of the divine is a clear marker of the interrelationship of these texts; cf. Y. Zakovitch, 'Assimilation in Biblical Narratives' in Tigay (ed.), *Empirical Models for the Development of the Hebrew Bible*, pp. 175–96 (192–5); idem, *Life of Samson*, pp. 55–8.

the group as well as individuals.[13] Yet despite its central role in the Pentateuchal literature, it is mentioned only occasionally elsewhere.[14] Elijah's sojourn to Sinai/Horeb[15] marks the only appearance of a biblical figure at this site after Moses.

Secondly, while the arrival of another prophet at Sinai would be cause enough for reflection, Elijah, like Moses, experiences a theophany there, at what is often taken to be the locus of Moses' divine encounter in Exod. 33.[16] The encounter at Sinai/Horeb marks an important turning point in the individual lives of the prophets, which will in turn have substantial ramifications for the Israelites as well. The use of motifs such as thunder and lightning, hiding the face, and standing on the (cleft of the) rock, all come to emphasize the interrelationship between the two theophanies. The confluence of the two texts is celebrated in midrashic literature with an elaborate description of the similarities (both real and apparent) between Moses and Elijah.[17] The thrust of this midrash is that Moses and Elijah were equal in nearly every matter except one, where Moses was superior.[18] Building upon this important difference, most modern readers have understood 1 Kgs 19 as a reflection of Exod. 33, and Elijah as a second, if less perfect, Moses.[19] An intertextual approach should not, however, restrict itself to reading influence in a single direction, but should explore the ways in which each text can be read in light of the other. It is no less important to ask how the Elijah theophany adds to our understanding of Exod. 33 as well. While both similarity and difference will concern us here, it is the latter which will be of greater value. Beyond the association of the two prophets is the question of the relationship between these two texts –

13. On the Sinai traditions in the Bible see E.W. Nicholson, *Exodus and Sinai in History and Tradition* (Oxford: Oxford University Press, 1973); R. Cohn, *The Shape of Sacred Space* Chico, CA: Scholars Press, 1981); R. Clifford, *The Cosmic Mountain in Canaan and the Old Testament* (Cambridge: Harvard University Press, 1972).

14. Cf. Judg. 5.5; Ps. 68.9,18; Neh. 9.13.

15. 1 Kgs 19 refers to Horeb, which is understood as the Deuteronomic name for Sinai. Zakovitch ('A Still Small Voice', p. 334) understands the use of the name in relation to חרב (sword) in 1 Kgs 19.14,17 (cf. *Exod. Rab.* 51:8).

16. The use of המערה in 1 Kgs 19.9 is often taken to refer precisely the rock on which Moses stood in Exod. 33. Cf. Simon, *Prophetic Narratives*, p. 271; Zakovitch, *"And You Shall Tell Your Son"*, p. 71; cf. already *BT* Pesachim 54a; Megillah 19b.

17. See *Pesikta Rabbati* 4.

18. YHWH told Moses to remain with him at Sinai (Deut. 5.28), but Elijah met with YHWH's rebuke: 'What do you want here, Elijah?' (1 Kgs 19.9). This difference will be discussed in detail below.

19. See G. Fohrer, *Elia* (Zurich: Zwingli-Verlag, 1957), pp. 55ff.; R. Carroll, 'The Elijah-Elisha Sagas: Some Remarks on Prophetic Succession in Ancient Israel', *VT* 19 (1969), pp. 400–15; R.A. Carlson, 'Elie a l'Horeb', *VT* 19 (1969), pp. 416–39; Zakovitch, 'A Still Small Voice', pp. 344–5; Simon, *Prophetic Narratives*, pp. 211–14.

the direction of influence, the image of the prophet, and their understanding of the Sinaitic revelation.

In order to accomplish this, it will be necessary first to sketch a number
of points of similarity and difference between Moses and Elijah: Their
relationship to YHWH, their connection with the people, their uniqueness
as prophetic figures, and the nature of the theophany reflected in both
texts. Following this we will examine a number of different ways of
understanding the relationship between the two texts.

a. *Relationship to the People.*
Both Moses and Elijah see their personal fate as closely bound up with the
people, but with significant differences. Both leave the people at the
command of YHWH – Moses to Sinai, and Elijah to Zarafat in 1 Kgs 17.
And both return to confront the idolatry of the people and to combat it –
Moses in Exod. 32 and Elijah in 1 Kgs 18.[20] Both figures seek out YHWH
at Sinai/Horeb in response to the people's apostasy. But beyond these
similarities they have very different types of relationship with the people.

The attitude of Moses toward the people in these chapters is truly
exceptional. His statement מחני נא מספרך (Exod. 32.32 – 'Wipe me out of
your book') is unparalleled in the Bible as a statement of willingness to
sacrifice himself for the sake of the people. In Exod. 33.12–17 he capitalizes
on YHWH's affection for him in order to restore a closer relationship
between YHWH and the people. The interweaving of his personal
situation with the fate of the people is apparent in nearly every verse of
this dialogue, from וראה כי עמך הגוי הזה in 33.12–13 ('Look, this nation is
your people'),[21] to the rejection of YHWH's offer והנחתי לך in 33.14 in
favor of אל תעלנו in 33.15,[22] to the repetition of אני ועמך in 33.16.[23] At the
conclusion of the theophany Moses returns to the people with tokens of
externalization – the tablets and the veil – which emphasize his desire to
involve the people in the covenantal process.[24] In stark contrast to this we
see a much harsher picture of this relationship when Moses is 'on the
ground' confronting the Israelites. While the breaking of the tablets in
32.19 may be an understandable emotional response to the sight of

20.   On parallels between Exod. 32–24 and 1 Kgs 17–19 see below.
21.   This word ראה appears at the beginning and end of Moses' speech in vv. 12–13, even
though the rest of his words focus on his own personal relationship with YHWH.
22.   The change of focus from the singular to the plural offers the best explanation of
Moses' refusal of YHWH's apparent concession. YHWH offers to accompany Moses, but
Moses holds out for divine accompaniment for the entire people. Cf. Ibn Ezra *ad loc.*
23.   Moses' exceptional devotion to the people is contrasted with the absence of any
mention of the people on YHWH's part. Even in his closing statement in 33.17 YHWH
reiterates his attachment to Moses without referring to the Israelites.
24.   See chapter 5 on externalization.

apostasy, Moses' command to the people to kill 'every man his brother, his neighbour, and his kin' (32.27) is exceptionally harsh. The violence of this act is given further weight by the language of 32.29, juxtaposing the command to slay with the language of blessing. Despite this, while both sides of his relationship to the people are present, Moses' concern for their welfare is brought out more strongly.

Elijah's relationship with the people is of a different nature, on the one hand more tolerant of their forays into idol worship and at the same time displaying a harsher attitude toward them. In speaking of the people to YHWH in 1 Kgs 19.10 he has only bad things to say about them. They are to blame for all his misfortunes, being the subject of three consecutive sentences of harsh accusation. In sharp contrast to his own zeal for YHWH, they have abandoned the covenant, destroyed altars and murdered prophets. In light of Moses' devotion to the people when speaking to YHWH in Exod. 32–33, Elijah's vilification of their behavior here is all the more striking. His repetition of these accusations in 1 Kgs 19.14 gives further emphasis to this harshness. He makes no concessions to their situation, despite the fact that the narrator places the blame for at least some of these actions at the feet of Jezebel. Moreover, while the narrator makes it clear that his flight to the desert is a response to Jezebel's threats, Elijah gives the impression that it is the people who have driven him to this act of desperation.

Despite this verbal asperity, when Elijah actually confronts the people in 1 Kgs 18 he offers them a demonstration instead of castigation. A model of positive reinforcement takes the place of punishment, enticing them with the promise of a contest, enlisting their help in rebuilding the destroyed sanctuary, and putting on a display of divine fireworks which turns their hearts around. Their sin of following Baal is of a similar nature to the apparent idolatry of the Golden Calf,[25] yet Elijah doesn't punish them. Instead we see a virtual reversal of Moses' strategy in Exod. 32. Moses has only good things to say about the people when pleading with YHWH, but in his confrontation with the people he can be harshly critical, even to the point of violence. Elijah, on the other hand, censures the people when speaking to YHWH, but in his actual encounter with them he is far more generous.

b. *Relationship to YHWH*
The intimacy between Moses and YHWH is incomparably close in Exod. 32–34, as brought out both by Moses' daring request in Exod. 33.18 –

---

25. The question of the nature of Israel's sin in Exod. 32 has been the subject of much interpretation, ancient and modern. See Childs, *Exodus*, pp. 574–9 and the literature cited there.

'show me your *kavod*' – as well as by YHWH's response in 33.19–23. Moses is praised explicitly by YHWH as having found favor in his eyes (33.17), a sentiment otherwise reserved for Noah alone (Gen. 6.8). Similarly unusual is YHWH's use of the verb ידע with respect to Moses in 33.17, used elsewhere to describe his relationship with an individual only with Abraham (Gen. 18.19) and Jeremiah (Jer. 1.5).[26] This familiarity between the two is reflected in Moses' willingness to utilize YHWH's attachment to him order to plead for the people's welfare, employing a degree of flattery and manipulation not found elsewhere in prophetic prayer. One sees this quite clearly in the case he presents for Israel's defense in Exod. 32.11–14, as well as in his pursuit of a divinely granted pardon in 33.12–17.[27] Moreover, the individual revelation which he receives exceeds any other theophany in the Bible in YHWH's concession to Moses' nearness, in the revelation of the divine attributes, and in the exceptional aftermath of Moses' shining face. The nature of the intercourse between Moses and YHWH is described repeatedly as a face to face encounter.[28] To be sure, Moses is also the recipient of divine rebuke and punishment, but in this particular pericope the closeness of his relationship to YHWH is unique in the Bible.

Elijah's connection to YHWH also displays a significant degree of intimacy which is demonstrated numerous times: In the pattern of command and obedience in 1 Kgs 17–18, in YHWH's caring for Elijah's nourishment during the drought, in dispatching his *malakh* in response to Elijah's request to die in 1 Kgs 19.4, and in the effectiveness of his prayers in 1 Kgs 17.20–21 and 18.36–37. In these prayers he uses familiar language in a manner similar to that of Moses in Exod. 32–33. In the first case he accuses YHWH of causing the death of the child he is trying to revive,[29] and in the second of being responsible for Israel's backsliding.[30] In both texts YHWH is clearly responsive to his prayers. But the only actual dialog between Elijah and YHWH, found in 1 Kgs 19.9–18, shows a different side of their relationship. Where Moses used the occasion of theophany to contend for the people, in Elijah's appearance at Horeb he argues *against*

---

26. The term is also used in prophetic literature to describe YHWH's relationship to Israel; cf. Hos. 5.3; 13.5; Amos. 3.2. On its meaning cf. Holladay, *Jeremiah*, vol. 1, p. 33.

27. On Exod. 32.11–14 see M. Greenberg, 'Moses' Intercessory Prayer', *Tantur Yearbook* (1977–78), pp. 21–36. On Exod. 33.12–17 see Moberly, *At the Mountain of God*, pp. 66–76; Muffs, 'Who Will Stand in the Breach?', pp. 14–16.

28. Cf. Exod. 33.11; Deut. 34.10; Num. 12.8.

29. Cf. Simon, *Prophetic Narratives*, pp. 165–166.

30. Cf. M. Greenberg, 'You Have Turned Their Hearts Backwards (I Kings 18.37),' *Studies in Aggadah, Targum, and Jewish Liturgy in Memory of Joseph Heinemann*, ed. J. Petuchowski and E. Fleischer, (Jerusalem: Magnes, 1981), pp. 52–66 (Hebrew). Contra, cf. Simon, *Prophetic Narratives*, pp. 187–8.

the people. Moreover, where YHWH was receptive to Moses' arguments in Exod. 33, here the response to Elijah is more equivocal. On the one hand, the gist of YHWH's response in vv. 15–18 is to order a violent response to the problem of Baal worship, emphasizing the use of the sword. But at the same time YHWH refutes Elijah's claim that all the people are to be punished, arguing for the existence of some 7,000 faithful. Moreover, while the question posed to Elijah in 19.9 – מה לך פה אליהו – 'What are you doing here, Elijah?' – offered Elijah a chance to explain his actions, its repetition in v. 13 following the theophany of the still small voice implies a rebuke of Elijah's claim. He is sent back to the people, but primarily in order to train his own replacement. Whatever closeness had developed in chapters 17–18 seems to have dissipated in the face of the aftermath of the theophany. Where Moses' response to theophany in Exod. 33–34 shows a deep understanding of YHWH's nature and intentions, Elijah's literal repetition of his earlier claim in 19.14 implies that the prophet has not understood the message in the theophany, and that communication between prophet and Deity has broken down.

c. *Aloneness/Uniqueness*

Both Moses and Elijah enjoy a singular status, yet they suffer from a situation of aloneness in relation to other humans. While Moses is often shown working in conjunction with others – Aaron, Joshua, the seventy elders – he is always dominant, at the center of things, in direct contact with YHWH. At Sinai this is seen most clearly in his unique role in the drama of the revelation both in Exod. 19–20[31] and in Exod. 24. In the former text his contact with YHWH separates him from the rest of the people, while in the latter he is initially part of a select contingent Aaron, Nadav, Avihu and the seventy elders. But where they remain at a distance after the theophany in 24.9–11, Moses is instructed to approach further (24.12–18), and this proximity to the numinous distinguishes him from all the rest. In Exodus 32–34 Moses stands completely alone in his encounter with YHWH at Sinai. The pattern of his ascents and descents in Exod. 32–34 shows him acting on his own initiative, inaugurating contact with YHWH and establishing the terms of their discourse. Here Moses' aloneness is the obverse of his uniqueness, as reflected both in the nature of this theophany, as well as in his ability to persuade YHWH to forgive Israel. Ultimately all other characters are present only as a foil for this incomparability.[32]

---

31. Cf. chapter 4.
32. See, for example, the comment of Childs, *Exodus*, p. 570, contrasting Moses' courage before YHWH with Aaron's conciliatory behaviour toward the people.

The positive aspect of this uniqueness is emphasized in most of Moses' encounters with YHWH, but the negative side, the solitude, comes to the fore primarily in Num. 11.4–35.[33] Here Moses complains that his singularity has led to a profound sense of isolation, not to mention a feeling of inadequacy reflected in his inability to produce what is necessary for the people.[34] Coupled with this is no small amount of doubt about YHWH's ability to perform as desired.[35] In what amounts to a reversal of the positive sentiment in Exod. 33, Moses complains that he has *not* found favor in YHWH's eyes (Num. 11.11). Indeed, he claims that the burden of solitary leadership reflects YHWH's mistreatment of him rather than his chosenness. His inability to provide for the people is coupled with a deeper, more thoroughgoing complaint of being unable 'to bear the burden of this people' in the fullest sense (11.14). This leads to an uncharacteristic moment of despair in 11.15, where Moses asks to be relieved of this task in a most extreme way – 'Kill me, rather, I beg you'. As in Exod. 33, Moses uses his personal situation in order to gain something for the people, but the context and the speech itself show another, darker side of Moses' persona.

If Moses is characterized more by uniqueness than by aloneness, Elijah displays the opposite side of the coin. He is profoundly alone in 1 Kgs 17–19, showing no emotional or organizational attachment to any prophetic group[36] or to any individual.[37] From his solitary sojourn in Nahal Keret (1 Kgs 17.3–7), to his uncomfortable encounter with the widow and her son (17.8–24), to his confrontation with Obadiah in 1 Kgs 18.7–15, he is constantly set apart, first by YHWH's commands to him, and then by his own words and behavior.[38] He describes himself to the people as a lone

---

33. See the discussion of this text in B. Levine, *Numbers 1–20*, pp. 319–27, 337–8; Milgrom, *Numbers*, pp. 376–86; D. Jobling, *The Sense of Biblical Narrative* (Sheffield: Sheffield Academic Press, 1978), pp. 27–62; B.D. Sommer, 'Reflecting on Moses: The Redaction of Numbers 11', *JBL* 118 (1999), pp. 601–24; Licht, *Numbers*, vol 2, pp. 17–13; H. Fisch, ' "Eldad and Medad are Prophesying in the Camp" – Structural Analysis of Numbers XI', *Studies in Bible and Exegesis*, vol. 2 (Ramat Gan, 1986) pp. 45–55 (Hebrew).

34. On the unity of Num. 11.11–15 see Savran, *Telling and Retelling*, pp. 68–9; 94–6; Sommer, 'Reflecting on Moses', pp. 606–8.

35. Cf. Sommer, 'Reflecting on Moses', pp. 613–14; Rashi on Num. 11.22.

36. Though he is obviously the leader of such a prophetic group in II Kgs 2. Cf. J.G. Williams, 'The Prophetic Father: A Brief Explanation of the Term "Sons of the Prophets" ', *JBL* 85 (1966), pp. 344–8 (345).

37. The account of Elijah's commissioning of Elisha is similarly marked by Elijah's emotional distance from Elisha. Cf. Y. Shemesh, 'Footsteps of the Oxen', pp. 85–6.

38. Note the stiffness in his interaction with the widow in 1 Kgs 17, as well as her hostility towards him throughout most of the encounter. His interchange with Obadiah is marked by accusation and by defensiveness by Obadiah. Simon, *Prophetic Narratives*, p. 313 n. 52, compares this situation to the confrontation between Moses and the Israelite foremen in Exod. 5.21. In both texts the prophet places those who side with him in an impossible position

figure (18.22 – 'I am the only prophet of the Lord left'), and sets himself in opposition to the prophets of Baal. While there is a temporary joining of forces with the Israelites around the rebuilding of the altar (18.30) and the slaughter of the Baal prophets (18.40), this is offset by his solitary behavior praying for rain (18.42–45) and in his running alone before Ahab's chariot (18.46).

While this aloneness/singularity has a triumphal aspect in 1 Kgs 17–18, it takes a different turn in the subsequent chapter. If to this point Elijah's aloneness has marked him as uniquely chosen, 1 Kgs 19 describes his isolation as the result of being pursued and persecuted by Jezebel. Elijah carries this isolation to an extreme position, separating himself from human company by fleeing to the south and dismissing his servant in v. 3, preliminary to asking YHWH to take his life.[39] Elijah's explanation, that he is no better than his fathers, expresses his profound disappointment at not having been as singular as he would have wished to be. While it is possible to read this as a general complaint with no specific comparison intended,[40] it is best taken as a reference to Moses' despair and request to die in Num. 11.11–15.[41]

Elijah seems to revel in this sense of isolation once he is at Horeb. In his speech in 1 Kgs 19.10, where he explains his plight, he emphasizes the opposition between the people and himself. *He alone* has been zealous for YHWH.[42] Where Elijah's mention of his singularity in 18.22 is meant to heighten the contest between the one and the many, his repetition of the

---

vis-a-vis the ruling power. Elijah's interaction with Ahab here varies from outright hostility in the first part of the chapter (18.17–18), to apparent support for the king in the last section (18.46).

39.   There is some manuscript evidence for seeing in v. 3 a statement about Elijah's fear, reading וַיִּרָא - 'he was afraid' instead of MT וַיַּרְא 'he saw'. See Simon, *Prophetic Narratives*, p. 301; Cogan, *I Kings*, p. 450. While the phrase וַיֵּלֶךְ אֶל נַפְשׁוֹ finds a close parallel in Gen. 19.17, Zakovitch suggests a more literal reading, in which Elijah becomes entirely self-absorbed, goes into himself ('A Still Small Voice', p. 332). Instead of describing a limited degree of anxiety about his prophetic calling, Elijah's request to die recalls Jonah more than Moses; see the comments of Magonet, *Form and Meaning*, pp. 67–9. Elijah's anxiety is focussed entirely around Jezebel's threat.

40.   So Simon, *Prophetic Narratives*, p. 202. It could also be a reference to his fellow prophets who have died at the hands of Jezebel or to the patriarchs whom he invoked in his prayer in 18.36.

41.   This trope of the prophet asking to die is also found in Jonah 4 and in Jeremiah's laments, esp. Jer. 20.14–18. See the discussion in J.M. Sasson, *Jonah* (AB; N.Y.: Doubleday, 1990), pp. 283–6.

42.   This phrase also singles out Elijah as uniquely devoted. Most notable among those who are described as zealous is YHWH, who defines himself as אֵל קַנָּא in Exod. 20.2 (here associated with exclusivity). Moreover, the zealousness of the priest Phinehas ben Eleazar is connected with exclusive worship of YHWH in Num. 25.11,13. On this connection cf. Simon, *Prophetic Narratives*, p. 205.

phrase in 19.10 highlights his sense of persecution by the people. But
YHWH's response in vv. 15–18 undercuts both his aloneness and his
uniqueness. Elijah is told that he is not alone among a hostile people, but
that there still remains a large number faithful to YHWH. Solitude is not
an indication of his greatness, but of his insufficiency. He is told that he
must enlist others to help him accomplish the task of eradicating Baal
worship. Most telling of all, he is called to anoint his own successor, Elisha
ben Shaphat, indicating that Elijah is being relieved of his prophetic role.
Where Moses' complaint about his solitude was answered by YHWH
without compromising his uniqueness, the response to Elijah's complaint is
that he is to be replaced.

d. *The Nature of the Theophany*

The centerpieces of Exod. 33 and 1 Kgs 19 are the theophanies themselves.
In both cases it is not an initial encounter, but a mid-career event intended
to resolve a crisis in the public life of the prophet. These theophanies are
not initiated by YHWH, but are the result of human initiative, albeit in
different ways. In addition, both texts contain an explicit repudiation of
direct visual theophany to individuals who have had frequent contact with
YHWH prior to this event. Where Exod. 33.18–23 focuses on YHWH's
qualification of Moses' request for exceptional visual revelation, 1 Kgs 19
recounts the frustration of the prophet's expectations in the denial of the
storm theophany. While the qualification of the visual aspect of the
theophany is found in many theophany narratives, in these two cases this
restraint is unusually explicit.

The theophany in Exod. 33–34 is a multistage affair, beginning *in medias
res* with Moses' request for YHWH's forgiveness of the people after the
golden calf episode (Exod. 32). At first, it is Moses who initiates the
dialogue and determines the tone of the discourse. This is particularly
noticeable in his argument in 33.12–17, where he modifies his extreme
words in 32.32 ('Erase me from your book') in favour of a more controlled
rhetoric of persuasion, to which YHWH accedes in 33.17.[43] The
subsequent negotiation about the nature of the theophany which is to
take place (33.18–23) moves the discussion to a new level. Only here does
YHWH describe the permissible parameters of theophany, what he will
and will not do, what can and what cannot be seen. Moses' request to see
YHWH's *kavod* is not granted, but the invitation to inhabit a uniquely
chosen space (הנה מקום אתי) and the gesture of divine protectiveness (עליך

---

43. See the insightful and sensitive discussions of Moses' argument here in Moberly, *At
the Mountain of God*, pp. 66–76; Muilenburg, 'The Intercession of the Covenant Mediator',
pp. 159–81.

ושכתי כפי)[44] soften the refusal and accentuate the uncommon intimacy of the moment.

The actual theophany which follows in Exod. 34 differs from the previous chapter in that YHWH clearly regains the initiative and instructs Moses what he may and may not do. Moses is to carve the new set of tablets, but it is YHWH who will inscribe them.[45] In keeping with Exod. 33.21 these directives include specific details about where Moses is to stand in preparation for the theophany in 34.2.[46] The climactic moment of the theophany in 34.6–7 is an actualization of what is forecast in 33.19. YHWH causes his face to pass by (ויעבר ה' על פניו), and proclaims his essence as merciful and forgiving (רחום וחנון).[47] The idea of divine forbearance is the very heart of this revelation – all of YHWH's self-description in 34.6–7 is bound up with the question of forgiveness.[48] In contradistinction to other theophany narratives in which YHWH's words are usually descriptive of the fate of the human protagonist, here YHWH describes what the Bible understands to be his essential nature as a forgiving God.[49] In his analysis of this text Muffs argues convincingly that even the idea of deferred punishment is emblematic of divine mercy, and is entirely appropriate to the context of seeking forgiveness for the people.[50] When read as the continuation of Moses' request in Exod. 33.19–23, the 'goodness' which YHWH has promised to reveal is not reflected in a visual spectacle, but in the revelation of divine attributes, aspects of character rather than ocular representation.[51] Regardless of whether or not this reflects the *kavod* which

---

44.   M. Malul, 'כפי (Ex 33,22) and בחפניו (Prov 30,4): Hand or Skirt?', *ZAW* 109 (1997), pp. 356–68, suggests reading כנפיו here, in keeping with the tradition of a sheltering wing in Exod. 25.20; 37.9; 1 Kgs 8.7.

45.   On the relationship of Exod. 34.1 to 34.27–28 cf. Moberly, *At the Mountain of God*, pp. 103–5; Childs, *Exodus*, p. 615.

46.   The prohibition of the presence of other people or animals recalls Exod. 19.12–13, but the emphasis here is on Moses' singularity. cf. Moberly, *At the Mountain of God*, p. 84.

47.   On the question of the identity of the speaker in 34.6 see Childs, *Exodus*, p. 603; Moberly, *At the Mountain of God*, pp. 85–6.

48.   In contrast to Exod. 20.5–6 the idea of mercy has priority here and is expanded in significant ways. Moberly (*At The Mountain of God*, p. 88) suggests that, in contrast to 20.6, the absence of a clause requiring Israel's obedience indicates that divine goodness is available to Israel even in the face of disobedience.

49.   As an indication of the importance of this text within biblical tradition see the discussions of the exegetical development of Exod. 34.6–7 in J. Scharbert, 'Formgeschichte und Exegese von Ex. 34, 6f. und seiner Parallelen', *Biblica* 38 (1957), pp. 130–50; M. Fishbane, *Biblical Interpretation in Ancient Israel* (Oxford: Oxford University Press, 1985), pp. 335–50; Dozeman, 'Inner-Biblical Interpretation', pp. 207–33.

50.   Cf. Y. Muffs, 'Who Will Stand in the Breach?', pp. 9–46.

51.   The only visual component mentioned here is the cloud in 34.5.

Moses asked to see, he is privy to a truly rare moment of divine self-disclosure.

Moses' response to this divine self-revelation reflects his complete acceptance of YHWH's response. His use of the language of 'finding favour in God's eyes' in 34.9, as well as his repeated request for divine accompaniment on the journey, further cement the connection with 33.12–17. YHWH is to forgive Israel not simply because he cares about Moses, but because of his nature as a gracious and compassionate Deity. In this sense the reactions to the theophany confirm the roles established for Moses and for YHWH: Moses is the successful covenant mediator and YHWH is the gracious, forgiving Deity. The conclusion of the narrative, describing his shining face upon his return to the Israelites (34.29–35), returns Moses to his central position among the people.

In contrast to Exod. 33, YHWH reveals very little of himself in 1 Kgs 19, and what he does reveal is unfolded gradually. The graduated nature of this theophany is manifest first in Elijah's double encounter with a *malakh* prior to his arrival at Horeb, first in 19.5 then again in 19.7. These two moments are not identical; in the first the *malakh* is not attributed to YHWH, while in 19.7 Elijah recognizes him as such.[52] They should be seen as preludes to the direct encounter with YHWH, as should Elijah's 40-day fast in v. 8.[53] In contrast to Exod. 34.28, where the 40-day period of divine sustenance is meant to highlight the miraculous nature of the experience, here it occurs as preparation for the central theophany.[54]

---

52.   The lack of specific identification as a messenger of YHWH, coupled with Elijah's return to sleep in 19.6, betray Elijah's lack of awareness of his identity. The use of הנה in vv. 5–6 indicates Elijah's perspective; cf. Simon, *Prophetic Narratives*, p. 203.

53.   There is a certain degree of rebuke in the angel's use of רב in v. 7. In contrast to Elijah's use of the term as 'too much' in his plea in v. 4, here it means 'a long way': 'You have a long way to go before you can retire from this task.' But does the angel mean 'a long way' back to Israel, or 'a long way' to Sinai? If it is YHWH's idea to go to Sinai, then Elijah is being summoned by YHWH to receive a divine message. (Simon, *Prophetic Narratives*, p. 203). But if it is entirely Elijah's own idea, then his actions indicate a rejection of the angel's message, and his imitation of Moses seems almost artificial. As Robinson points out ('Elijah at Horeb', p. 519), Beer Sheva to Sinai is hardly a 40-day trek. Does Elijah stretch out the journey to fit the Mosaic period of 40 days? Moreover, Robinson suggests that Elijah decides to eat only food given by God, the better to emulate Moses' abstention from food and drink during his 40 days and nights on the mountain. This last point is too extreme; it would be better to attribute the forty-day period to a narrator or an editor who wanted to emphasize the Mosaic parallel in a positive sense.

54.   Both Exodus and Deuteronomy place Moses on the mountain for a period of 40 days (Exod. 24.18; 24.28; Deut. 9.9,18,25). In these texts refraining from eating and drinking is not preparation for an encounter with the divine, but an essential part of that encounter. Conversely it is very likely that the 40 day period in 1 Kgs 19.8 is meant to parallel the 40-year sojourn in the desert, which Elijah travels in reverse (cf. Carlson, 'Elie a l'Horeb', p. 432). This is not unlike the pattern of Elijah and Elisha in 2 Kgs 2.1–18, where they pass through Gilgal

Beyond the mention of the 40-day fast, the theophany at Horeb has additional points of contact with Moses' experience at Sinai in Exodus. As with Moses, Elijah and YHWH have an exchange of words both before (1 Kgs 19.9–10) and after (19.13–14) the theophany. Elijah's physical location in the cave on the mountain recalls Moses' stance before YHWH in Exod. 33.21, and his reaction of hiding his face recalls YHWH's promise to shield Moses in 33.22. As in Exod. 33.21, the theophanic moment is punctuated with הנה. The voice before and after the theophany is introduced by הנה in vv. 9 and 13, and the appearance of YHWH in v. 11 is likewise introduced by the phrase הנה ה' עבר.[55] As in Exod. 33.19–23 the description of the theophany is forecast, though in 1 Kgs 19 the actual occurrence of the theophany seems to be understood elliptically.[56] The sense of anticipation which is encouraged by this description dovetails nicely with the gradation of divine revelation within the narrative.

This anticipation is enhanced in 19.11 by the longish description of the wind, whose destructive power is witnessed by Elijah in anticipation of the coming of the divine. The phrase לפני ה' usually functions as a spatial indication of relationship to the numinous, particularly in priestly texts,[57] and this sense may well reflect Elijah's expectation. However, the immediate negation of this – לא ברוח ה' – frustrates this expectation, and the very next word, אחרי, makes it clear that לפני ה' is to be understood in a temporal sense as well.[58] The progression of phenomena detailed here actually prolong the experience for an unspecified period of time. While the

and Jericho before crossing the Jordan. This is meant to retrace the path of Joshua's entrance into the land in preparation for Elijah's appointment of Elisha – a clear parallel to Moses' appointment of Joshua. Cf. Carroll, 'The Elijah-Elisha Sagas', p. 411; J. Lundbom, 'Elijah's Chariot Ride', *JJS* 24 (1973), pp. 39–55.

55. Cf. Exod. 33.21. The use of the verb עבר (22, 33.19) to describe YHWH's presence is another thread linking 1 Kgs 19 and Exod. 33–34; see also Gen. 15.17; Num. 22.26.

56. Much has been made of the fact that the description in 19.11–12 is anticipatory, and the enactment of this forecast is nowhere explicitly stated. The most extreme position is taken by Robinson ('Elijah at Horeb', p. 521) who sees the fulfillment of the forecast only in YHWH's anticlimactic statement in 13b, 'What are you doing here Elijah?'. Zakovitch ('A Still Small Voice', p. 341) understands the theophany to have taken place as it is forecast, but sees the description of the enactment is unnecessary. Simon (*Prophetic Narratives*, p. 214) sees the parallel with Exod. 33 as decisive – in both texts there is forecast with no statement of enactment. However, Exod. 34 does serve as the enactment of the forecast theophany in 33.19–23, giving a sense of completion to the experience which is lacking in Kings. Most suggestive is the solution offered by Walsh, *I Kings* p. 275: 'The description may fulfill a double function: it contains Yahweh's words anticipating the theophany; but it also serves as an implicit description of the events as they unfold, in order to avoid a repetition of details which would weaken the power of the images.' On the narrative effects of forecasting in repetitive structures in biblical narrative cf. M. Sternberg, *Poetics*, pp. 375ff.

57. See the discussion of the term in *TDOT*, vol.11, pp. 609–11.

58. This sense is less usual in the Bible; cf. Isa. 43.10.

combination of wind, earthquake and fire is a standard grouping for theophanic descriptions in both narrative and poetic traditions,[59] here they are noteworthy for what they *don't* contain. Theophany here is characterized more by absence than by presence, for even when the text reaches its climax in קול דממה דקה it is not clear if what is described is a finely perceived sound or a distinct silence.

What does Elijah experience here? There must be some audial element, for in v. 13 Elijah responds to what he hears (כשמע) by covering his face. If דממה is understood as 'silence',[60] then we might take דקה to indicate something like a 'fine' silence, in keeping with the sense of the word as 'finely ground'.[61] The deliberate application of a concrete term to a sound (or a silence) presents the reader with an audial oxymoron similar to that found in other theophany narratives, such as the seeing of sound in Exod. 20.15 and its interpretation in Deut. 4 'You saw no image but a sound'.[62] If, on the other hand, דממה is understood with Akk. *damamu*, 'to roar' or 'to moan', then the audible nature of the sound is more understandable.[63] The occurrence of דממה וקול in Job 4.16 indicates a whispering sound, which is more appropriate to the context than wailing or roaring.[64] While Elijah's perception of it is described as audial in v. 13, his physical response of covering his face is as if he is responding to something visual. The effect of both senses together recalls the response of the Israelites to the Sinai theophany in Exod. 20.15 'All the people saw the sounds...', a synaesthetic reaction unique to the perception of theophany at Sinai. Various contextual explanations of this sound/silence have been suggested,[65] but the unusual locution, following upon the rejection of the

59. Cf. Judg. 5.4–5., 2 Sam. 22.8–16 (= Psa. 18.8–16); Pss. 29.3–9; 68.8–9; 97.3–4; 104.4. Cf. Hiebert, 'Theophany in the OT', pp. 505–11; J. Jeremias, *Theophanie*; F.M. Cross, *Canaanite Myth and Israelite Epic*, pp. 147–77. Cf also the discussion of these sources in Van Seters, *The Life of Moses*, pp. 254–63.

60. E.g. Lev. 10.3; Amos. 5.13; Ps. 4.5.

61. Elsewhere the term is always applied to physical objects – sheaves (Gen. 41.6–7, 23–24); cows (Gen. 41.3–4); dust (Isa. 29.5; 40.15), and frost (Exod. 16.14). The one possible exception would be the root דכא in Ps. 93.3, indicating the roaring of the sea. But the equivalence of the two roots is far from certain. Cf. Robinson, 'Elijah at Horeb', p. 522 n. 8.

62. Cf. Carasik, 'To See a Sound', pp. 262–5; a similar paradox might also be conveyed in visual terms in Exod. 3.2, by the burning bush which is not consumed.

63. Cf. Simon, *Prophetic Narratives*, p. 213; Sommer, 'Revelation at Sinai', p. 443, n. 50.

64. Cf. Zakovitch, 'A Still Small Voice', p. 340. Robinson ('Elijah at Horeb', p. 257) cites Job 26.14 as a further indication of limited audial perception of the divine. B.H. Levine, 'Silence, Sound, and the Phenomenology of Mourning', p. 101, translates this as 'a droning voice' (with credit to H.L. Ginsberg), and prefers to follow the NJPS translation 'a soft, murmuring sound', deriving the noun from *d-m-m* II, 'to moan, sigh, mourn'.

65. Some examples: a polemic against the 'noisy' Sinai theophany to 'correct' its pagan associations (Cross, *Cannanite Myth and Israelite Epic*, pp. 193–4; Jeremias, *Theophanie*, p. 65); a parallel between the revelation and YHWH's reply to Elijah in vv. 15–18 hints at

familiar attributes of theophany, would seem to locate primary significance in its own ambivalent expression. The presence of YHWH ultimately cannot be reduced to naturalistic description, and is best expressed in paradoxical language.

2. *I Kings 19 and Exodus 33 as Mirror Images.*

Given the number of points of similarity and contrast between Moses and Elijah, the intertextual reading which immediately suggests itself is to see the two theophanies as direct reflections of one another. Since the theophany in Exodus 33–34 marks the conclusion of the Golden Calf pericope, it is inextricably tied to the role of the prophet as intercessor. The threat to the continuation of the people is so great, and Moses' success is so impressive, that this narrative serves as a foundational text for defining the nature of prophetic intercession.[66] Moses' overwhelming concern for the people is expressed in his attempt to persuade YHWH to forgive, in his refusal to abandon them despite their rejection of him, and in his return to their ranks with the tablets of the renewed covenant in Exod. 34.29–35. The function of the theophany in Exod. 34 is to confirm the roles of YHWH and Moses as forgiving Deity and covenant mediator respectively. There is no better illustration of the intertwined relationship between the two than the singular phenomenon of Moses' shining face in Exod. 34.29–24, where both his role and his appearance mimic YHWH's fiery revelation at Sinai.

1 Kings 19 is also set in the context of apostasy and prophetic intercession in the larger pericope of 1 Kgs 17–19, and here too the prophet succeeds in moving Israel to repentance and YHWH to conciliation. However, even the most generous reading of Elijah falls short of the figure of Moses. When 1 Kgs 19 is read in light of Exod. 33, Elijah approaches the Mosaic ideal but cannot equal it.[67] Where Moses singlehandedly brings about a change in YHWH's attitude toward the people, and returns both sides to the covenantal framework, Elijah's achievements are much more limited. Moses returns to the people to remain the unchallenged leader who has no peer, but Elijah must anoint a series of figures to help carry out YHWH's task. Where Moses' authority is affirmed, even strengthened by the end of Exod. 34, Elijah's position has been undermined. Moses invests

---

YHWH's displeasure with Elijah (Zakovitch, 'A Still Small Voice', pp. 344); a warning to Elijah that YHWH will not always intercede on his behalf in miraculous ways (Hauser and Gregory, *From Carmel to Horeb*, p. 70); a sign of support for Elijah to encourage him in his prophetic task (Simon, *Prophetic Narratives*, p. 213).

66. Cf. Muffs, 'Who Will Stand in the Breach?', pp. 11–16.

67. Even in the case of *Pesiqta Rabbati* 4, where Elijah and Moses are deemed virtual equivalents, there is a distinct difference in YHWH's receptivity to the two figures, to Elijah's disadvantage.

Joshua as his successor only towards the end of his career, but Elijah must anoint his own replacement immediately.

The difference is also noticeable in the behaviour of the characters themselves. Where Moses is ever responsive to divine commands, Elijah has to be awakened twice by the angelic emissary, the only recipient of a theophany who is not immediately attentive.[68] Moreover, Moses puts his life on the line for the people, while Elijah asks that his life be ended for personal reasons. Fleeing from Jezebel, he also seems to be fleeing from the responsibility of the prophetic task, leaving a job half done at best. Moses too asks to be put out of his misery in Num. 11.11–15, but, as Zakovitch points out, the difference is very revealing: Moses asks to die because he felt he could not bear the burden of the people alone. Elijah emphasizes his aloneness (1 Kgs 19.11,14) in that he chooses to separate himself from the people because of their behaviour.[69] Moses, however, describes his singularity before YHWH only in order to save the people.[70] Where Moses is completely identified with the idea of forgiveness associated with YHWH's self-revelation in 34.6–7, Elijah's description of himself in 19.11,14 calls for the punishment of the people.[71] The comparison with Jonah suggested by the Mekhilta is most telling: Both prophets are criticized for being unable to find the proper balance between concern for the people and identification with YHWH.[72]

The contrast in the description of the theophany adds to this unfavorable view of Elijah. The idea of a revelation manqué has often been taken as a critique of Elijah; where YHWH reveals himself to Moses by self-disclosure in Exod. 34 Elijah gets only a 'negative' theophany. Instead of defining who YHWH is, the theophany defines where YHWH is not. Read in light of Exod. 33–34 this seems to be a rebuke to the recalcitrant prophet, a refutation of his expectations and a critique of his methods.[73] Elijah's literal repetition of his claims in 19.14 indicates that the

---

68. Samuel does not recognize that it is YHWH who speaks to him, but he is nonetheless immediately responsive to Eli. Even Balaam, similarly unaware of the presence of the *malakh*, reacts quickly and decisively to the evasive actions of the she-ass. The comparison of this double awakening to YHWH's miraculous feeding of Elijah in 1 Kgs 17 (Cohn, 'Literary Logic', p. 346; Simon, *Prophetic Narratives*, p. 204) only makes the discrepancy more apparent. There Elijah is immediately responsive (twice); here he resumes his sleep. Walsh, *I Kings*, p. 288 notes that Elijah is also less than obedient in not going out of the cave to experience the theophany 1 Kgs 19.13.

69. Zakovitch, 'A Still Small Voice', p. 332; Gregory and Hauser, *From Carmel to Horeb*, pp. 145f.

70. Robinson, 'Elijah at Horeb', p. 529; Walsh, *I Kings*, p. 288.

71. Zakovitch, 'A Still Small Voice', p. 345.

72. *Mekhilta* Bo, 1.

73. Zakovitch, 'A Still Small Voice', pp. 343; Uffenheimer, *Ancient Prophecy in Israel*, p. 233; Hauser and Gregory, *From Carmel to Horeb*, pp. 74–7.

prophet has been unaffected by the theophany he has just witnessed, and that he has not understood the message which YHWH was trying to convey to him.[74]

The upshot of the comparison is to reinforce what *Pesikta Rabbati* had already stated: Elijah may be good, but he is not Moses *redividus*. The extensive parallels between the two figures may enhance his standing in 1 Kgs 17–18, but seem to have the opposite effect in 1 Kgs 19.[75] This reading of the two texts leads to the conclusion that Moses is unique, and Elijah is a distant second. Other prophets may fit the Mosaic model of intercession, but no one can approach YHWH as Moses does, try as they might to emulate his actions.[76]

But if our reading points in the opposite direction, and we read Exod. 33 in light of 1 Kgs 19, a different dynamic emerges.[77] First, the difficulty of Elijah's situation becomes defined more sharply. Where Moses has to deal only with the people's sin and recalcitrance, Elijah must also battle a hostile monarchy and face active persecution by political forces. From this vantage point Elijah's wish to die does not simply reflect inadequacy born of frustration, but it is a principled act of protest against YHWH's limited response to the threat posed by Ahab and Jezebel. Clearly the drought in 17.1 and the subsequent bringing of rain in 18.45 are not sufficient to bring about any lasting change, neither in effecting popular opinion nor in garnering political support. Like Jonah who wishes to die of genuine disagreement with YHWH's policy of forgiveness towards Nineveh,[78] Elijah is unwilling to continue without a full hearing from YHWH. His request to die is not motivated simply by fear of Jezebel, but results from a profound disappointment with the limited success of his prophetic task. By contrast, Moses' request to be erased from YHWH's book (Exod. 32.32) appears to be more a gesture of rebellion than real despair.[79] In Exod. 32–34 neither YHWH nor the people exhibit the same

74. Cogan, *I Kings*, p. 457.

75. Walsh, *I Kings*, p. 288.

76. Amos, for example, acts as intercessor in Amos. 7.1–8.3, but he is successful only half the time. On the comparison between Jeremiah and Moses cf. Holladay, 'Jeremiah and Moses', pp. 17–27; idem, 'Jeremiah's Self-Understanding', pp. 153–64.

77. Neither text can be dated so unequivocally that one can assume a single vector of influence. On the dating of Exod. 32–34 cf. Childs, *Exodus*, pp. 604–10; Van Seters, *The Life of Moses*, pp. 290–318; on the dating of 1 Kgs. 19 see Rofe, *The Prophetical Stories*, p. 188; Long, *1 Kings*, p. 202. Moreover, the model of intertextuality applied here does not limit itself to influence in a single direction; see the comments by Dozeman, 'Inner Biblical Interpretation', pp. 208–9 and by Savran, 'Beastly Speech', p. 37.

78. See the interpretation of S. Frolov, 'Returning the Ticket: God and his Prophet in the Book of Jonah', *JSOT* 86 (1999), pp. 85–105.

79. Read this way even Moses' request to die in Num. 11 garners less sympathy than Elijah's request to die in the desert. One could argue that Moses works in a protected

sort of stubborn opposition as that encountered by Elijah. Elijah *in extremis* is a much more compelling figure than Moses, whose emotional reactions are rarely indicated in the text.[80]

Likewise, the notion of aloneness/uniqueness takes on a different dimension when Moses is understood in light of Elijah. As noted above, Elijah's aloneness is one of his defining characteristics, and the change which he is forced to undergo as a result of the theophany modifies this tendency. Elijah is compelled to work with others in order to achieve the goals set out for him. This change is hinted at by his instrumental use of Obadiah and Ahab in 1 Kgs 18, but expressed more fully in the command to anoint his three 'helpers' – Hazael, Jehu and Elisha. The brief description of the initiation of Elisha in 1 Kgs 19.19–21 indicates Elijah's willingness to accept the need for giving up his aloneness in a way that Moses is not able to emulate.[81] By contrast, Moses' singularity does not seem to allow for much change, and as such his theophanic encounter does not result in any significant shift in his character. In Exod. 32–34 Moses works entirely by himself, sharing power with no one and controlling everyone. Joshua is present in Exod. 32–34 as an assistant to Moses, occasionally helping, but with no indication that he will be Moses' successor.

A further reflection of this question of singularity can be seen in the role of the *malakh* in the two texts. In the case of Elijah, the graduated theophany mentioned earlier requires the use of angelic intermediaries, first to respond to his wish to die, and then to set him on the path to Horeb (1 Kgs 19.5–7). Elijah's acceptance of the role of the *malakh* foreshadows the need to accept the role of other intermediaries – Elisha, Hazael and Jehu – at the end on the chapter. Moses, by contrast, rejects the very notion of a *malakh* as a means of mediation between God and people. In Exod. 32.34; 33.2 YHWH promises (threatens?) to send a *malakh* to accompany Israel in his stead, and much of Moses' efforts are spent in trying to derail this additional level of mediation. This is seen in the

---

framework – the success of the plagues in Egypt are a foregone conclusion, and the Israelites in the desert have no competing political forces to fight them. Moses may be alone in his role, but Elijah suffers persecution with much less divine support.

80.   Simon, *Prophetic Narratives*, pp. 209–10, compares Elijah favorably to Jeremiah, and sees 1 Kgs 19 as a narrative of recommissioning similar to Jer. 12.1–6; 15.10–21 and Isa. 49.1–6. While the relationship of 1 Kgs 19 to this 'subgenre' is not entirely convincing, Simon's analysis is useful in bringing out some of the more positive aspect of Elijah's behaviour in this chapter.

81.   Even in Exod. 18 and Num. 11, where Moses chooses a number of assistants to aid him in handling the burden of the people, Moses retains his singularity, and continues to concentrate all power around himself. Despite the generous gesture to Joshua in Num. 11.29 – 'would that all the Lord's people were prophets' – Num. 12.6–8 makes it clear that Moses' prophetic status is categorically different.

elaborate rhetorical argument of 33.12–17, as well as in Moses' final comment in 34.9. In Moses' view, the presence of the *malakh* dilutes the sense of divine presence and threatens his singularity. In the case of Elijah, without the appearance of the *malakh* he would never have arrived at Horeb. In this reading of the two texts, Elijah's situation points up questions about the character of Moses which otherwise might have been overlooked.

3. *Exodus 33 and 1 Kings 19 as Reflexes of the Initial Sinai Theophany.*

The above intertextual readings uncover important differences in the situations of Moses and Elijah, viewing one prophet over against the other in an almost competitive fashion. Yet there must be more to the similarity between the texts than a negative evaluation of Elijah. In the context of 1 Kgs 17–19. one must ask why Elijah would be the object of such severe criticism, more so than any other prophet (with the possible exception of Jonah). When 1 Kgs 19 is read together with chapters 17–18, we see that Elijah scores impressive victories in these chapters. Moreover, he continues to work successfully as a prophet in 1 Kgs 21 and 2 Kgs 1. If Elijah is here rebuked and replaced, why does he reappear in a favorable light in subsequent chapters? Would not the editor of Kings have noticed the incongruity and reordered the chapters?[82] Since the comparison between Elijah and Moses is entirely positive in chapters 17–18, one must ask if it is likely that the narrator would turn against Elijah in chapter 19. And when this chapter is read in the light of other theophany narratives, we must ask why, only here, is visual theophany invoked in order to indicate the *failure* of the prophet, and perhaps to signal his removal? It makes little sense to argue that the theophany at Horeb is anticlimactic, when every theophany which we have explored serves as the climactic moment of the narrative in which it is embedded. The attempt to attribute an overinflated ego to Elijah is similarly unconvincing.[83] Comparable objections could be brought against the second reading which privileges Elijah over Moses: given Moses' unequalled standing, how can one explain his being compared negatively with Elijah?

---

82.   See the discussion of the placement of 1 Kgs 19 relative to chapters 17–18 in U. Simon, 'Elijah's Fight against Baal Worship: Unity and Structure of the Story (1 Kings 17–18)', *Studies in Bible and Exegesis*, vol. 1 (Ramat Gan: Bar Ilan, 1980), pp. 51–118 (55–63) (Hebrew); J. Gray, *I and II Kings* (OTL; 2nd edn.; Philadelphia: Westminster, 1975), p. 405.

83.   Cf. Hauser and Gregory, *From Carmel to Horeb*, p. 146; Walsh, *I Kings*, p. 289; Robinson, 'Elijah at Horeb', p. 519.

We therefore suggest an additional intertextual reading, one which views the two texts not as mirror images of one another, but as alternative reactions to the Sinai theophany in Exod. 19–24. Both come to offer an answer to a major unanswered question of the Sinaitic covenant – How will YHWH respond to disobedience to the covenant? And what will be the role of the prophet in this response? Is the prophet primarily on the side of YHWH or on the side of the people? The threat of punishment for idol worship is mentioned in Exod. 20, but does disobedience indicate dissolution of the covenant? YHWH has described himself as אל קנא, but it is not clear how this zealousness will be expressed. It is our contention that Exod. 33 (in the context of Exod. 32–34) and 1 Kgs 19 (or more correctly 17–19) respond to these crucial questions in different ways.

Both sections have structural parallels: They are each discrete literary entities[84] which begin with a major act of apostasy – the Golden Calf episode in Exod. 32, and what we subsequently learn to be Jezebel's sponsorship of the Baal cult and the killing of YHWH prophets.[85] In both cases there is a counterattack by the prophet: Moses descends the mountain, breaks the tablets, and destroys the calf (presumably together with the altar of 32.5). His punishment of the people culminates in the slaughter of a large number of Israelites by their own brethren. Elijah's response initially takes a somewhat different form, beginning with the announcement of the drought in 1 Kgs 17.1. In 1 Kgs 18 he rebuilds the altar upon which he offers a sacrifice, which leads to the Israelites' moment of repentance in 18.38.[86] Here too there is a wholesale blood-letting of the Israelites by their own brethren.[87] As in Exod. 32, it is the prophet who leads the slaughter. In both texts prophetic prayer plays an important role in persuading YHWH to respond favorably despite Israel's sin, including the unusual formulation 'Abraham, Isaac and Israel' (Exod. 32.14; 1 Kgs 18.36). Following this is the prophet's attempt to influence YHWH in his response to the people. In Exod. 33–34 Moses encourages forgiveness, while in 1 Kgs 19 Elijah urges punishment of the people. In both cases

---

84.   On the editing of Exod. 32–34 as a discrete unit cf. Childs, *Exodus*, pp. 557–62; Moberly, *At The Mountain of God*, pp. 182–6. On 1 Kgs 17–19 as a unit cf. Cohn, 'Literary Logic', pp. 333–4; Cogan, *1 Kings*, p. 430; Simon, *Prophetic Narratives*, pp. 155–8.

85.   Cf. Hauser and Gregory, *From Carmel to Horeb*, pp. 144–6.

86.   The Rabbis were well aware of the parallels between the texts as they assigned 1 Kgs 18 as the reading from the prophets to accompany the story of the Golden Calf. Cf. further *Exod. Rab.* 44:1.

87.   Cf. Simon, *Prophetic Narratives*, p. 191; Cogan *1 Kings*, p. 444. We should not assume that the these Baal prophets were imported from Phoenicia. They themselves are Israelites, and their act of apostasy is similar to that of the Exodus generation with the Golden Calf.

there is a theophany in which YHWH accepts the prophet's argument, albeit with certain reservations.[88]

But the differences between the two texts describe how each responds to the apostasy of the people in its own way. The response to the question of covenant breach proposed by Exod. 32–34 is that an outburst of divine anger can be surmounted by forgiveness, given the concerted efforts of prophetic intercession. Overcoming this anger takes place in graduated stages. Moses' intercession in 32.11–14 prevails over the immediate desire to destroy the people (32.15). Moses' second negotiation in 32.30 meets with less dramatic success, as YHWH promises to continue the people's journey, but only with the accompaniment of a *malakh*. The third, climactic intervention can be seen first in Moses' negotiation with YHWH in 33.12–17, by YHWH's response in 33.19, and by YHWH's self-description in 34.6–7 as a God of forgiveness. Moses' role here is primarily to act as the people's advocate, a task which he fulfills faithfully throughout these chapters. That the people are guilty is made clear in 34.9,[89] yet despite their guilt, YHWH's response is one of forgiveness and adoption of the people (ונחלתנו). Threat and punishment are not entirely foregone, as seen first in the harsh punishment in 32.27–28, and then in YHWH's reiteration of his identity as אל קנא in 34.14. But at this point zealousness is redirected towards the threat of idolatry from Canaanite sources. Whatever the hypothetical sources of the Golden Calf apostasy,[90] idolatry has now been more clearly defined as tied to the land of Canaan, and is not intrinsic to the Israelites.

By contrast 1 Kgs 19 shows both prophet and Deity advocating a harsher response to covenantal disobedience. Elijah's stance vis-a-vis the people is not one of intercession but of condemnation. He does not sympathize with their situation, but condemns them explicitly for his

---

88. Walsh, *I Kings*, pp. 284ff., develops some of these parallels in suggestive ways. He notes the similarities between Exod. 24 and 1 Kgs 18: the construction of an altar, the use of water/blood to anoint the altar, the covenantal meal in Exod. 24.9–11 and the commands to Ahab to 'Go up, eat and drink'. Moreover, there is a thematic connection between Elijah's prayer in 1 Kgs 18.37 and Moses' prayer in Exod. 32.11–13 – YHWH must respond for the sake of his own name. M. Fishbane, *Haftaroth* (JPS; Philadelphia: JPS, 2002), p. 139, notes the wordplay of sound and silence between the texts. Moses comments that the noises which arise from the camp are not (אין) the sounds (קול ענות) of war or victory, but of revelry (32.18). In 1 Kgs 18.29 when the prophets of Baal call out to their god, 'there was no response' (ענה אין קול ואין), but when Elijah calls out to YHWH in 18.37 he says 'answer me' (ענני).

89. I understand כי here as 'although'; cf. the discussion of the term in Moberly, *At the Mountain of God*, p. 90.

90. On the background of the calf cf. Childs, *Exodus*, pp. 565–76; M. Aberbach and L. Smolar, 'Aaron, Jeroboam and the Golden Calves', *JBL* 86 (1967), pp. 129–40; J.M. Sasson, 'Bovine Symbolism in the Exodus Narrative', *VT* 18 (1968), pp. 380–7.

persecution and for Israel's disarray. Jezebel (and Ahab) may be accused by the narrator, but Elijah places the blame squarely upon the people's shoulders. Both prophets interpret the second commandment, but where Exod. 34.6–7 rereads YHWH's self-description in Exod. 20.5–6 as the exemplar of a forgiving God, Elijah's self-description as קנא קנאתי in 1 Kgs 19.10 reinforces the more severe side of the Deity as אל קנא. His repetition of this claim in 19.13 emphasizes that, despite YHWH's theophany, he still sees the people as the primary defendant, and implicitly argues for their punishment (and his own vindication). YHWH basically accepts Elijah's demand and orders the anointing of three figures who will punish with the sword. Zakovitch's claim that Horeb is used here to emphasize the punitive aspect of YHWH's command to Elijah brings out this out forcefully. Sinai is no longer the place of the bush symbolizing covenant (סני/סנה), but rather it is termed Horeb, the site of the punishing sword.[91] YHWH tempers Elijah's complete condemnation of the people by claiming for himself a large number of Israelites who do not accept Baal, but he is essentially in agreement with Elijah. Disobedience to the covenant is to be met not with forgiveness but with punishment, and it is the job of the prophet to anoint those figures – Elisha, Hazael and Jehu – who will carry it out.

Another important aspect of both narratives is to be found in the reinterpretation of the theophany itself. As discussed above, Exod. 19–20 leaves unresolved the question as to whether the people were privy to a direct revelation from YHWH, or whether everything was transmitted via Moses.[92] Both Exod. 33–34 and 1 Kgs 19 make it abundantly clear that, whatever the people heard at Sinai, YHWH's command is brought to the people only through the prophet. In neither narrative are the people part of the drama of theophany.[93] Upon his return in Exod. 34.28–35. Moses enacts the role of YHWH in delivering the revelation to the people, replete with the tablets of the law and a transfigured face.[94] In 1 Kgs 19, only Elijah can convey YHWH's message to the people, for both prophet and king will be anointed by him.

1 Kgs 19 carries this process still further. Where the theophany in Exod. 34 basically recapitulates the event described in Exod. 19–20 in emphasizing a visual experience, 1 Kgs 19 'refines' the Sinai theophany traditions by separating YHWH from the forces of nature in an explicit

91. Zakovitch, 'A Still Small Voice', p. 334.
92. See discussion in Chapter 4.
93. At most, the people experience fire from heaven in 1 Kgs 18.38–39, but this type of revelation, like that reported in Lev. 9.24, is hardly the same as the verbal revelation discussed here. Cf. the discussion of the priestly account of the Sinai revelation in Schwartz, 'The Priestly Account of the Theophany', pp. 103–34.
94. See the discussion of this text in Chapter 5.

fashion. While the downplaying of the visual factor is consistent with a number of other texts we have examined,[95] nowhere else is there such an explicit rejection of these elements in favor of the verbal. Whether this reworking was a response to the syncretizing phenomena of the Baal cult,[96] or a clarification of the question of how the divine voice manifests itself,[97] it is clear that the return to Horeb reinterprets the earlier experience.[98] Moreover, this rarefied experience of the numinous must be read in conjunction with 1 Kgs 18. There, YHWH reveals himself in fire, one of the standard divine manifestations which are appropriate for the masses. But Elijah's experience of YHWH at Horeb indicates that YHWH's real essence is to be found in articulated silence, not in the noise of theophanic pyrotechnics.[99]

The two texts represent the two faces of the idea of the covenant mediator. If Exod. 32–34 develops the image of the all-powerful prophet who is capable of persuading both YHWH and Israel, 1 Kgs 19 develops the notion of the beleaguered prophet who must find ways to fight a recalcitrant people. In Exod. 32–34 Moses continues the model of Exod. 20.18–21, concerned with the welfare of the people, and willing to speak with YHWH on their behalf. Elijah represents the persecuted prophet, beset by political and popular forces which he cannot control. This distinction is exemplified in the difference between the concluding sections of the two texts. In Exod. 34.29–35 Moses is at his most singular, bringing the tablets to the people, and serving as a continuing conduit of revelation for the people. Joshua is nowhere to be seen, as Moses is indispensable for the people's survival. By contrast the anointing of Elisha in 1 Kgs 19.19–21, together with the plan to involve the political figures Jehu and Hazael, indicate Elijah's singularity is at an end. To the question of how the covenant is to be perpetuated we have two answers. Exod. 34 sees the covenant as bound up exclusively with Moses – only he can mediate it.[100] 1 Kgs 19, on the other hand, suggests that the covenant will maintain itself regardless of the type of prophetic leader. There will never be another

---

95.   E.g. 1 Sam. 3 and Jer. 1.

96.   Cf. F.C. Fensham, 'A Few Observations on the Polarization Between Baal and Yahweh in I Kings 17–19,' *ZAW* 92 (1980), pp. 227–36; Jeremias, *Theophanie*, p. 65; Cross, *Canaanite Myth and Israelite Epic*, pp. 192–4.

97.   See the discussion of the people's reaction in Exod. 20.15–18 in Chapter 5. Sommer, 'Revelation at Sinai', pp. 441ff., invokes 1 Kgs 19.12–13 as support for the interpretation that YHWH did not speak to the people at Sinai.

98.   Cf. Sommer, 'Revelation at Sinai', p. 442.

99.   Sommer, 'Revelation at Sinai' p. 444, points to Job 4.16 as further indication of a similar type of revelation.

100.   Deut. 5 and 18 are a subsequent development of this; all subsequent leaders will be in the model of Moses.

Moses, but there will be an Elijah and an Elisha, who reshape the covenantal ideal in new ways.[101]

---

101. On the covenantal ideal represented by these prophets see Uffenheimer, *Ancient Prophecy in Israel*, pp. 173–277; J. Blenkinsopp, *A History of Prophecy in Israel* (London: SPCK, 1984), pp. 68–79.

Chapter 8

FROM THEOPHANY NARRATIVE TO DIVINE JOURNEY

As the biblical period draws toward its end the Bible attests to a significant change in the nature of contact between the human and the divine, both in form and in content. The most noticeable casualty of this change was prophecy. After the destruction of the temple, the lament literature speaks of the (temporary) disappearance of prophecy (Lam. 2.9; Ps. 74.9), and even when it is renewed in the post-exilic period it never regains its former glory.[1] The popular dissatisfaction with the lack of fulfillment of oracles of restoration led to a lowering of the status of prophecy and to a change in the way prophecy was perceived.[2] Along with the increasing anonymity of the prophet and the growth of the deutero-prophetic literature was a tendency to see prophecy as the possession of all Israel.[3] Divine inspiration was now seen as the force behind written activity (Ezra, the scribes) and musical activity (the Levites in Chronicles).[4] In post-exilic literature the

1. Rabbinic teaching sees the end of prophecy after the last of the Twelve (*Tos.* Sotah 13:2–3) but significant changes take place before this, and prophecy continues (albeit in a modified fashion) afterwards as well. See the discussion in F. Greenspahn, 'Why Prophecy Ceased', *JBL* 108 (1989), pp. 37–49. Among the reasons suggested for the decline of prophecy are: dissatisfaction with the lack of reliable criteria for distinguishing true prophecy from false (J. Crenshaw *Prophetic Conflict:Its Effect upon Israelite Religion* (BZAW 124; Berlin: de Gruyter, 1977), pp. 93–4); a profound disillusionment with prophecy after the failure of the prophecies of the return to materialize, which in turn led to the growth of apocalyptic literature (R.P. Carroll, *When Prophecy Failed* (N.Y.: Seabury Press, 1979), pp. 184–213); the disappearance of the institution of the monarchy (Cross, *Canaanite Myth and Israelite Epic*, p. 223); the canonization of the prophetic writings about the destruction which led to a valuation of written over oral prophecy (R. Mason, 'The Prophets of the Restoration', in Coggins, Phillips, and Knibb (eds.), *Israel's Prophetic Tradition*, pp. 137–54 (141)). See the discussion of this literature in W.G. Schniedewind, *The Word of God in Transition: From Prophet to Exegete in the Second Temple Period* (Sheffield: Sheffield Academic Press, 1995), pp. 14–22.

2. J. Blenkinsopp, (*Prophecy and Canon* (Notre Dame: University of Notre Dame, 1977) describes these new developments as 'scribal prophecy' and 'clerical prophecy'; see pp. 109–38, esp. p. 111.

3. E.g. Isa. 42:1; 49:1–6; Joel 3.1; cf. Wilson, *Prophecy and Society in Ancient Israel*, p. 307.

4. Cf. D. Peterson, *Late Biblical Prophecy* (Missoula, Mt.: Scholars Press, 1977), pp. 55–96; Schneidewind, *The Word of God in Transition*, pp. 130–88.

term *malakh* refers not only to a divine emissary, but to a human prophet as well.[5] The role of the otherworldly *malakh* in Chronicles was enhanced, becoming the essential mediator of divine revelation in apocalyptic literature.[6] Moreover, the transition from prophetic to apocalyptic thought brought with it additional changes in the prophetic message as well as in the prophetic role.[7]

Theophany traditions were also affected by these changes, resulting in a reduction of the number of theophany narratives, and in substantial modification when they do appear. This chapter will point out certain tendencies in the representation of theophany in the post-exilic period, but, in contrast with previous chapters, will not engage in an extended analysis of specific texts. With the exception of Daniel (which will be discussed below), there are no theophany narratives directed at individuals along the models which we have examined in previous chapters. YHWH appears in theophanic fashion a number of times in Chronicles, but only in connection with the dedication of Solomon's Temple. According to 2 Chron. 5.11–14 the cloud which represents the divine presence is stationed in the temple before the priests, and in 2 Chron. 7.1–3 the *kavod* appears before all the people at the conclusion of Solomon's dedicatory prayer. These texts are, however, highly derivative, and are constructed along the lines of the parallel text from 1 Kgs 8.10–11, with the addition of references to the dedication of the Tabernacle in Exod. 40.34–35 and Lev. 9.23–24.[8] None of these texts describe an original theophany event with interaction between the human and the divine, similar to what was seen in the pre-exilic literature. Those changes which have been introduced into the text reflect the Chronicler's tendency to harmonize Israel's religious life with the written Torah and with his particular ideology.[9] In like fashion the Chronicler has taken over the story of Solomon's theophany at Gibeon directly from 1 Kgs 3.5–14, just as the revelation to Solomon in 2 Chron.

---

5. E.g. 2 Chron. 36.15–16; Hag. 1.13; Mal. 1.1; 3.1; cf. Schneidewind, *The Word of God*, pp. 81–4; N.G. Cohen. 'From *Nabi* to *Mal'ak* to "Ancient Figure" ', *JJS* 36 (1985), pp. 12–24 (16–22).

6. Cf. 1 Chron. 21 for such an enhanced role of the *malakh*; cf. Schneidewind, *The Word of God in Transition*, p. 65.

7. See P. Hanson, *The Dawn of Apocalyptic* (Philadelphia: Fortress, 1975), pp. 1–31, for a discussion of the shift from prophetic eschatology to apocalyptic eschatology; cf. Blenkinsopp, *A History of Prophecy in Israel*, pp. 255–67.

8. See S. Japhet, *The Ideology of the Book of Chronicles and its Place in Biblical Thought* (Frankfurt: Peter Lang, 1989), pp. 72–4. Note also the similarity to the revelation in fire to Elijah in 1 Kgs 18.37–38 (pp. 83–5).

9. Cf. I.L. Seeligman, 'The Beginnings of Midrash in the Book of Chronicles', *Studies in Biblical Literature* (Jerusalem: Magnes, 1992), pp. 459–74; on the Chronicler's use of 'all the people' cf. Japhet, *Ideology of Chronicles*, pp. 270–78.

7.12–22 is based clearly on 1 Kgs 9.2–9.[10] While David reports having had a verbal revelation from YHWH in 1 Chron. 22.8–10 and 28.3, and is witness to a fiery revelation in 1 Chron. 21.26, the text of 2 Chron. 3.1 is ambiguous as to whether YHWH actually appears to David.[11] Thus, while the Chronicler recasts David in the image of Moses, he refrains from ascribing to David a more fully developed theophanic encounter, and restricts him to indirect means of contact with the divine.[12]

Further examples of the change in the nature of contact with the divine can be seen with the prophets Zechariah and Daniel. In contrast with earlier prophets who have direct visual contact with YHWH, both speak only with a *malakh,* and Zechariah in particular displays the growing distance between heaven and earth by his inability to interpret the symbolic visions which he sees.[13] While prophets like Jeremiah or Amos do not experience similar difficulties, Zechariah finds the divine message to be impenetrable without the help of a heavenly guide. The ease which characterises divine-human communication in the First Temple period is no longer present. A less personal aspect of the divine, associated with Wisdom Literature, comes to the fore during this period, marking an emphasis on personal piety in place of group revelation.[14] It is hardly accidental some of the most extensive theophanic descriptions in post-exilic literature occur in the book of Job, which is concerned entirely with questions of personal piety.[15]

10. See I. Kalimi, *The Book of Chronicles: Historical Writings and Literary Devices* (Jerusalem: Mossad Bialik, 2000), p. 57; Japhet, *I and II Chronicles,* pp. 530–32.

11. S. Japhet, with most commentators, follows the LXX reading here which adds YHWH as the subject of נראה (*I and II Chronicles,* pp. 550–2). But cf. Ehrlich, *Randglossen* VII, pp. 355–6, and Schneidewind, pp. 200–2.

12. In 1 Chron. 14.10 David inquires of YHWH by indirect means (compare 1 Sam. 23.9–12 and 1 Sam. 30.7–8); the oracle about kingship is transmitted by Nathan in 1 Chron. 17.3–15; communication with YHWH regarding the plague on Israel is accomplished through the prophet Gad in 1 Chron. 21.10,18.

13. This is particularly noticeable in Zech. 4.5, 13, where Zech confesses his lack of understanding of the symbols to the interpreting angel. Cf. C.L. Meyers, E.M. Meyers, *Haggai, Zechariah 1–8* (AB; N.Y.: Doubleday, 1987), p. 241; Niditch, *The Symbolic Vision,* p. 96.

14. Cf. R. Albertz, *A History of Israelite Religion in the Old Testament Period* (OTL; 2 vols.; Louisville: Westminster John Knox, 1994), vol. II, pp. 511–17.

15. This theophany in Job 38–41 utilizes the basic form of the theophany narrative: Job is effectively separated from his friends (and the rest of society) in the chapters which preceded the theophany. There is a limited visual perception (the whirlwind) which accords with descriptions of theophany earlier in the Bible. YHWH's speech is much longer and more involved that any other theophany, and Job's response is one of complete self-abasement. Cf. also Eliphaz' description of a night vision in Job 4.12–16 and the discussion in Clines, *Job 1–20,* pp. 128–31; G.V. Smith, 'Job iv 12–21: Is it Eliphaz's Vision?', *VT* 40 (1990), pp. 453–63.

1. *Revelation and Torah*

One of the main elements which comes to bridge the distance between the human and the divine is the idea of Torah, which, by the Rabbinic period, has become the primary conduit for divine–human contact. This process asserts itself noticeably in the post-exilic period with emergence of the canonized Torah under the leadership of Ezra.[16] Where the phrase דרש was used earlier to describe seeking out a divine oracle (e.g. Gen. 25.22; 1 Kgs 14.1),[17] in the post-exilic period it is used for inquiring into Torah for an answer to a question, and subsequently, in Rabbinic literature, as 'to interpret'.[18] This change can be sensed already in Psalm 19, where Torah comes to complement YHWH as cosmic deity, who is closely identified with the sun in 19.1–7, and in Psalm 1, where the way of Torah is the chosen path for success in life.[19] It is unclear exactly when this process begins,[20] but a significant developmental step has been demonstrated by Yehoshua Amir in his important study of Psalm 119.[21] The psalm is an elaborate eightfold acrostic which refers to Torah with a range of synonyms in nearly every one of its 176 verses.[22] Amir has drawn attention to the fact that many phrases in the psalm, which are elsewhere descriptive of a direct relationship to YHWH, are used here to portray the psalmist's relationship to Torah. While raising up one's hands in prayer is always directed toward YHWH,[23] in Ps. 119.48 the psalm lifts his hands towards YHWH's *commandments*. The normative object of trust (בטח) in the Bible is YHWH,[24] and the most common object of belief (האמן) is also YHWH,[25] yet our psalmist declares 'I have trusted (בטחתי) in your *word*' (119.42) and 'I have faith in your *commandments*' (119.66). In a similar fashion, where the idiom 'hiding the face' is used to indicate a breakdown of the

---

16. On the development of the idea of Torah in the biblical period see M. Fishbane, 'Torah', *EM* vol. 8, pp. 469–83 (Hebrew).

17. *TDOT*, vol. 3, p. 302.

18. *TDOT* Vol. 3, p. 306; Y. Amir, 'The Place of Psalm 119 in Biblical Thought', in Uffenheimer (ed.), *Bible Studies: Y.M. Grintz in Memoriam, Te'udah* vol. 2, pp. 57–81 (75–9) (Hebrew).

19. Cf. Albertz, *History of Old Testament Religion*, pp. 556–63.

20. The beginnings of this process are often identified with the Deuteronomic movement in the 8th-7th Cent. BCE; cf. Weinfeld, *Deuteronomy 1–11*, pp. 37–57.

21. Y. Amir, 'Psalm 119'. Cf. also D.N. Freedman, *Psalm 119: The Exaltation of Torah* (Winona Lake, IN: Eisenbrauns, 1999), pp. 87–92; J. Levenson, 'The Sources of Torah: Psalm 119 and the Modes of Revelation in Second Temple Judaism', in Miller *et al.* (eds.), *Ancient Israelite Religion: Essays in Honor of F.M. Cross*, pp. 559–74.

22. While the term תורה occurs most frequently (25 times), the other terms are not far behind: חוק (22), משפט (23), עדות (23), דבר (22), פקוד (21), מצוה (22), אמרה (19).

23. E.g. Lam. 2.19; Ps. 63.5.

24. E.g. Pss. 115.9; 118.8.

25. E.g. Gen. 15.6; Exod. 14.31.

relationship with YHWH, the psalmist pleads 'Do not hide your *commandments* from me' (119.19). Amir further demonstrates this with regard to the verbs שוה,[26] יחל,[27] אהב,[28] and דרש.[29] While it is unclear the extent to which the psalmist wishes to distinguish between YHWH and his Torah, the use of these terms in the psalm clearly demonstrates the shift in emphasis from pre-exilic descriptions of the relationship to the Deity. The large number of examples of this phenomenon in the psalm suggests that a mediated approach to YHWH by means of Torah has become significant by the time of this psalm. The psalmist's rhetoric effectively elevates Torah to a level which looks ahead to the Rabbinic understanding of Torah as the essential means for communicating the will of the Deity.[30]

This point can be sharpened with regard to a similar shift in the attitude toward theophany. In addition to the above terms, a number of expressions elsewhere associated with theophany are used by the author of Psalm 119 to describe the psalmist's relationship with Torah. For example, the verb הביט is used frequently to describe visual experience of the divine. Moses covers his face in Exod. 3.6 for he fears 'to look at God', and his experience of YHWH is described in Num. 12.6 as ותמנת ה' יביט – 'he beholds the image of YHWH'.[31] The speaker in Ps. 119 uses the phrase three times, to describe gazing at God's commandments (119.6), God's paths (119.15), and 'the wonders of your Torah' (119.18). Nowhere else are these aspects of Torah the objects of visual contemplation. The effect of these locutions is to place the visual experience of the divine at a certain remove when compared with other sections of the Bible. While one might translate הביט in these three verbs in a more figurative fashion, such as 'have regard for', the contrast with actual visual experience of the divine is striking. Amir may be correct in understanding this (and other expressions) as reflecting inspired interpretation of a written text, but our point still stands: Visual experience of the divine has now been reinterpreted as contemplation of an objectified aspect of the divine.[32] In a similar fashion, the phrase גלה עינים, to open the eyes, occurs twice in the

26. Contrast Ps. 16.8 with 119.30.
27. Contrast Ps. 130.5 with 119.74,81,114,147.
28. Contrast Deut. 6.6 with Ps. 119.97,165.
29. Contrast Gen. 25.22 with Ps. 119.45,94,155. On the development of this term see Y. Heinemann, 'On the Development of Terminology for the Interpretation of the Bible: דרש', *Leshonenu* 14 (1946), pp. 182–9 (Hebrew); A. Hurvitz, *The Transition Period in Biblical Hebrew* (Jerusalem: Magnes, 1972) (Hebrew), pp. 131–3.
30. Amir ('Psalm 119', p. 66) correctly points out that Torah in Ps. 119 is not seen as the exclusive means for approaching YHWH; cf. e.g. Ps. 119.2,10,40,174.
31. Cf. also Isa. 38.11; Ps. 34.6.
32. Levenson, 'The Sources of Torah', p. 573 n. 35, sees the verse as referring to actual visionary experience, but this seems unlikely; the object of the supposed vision here is verbal in form, if not actually textual in nature.

Bible. We encountered it in our discussion of Balaam's theophany in Num. 22.31 as a clear expression of visual theophany.[33] But in Ps. 119.18 the psalmist asks 'Open (גל) my eyes that I my look upon the wonders of your Torah.'[34]

Such gazing upon the text is not a contemplation of the object 'Torah', but rather a search for interpretation by inspired means.[35] This development underlines the shift from visual revelation to inspired interpretation as a further indication of the indirection of theophanic contact in the psalm.

An additional example of the reworking of visual language can be seen in Ps. 119.89, where the psalmist claims that: 'Your word, O Lord, is forever stationed (נצב) in the heavens'. We have seen this verb used frequently as a term for the visual representation of the divine.[36] While elsewhere it is YHWH who is located in the heavens, here his hypostasized דבר is the focus of the psalmist's attention.[37] In all these cases the reworking of literal expressions of theophany into a figurative mode of contact with the divine illustrates this tendency to distance oneself from the visual experience of the divine.[38] Albertz is correct in describing this as a new formulation of the psalmist's relationship to the divine, rather than as a displacement of YHWH. Moreover, in contrast to theophany narratives which limit this inspired relationship to the divine to the chosen few, the

---

33. Also note the phrase גלוי עינים in Num. 24.4,16 to indicate prophetic revelation.

34. Note the use of the phrase גלה אזן to indicate verbal prophetic revelation in 1 Sam. 9.15; 2 Sam. 7.27; 1 Chron. 17.25; cf. also Amos 3.7.

35. Fishbane has argued that the expression מתורתך should be understood 'from out of your Torah', implying exegesis of an existing text. This idea is reflected in the reworking of Ps. 119.18 in post-biblical literature, such as Ben Sira 3.20–22, 1QS 11.3,5–6 and 1QHod 8.19. Cf. Fishbane, *Biblical Interpretation*, pp. 539–42; idem, 'From Scribalism to Rabbinism: Perspectives on the Emergence of Classical Judaism', *The Garments of Torah*, (Bloomington: Indiana University Press, 1989), pp. 64–78 (67).

36. E.g. Gen. 28.13; Exod. 34.5; Num. 22.22, 23, 31, 34 (here a *malakh* is referred to, but the visual sense of the divine is clear); 1 Sam. 3.10; Amos. 7.7; 9.1; cf. also Gen 18.2.

37. It may be possible to see in 119.130 a reference to verbal revelation, as suggested by L.C. Allen (*Psalms 101–150* (WBC; Waco, Texas: Word, 1983), p. 179] following G. Driver ['Textual and Linguistic Problems of the Book of Psalms', *HTR* 29 (1936), pp. 171–92 (191–2)), who reads פתח on analogy with Akk. *pitu*, which carries with it a sense of revelation, as in Gilgamesh. XI:9 'I will open for you (*lu-up-te-ka*) a hidden word'. Similarly, Dahood understands this as an imperative 'Unfold your words which illuminate'. It is not out of the question to see here an allusion to prophetic speech and the opening of the mouth, as in Ezek. 3.27; 33.22; Num. 22.28.

38. Levenson, 'The Sources of Torah', p. 564, correctly draws a connection between the absence of a Mosaic-type teacher in Psalm 119 and the essence of the psalm as 'a prayer for illumination and revelation'. Like the theophany narratives, the psalmist's revelation comes directly from YHWH (through Torah), and not from a teacher of Torah. In contrast to the narratives we have studied, the source of the revelation is YHWH, but the vehicle of that revelation is Torah.

type of piety described in Psalm 119 implies a degree of democratization of this special relationship to the divine.[39] As with the other terms which Amir has described, these three expressions move us toward a Rabbinic understanding of revelation which is focused upon the process of exegesis of the written Torah. While it is unclear if the psalmist in Ps. 119 has the canonized Torah book in mind,[40] he describes a process of inspired interpretation of an existing text, rather than direct revelation from the mouth of the Deity as reflected in the theophany narratives.

The most well-known biblical text which describes this combination of exegesis and inspiration is Daniel chapter 9, where Daniel reinterprets Jeremiah's 70-year oracle. After praying at length, he is visited by the angel Gabriel who tells him בין בדבר והבן במראה – 'contemplate the text in order to grasp the vision' (9.23). But Daniel's intensive study of the Jeremiah text (Dan. 9.1–2) is of no avail without the advent of divine intervention in the form of a *malakh*. The interpreting angel approaches 'in flight'; the phrase מעף ביעף recalls the flight of the angel and his cleansing touch in Isa. 6.6–7, but here the touch grants inspiration for reading the text of Jeremiah.[41] Y. Blidstein has pointed out that a similar combination of divine inspiration and exegesis of received tradition constituted an important model of Torah learning in the Qumran community. While the Qumran texts do not describe precisely how such enlightenment was transmitted, the idea itself is reflected in texts like 1QH 12.6 'Like perfect dawn you have revealed yourself to me with perfect light', and 'You have shown me your wondrous mysteries' (– הודעתני ברזי פלאכה 1 QH 12.27).[42] Although the Rabbis saw Torah learning primarily as a product of human intellectual endeavor, Blidstein argues that this model of divinely inspired learning can nonetheless be found in certain Rabbinic texts.[43] In light of these developments it can be said that the fusion of exegesis and inspiration in

---

39. Albertz, *History of Israelite Religion*, p. 558.

40. Cf. Freedman, *Psalm 119* p. 91.

41. Cf. Fishbane, 'From Scribalism to Rabbinism', p. 68.

42. See also CD 1.11–12; 3.12–14; 5.20–6.11; 1QS 5.8–9; 1QPHab 7.4–5. Cf. G.W. Nickelsburg, 'The Nature and Function of Revelation in *1 Enoch*, *Jubilees* and some Qumranic Documents', in Chazon and Stone (eds.), *Pseudepigraphic Perspectives*, pp. 91–119 (112–118); G.E. Brooke 'Prophets and Prophecy', in VanderKam and Flint (eds.), *The Dead Sea Scroll after Fifty Years*, pp. 344–78 (373–6); M. Fishbane, 'Use, Authority and Interpretation of Mikra at Qumran', *Mikra: Compendium Rerum Iudicarum* (Cambridge: Cambridge University Press, 1989), pp. 339–78 (363–5); idem, 'From Scribalism to Rabbinism', pp. 73–8. N. Weider [*The Judean Scrolls and Karaism* (London: East and West Library, 1962), pp. 81–5] points out that what he terms 'illuminational exegesis' continued among the Karaites. Psalm 119.19 became an important Karaite prayer text, and the psalm as a whole had a central place in Karaite thought (pp. 206–9).

43. Y. Blidstein, 'Torah and Inspiration in the Scrolls from the Judean Desert and in Psalm 119', *BM* 62 (1975), pp. 378–82 (Hebrew); cf. *BT* Ber. 29a; *Sifre Numbers* 41.

Psalm 119 describes a development of the idea of revelation which grows out of the language of theophany narratives.

2. *Theophany in Daniel*

Chapters 7–12 of the book of Daniel describe a number of elaborate visionary encounters with the divine which display continuity with the theophany traditions we have been studying.[44] While these visionary experiences entail contact with a divine emissary, the descriptions in 7.9–14; 8.13–19; and 10.5–19 involve theophanic encounters as well. In Dan. 10.7–8 Daniel is singled out from among a group; he is privy to a vision which no one else perceives, though they are present at the same place (recalling Eli and Samuel in 1 Sam. 3). In all three texts the description of the visual encounter with the divine (or the divine emissary) is followed by a verbal revelation. These visual descriptions of the divine owe much to previous images of the divine, especially to Ezekiel: fire (7.10; 10.6), an enthroned Deity (7.9–10), ministering angels singing praises (7.10), and clouds as an indication of divine presence.[45] The sight of the Deity enthroned invites comparison with Isa. 6, and the sense of divine judgment is reminiscent of the throne vision of Micaiah in 1 Kgs 22.[46] The experience evokes in Daniel a response of amazement and trepidation, with greater emphasis on his fear and on the attendant support of the accompanying angel (8.17–18,27; 10.8–9,15). Daniel is struck dumb before the image of the divine, faints, and is revived by the touch of an angel (8.18; 10.15–19).[47] Moreover, he receives the traditional prophetic encouragement 'Fear not' twice in 10.12,19. Like Gideon in Judg. 6.23 he is told שלום לך, apparently to offset his fear of death in the face of a numinous encounter. In all these ways the description of the encounter in Daniel draws upon earlier theophany narratives.[48]

---

44. On the structure of the book of Daniel and on the differences between the two halves of the book cf. Collins, *Daniel*, pp. 24–60; L.F. Hartman, A.A. DiLella, *The Book of Daniel* (AB; N.Y.: Doubleday, 1978), pp. 9–18.

45. Cf. the fire imagery in Ezek. 1.4,13,27; the wheels of the chariot in Ezek. 1.15–21; the cloud in Ezek. 1.4; 10.3–4, and A. Lacocque, *The Book of Daniel* (Atlanta: John Knox, 1979), p. 146.

46. See I. Gruenwald, *Apocalyptic and Merkavah Mysticism* (Leiden: Brill, 1980), pp. 30–31; Niditch, *The Symbolic Vision in Biblical Tradition*, pp. 197–198.

47. Collins (*Daniel*, p. 338) notes that the term תרדמה is also used of Abraham's visionary sleep in Gen. 15.12 as well as in Elihu's vision report in Job 4.13.

48. On the reuse of motifs from Ezekiel's call narrative cf. Fishbane, 'From Scribalism to Rabbinism', p. 69. On the connections with Isa. 6 see Nicol, 'Isaiah and Daniel', pp. 501–5.

But there are also significant differences through which the book of Daniel reveals its kinship with apocalyptic literature.[49] In contrast to the sudden character of theophany which is common to nearly all theophany narratives, Daniel prepares himself for his visionary encounters. In Daniel 9.3 Daniel sets his face toward YHWH, 'devoting myself to prayer and supplication, in fasting, in sackcloth and ashes'.[50] And in 10.2–3, while Daniel's abstention from food, drink and oil is clearly penitential, it also serves as preparation for receiving a vision.[51] Daniel may be overwhelmed by the power and the content of these visions (7.15,28; 8.27) but he is not taken by surprise. H. Pedayah sees the development of this technique as one of the major differences between classical prophecy and apocalyptic – revelation doesn't simply happen, but is determined to a certain extent by the seeker.[52] In addition, specifying a location 'on the bank of the great river' (Dan. 10.4) indicates that Daniel seeks out a desired place for revelation, as we see in other apocalyptic texts as well.[53] While seeking out oracles from YHWH is also characteristic of pre-exilic prophetic behavior, the active pursuit of a visionary encounter as demonstrated in Daniel 9–10 signals a new departure.

As is common in apocalyptic literature, all of Daniel's encounters are mediated by angelic emissaries, and he has no direct contact with YHWH. While the *malakh* figured noticeably in theophany narratives, it was always clear that the *malakh* was speaking and acting for YHWH. But in Daniel the messages which are supplied are dictated by the angel, without any identifying formula such as 'Thus says YHWH'.[54] Nor are the visions preceded by a phrase like 'Thus the Lord showed me' (Amos 7–8). In the

---

49. On the development of apocalyptic literature cf. D.S. Russell, *The Meaning and Message of Jewish Apocalyptic* (London: SCM, Press, 1964), pp. 73–202; J.J. Collins, *The Apocalyptic Imagination* (Grand Rapids: Eerdmans, 1998), pp. 1–42; idem, *Apocalyptic: The Morphology of a Genre, Semeia* 14 (1979), pp. 1–20; Hanson, *Dawn of Apocalyptic*, pp. 1–31.

50. Hartman and Di Lella (*The Book of Daniel*, p. 241) note that the use of בקש here has the sense of seeking an oracle, as in 2 Sam. 21.2; Hos. 5.15. Lacocque (*Daniel* p. 182) suggests a parallel with Moses' fasting in Exod. 34.28; Deut. 9.9.

51. Cf. Collins, *Daniel*, p. 372. This is made even clearer in 10.12 'From the first day that you set your mind to get understanding, practicing abstinence before your God'. Hartman and DiLella [*Book of Daniel* p. 278] note that this becomes an accepted trope of preparation for vision in apocalyptic literature, as in 4 Ezra 9.24. Cf. Russell, *Jewish Apocalyptic*, pp. 169–173.

52. Pedayah, 'Seeing, Falling', p.258. While preparation for receiving an oracle is found in classical prophecy as well, the phenomenon is more extensive and more focused in apocalyptic literature.

53. Cf. 3 Baruch 1.2; 1 Enoch 13.7. I. Gruenwald, 'The Speculum and the Technique of the Prophetic and the Apocalyptic Vision', *BM* 40 (1970), pp. 95–7 (Hebrew), argues that the choice of a site by a body of water was conditioned by the idea of indirection, seeing the divine reflected in the water.

54. Cf. Russell, *Jewish Apocalyptic*, pp. 235–40.

one vision where YHWH is visually present (Dan. 7.9–14) He is perceived only at a great distance from Daniel. He is referred to not as YHWH or as 'my Lord', but by the magisterial title 'Ancient of Days', an expression which does not imply a close connection to Daniel.[55] The description of the fiery throne owes much to Ezek. 1, but here the throne does not move closer to Daniel. Rather, all the images attached to it emphasize distance and transcendence. The fiery river beneath the throne prevents approach, the profusion of ministering angels leaves no room for Daniel to join the throng, and the Deity is involved in an act of judgment in 7.10. The bestowing of authority upon the son of man, most likely an angelic figure, is also accomplished in a ceremonial fashion which does not allow for Daniel's involvement.[56] Daniel witnesses this contact with the son of man as a mere observer, not as a participant in the divine drama like Isaiah in his throne vision in Isa. 6. All this contributes to a sense of enormous distance between the human and the divine. The idea that there can be no direct encounter with the Deity will be developed further in subsequent apocalyptic literature.

This is brought out even more clearly in Dan. 10, where the Deity is not present, but the divine emissary himself is described in unusual terms. On the one hand, his linen clothing reminds one of the messenger in Ezekiel 9–10 and indicates a priestly function.[57] But further details of his appearance recall the splendor of the Deity – the imagery of gold in 10.5, the splendor of the angel's face and his burning eyes in 10.6.[58] The hand which touches Daniel in 10.10,16,18 is not that of YHWH as in Jeremiah and Ezekiel, but of the angelic figure alone. Despite the fact that Daniel sees an angel who is clearly not the Deity, his reactions of fainting and revival are much more extreme here. He requires no less than three separate 'touches' by the angel to revive him (10.10,16,18). Although the angel touches Daniel's mouth in 10.16 the purpose is not to purify him (Isaiah) or to place a prophetic message in his mouth (Jeremiah); the touch simply enables Daniel to voice his message of distress.[59] In contrast to the theophany

---

55. On the source of the expression in biblical and Ugaritic literature cf. Collins, *Daniel*, pp. 290, 301; Hartman and DiLella, *Book of Daniel* p. 218; Lacocque, *The Book of Daniel*, p. 142.

56. The angelic interpretation of the son of man by Collins [*Daniel*, pp. 304–10 (following J. Emerton, 'The Origin of the Son of Man Imagery', *JTS* 9 (1958), pp. 225–42), emphasizes the otherworldly character of the entire throne vision and accentuates the absence of human contact with the Deity. Contra, cf. Hartman and DiLella, *The Book of Daniel*, pp. 85–102.

57. Collins, *Daniel*, p. 373; M. Himmelfarb, *Ascent to Heaven in Jewish and Christian Apocalypses* (N.Y.: Oxford University Press, 1993), pp. 17–20.

58. J.E. Goldingay [*Daniel* (WBC; Dallas: Word, 1989), p. 291] describes Daniel here as 'someone almost seeing God and hearing God, and almost losing his life as a consequence'.

59. Hartman and DiLella, *Book of Daniel*, p. 284.

narratives, the contact with the Divine is at once more distant and yet more distressing.[60]

The conversations Daniel has with the angelic figures also differ from the human response to theophany discussed in Chapter 4. We find no expression of doubt or skepticism on Daniel's part, only an exaggerated sense of weakness in the face of the angel in Dan. 10. The presence of a number of angelic figures with different roles also represents a significant development from the more limited role of the *malakh* in the theophany narratives. That the angels can converse amongst themselves is clear from Dan. 8.13–16 and 12.5–9. Daniel's overhearing the conversation of the two angelic figures in 8.13–14 recalls Micaiah's overhearing unidentified (angelic) voices in 1 Kgs 22.20–22, but also anticipates the Rabbinic trope of eavesdropping on the divine found in later midrashic literature.[61] The unnamed angelic figure in Dan. 8.16 instructs Gabriel to enlighten Daniel about the vision he has seen. While Daniel's extensive contact with the angels emphasizes his distance from YHWH, these emissaries are also a rich source of information and interpretation about what is otherwise hidden from normal human understanding.[62]

The messages which are transmitted by the visions are conveyed by means of highly baroque symbolism and complex interpretation. We find here little of the directness of classical prophecy. The visions do not address the immediate situation of Daniel, but speak to a distant future, giving voice to an apocalyptic eschatology.[63] In contrast to the prophetic call narratives Daniel's role is not addressed, except for the command to preserve the message for a later time (8.26; 12.4,9). Like the visions of Proto-Zechariah, Daniel is unable to understand the complex imagery without a guide, as is made clear by the comments of the interpreting angel (7.16; 8.16; 10.14,20). Everything is clothed in layers of symbolism, and each image requires a key for interpretation. By contrast, even where the precise meaning of a given element of the visual aspect of the theophany narrative was open to debate (Jacob's ladder, Moses' thornbush), the symbols themselves emerge from the natural world and their basic sense is straightforward. Ezekiel's chariot vision moves beyond this directness to

60. Pedaya, 'Seeing, Falling'. pp. 256–7. Pedaya argues that the apocalyptic visionaries are more eager than their predecessors to see God, but Daniel exhibits the same mixture of fear and fascination which we discerned in most of the protagonists of the theophany narratives.

61. Cf. *BT* Berachot 18b; Yoma 77a; Hagiga 15a, 16a; Sanhedrin 89b; *Deut. Rab.* Va'ethanan; *Tanhuma* Va'ethanan 6; *PRE* 6.

62. On the developing role of angels in apocalyptic literature cf. Russell, *Jewish Apocalyptic* pp. 235–62; Himmelfarb, *Ascent to Heaven*, pp. 69–70; C. Newsom, *Songs of the Sabbath Sacrifice: A Critical Edition* (HSS, 27; Atlanta: Scholars Press, 1985), pp. 23–38; idem, 'Angels', pp. 251–3.

63. Cf. Collins, *Daniel*, pp. 52–61; Niditch, *Symbolic Vision*, p. 247.

reveal a more complex set of visual images, but the world of Daniel's visual symbols is far more mysterious and multifarious.

In contrast to the final stage of the theophany type-scene, these narratives in Daniel offer no real indication of externalization, of the return of the prophet to transmit the message, or to assume a societal role related to the revelation.[64] In 8.27 Daniel returns to the king's service, but this is mentioned to indicate the discrepancy between his outer and inner states. If the prophet has been changed by the experiences he has undergone, there is little indication that he will express this transformation before the people. Rather, there is a greater focus on the prophet's own internal feelings, particular on his sense of being confused by the vision and bewildered by the interpretation (7.28; 8.27; 12.5). Herein lies yet another contrast with the theophany narratives: Daniel's sense of unease results from his inability to understand the meaning of the visions, and not from a sense of dismay at the content of the revelation, as shown by Isaiah in Isa. 6.11.[65] The numinous is no less present for Daniel than for Jacob or Samuel, but the terms of the theophanic encounter have changed significantly.

3. *Ascent to Heaven*

The pseudepigraphal book of *1 Enoch*, or more precisely the section known as *The Book of the Watchers*, partakes of the theophany tradition from Ezekiel and Daniel, and points in new and important directions.[66] Before being taken up to heaven, Enoch is approached by a group of fallen angels and asked to intercede with God on their behalf. 1 *En*. 14 describes the subsequent theophanic encounter with the Deity in a manner which has much in common with its biblical predecessors.[67] Enoch experiences many of the familiar aspects of biblical theophany – clouds, lightning, *cherubim*,

---

64. This is in marked contrast with Daniel's roles as courtier and dream interpreter in Daniel 1–6, where (with the exception of 4.16) the narrator gives no inside views of Daniel's state of mind.

65. Collins, *Daniel*, p. 342.

66. On the book of *Enoch* and the Enoch literature see J.C. VanderKam, *Enoch and the Growth of An Apocalyptic Tradition* (CBQMS, 16; Washington, DC: Catholic Biblical Association of America, 1984), pp. 110–40; G.W. Nickelsburg, *1 Enoch* (Hermeneia; Minneapolis: Fortress, 2001); Collins, *The Apocalyptic Imagination*, pp. 43–79; on the dating of the *Book of the Watchers* (*Enoch* 1–36) prior to Daniel 7–12 on the basis of fragments found at Qumran cf. VanderKam, *Enoch*, pp. 111–14.

67. The earlier theophany described in 1 Enoch 1.3–8 follows the pattern of the poetic theophany such as Hab. 3, and lacks the component of interaction with the divine. See J. VanderKam, 'The Theophany of Enoch i, 3b-7, 9', *VT* 23 (1973), pp. 129–50.

a divine throne, and a glimpse of the 'Great Glory' as the ultimate vision.[68]
Like Isaiah and Ezekiel before him, the throne vision in *1 En.* 14 can be
read as a prophetic call,[69] but unlike any other recipient of a theophany
Enoch ascends to heaven in order to receive this mandate. This is the first
case of ascent in Jewish literature, and it heralds a significant mutation of
the idea of theophany, which will gain currency in both apocalyptic
literature and the Merkavah tradition.[70]

In contrast to the passivity of Ezekiel and Daniel in their throne
visions, Enoch actively wanders through a heavenly temple;[71] the
structures he discovers are stationary while he moves through them.
While Enoch is indebted to Ezekiel's chariot vision in language and
imagery,[72] the idea of a journey here is completely new, and represents a
shift from other theophany narratives in which the vision (and the Deity)
comes to the human protagonist. Enoch is initially passive, as divine
winds carry him up to heaven (1 *En.* 14.8). But after this Enoch actively
engages the components of this vision. Nickelsburg points out the unusual
number of active verbs describing Enoch: he 'entered' heaven, 'drew near'
the wall of hailstones, 'went into' the tongues of fire, and then 'went into'
the two houses, all on his own initiative and by his own power. 'Enoch
does not simply *see* the house made of hailstones and snow and
surrounded with fire... he *experiences* its *peculiarity*'.[73] The vision follows
the model of Ezekiel's chariot vision in the gradual unfolding of its
numinous elements, but here the dramatic aspect is much greater, moving
from one spectacle to the next with increasing intensity. Moreover, Enoch
must pass through a series of protective barriers which shield the divine, a
process which recalls the trials of a hero like Gilgamesh more than the call
of a biblical prophet.[74] While Enoch's sense of *angst* in the face of the
vision is emphasized, it does not paralyze him, and his intense desire to
experience the numinous is brought out by the active description of his

---

68. Enoch's vision is also much more detailed, and contains new elements as well. While
certain images can be traced to biblical antecedents – e.g. the hailstones in 14.9 and the קרח in
Ezek. 1.22 – descriptions such as the simultaneous mixture of heat and cold in 14.13 are
original to him.

69. G.W. Nickelsburg, 'Enoch Levi and Peter: Recipients of Revelation in the Upper
Gallilee', *JBL* 100 (1981), pp. 575–600 (576).

70. Cf. M. Himmelfarb, 'From Prophecy to Apocalypse: The *Book of the Watchers* and
Tours of Heaven', in Green (ed.), *Jewish Spirituality*, vol. 1, pp. 145–65 (146).

71. On the structure of this temple cf. Nickelsburg, *1 Enoch*, pp. 263–4.

72. Gruenwald [*Apocalyptic and Merkavah Mysticism*, p. 35] traces the throne imagery to
Ezek. 1.26, and the wheels of the throne to Ezek. 1.16; Nickelsburg [*1 Enoch*, p. 254] also
points out connections with Ezek. 40–44.

73. Nickelsburg, 'Enoch, Levi and Peter', p. 580.

74. Cf. VanderKam, *Enoch*, p. 175.

progress.[75] The depiction of the throne which Enoch sees in 14.18–19 is much more forbidding than Daniel's sketch of the tongues of flame in Dan. 7.9. While Enoch has an equivalent reaction of fear and trembling, he nonetheless has direct verbal and visual contact with the Deity. On the one hand Enoch declares that no angel could approach the Great Glory, yet he himself is privileged to be addressed directly by God.[76]

Most of the book of *Enoch* and much of the apocalyptic literature is given over to this new form of encounter with the divine. Instead of extended contact with the Deity, the experience described by these texts involve extensive tours of the heavenly precincts.[77] Enoch's revelation in *1 En.* 14 is a stage on the way to his ascending higher than the angels.[78] In other apocalypses human figures are described as being transformed into angels.[79] YHWH's refusal to descend to the earth (after his departure from the Temple in Ezek. 11) has not led to a deterioration of the relationship with the divine, but to new ways of defining that relationship. The ascent to heaven is the obverse of the process of biblical theophany, describing a unique way of mediating the distance between heaven and earth. Enoch is the prototype for such an ascent, and he is but the first in a line which continues through the apocalyptic literature to the Hekhalot texts and Merkavah mysticism, where instructions for achieving the experience of ascent are related.[80]

The decline of prophecy and the rise of apocalyptic has often been seen to reflect an ever-growing distance between the human and the divine, a situation in which the gap between heaven and earth has been filled with myriads of angels, but whose presence actually clogs the channels of communication. Insofar as the Deity is virtually inaccessible to humans, the close interaction between the human and the divine as reflected in the theophany traditions of the Hebrew Bible is seen to have diminished drastically.[81] But if the natural continuation of the biblical theophany

75. Cf. Pedayah ['Seeing, Falling' p. 257] suggests that a greater desire to experience the divine in its fullness differentiates the apocalyptic and Hekhalot texts from their biblical predecessors.

76. Gruenwald sees this as a prototype of Merkavah ascent, since Enoch goes unaccompanied by an angel and, unlike Daniel, is spoken to directly by God; cf. *Apocalyptic and Merkavah Mysticism*, p. 36. Nickelsburg, however, [*1 Enoch*, p. 265] claims that v. 22 indicates that some angels can in fact approach the Deity. According to Pedayah, ['Seeing, Falling', p. 252] the text is deliberately ambiguous about whether or Enoch actually saw God.

77. See the range of journeys described in J.J. Collins, 'Jewish Apocalypses', *Semeia* 14 (1979), pp. 36–43; Himmelfarb, *Ascent to Heaven*, pp. 29–46.

78. In *2 Enoch* 22 he actually joins the angels, and in *3 Enoch* (*Sefer Hekhalot*) he becomes the angel Metatron.

79. Cf. Himmelfarb, *Ascent to Heaven*, pp. 47–71.

80. See M. Himmelfarb, 'Heavenly Ascent and the Relationship of the Apocalypses and the *Hekhalot* Literature', *HUCA* 59 (1988), pp. 73–100.

81. E.g. M. Hengel, *Judaism and Hellenism* (2 vols.; Philadelphia: Fortress, 1974), vol. 1, p. 233.

tradition is to be found in the literature of apocalypticism and early mysticism, then the heavens are opened up to human visitation, and reveal their mysteries to select humans in new ways.[82] Martha Himmelfarb has suggested that the multiplication of angels should be seen not as closing off the opportunity for encounter with the numinous, but as a broadening of the conduit of communication between the human and the divine. In the theophany narrative we have seen how the Deity descended to earth out of a desire to communicate with Israel and to direct their future. She argues that, in a complementary fashion, 'the ascent apocalypses make greater claims for the nature of humanity; human beings, whether all the righteous or a single inspiring example, have the potential to become like angels, or even greater than the angels.'[83] The waning of the theophany narrative in the Bible leads to the opening of the *Book of the Watchers*, to Enoch, and to the many figures who ascend to heaven, not to challenge the angels, but to seek out the divine.

Despite the similarities between the pre-exilic and post-exilic theophany traditions outlined above, it is clear that something exceptional in the relationship with the numinous has changed irrevocably. What was demonstrated continuously in the theophany narratives was the possibility of an encounter between YHWH and a wide variety of individuals – men and women, prophets, patriarchs and judges. It would be incorrect to claim that a direct encounter with YHWH could be experienced by all Israel. The very idea of Sinai as a one-time event, never to be re-enacted, demonstrates how unusual the experience of the divine was. The ambivalence in the Exodus account as to what precisely Israel saw and heard at Sinai underscores the sense of an unrecoverable moment. Yet the variety of texts, personalities, and roles that we find in these theophany traditions indicate that the Deity was accessible in a wide variety of circumstances, and that this availability was central to Israel's relationship to YHWH. What the theophany narratives illustrate clearly, perhaps more than any other group of biblical texts, is the sense that YHWH both desires and actively seeks out such communication. For the most part it is not human initiative which dominates here, but rather the impetus of the Deity to communicate directly with chosen individuals. The message communicated is certainly of great importance, but it is the method of communication which is exceptional here, the pattern of overture and response, of hesitation and reassurance. In all these senses, the theophany narratives offer us a glimpse of a unique moment of intimacy in the ongoing relationship of YHWH and Israel.

82. Cf. Gruenwald, *Apocalyptic and Merkavah Mysticism*, pp. 8–16.
83. M. Himmelfarb, *Ascent to Heaven*, p. 71.

BIBLIOGRAPHY

Aberbach, M., and Smolar, L., 'Aaron, Jeroboam and the Golden Calves', *JBL* 86 (1967), pp. 129–40.

Ackerman, S., 'Is Miriam Also Among the Prophets (And Is Zipporah Among the Priests?)', *JBL* 121 (2002), pp. 47–80.

— 'The Deception of Isaac, Jacob's Dream at Bethel, and Incubation on an Animal Skin', in Anderson and Olyan (eds.), *Priesthood and Cult in Ancient Israel*, pp. 92–120.

Ackroyd, P.R., and B. Lindars (eds.), *Words and Meanings: Essays Presented to David Winton Thomas* (Cambridge: Cambridge University Press, 1968).

Ahituv S., *Joshua*, (Jerusalem: Magnes, 1995) (Hebrew).

— 'The Countenance of God' in Cogan *et al* (eds.), *Tehillah LeMoshe: Biblical and Judaic Studies in Honor of Moshe Greenberg*, pp. 3*-13* (Hebrew).

Albertz, R., *A History of Israelite Religion in the Old Testament Period*, (OTL; 2 vols.; Louisville: Westminster John Knox, 1994).

Alexander, T.D., 'The Hagar Traditions in Genesis XVI and XXI', in Emerton (ed.), *Studies in the Pentateuch*, pp. 131–48.

Allen, L.C., *Ezekiel 1–19* (WBC; Waco, Texas: Word, 1994).

— *Psalms 101–50* (WBC; Waco, Texas: Word, 1983).

— 'The Structure and Intention of Ezekiel 1', *VT* 43 (1993), pp. 145–61.

Alter, R., 'How Convention Helps us Read: The Case of the Bible's Annunciation Type-Scene', *Prooftexts* 3 (1983), pp. 115–30.

— *The Art of Biblical Narrative* (N.Y.: Basic Books, 1981).

Amir, Y., 'The Place of Psalm 119 in Biblical Thought', in Uffenheimer (ed.), *Bible Studies: Y.M. Grintz in Memoriam, Te'udah* vol. 2, pp. 57–81 (Hebrew).

Amit, Y., 'Bochim, Bethel, and the Hidden Polemic (Judg 2,1–5)', in Galil and Weinfeld (eds.), *Studies in Historical Geography and Biblical Historiography*, pp. 121–31.

— ' "Manoah Promptly Followed his Wife" (Judges 13:11): On the Place of the Woman in the Birth Narratives', in Brenner (ed.), *A Feminist Companion to Judges*, pp. 146–56.

— *The Book of Judges: The Art of Editing* (Jerusalem: Mossad Bialik, 1992) (Hebrew).

— 'The Story of Samuel's Commission to Prophecy in Light of Prophetic Thought', in Luria (ed.), *Sepher Moshe Goldstein*, pp. 29–39 (Hebrew).

Anderson B. and W. Harrelson, (eds.), *Israel's Prophetic Heritage*, (N.Y.: Harper and Row, 1962).

Anderson, F.I., *The Sentence in Biblical Hebrew*, (The Hague: Mouton, 1974).

Anderson, G.A., and S.M. Olyan (eds.), *Priesthood and Cult in Ancient Israel*, (Sheffield: Sheffield Academic Press, 1991).

Assmann, J., and G.G. Stroumsa (eds.), *Transformations of the Inner Self in Ancient Religions* (Leiden: Brill, 1999).

Auerbach, E. *Mimesis* (trans. W.R. Trask; Princeton: Princeton University Press, 1953).

Avishur, Y., 'On the Demonic Nature of the Bridegroom of Blood Story (Exod. 4:24–26)', *Eshel Beer Sheva* 2 (1981), pp. 1–17 (Hebrew).

Avishur, Y. and J. Blau, (eds.), *Studies in the Bible and the Ancient Near East Presented to Samuel Loewenstamm* (2 vols.; Jerusalem: Rubenstein, 1978).

Bal, M., *Lethal Love*, (Bloomington: Indiana University Press, 1987).

Bar-Efrat, S., *The Art of the Biblical Story* (Tel Aviv: Sifriat Poalim, 1979).

Bar, S., *A Letter That Has Not Been Read: Dreams in the Hebrew Bible* (Cincinnati: HUC Press, 2001).

Barr, J., 'Theophany and Anthropomorphism in the Old Testament', *VTS* 7 (1959), pp. 31–8.

Barrick, W.B., *et al.* (eds.), *In the Shelter of Elyon* (JSOTS. 31; Sheffield: JSOT Press, 1984).

Baudissin, W.W.G., '"Gott schauen" in der attestamentliche Religion', *Archiv fur Religionswissenschaft* 18 (1915), pp. 173–239.

Beale, G.K., 'Isaiah VI 9–13; A Retributive Taunt Against Idolatry', *VT* 41 (1991), pp. 257–78.

Bell, C., *Ritual: Perspectives and Dimensions* (New York: Oxford University Press, 1997).

Ben-Tulilah, J. (ed.), *Shai Lehadasah – Studies in Hebrew Language and Jewish Languages*, (Beer Sheva: Ben Gurion University, 1997).

Bergen, W.J., *Elisha and the End of Prophetism* (Sheffield: Sheffield Academic Press, 1999).

Berlin, A., *Poetics and Interpretation of Biblical Narrative* (Sheffield: Almond Press, 1983).

Berlin, A., 'Numinous *Nomos*: On the Relationship Between Law and Narrative', in Olyan and Culley (eds.), *'A Wise and Discerning Mind': Essays in Honor of Burke O. Long*, pp. 25–31.

Bird, P., 'The Place of Women in the Israelite Cultus', in Miller *et al.* (eds.), *Ancient Israelite Religion: Essays in Honor of F.M. Cross*, pp. 397–419.

Blenkinsopp, J., *A History of Prophecy in Israel* (London: SPCK, 1984).

— *Isaiah 1–39* (AB; N.Y.: Doubleday, 2000).

— *Prophecy and Canon* (Notre Dame: University of Notre Dame, 1977).

Blidstein, Y., 'Torah and Inspiration in the Scrolls from the Judean Desert and in Psalm 119', *BM* 62 (1975), pp. 378–82 (Hebrew).

Block, D.I., 'Text and Emotion: A Study in the "Corruptions" in Ezekiel's Inaugural Vision (Ezekiel 1:4–28)', *CBQ* 50 (1988), pp. 418–42.

— *The Book of Ezekiel: Chapters 1–24* (Grand Rapids, MI: Eerdmans, 1974).

Bogaert, P-M. (ed.), *Le Livre de Jeremie* (Leuven: Leuven University Press, 1981).

Boling, J.G., *Judges* (AB; Garden City, NY: Doubleday, 1975).

Botterweck, G.J. and H. Ringgren (eds.), *Theological Dictionary of the Old Testament* (Grand Rapids, MI: Eerdmans, 1974-).

Booij, Th., 'Hagar's Words in Genesis XVI 13B', *VT* 30 (1980), pp. 1–7.

— 'Mountain and Theophany in the Sinai Narrative', *Biblica* 65 (1984), pp. 1–26.

Boyarin, D., 'The Eye in the Torah: Ocular Desire in the Midrashic Hermeneutic', *Critical Inquiry* 16 (1990), pp. 532–50.

Brenner, A. (ed.), *A Feminist Companion to Judges* (Sheffield: Sheffield Academic Press, 1993).

Brodsky, H., 'Bethel', *ABD* I, pp. 710–12.

Brooke, G.E., 'Prophets and Prophecy', in VanderKam and Flint (eds.), *The Dead Sea Scroll after Fifty Years*, pp. 344–78.

Buber, M., *Moses* (N.Y.: Harper and Row, 1958).

— *The Prophetic Faith* (N.Y.: Harper and Row, 1949).

Calloway, M., *Sing, O Barren One* (Decatur, GA: Scholars Press, 1986).

Carasik, M., 'To See a Sound: A Deuteronomic Rereading of Exodus 20:15', *Prooftexts* 19 (1999), pp. 257–65.

Carlson, R.A., 'Elie a l'Horeb,' *VT* 19 (1969), pp. 416–39.

Carroll, R.P., *Jeremiah* (OTL; Philadelphia: Westminster, 1986).

— 'Strange Fire', *JSOT* 61 (1994), pp. 39–58.

— 'The Elijah-Elisha Sagas: Some Remarks on Prophetic Succession in Ancient Israel', *VT* 19 (1969), pp. 400–15.

— *When Prophecy Failed* (N.Y.: Seabury, 1979).

Cartledge, T., *Vows in the Hebrew Bible and the Ancient Near East* (Sheffield: Sheffield Academic Press, 1992).

Cassuto, U., *Commentary on the Book of Exodus* (Jerusalem: Magnes, 1952).

Chazon, E.G. and M. Stone (eds.), *Pseudepigraphic Perspectives* (Leiden: Brill, 1999).

Chernus, I., 'Visions of God in Merkabah Mysticism', *JSJ* 13 (1982), pp. 123–46.

Childs, B.S., 'Anticipatory Titles in Hebrew Narrative', in Rofe, A., and Y. Zakovitch, (eds.), *Isaac Leo Seeligmann Volume*, vol. 3, pp. 57–65.

— *Isaiah 1–39* (OTL; Louisville, KY: Westminster, 2001).

— *The Book of Exodus* (OTL; Philadelphia: Westminster, 1974).

Clifford, R. *The Cosmic Mountain in Canaan and the Old Testament* (Cambridge MA.: Harvard University Press, 1972).

Clines, D., *Job 1–20*, (WBC; Waco, Texas: Word, 1989).

Coats, G.W., 'The King's Loyal Opposition: Obedience and Authority in Exod. 32–34', in Long and Coats (eds.), *Canon and Authority*, pp. 91–109.

Cogan, M., *I Kings* (AB; N.Y.: Doubleday, 2000).

Cogan, M. *et al* (eds.), *Tehillah LeMoshe: Biblical and Judaic Studies in Honor of Moshe Greenberg* (Winona Lake, IN: Eisenbrauns, 1997).

Coggins, R., Phillips, A., and Knibb, M. (eds.), *Israel's Prophetic Tradition* (Cambridge: Cambridge University Press, 1982).

Cohen, C., 'The Literary Motif of Jacob's Ladder', in Ben-Tulilah (ed.), *Shai Lehadasah – Studies in Hebrew Language and Jewish Languages*, pp. 15–26 (Hebrew).

Cohen, N.G., 'From *Nabi* to *Mal'ak* to "Ancient Figure" ', *JJS* 36 (1985), pp. 12–24.

Cohn, R.L., 'The Literary Logic of I Kings 17–19', *JBL* 101 (1982), pp. 333–50.
— *The Shape of Sacred Space* (Chico, CA: Scholars Press, 1981).
Collins, J.J., *Daniel* (Hermeneia; Minneapolis: Fortress, 1993).
— 'Jewish Apocalypses', *Semeia* 14 (1979), pp. 21–59.
— *The Apocalyptic Imagination* (Grand Rapids: Eerdmans, 1998).
Collins, J.J. (ed.), *Apocalyptic: The Morphology of a Genre*, *Semeia* 14, (1979).
Cook, J.A., 'The Theophanies of Gideon and Manoah', *JTS* 28 (1927), pp. 363–83.
Coote, R.B., 'The Meaning of the Name Israel', *HTR* 65 (1972), pp. 137–46.
— 'Yahweh Recalls Elijah,' in Halpern and Levenson (eds.), *Traditions in Transformation*, pp. 115–20.
Crenshaw J., *Prophetic Conflict:Its Effect upon Israelite Religion* (BZAW 124; Berlin: de Gruyter, 1977).
Cross, F.M., *Canaanite Myth and Hebrew Epic* (Cambridge: Harvard University Press, 1973).
Dan, J., *On Sanctity* (Jerusalem: Magnes, 1997 (Hebrew).
Davis, E.F., *Swallowing The Scroll* (Sheffield: Almond Press, 1989).
Day, P.L., *An Adversary in Heaven: 'Satan' in the Hebrew Bible* (Atlanta: Scholars Press, 1988).
Dozeman, T.B., *God on the Mountain* (Atlanta: Scholars Press, 1989).
— 'Inner-Biblical Interpretation of YHWH's Gracious and Compassionate Character', *JBL* 108 (1989), pp. 207–33.
— 'Masking Moses and Mosaic Authority in Torah', *JBL* 119 (2000), pp. 21–45.
Driver, G.R., 'Ezekiel's Inaugural Vision', *VT* 1 (1951), pp. 60–2.
— 'Isaiah 6:1 "His Train Filled the Temple" ', in Goedicke (ed.), *Near Eastern Studies in Honor of W.F. Albright*, pp. 87–96.
— 'Textual and Linguistic Problems of the Book of Psalms', *HTR* 29 (1936), pp. 171–92.
Driver, S.R., *A Treatise on the Use of the Tenses in Hebrew* (London: Oxford University Press, 1892).
Durham, J.I., *Exodus* (WBC; Waco, Texas: Word, 1987).
Ehrlich, U., *The Non-Verbal Language of Jewish Prayer* (Jerusalem: Magnes, 2003) (Hebrew).
Ehrlich, A., *Mikra Ki-Pheshuto* (3 vols.; N.Y.: Ktav, 1969) (Hebrew).
— *Randglossen zur hebräischen Bibel* (7 vols.; Leipzig: J.C. Hinrichs, 1908–14).
Ehrlich, E.L., *Der Traum im alten Testament* (*BZAW*, 73; Berlin: Topelmann, 1953).
Eichrodt, W., *Theology of the Old Testament* (2 vols.; trans. J.A. Baker; OTL; Philadelphia: Westminster, 1961).
Eilberg-Schwartz, H., *God's Phallus and Other Problems for Men and Monotheism* (Boston: Beacon, 1994).
— *The Savage in Judaism* (Bloomington, IN: Indiana University Press, 1990).
Elat, M., *Samuel and the Foundation of Kingship in Israel* (Jerusalem: Magnes, 1998. (Hebrew)
Eliade, M., *Myth and Reality* (N.Y.: Harper and Row, 1963).
— *The Sacred and the Profane* (N.Y.: Harper and Row, 1961).
Emerton, J., 'The Origin of the Son of Man Imagery', *JTS* 9 (1958), pp. 225–42.
Emerton, J. (ed.), *Studies in the Pentateuch* (*VTS*; Leiden: Brill, 1990).

Eslinger, L., *Kingship of God in Crisis* (Decatur, GA: JSOT Press, 1985).
— 'The Infinite in a Finite Organical Perception', *VT* 45 (1995), pp. 145–73.
— 'Inner-Biblical Exegesis and Inner-Biblical Allusion: The Question of Category', *VT* 42 (1992), pp. 47–58.
Exum, J. Cheryl, 'Promise and Fulfillment: Narrative Art in Judges 13', *JBL* 99 (1980), pp. 43–59.
— 'The Theological Dimensions of the Samson Saga' *VT* 33 (1983), pp. 30–45.
Exum, J. Cheryl (ed.), *Signs and Wonders* (Semeia Studies; Decatur, GA: Scholars Press, 1989).
Fensham, F.C., 'A Few Observations on the Polarization Between Baal and Yahweh in I Kings 17–19,' *ZAW* 92 (1980), pp. 227–36.
Fewell, D.N., *Reading Between Texts: Intertextuality and the Hebrew Bible* (Louisville: Westminster John Knox, 1992).
Fidler, R., 'The Dream Theophany in the Bible', unpublished doctoral dissertation, Hebrew University, Jerusalem, 1996 (Hebrew).
— 'The Shiloh Theophany – A Case Study of a Liminal Report', *WCJS* 12 (1999), pp. 99–107 (Hebrew).
Fishbane, M., 'A Wretched Thing of Shame, a Mere Belly', in Polzin (ed.), *The Biblical Mosaic*, pp. 169–98.
— 'Composition and Structure in the Jacob Cycle', *JJS* 26 (1975), pp. 15–38.
— 'From Scribalism to Rabbinism: Perspectives on the Emergence of Classical Judaism', *The Garments of Torah*, (Bloomington: Indiana University Press, 1989), pp. 64–78.
— *Haftaroth* (JPS; Philadelphia: Jewish Publication Society, 2002).
— 'I Samuel 3: Historical Narrative and Narrative Poetics', in Gros Louis, K.R.R. (ed.), *Literary Interpretations of Biblical Narratives*, vol. 2, pp. 191–203.
— *Biblical Interpretation in Ancient Israel* (Oxford: Oxford University Press, 1985).
— 'The Biblical OT', *Shnaton* 1 (1975), pp. 213–34 (Hebrew).
— 'Torah', *EM* Vol. 8, pp. 469–83 (Hebrew).
— 'Use, Authority and Interpretation of Mikra at Qumran', *Mikra: Compendium Rerum Iudicarum* (Cambridge: Cambridge University Press, 1989), pp. 339–77.
Fisch, H., ' "Eldad and Medad are Prophesying in the Camp" – Structural Analysis of Numbers XI', *Studies in Bible and Exegesis* vol. 2, (Ramat Gan, 1986), pp. 45–55 (Hebrew).
Flanagan, J.W., 'Social Transformation and Ritual in 2 Samuel 6', in Meyers and O'Connor (eds.), *The Word of the Lord Shall Go Forth: Essays in Honor of David Noel Freedman*, pp. 361–72.
Fohrer, G., *Elia* (Zurich: Zwingli-Verlag, 1957).
Fokkelmann, J.P., *Narrative Art and Poetry in the Books of Samuel*, vol. 4, *Vow and Desire* (Assen: Van Gorcum, 1993).
— *Narrative Art in Genesis* (Amsterdam: van Gorcum, 1975).
Fox, E., *The Five Books of Moses* (N.Y.: Schocken, 1995).
Fox, M., *Character and Ideology in the Book of Esther* (Columbia, SC: Univ. of South Carolina Press, 1991).
Fox, M. *et al.* (eds.), *Texts, Temples, and Traditions: A Tribute to Menahem Haran* (Winona Lake, IN: Eisenbrauns, 1996).

Freedman, D.N., *Psalm 119: The Exaltation of Torah* (Winona Lake, IN: Eisenbrauns, 1999).

Friedman, R., 'The Biblical Expression *Mastir Panim*', *HAR* 1 (1977), pp. 139–47.

Frolov, S., 'Returning the Ticket: God and his Prophet in the Book of Jonah', *JSOT* 86 (1999), pp. 85–105.

— 'The Other Side of the Jabbok: Genesis 32 as a Fiasco of Patriarchy', *JSOT* 91 (2000), pp. 41–59.

Frymer-Kensky, T., *In The Wake of the Goddesses* (N.Y.: Free Press, 1992).

Fuchs, E., *Sexual Politics in the Biblical Narrative* (JSOTS, 310; Sheffield: Sheffield Academic Press, 2000).

— 'The Literary Characterization of Mothers and Sexual Politics in the Hebrew Bible', *Semeia* 46 (1989), pp. 151–66.

Fück, H.J. (ed.), *Festschrift Otto Eissfeldt* (Halle: Max Niemeyer, 1947).

Galil, G., and M. Weinfeld, (eds.), *Studies in Historical Geography and Biblical Historiography* (*VTS*, 81; Leiden: Brill, 2000).

Gelander, S., *Art and Idea in Biblical Narrative* (Tel Aviv: Hakibbutz Hameuchad, 1997) (Hebrew).

— *David and His God* (Jerusalem: Simor, 1991).

Geller, S.A., *Sacred Enigmas* (N.Y.: Routledge, 1996).

— 'The Struggle at the Jabbok', *JANES* 14 (1982), pp. 37–60.

Gerstenberger, E., *Leviticus* (Louisville, KY: John Knox, 1996).

Gilula, M., 'An Egyptian Parallel to Jer. 1:4–5', *VT* 17 (1967), p. 114.

Gitay, Y., *Isaiah and His Audience* (Assen: Van Gorcum, 1991).

Glazov, G.Y., *The Bridling of the Tongue and the Opening of the Mouth in Biblical Prophecy* (JSOTS 311; Sheffield: Sheffield Academic Press, 2001).

Gnuse, R., 'A Reconsideration of the Form-Critical Structure of I Samuel 3: An Ancient Near Eastern Dream Theophany', *BZ* 29 (1985), pp. 379–90.

— *The Dream Theophany of Samuel* (Lanham, MD: University Press of America, 1984).

Goedicke, H. (ed.), *Near Eastern Studies in Honor of W.F. Albright* (Baltimore and London: Johns Hopkins Press, 1971).

Goldingay, J.E., *Daniel* (WBC; Dallas: Word Books, 1989).

Good, E.M., *In Turns of Tempest* (Stanford: Stanford University Press, 1990).

Gorman, F.H. Jr., *The Ideology of Ritual* (Sheffield: Sheffield Academic Press, 1990).

Gray, G.B., *A Critical and Exegetical Commentary on the Book of Numbers* (Edinburgh: T. & T. Clark, 1903).

Gray, J., *I and II Kings* (OTL; 2nd edn.; Philadelphia: Westminster, 1975).

Green, A. (ed.), *Jewish Spirituality* (vol. 1; N.Y.: Crossroad, 1986).

Greenberg, M., *Ezekiel 1–20* (AB; N.Y.: Doubleday, 1983).

— 'Moses' Intercessory Prayer', *Tantur Yearbook* (1977–78), pp. 21–36.

— 'נסה in Exod. 20:20', *JBL* 79 (1960), pp. 273–6.

— *Understanding Exodus* (N.Y.: Behrman House, 1969).

— 'You Have Turned Their Hearts Backwards (I Kings 18:37),' in Petuchowski and Fleisher (eds.), *Studies in Aggadah, Targum, and Jewish Liturgy in Memory of Joseph Heinemann*, pp. 52–66 (Hebrew).

Greenspahn, F., 'Why Prophecy Ceased', *JBL* 108 (1989), pp. 37–49.

Greenstein, E., 'Deconstruction and Biblical Narrative', *Prooftexts* 9 (1989), pp. 43–71.

— 'The Riddle of Samson', *Prooftexts* 1 (1981), pp. 237–60.

Gros Louis, K.R.R. (ed.), *Literary Interpretations of Biblical Narratives*, (vol. II, Nashville: Abingdon, 1982).

Gruber, M., 'The Many Faces of *Nasa' Panim* "Lift up the Face"', *The Motherhood of God and Other Studies* (Atlanta: Scholars Press, 1992), pp. 173–83.

Gruenwald, I., *Apocalyptic and Merkavah Mysticism* (Leiden: Brill, 1980).

— *From Apocalypticism to Gnosticism* (Frankfurt: Peter Lang, 1988).

— 'The Speculum and the Technique of the Prophetic and the Apocalyptic Vision', *BM* 40 (1970), pp. 95–7 (Hebrew).

Gunn, D.M., 'Narrative Patterns and Oral Traditions in Judges and Samuel', *VT* 24 (1974), pp. 286–317.

Habel, N., 'The Form and Significance of the Call Narratives', *ZAW* 77 (1965), pp. 297–323.

Halperin, D., 'The Exegetical Character of Ezek. X:9–17', *VT* 26 (1976), pp. 129–41.

Halpern, B. and Levenson, J.D. (eds.), *Traditions in Transformation* (Winona Lake, IN: Eisenbrauns, 1981).

Hanson, P., *The Dawn of Apocalyptic* (Philadelphia: Fortress, 1975).

Haran, M., 'Ma'aser', *EM* vol. 5, pp. 204–12 (Hebrew).

— *Temples and Temple Service in Ancient Israel* (Oxford: Oxford University Press, 1978).

— 'The Shining of Moses' Face: A Case Study in Ancient Near Eastern Iconography', in Barrick, W.B., *et al.* (eds.), *In the Shelter of Elyon*, pp. 150–73.

Harland, P.J., and C.T.R. Hayward (eds.), *New Heaven and New Earth: Prophecy and the Millenium* (*VTS*, 77; Leiden: Brill, 1999).

Hartman, L.F., A.A. DiLella, *The Book of Daniel* (AB; N.Y.: Doubleday, 1978).

Hauser, A.J., R. Gregory, *From Carmel to Horeb*, (Sheffield: Almond Press, 1990).

Heinemann, Y., 'On the Development of Terminology for the Interpretation of the Bible: דרש', *Leshonenu* 14 (1946), pp. 182–9 (Hebrew).

Hengel, M., *Judaism and Hellenism* (2 vols., trans. J. Bowden, Philadelphia: Fortress, 1974).

Herr, D.D., 'Variations of a Pattern: I Kings 19,' *JBL* 104 (1985), pp. 292–4.

Hertzberg, H.W., *I and II Samuel* (OTL; Philadelphia: Westminster, 1960).

Hiebert, T., 'Theophany in the OT', *ABD* vol. VI, pp. 505–11.

— *The Yahwist's Landscape* (N.Y.: Oxford University Press, 1996).

Himmelfarb, M., *Ascent to Heaven in Jewish and Christian Apocalypses* (N.Y.: Oxford University Press, 1993).

— 'From Prophecy to Apocalypse: The *Book of the Watchers* and Tours of Heaven', in Green (ed.), *Jewish Spirituality*, vol. 1, pp. 145–65.

— 'Heavenly Ascent and the Relationship of the Apocalypses and the *Hekhalot* Literature', *HUCA* 59 (1988), pp. 73–100.

Hoffmann, Y., *Jeremiah* (2 vols.; Tel Aviv: Am Oved, 2001) (Hebrew).

Hoffmann, Y. and F. Polak (eds,), *Or Leya'akov* (Jerusalem: Mossad Bialik, 1997).

Holladay, W.L., *Jeremiah 1–2* (Minneapolis: Fortress, 1989).
— 'Jeremiah and Moses: Further Observations', *JBL* 85 (1966), pp. 17–27.
— 'The Background of Jeremiah's Self-Understanding: Moses, Samuel, and Psalm 22', *JBL* 83 (1964), pp. 153–64.
Houtman, C., *Exodus*, Vol. 3, (Leuven: Peeters, 2000).
— 'What Did Jacob See in His Dream at Bethel?', *VT* 27 (1977), pp. 337–51.
Huffmon, H., 'The Treaty Background of Hebrew ידע', *BASOR* 181 (1966), pp. 31–7.
Hurowitz, V.A., 'Eli's Adjuration of Samuel's Initiation Oath (I Sam. 3:17–18) in Light of a 'Diviner's Protocol' from Mari (AEM I/1,1)', *VT* 44 (1994), pp. 483–97.
— *I Have Built You an Exalted House* (*JSOTS*, 115; Sheffield: Sheffield Academic Press, 1992).
— 'Isaiah's Impure Lips and Their Purification in Light of Akkadian Sources', *HUCA* 60 (1990), pp. 39–89.
Hurvitz, A., *The Transition Period in Biblical Hebrew* (Jerusalem: Magnes, 1972) (Hebrew).
Husser, J-M, *Dreams and Dream Narratives in the Biblical World* (Sheffield: Sheffield Academic Press, 1999).
Idinopolus, T.A. and E.A. Yonan (eds.), *The Sacred and its Scholars* (Studies in the History of Religions, 73; Leiden: Brill, 1996).
Irvin, D., *Mytharion* (Neukirchner: Neukirchner Verlag, 1978).
Jacob, B., *The Second Book of the Bible: Exodus* (trans. W. Jacob; Hoboken, NJ: Ktav, 1992).
Jantzen, J.G., '"Samuel Opened the Doors of the House of Yahweh" (I Sam. 3:15)', *JSOT* 26 (1983), pp. 89–96.
Japhet, S., *I and II Chronicles* (OTL; Louisville: Westminster, 1993).
— 'Some Biblical Concepts of Sacred Space', in Kedar and Werblowsky (eds.), *Sacred Space: Shrine, City, Land*, pp. 55–72.
— *The Ideology of the Book of Chronicles and its Place in Biblical Thought* (Frankfurt: Peter Lang, 1989).
Japhet, S. (ed.), *Studies in Bible* (Scripta Hierosolymitana, 31; Jerusalem: Magnes, 1986).
— *The Bible in Light of its Interpreters: The Sarah Kamin Memorial Volume* (Jerusalem: Magnes, 1994).
Jeremias, J., *Theophanie: Die Geschichte einer alttestamentlichen Gattung* (Neukirchen-Vluyn: Neukirchener Verlag, 1965).
Jobling, D., *The Sense of Biblical Narrative* (Sheffield: Sheffield Academic Press, 1978).
Johnson, A.R., 'Aspects of the Word Panim in the OT', in Fück (ed.), *Festschrift Otto Eissfeldt*, pp. 155–60.
Joines, K., 'Winged Serpents in Isaiah's Inaugural Vision', *JBL* 86 (1967), pp. 410–5.
Kalimi, I., *The Book of Chronicles: Historical Writings and Literary Devices* (Jerusalem: Mossad Bialik, 2000) (Hebrew).
Kaufmann, Y., *The Book of Joshua* (Kiryat Sepher: Jerusalem, 1976) (Hebrew).
— *The Book of Judges* (Kiryat Sepher: Jerusalem, 1973) (Hebrew).

Kedar. B.Z., and R.J.Z. Werblowsky (eds.), *Sacred Space: Shrine, City, Land* (Jerusalem: Israel Academy of Sciences and Humanities, 1998).

Keel, O., C. Euhlinger, *Gods, Goddesses and Images of God* (Minneapolis: Fortress, 1998).

Knierem, R., 'The Vocation of Isaiah', *VT*18 (1968), pp. 47–68.

Knohl, I., *The Sanctuary of Silence* (Minneapolis: Fortress, 1995).

Kochan, L., *Beyond the Graven Image* (London: Macmillan, 1997).

Koenen, K., 'Wer sieht wen? Zur Textgeschichte von Gen. 16:13', *VT* 38 (1988), pp. 468–74.

Kogut, S., 'On the Meaning and Syntactical Status of הנה in Biblical Hebrew', in Japhet, *Studies in Bible*, pp. 133–54.

Komlosh, Y., 'Ezekiel's Silence at the Beginning of his Prophecy', in Luria (ed.), *Zer Ligevurot: Shazar Jubilee Volume*, pp. 279–83 (Hebrew).

Korpel, M.C.A., *A Rift in the Clouds: Ugaritic and Hebrew Descriptions of the Divine* (Muenster: Ugaritverlag, 1990).

Kugel, J.L., *The God of Old* (N.Y.: Free Press, 2003).

Kuntz, K., *The Self-Revelation of God* (Philadelphia: Westminster, 1967).

Kutscher, R., 'The Mesopotamian God Zaqar and the Pillar in Jacob's Dream', *Beer Sheva* 3 (1988), pp. 125–30 (Hebrew).

Kutsko, J.F., 'Ezekiel's Anthropology and its Ethical Implications', in Odell and Strong (eds.), *The Book of Ezekiel: Theological and Anthropological Perspectives*, pp. 119–41.

Lacocque, A., *The Book of Daniel* (trans. D. Pellauer; Atlanta: John Knox, 1979).

Landy, F., 'Narrative Techniques and Symbolic Transactions in the Akedah', in Exum (ed.), *Signs and Wonders*, pp. 1–40.

— 'Strategies of Concentration and Diffusion in Isaiah 6', *Biblical Interpretation* 7 (1999), pp. 58–86.

— 'Vision and Voice in Isaiah', *JSOT* 88 (2000), pp. 19–25.

Lang, B. (ed.), *Anthropological Approaches to the Old Testament* (Philadelphia: Fortress, 1985).

Lawrie, D., 'Telling of(f) Prophets', *JNSL* 23 (1997), pp. 163–80.

Leach, E., 'The Logic of Sacrifice', in B. Lang (ed.), *Anthropological Approaches to the Old Testament*, pp. 136–48.

Leibowitz, N., *Studies in Shemot* (Jerusalem: Jewish Agency, 1976) (Hebrew).

Levenson, J.D., *The Death and Resurrection of the Beloved Son* (New Haven: Yale University Press, 1993).

— 'The Jerusalem Temple in Devotional and Visionary Experience', in Green (ed.), *Jewish Spirituality*, vol. 1, pp. 32–61.

— 'The Sources of Torah: Psalm 119 and the Modes of Revelation in Second Temple Judaism', in Miller *et al.* (eds.), *Ancient Israelite Religion*, pp. 559–74.

Levine, B., *Numbers 1–20* (AB; N.Y.: Doubleday, 1993).

— *Numbers 21–36* (AB; N.Y.: Doubleday, 2000).

— 'Silence, Sound, and the Phenomenology of Mourning in Ancient Israel', *JANES* 22 (1993), pp. 89–106.

Lewin, E. Davis, 'Arguing for Authority; A Rhetorical Study of Jeremiah 1:4–19 and 20:7–18', *JSOT* 32 (1985), pp. 105–19.

Lichtenstein, M., 'Dream Theophany and the 'E' Document', *JANES* 1–2 (1969), pp. 45–54.

Licht, J., *A Commentary on the Book of Numbers*, Vol. 3 (Jerusalem: Magnes, 1995) (Hebrew).

— 'Holy, Holiness', *EM* vol. 7, col. 43–62 (Hebrew).

— 'Malakh, Malakhim', *EM* vol. 4, pp. 975–990 (Hebrew).

— 'The Revelation of God's Presence at Sinai', in Avishur and Blau (eds.), *Studies in the Bible and the Ancient Near East Presented to Samuel Loewenstamm*, vol. 1, pp. 251–67. (Hebrew).

Lindblom J., 'Theophanies in Holy Places in Hebrew Religion', *HUCA* 32 (1961), pp. 91–106.

— 'Wisdom in the OT Prophets', *VTS* 3 (1955), pp. 192–204.

Lipton, D., *Revisions of the Night* (Sheffield: Sheffield Academic Press, 1999).

Loewenstamm, S.E., 'Gid Hannasheh', *EM* vol. 2, col. 480–1 (Hebrew).

— 'The Upheaval of Nature During Theophany', in *Oz Ledavid* (Jerusalem: Society for Biblical Study, 1964), pp. 508–20 (Hebrew).

Long, B.O., *I Kings with an Introduction to Historical Literature* (FOTL; Grand Rapids, MI: Eerdmans, 1984).

— 'Reports of Visions among the Prophets', *JBL* 95 (1976), pp. 353–65.

Long, B. and Coats, G. (eds.), *Canon and Authority* (Philadelphia: Fortress, 1977).

Lopez, F.G., 'Election-Vocation D'Israel et De Jeremie: Deuteronome VII et Jeremie I', *VT* 35 (1985), pp. 1–12.

Lundbom, J., 'Elijah's Chariot Ride', *JJS* 24 (1973), pp. 39–55.

— 'God's use of *Idem per Idem* to Terminate Debate', *HTR* 71 (1978), pp. 193–201.

— *Jeremiah 1–20* (AB; N.Y.: Doubleday, 1999).

— 'Rhetorical Structures in Jeremiah 1', *ZAW* 103 (1991) pp. 193–210.

Luria, B.Z. (ed.), *Sepher Moshe Goldstein* (Tel Aviv: Society for Bible Research, 1987).

— *Zer Legevurot: Shazar Jubilee Volume* (Jerusalem: Israel Society for Biblical Research, 1973).

Lust, J., 'A Gentle Breeze (I Kings 19)', *VT* 25 (1975), pp. 110–5.

Luzzato, S.D., *Commentary to The Book of Isaiah* (Tel Aviv: Dvir, 1970) (Hebrew).

— *Commentary to the Pentateuch* (Tel Aviv: Dvir, 1965) (Hebrew).

Mack, H., "Maqel Shaqed Ani Ro'eh", *BM* 39 (1994), pp. 269–75 (Hebrew).

Magnes, J. and S. Gittin (eds.), *Hesed Ve'emet – Studies in Honor of E.S. Freidrichs* (Atlanta: Scholars Press, 1998).

Magonet, J., *Form and Meaning: Studies in Literary Techniques in the Book of Jonah* (Bern: Herbert Lang, 1976).

— 'The Structure of Isaiah 6', *WCJS* 9 (1986), pp. 91–7.

Malul, M., כפי (Exod. 33:22) and בחפניו (Prov. 30:4): Hand or Skirt?', *ZAW* 109 (1997), pp. 356–68.

Mann, T.W., *Divine Presence and Divine Guidance in Israelite Traditions* (Baltimore: Johns Hopkins University Press, 1977).

Marks, H., 'On Prophetic Stammering', in Schwartz (ed.), *The Book and the Text*, pp. 61–80.

Mason, R., 'The Prophets of the Restoration', in Coggins, Phillips, and Knibb (eds.), *Israel's Prophetic Tradition*, pp. 137–54.

Mays, H., 'Some Connotations of *Mayim Rabbim*', *JBL* 74 (1955), pp. 9–21.

McCarter, K.P., *I Samuel* (AB; Garden City, N.Y.: Doubleday, 1980).

— *II Samuel* (AB; Garden City, N.Y.: Doubleday, 1984).

McKane, W., *Jeremiah* (ICC; 2 vols.; Edinburgh: T&T Clark, 1986).

McKay, H.A., 'Jacob Makes it Across the Jabbok', *JSOT* 38 (1987), pp. 3–13.

McLaughlin, J.L., 'Their Hearts Were Hardened: The Use of Isaiah 6:9–10 in the Book of Isaiah', *Biblica* 75 (1994), pp. 1–25.

Meier, S.A., *Speaking of Speaking: Marking Direct Discourse in the Hebrew Bible* (Leiden: Brill, 1992).

Mendenhall, G., *The Tenth Generation* (Baltimore: Johns Hopkins University Press, 1973).

Merkur, D., 'The Numinous as a Category of Values', in Idinopolus and Yonan (eds.), *The Sacred and its Scholars* (Leiden: Brill, 1996), pp. 104–23.

Mettinger, T.N.D., *No Graven Image?* (Stockholm: Almqvist and Wiksell, 1995).

Meyers, C., *The Tabernacle Menorah* (Missoula, MT: Scholars Press, 1976).

— 'Temple, Jerusalem', *ABD* vol. 6, pp. 355–8.

Meyers, C.L., Meyers, E.M., *Haggai, Zechariah 1–8* (AB; N.Y.: Doubleday, 1987).

Meyers, C., and O'Connor, M.P. (eds.), *The Word of the Lord Shall Go Forth: Essays in Honor of David Noel Freedman* (Winona Lake, IN: Eisenbrauns: 1983).

Milgrom, J., *Cult and Conscience* (Leiden: Brill, 1976).

— *Leviticus 1–16* (AB; N.Y.: Doubleday, 1991).

— *Leviticus 23–27* (AB; N.Y.: Doubleday, 2000).

— *Numbers* (Philadelphia: Jewish Publication Society, 1990).

Miller, P.D. *et al.* (eds.), *Ancient Israelite Religion: Essays in Honor of F.M. Cross* (Philadelphia: Fortress, 1987).

Moberly, R.W.L., *At The Mountain of God* (JSOTS, 22; Sheffield: Sheffield Academic Press, 1983.

— 'On Learning to Be a True Prophet: The Story of Balaam and his Ass', in Harland and Hayward (eds.), *New Heaven and New Earth: Prophecy and the Millenium*, pp. 1–17.

Moore, M.S., *The Balaam Traditions: Their Character and Development* (Atlanta: Scholars Press, 1990).

Muffs, Y., 'Who Will Stand in the Breach?', in *Love and Joy* (N.Y.: Jewish Theological Seminary of America, 1992), pp. 9–48.

Muilenburg, J., 'Form Criticism and Beyond', *JBL* 88 (1969), pp. 1–18.

— 'The Intercession of the Covenant Mediator', in Ackroyd and Lindars (eds.), *Words and Meanings: Essays Presented to David Winton Thomas*, pp. 159–81.

Ne'eman, N., 'Bethel and Beth-Aven', *Zion* 50 (1985), pp. 15–25 (Hebrew).

Neff, R.W., 'The Birth and Election of Isaac in the Priestly Tradition', *Biblical Research* 15 (1970), pp. 5–18.

Nelson, R.D., *Joshua* (OTL; Louisville, KY: Westminster, 1997).

Newman, M., 'The Prophetic Call of Samuel', in Anderson and Harrelson, (eds.), *Israel's Prophetic Heritage*, pp. 86–97.

Newsom, C., 'Angels', *ABD* vol. 1, pp. 248–53.

— *Songs of the Sabbath Sacrifice: A Critical Edition* (HSS, 27; Atlanta: Scholars Press, 1985).

Nicholson, E.W., *Exodus and Sinai in History and Tradition* (Oxford: Oxford University Press, 1973).
— 'The Antiquity of the Tradition in Exodus XXIV 9–11', *VT* 25 (1975), pp. 69–79.
— 'The Interpretation of Exodus XXIV 9–11', *VT* 24 (1974), pp. 77–94.
— 'The Origin of the Tradition in Exodus XXIV 9–11', *VT* 26 (1976), pp. 148–60.
Nickelsburg, G.W., *1 Enoch* (Hermeneia; Minneapolis: Fortress, 2001).
— 'Enoch Levi and Peter: Recipients of Revelation in the Upper Gallilee', *JBL* 100 (1981), pp. 575–600.
— 'The Nature and Function of Revelation in 1 Enoch, Jubilees and some Qumranic Documents', in Chazon and Stone, *Pseudepigraphic Perspectives*, pp. 91–119.
Nicol, G.G., 'Isaiah and Daniel', *VT* 29 (1979), pp. 501–5.
Niditch, S., *The Symbolic Vision in Biblical Tradition* (Chico, CA: Scholars Press, 1983).
Noth, M., *Numbers* (Philadelphia: Westminster, 1968).
Oblath, M., ' "To Sleep, Perchance to Dream": What Jacob Saw at Bethel', *JSOT* 95 (2001), pp. 117–26.
Odell, M.S., 'You Are What You Eat: Ezekiel and the Scroll', *JBL* 117 (1998), pp. 229–48.
Odell, M.S., and J.T. Strong (eds.), *The Book of Ezekiel: Theological and Anthropological Perspectives* (Atlanta: Society of Biblical Literature, 2000).
Olyan, S.M., ' "To Uproot and to Pull Down, to Build and to Plant": Jer. 1:10 and its Earliest Interpreters', in Magnes and Gittin (eds.), *Hesed Ve'emet – Studies in Honor of E.S. Freirichs*, pp. 63–72.
Olyan, S.M. and Culley, R.C. (eds.), *'A Wise and Discerning Mind': Essays in Honor of Burke O. Long* (Providence, RI: Brown Judaic Studies, 2000).
Oppenheim, A.L., 'Akkadian *pul(u)h(t)u* and *melammu*', *JAOS* 63–64 (1943), pp. 31–4.
— *The Interpretation of Dreams in the Ancient Near East* (Transactions of the American Philosophical Society, n.s. 46; Philadelphia: American Philosophical Society. 1956).
Otto, R., *The Idea of the Holy* (trans. J.W. Harvey; London: Oxford University Press, 1950).
Pardes, I., *Countertraditions in The Bible* (Cambridge: Harvard University Press, 1992).
— *The Biography of Ancient Israel* (Berkeley: University of California Press, 2000).
Parunak, H. Van Dyke, 'The Literary Architecture of Ezekiel's *Mar'ot 'Elohim*', *JBL* 99 (1980), pp. 61–74.
Paul, S. 'Deutero-Isaiah and Cuneiform Royal Inscriptions', *JAOS* 88 (1968), pp. 180–6.
— 'Prophets and Prophecy', *EJ* vol. 13, col. 1150–75.
— *The Laws of the Book of the Covenant in Light of Cuneiform and Biblical Law* (*VTS*, 18; Leiden: Brill, 1970).
Pedaya, H., 'Seeing, Falling, Song: The Yearning to See God and the Element of the Spirit in Early Jewish Mysticism', *Asufot* vol. 9 (1985), pp. 237–77 (Hebrew).

— *Vision and Speech: Models of Revelatory Experience in Jewish Mysticism* (Los Angeles: Cherub Press, 2002) (Hebrew).

Peleg, Y., 'Going Up and Going Down: A Key to Interpreting Jacob's Dream', unpublished doctoral dissertation, Schechter Institute of Jewish Studies, Jerusalem, 2000 (Hebrew).

Peterson, D.L., *Late Biblical Prophecy* (Missoula, Mt.: Scholars Press, 1977).

— *The Roles of Israel's Prophets* (Sheffield: JSOT Press, 1980).

Petuchowski, J., and Fleischer, E. (eds.), *Studies in Aggadah, Targum, and Jewish Liturgy in Memory of Joseph Heinemann* (Jerusalem: Magnes, 1981).

Polak, F., *Biblical Narrative: Aspects of Art and Design* (Jerusalem: Mossad Bialik, 1994) (Hebrew).

— 'The Messenger of God and the Dialectic of Revelation', in Hoffmann and Polak (eds.), *Or Leya'akov*, pp. 14–30.

— 'Theophany and Mediator', in M. Vervenne (ed.), *Studies in the Book of Exodus*, pp. 113–47.

Polzin, R., *Moses and the Deuteronomist* (N.Y.: Seabury, 1980).

Polzin, R. and E. Rothman (eds.), *The Biblical Mosaic* (Philadelphia: Scholars Press, 1982).

Propp, W.C., *Exodus 1–18* (AB, N.Y.: Doubleday, 1999).

— 'That Bloody Bridegroom (Exodus iv:24–26)', *VT* 43 (1993), pp. 495–518.

— 'The Skin of Moses' Face – Transfigured or Disfigured?', *CBQ* 49 (1987), pp. 375–86.

von Rad, G., *Deuteronomy* (OTL; Philadelphia: Westminster, 1966).

— *Genesis* (OTL; Philadelphia: Westminster, 1972).

— *Old Testament Theology* (2 vols; trans. D.M.G. Stalker; San Francisco: Harper, 1962).

— 'The Deuteronomistic Theology of History in the Book of Kings', *Studies in Deuteronomy* (London: SCM, 1953), pp. 74–91.

Rappaport, R., 'The Obvious Meaning of Ritual', *Ecology, Meaning and Religion* (Richmond, CA: North Atlantic Books, 1979).

Reinhartz, A., 'Samson's Mother: An Unnamed Protagonist', *JSOT* 55 (1992), pp. 25–37.

— *Why Ask My Name?* (N.Y.: Oxford University Press, 1998).

Renaud, B., 'Jer. 1: Structure et Theologie de la Redaction', in Bogaert (ed.), *Le Livre de Jeremie*, pp. 177–96.

Rentdorff, R., 'Jakob in Bethel', in Rofe and Y. Zakovitch (eds.), *Isaac Leo Seeligmann Volume*, vol. 3, pp. 115–27.

Richter, W., *Die sogennanten vorprophetischen Berufungsberichte* (Gottingen: Vanderhoek und Ruprecht, 1970).

Roberts, J.J.M., 'Double Entendre in First Isaiah', *CBQ* 54 (1992), pp. 39–48.

— 'The Hand of Yahweh', *VT* 21 (1971), pp. 244–51.

Robinson, B., 'Elijah at Horeb', *RB* 98 (1991), pp. 513–36.

— 'Moses at the Burning Bush', *JSOT* 75 (1997), pp. 107–22.

— 'The Jealousy of Miriam: A Note on Num. 12', *ZAW* 101 (1981), pp. 428–32.

— 'Zipporah to the Rescue: A Contextual Study of Exodus 4,24–6', *VT* 36 (1986), pp. 447–61.

Rofe, A., *The Book of Balaam* (Jerusalem: Simor, 1980) (Hebrew).

— *The Belief in Angels in the Bible and in Early Israel* (Jerusalem: Makor, 1979) (Hebrew).
— 'The Monotheistic Argumentation in Deut. 4:32–40, Contents, Composition and Text', *VT* 35 (1985), pp. 434–45.
— *The Prophetical Stories* (Jerusalem: Magnes, 1988).
Rofe., A. and Y. Zakovitch, (eds.), *Isaac Leo Seeligmann Volume* (3 vols; Jerusalem: Rubenstein, 1983).
Rudin-O'Brasky, T., *The Patriarchs in Hebron and Sodom (Genesis 18–19)* (Jerusalem: Simor, 1982) (Hebrew).
Russell, D.S., *The Meaning and Message of Jewish Apocalyptic* (London: SCM, 1964).
Saggs, H.W.F., *The Encounter with the Divine in Mesopotamia and Israel* (London: Athlone, 1978).
Sarna, N.M., *Exploring Exodus* (N.Y.: Schocken Books, 1986).
— *Genesis* (JPS; Philadephia: Jewish Publication Society, 1989).
— *Understanding Genesis* (New York: Schocken, 1965).
Sasson, J.M., 'Bovine Symbolism in the Exodus Narrative', *VT* 18 (1968), pp. 380–7.
— *Jonah* (AB; N.Y.: Doubleday, 1990).
Savran, G., 'Beastly Speech: Intertextuality, Balaam's Ass and the Garden of Eden', *JSOT* 64 (1994), pp. 33–55.
— *Telling and Retelling* (Bloomington: Indiana University Press, 1988).
Scharbert, J., 'Formgeschichte und Exegese von Ex. 34, 6f. und seiner Parallelen', *Biblica* 38 (1957), pp. 130–50.
Schinkel, D., 'Mirjam als Aussätzige? Zwei Bemerkungen zu Num. 12', *ZAW* 115 (2003), pp. 94–101.
Schmidt, N.F. and Nel, P.J. 'Theophany as Type-Scene in the Hebrew Bible', *Journal for Semitics* 11 (2002), pp. 256–81.
Schniedewind, W.G., *The Word of God in Transition: From Prophet to Exegete in the Second Temple Period* (Sheffield: Sheffield Academic Press, 1995).
Scholem, G., 'Revelation and Tradition as Religious Categories in Judaism', *The Messianic Ideal in Judaism* (N.Y.: Schocken, 1971), pp. 282–303.
Schwartz, B., ' "I am the Lord" and "You Shall Have no Other Gods" Were Heard from the Mouth of the Almighty: On the Evolution of an Interpretation', in Japhet (ed.), *The Bible in Light of its Interpreters: The Sarah Kamin Memorial Volume*, pp. 170–97 (Hebrew).
— 'The Concentric Structure of Ezekiel 2:1–3:15', *WCJS* 10 (1990), pp. 107–14.
— 'The Priestly Account of the Theophany and Lawgiving at Sinai', in Fox *et al*, (eds.), *Texts, Temples, and Traditions: A Tribute to Menahem Haran*, pp. 103–34.
Schwartz, R. (ed.), *The Book and the Text: The Bible and Literary Theory* (Cambridge: Basil Blackwell, 1990).
Schulman, D., *The Hungry God* (Chicago: University of Chicago, 1993).
Seeligman, I.L., 'The Beginnings of Midrash in the Book of Chronicles', *Studies in Biblical Literature* (Jerusalem: Magnes, 1992), pp. 459–74 (Hebrew).
Segal, M.H., 'Prophet, Lookout, Reprover', in *Masoret Ubiqqoret* (Jerusalem: Kiryat Sepher, 1957), pp. 150–9 (Hebrew).

— *The Books of Samuel* (Jerusalem: Kiryat Sefer, 1968 (Hebrew)).

Segal, P., 'The Divine Verdict of Leviticus 10:3', *VT* 39 (1989), pp. 90–5.

Seitz, C., 'The Prophet Moses and the Canonical Shape of Jeremiah', *ZAW* 101 (1989), pp. 3–27.

Sharp, C.J., 'The Call of Jeremiah and Diaspora Politics', *JBL* 119 (2000), pp. 421–38.

Shemesh, Y., 'From Following the Footsteps of the Oxen to Following the Footsteps of Elijah – The Appointment of Elisha as Elijah's Servant (I Kings 19:19–21)', *Studies in Bible and Exegesis*, Vol. 5 (Ramat Gan: Bar Ilan, 2000), pp. 73–93 (Hebrew).

Shiloah, M., 'Vayyo'mer...Vayyo'mer', in Weiser and Luria (eds.), *Sefer Korngrin*, pp. 251–67 (Hebrew).

Simon, U., 'Elijah's Fight against Baal Worship: Unity and Structure of the Story (I Kings 17–18)', *Studies in Bible and Exegesis*, Vol. 1 (Ramat Gan: Bar Ilan, 1980), pp. 51–118. (Hebrew)

— *Reading Prophetic Narratives* (Bloomington: Indiana University Press, 1997).

Smith, G.V., 'Job iv 12–21: Is it Eliphaz's Vision?', *VT* 40 (1990), pp. 453–63.

Smith, J.Z., *Imagining Religion* (Chicago: University of Chicago, 1982).

— *To Take Place: Toward Theory in Ritual* (Chicago: University of Chicago, 1987).

Smith, M.S., 'Divine Form and Size in Ugarit and Pre-Israelite Religion', *ZAW* 100 (1988), pp. 424–7.

— '"Seeing God" in the Psalms: The Background to the Beatific Vision in the Bible', *CBQ* 50 (1988), pp. 171–83.

— *The Pilgrimage Pattern in Exodus*, (Sheffield: Sheffield Academic Press, 1997).

— *The Origins of Biblical Monotheism*, (N.Y.: Oxford University Press, 2000).

Smith, S.H., '"Heel and Thigh": The Concept of Sexuality in the Jacob-Esau Narratives', *VT* 40 (1990), pp. 464–73.

Sommer, B.D., *A Prophet Reads Scripture* (Stanford: Stanford University Press, 1998).

— 'Reflecting on Moses: The Redaction of Numbers 11', *JBL* 118 (1999), pp. 601–24.

— 'Revelation at Sinai in the Hebrew Bible and in Jewish Theology', *JR* 79 (1999), pp. 422–51.

Speiser, E.A., *Genesis* (AB; Garden City, N.Y.: Doubleday, 1964).

Stahl, N., *Law and Liminality in the Bible* (Sheffield: Sheffield Academic Press, 1995).

Sternberg, M., *The Poetics of Biblical Narrative*, (Bloomington: Indiana University Press, 1985).

Stolz, F., 'Dimensions and Transformations of Purification Ideas', in Assmann and Stroumsa (eds.), *Transformations of the Inner Self in Ancient Religions*, pp. 211–29.

Talmon, S., 'An Apparently Redundant MT Reading – Jeremiah 1:18', *Textus* 8 (1973), pp. 160–3.

— 'Hatan Damim' *EI* 3 (1954), pp. 93–6 (Hebrew).

— 'The Concept of Revelation in Biblical Times', *Literary Studies in the Hebrew Bible* (Jerusalem: Magnes, 1993), pp. 192–215.

Terrien, S., *The Elusive Presence* (San Francisco: Harper Collins, 1983).

Tigay, J.H. (ed.), *Empirical Models for the Development of the Hebrew Bible* (Philadelphia: 1985).

Tigay, J.H., *Deuteronomy* (*JPS*; Philadelphia: Jewish Publication Society, 1996).

Toeg, A., *Lawgiving at Sinai* (Jerusalem: Magnes, 1977) (Hebrew).

Toorn, K. van der, 'Did Jeremiah See Aaron's Staff?', *JSOT* 43 (1989), pp. 83–94.

Trible, P., 'Bringing Miriam out of the Shadows', *Bible Review* 5,1 (1989), pp. 15–25, 34.

Tsevat, M., 'The Throne Vision of Isaiah', *The Meaning of the Book of Job and Other Essays* (New York: Ktav, 1980), pp. 155–76.

Tucker, G., D. Petersen, and R. Wilson (eds.), *Canon, Theology, and Old Testament Interpretation* (Philadelphia: Fortress, 1988).

Uffenheimer, A. and A. Kasher (eds.), *Dor LeDor* (Jerusalem: Mossad Bialik, 1995).

Uffenheimer, B., *Ancient Prophecy in Israel* (Jerusalem: Magnes, 1973) (Hebrew).

— *Classical Prophecy* (Jerusalem: Magnes, 2001) (Hebrew).

— 'Ma'aseh Merkavah', *EM* vol. 5, pp. 199–203 (Hebrew).

— 'Nevu'ah, Navi', *EM* vol. 5, pp. 690–731 (Hebrew).

— 'The Commission of Ezekiel and his Early Prophecy', in Uffenheimer and Kasher, *Dor LeDor*, pp. 27–55 (Hebrew).

— 'The Commission of Isaiah and its Development in Rabbinic Tradition', in Uffenheimer, *The Bible and the History of Israel*, pp. 18–50 (Hebrew).

— 'The Method of Rudolf Otto and Prophetic Consciousness', *BM* 38 (1993), pp. 1–13 (Hebrew).

Uffenheimer, B. (ed.), *The Bible and the History of Israel* (Tel Aviv: Tel Aviv University, 1972).

Uffenheimer, B. (ed.), *Bible Studies: Y.M. Grintz in Memoriam* (*Te'udah*; vol. 2; Tel Aviv: Hakibbutz Hemeuchad, 1982).

Vanderhooft, D., 'Dwelling Beneath the Sacred Place: A Proposal for Reading II Sam. 7:10', *JBL* 118 (1999), pp. 625–33.

VanderKam, J., *Enoch and the Growth of An Apocalyptic Tradition* (CBQMS, 16; Washington, DC: Catholic Biblical Association of America, 1984).

— 'The Theophany of Enoch i, 3b-7, 9', *VT* 23 (1973), pp. 129–50.

VanderKam, J. and P.W. Flint, (eds.), *The Dead Sea Scroll after Fifty Years* (Leiden: Brill, 1999).

Van Seters, J., *Abraham in History and Tradition* (New Haven: Yale University Press, 1975).

— 'Comparing Scripture with Scripture: Some Observations on the Sinai Pericope in Exod. 19–24', in Tucker, Petersen and Wilson (eds.), *Canon, Theology, and Old Testament Interpretation*, pp. 111–30.

— *The Life of Moses: The Yahwist as Historian in Exodus-Numbers* (Kampen: Kok Pharos, 1994).

Vervenne M. (ed.), *Studies in the Book of Exodus* (Leuven: Leuven University Press, 1993)

Vriezen, Th.C., 'The Exegesis of Exodus xxiv 9–11', *OTS* 17 (1972), pp. 100–33.

Waldman, N.M., 'God's Ways – A Comparative Note', *JQR* 70 (1979–80), pp. 67–72.

Walsh, J.T., *1 Kings* (Berit Olam; Liturgical Press: Collegeville, MN, 1996).

Watson, W.G.E., 'The Structure of 1 Sam. 3', *BZ* 29 (1994), pp. 90–3.

Weider, N., *The Judean Scrolls and Karaism* (London: East and West Library, 1962).

Weinfeld, M., *Deuteronomy 1–11* (AB; New York: Doubleday, 1991).

— *Deuteronomy and the Deuteronomic School* (Oxford: Oxford University Press, 1972).

— 'Presence, Divine', *EJ* vol. 13, col. 1015–20.

— 'Tithe', *EJ* vol. 15, col. 1156–62.

Weiser, A. and B.Z. Luria (eds.), *Sefer Korngrin* (Jerusalem: Niv, 1964).

Weismann, Z., 'Elijah's Mantle and the Consecration of Elisha', *Shnaton* 2 (1977), pp. 93–9 (Hebrew).

— *From Jacob to Israel* (Jerusalem: Magnes, 1986) (Hebrew).

Weiss, M., 'Image and Voice in Prophetic Vision', *WCJS* 6 (1973), pp. 91–9 (Hebrew).

— *The Bible From Within* (Jerusalem: Magnes, 1984).

Wenham, G., *Genesis 16–50* (WBC; Waco, TX: Word, 1984).

Werblowsky, R.J.Z., 'Anthropomorphism', *Encyclopedia of Religion* (New York, 1987), vol. 1, pp. 316–20.

Westermann, C., *Genesis 1–11* (trans. J.J. Scullion; Minneapolis: Augsburg, 1984).

— *Genesis 12–36* (trans. J.J. Scullion; Minneapolis: Augsburg, 1985).

White, H., 'The Initiation Legend of Ishmael', *ZAW* 87 (1975), pp. 267–306.

Wicke, D.W., 'The Structure of 1 Sam. 3: Another View', *BZ* 30 (1995), pp. 256–8.

Wieringen, A.L.H.M., *The Implied Reader in Isaiah 6–12* (Leiden: Brill, 1998).

Williams, J.G., 'The Prophetic Father: A Brief Explanation of the Term "Sons of the Prophets"', *JBL* 85 (1966), pp. 344–8.

Wilson, I., *Out of the Midst of the Fire: Divine Presence in Deuteronomy* (Atlanta: Scholars Press, 1995).

Wilson, R.R., *Prophecy and Society in Ancient Israel* (Philadelphia: Fortress, 1980).

van Wolde, E., 'Texts in Dialogue with Texts: Intertextuality in the Ruth and Tamar Narratives', *Biblical Interpretation* 5 (1997), pp. 1–28.

Wolf-Monson, T., '"Nofel Vegalu'i Einayim"', *BM* 47 (2002), pp. 237–56 (Hebrew).

Wolfson, E., *Through a Speculum that Shines* (Princeton: Princeton University Press, 1994).

Wyatt, N., 'The Significance of the Burning Bush', *VT* 36 (1986), pp. 361–5.

— 'Where Did Jacob Dream His Dream?', *JSOT* 2 (1990), pp. 44–57.

Zakovitch, Y., '"Aleh Qereah, Aleh Qereah" – Circles of Interpretation in Biblical Narrative', *Jerusalem Studies in Hebrew Literature*, vol. 5, (1985), pp. 7–23 (Hebrew).

— 'Assimilation in Biblical Narratives' in Tigay (ed.), *Empirical Models for the Development of the Hebrew Bible*, pp. 175–96.

— '"And You Shall Tell Your Son"' (Jerusalem: Magnes, 1991).

— '"A Still Small Voice": Form and Content in I Kings 19', *Tarbitz* 51 (1982), pp. 329–46 (Hebrew).

— 'For Three, and for Four', (Jerusalem: Makor, 1979) (Hebrew).

— *The Life of Samson* (Jerusalem: Magnes, 1982) (Hebrew).

— *Through the Looking Glass: Reflection Stories in the Bible* (Tel Aviv: Hakibbutz Hameuchad, 1995) (Hebrew).

— 'Yabok, Peniel, Mahanaim, Bet El', *Ariel* 100–1 (1994), pp. 191–204 (Hebrew).

Zimmerli, W., *Ezekiel 1–2* (2 vols.; trans. R.E. Clements; Hermeneia; Philadelphia: Fortress, 1979).

— 'Visionary Experience in Jeremiah', in Coggins, Phillips, and Knibb, (eds.), *Israel's Prophetic Tradition*, pp. 95–118.

INDEX

INDEX OF REFERENCES

BIBLE

OTHER ANCIENT REFERENCES

INDEX OF AUTHORS